Rise of the Vulcans

James Mann

RISE OF THE VULCANS

THE HISTORY OF BUSH'S WAR CABINET

VIKING

VIKING
Published by the Penguin Group
Penguin Group (USA) Inc., 375 Hudson Street,
New York, New York 10014, U.S.A.
Penguin Books Ltd, 80 Strand, London WC2R 0RL, England
Penguin Books Australia Ltd, 250 Camberwell Road, Camberwell,
Victoria 3124, Australia
Penguin Books Canada Ltd, 10 Alcorn Avenue,
Toronto, Ontario, Canada M4V 3B2
Penguin Books India (P) Ltd, 11 Community Centre, Panchsheel Park,
New Delhi – 110 017, India
Penguin Books (N.Z.) Ltd, Cnr Rosedale and Airborne Roads, Albany,
Auckland, New Zealand
Penguin Books (South Africa) (Pty) Ltd, 24 Sturdee Avenue,
Rosebank, Johannesburg 2196, South Africa

Penguin Books Ltd, Registered Offices:
80 Strand, London WC2R 0RL, England

First published in 2004 by Viking Penguin,
a member of Penguin Group (USA) Inc.

10 9 8 7 6 5 4 3 2 1

LIBRARY OF CONGRESS CATALOGING-IN-PUBLICATION DATA
Mann, Jim
Rise of the Vulcans: the history of Bush's war cabinet / James Mann.
p.   cm.
Includes index.
ISBN 0-670-03299-9
1. United States—Foreign relations—2001–   2.United States—Military policy.   3. United
States—Politics and goverment—2001–   4. Bush, George W. (George Walker), 1946—
Friends and associates.   5. Cabinet officers—United States—Biography.   6. Presidents—
United States—Staff—Biography.   7. Political consultants—United States—Biography.
I. Title.
E902.M345 2004
327.73'0092'2—dc22   2003065765

This book is printed on acid-free paper. ∞

Printed in the United States of America
Set in Adobe Garamond
Designed by Francesca Belanger

To my mother,
Peggy Mann,
who has inspired all of us
with the virtues of perseverance
and her love of life

Contents

Introduction

As GEORGE W. BUSH campaigned for the presidency in 1999 and 2000, he gradually settled upon a consistent theme. Seeking to deflect questions about his lack of experience in foreign policy, he explained again and again that he possessed an eminent group of advisers, one with vastly more experience than the Democrats. Most of these advisers had already served at the highest levels of government during his father's administration, in the heady days of the collapse of the Soviet Union and the first Gulf War against Iraq. Some of the advisers had served in the Reagan administration; some had even worked in the 1970s for Richard Nixon and Gerald Ford.

Whenever the younger Bush stumbled over details—as he did, for example, when an ambush-style "pop quiz" by a television reporter demonstrated that he couldn't name the leaders of Pakistan or India[1]—the candidate could argue that what mattered was a president's ability to select good people. "I've got one of the finest foreign policy teams ever assembled," he said in response to one Democratic challenge.[2] He pointed to the men and women supporting him, such as his vice presidential nominee, Dick Cheney, Colin Powell, Condoleezza Rice, Paul Wolfowitz and Richard Armitage, as symbols of continuity and stability. This group of advisers became, for all practical purposes, Bush's principal foreign policy plank in his first race for the White House. His message was not so much what he would do as whom he would appoint.

During the campaign Bush's foreign policy advisers came up with a nickname to describe themselves. They dubbed their team the Vulcans, in honor of the Roman god of fire, the forge and metalwork. Rice, who was serving as foreign policy coordinator for the Bush campaign, had been raised in Birmingham, Alabama, where a mammoth fifty-six-foot statue of Vulcan on a hill overlooking downtown paid homage to the city's steel industry. The name had started as a joke, but it caught on, and the campaign group began to use it in public. That word, *Vulcans,* captured perfectly the image the Bush foreign policy team sought to convey, a sense of power, toughness, resilience and durability. (Ironically, Birmingham's statue of Vulcan was taken down for repairs in 1999 because it was beginning to fall apart, a detail that the Bush team understandably did not emphasize when it began employing the metaphor.)

To no one's surprise, once Bush became president-elect, he turned to this same group of veterans to fill most of the top jobs. By the time the new administration's foreign policy team was assembled in early 2001, it had the feel of a class reunion. Most of its members had already worked closely alongside one another in previous administrations, and the ties among them were close, intricate and overlapping.

Donald Rumsfeld, the new defense secretary, had first worked alongside Cheney more than three decades earlier, when Cheney served as Rumsfeld's administrative assistant in the Nixon administration. Cheney, as defense secretary in the first Bush administration, had selected Colin Powell (over several more senior generals) to be the chairman of the Joint Chiefs of Staff and had served with him for three years. Richard Armitage, the new deputy secretary of state, had worked with Powell when the two men helped run the Pentagon in the Reagan administration. Paul Wolfowitz, the new deputy secretary of defense in 2001, had collaborated closely with Armitage when the two men were responsible for America's relations with Asia under Reagan. Wolfowitz had also served in the Pentagon as a top aide to Cheney. During the 1990s, when the Republicans were out of power, Wolfowitz had served on a prominent missile commission headed by Rumsfeld, and Armitage had run a small private consulting firm that employed Cheney's daughter.

By 2001 the Republicans had already controlled the White House for twenty of the previous thirty-two years. Their frequent successes in presidential politics had opened the way for ambitious Republicans such as the Vulcans to accumulate more years of on-the-job experience in foreign policy than their counterparts in the Democratic party. They had a long history, a collective memory. Even the two youngest members of the Bush foreign policy team of 2001—the president himself and Rice, his national security adviser—possessed extraordinarily close ties to this legacy of the past. Bush's father of course had been president of the United States and before that had served as director of central intelligence and U.S. vice president. Rice had had the arduous task of coordinating policy toward the Soviet Union in the first Bush administration; she had been carefully groomed as a protégée by Brent Scowcroft, the elder Bush's national security adviser.

The interconnecting relationships and the overhang of the past extended down through the ranks of the faithful. The aides and disciples of the top leaders had also toiled and advanced together through the series of past Republican administrations. Some of them shuffled back and forth from one boss to another. I. Lewis (Scooter) Libby, Vice President Cheney's new chief of staff, had been an undergraduate student of Wolfowitz's at Yale University three decades earlier and had served as an aide to Wolfowitz for more than a decade during the Reagan and first Bush administrations. Several members of Rice's new National Security Council team had worked previously for Cheney, Wolfowitz or Armitage.

Because of this legacy, as the Republicans prepared to return to power in 2001, there were suggestions that America's relations with the world were about to be restored to what they had been in the first Bush administration. During the same week, *New York Times* columnists Maureen Dowd and Thomas L. Friedman chose the same word, *retreads,* to describe the people surrounding Bush. "George II was an obedient son who emulated his father, the old king, in all respects," wrote Dowd a few weeks later. "He felt no need to put his own stamp on his monarchy."[3]

Such perceptions extended well beyond the realm of newspaper columns. Overseas many foreign governments and scholars basked in a sense of security that a new Bush administration would follow largely along the lines of the previous one and that its policies would be predictable. Its veterans were thought to care about great power diplomacy, not moral crusades; about maintaining stability, not changing the world. "The Republicans are generally better at foreign and security policy than the Democrats," observed Yang Jiemian of the Shanghai Institute for International Studies.[4]

These predictions of restoration and continuity were soon shown to be wrong. From its first months in office the new Bush foreign policy team made clear that it would deal with the world in new ways. Its style was, from the outset, at variance with that of the first Bush administration. During the first nine months of 2001 the new administration adopted a more confrontational approach to dealing with North Korea and with China. It quickly pressed forward with plans to develop a missile defense system, despite the uneasiness of its European allies. It displayed a pronounced skepticism about the value of international agreements and treaties that it believed were not in the American interest.

The administration's distinctive approach to the world became considerably more pronounced after the terrorist attacks on the World Trade Center and the Pentagon on September 11, 2001. Over the following year the Vulcans put forth a remarkable series of new doctrines and ideas, ones that represented a dramatic break with the foreign policies and strategies of the past. In dealing with hostile powers, the Bush administration decided that the United States would no longer hold to the policies of containment and deterrence that had been the fundamental tenets of the cold war. Instead the United States would be willing to start a war through a preemptive attack. In the Middle East, where the United States had for decades worked closely with such authoritarian regimes as Saudi Arabia, the Bush administration broke precedent by openly espousing the cause of democracy and by talking about the political transformation of the entire region.

These developments represented something more profound than a minor change of direction from one Republican administration to another. They represented an epochal change, the flowering of a new view of America's status and role in the world. The vision was that of an unchallengeable America, a United States whose military power was so awesome that it no longer needed to make compromises or accommodations (unless it chose to do so) with any other nation or groups of countries.

This new worldview represented the culmination of ideas and dreams that had been evolving in Republican administrations for more than three decades. Their intellectual origins can be traced back to the Reagan administration and, still earlier, to events in the Ford administration—notably, to the responses to the American defeat in Vietnam and to Richard Nixon and Henry Kissinger's pursuit of détente with the Soviet Union.

Several of the Vulcans had begun their careers in Washington in reaction to those two developments. Three top officials of the George W. Bush administration—Rumsfeld, Cheney and Wolfowitz—had been participants in the debates over détente. Two others, Powell and Armitage, had served in the military in Vietnam. As these men rose through the ranks of Washington's foreign policy apparatus, they kept in mind the lessons and experiences of the 1970s: The United States should build up its military power, regain popular support for the armed forces and advance democratic ideals in such a way as to confront and, where possible, overwhelm its leading adversaries.

As a group the Vulcans embodied a unique generation in American foreign policy, one every bit as distinctive as the "Wise Men" (such as Dean Acheson, George Kennan, Averell Harriman and John McCloy) who created a new American foreign policy at the end of World War II or the "Best and Brightest" (the Kennedys, Robert McNamara, the Bundys and Rostows) who prosecuted the Vietnam War in the 1960s.[5]

The Wise Men had come to government from the worlds of business, banking and international law; their spiritual home was Wall Street and the network of investment banks and law firms connected to it. The Best and Brightest had come to government with strong backgrounds in academia; their spiritual home was Cambridge, Massachusetts, and the Harvard campus where many of them had studied or taught.

The Vulcans were the military generation. Their wellspring, the common institution in their careers, was the Pentagon. The top levels of the foreign policy team that took office in 2001 included two former secretaries of defense (Cheney and Rumsfeld), one former chairman of the Joint Chiefs of Staff (Powell), one former undersecretary of defense (Wolfowitz) and one former assistant secretary of defense (Armitage). Even Rice had started her career in Washington with a stint at the Pentagon, working for the Joint Chiefs of Staff.

In the 1940s the Wise Men had concentrated on constructing institutions, both international and in Washington, that would help preserve democracy and capitalism in a threatened Europe. For institution building, their skills of law and business proved invaluable. Kennedy's Best and Brightest had attempted, with less success, to make use of their academic expertise to extend American influence in the third world and counter what they saw as Communist movements in Asia and Africa.

The Vulcans were different. They were focused above all on American military power. In the 1970s and early 1980s their goal was to help the armed forces recover and rebuild after Vietnam. In the late 1980s and early 1990s they attempted to figure out when and how America's revitalized military power should be employed. By the first years of the twenty-first century, with U.S. war-making abilities beyond question, they were trying to sketch out a new role for America, one that took into account the overwhelming gulf between America's military power and that of any other nation.

The Vulcans represented the generation that bridged what are commonly depicted as two separate and distinct periods of modern history: cold war and post–cold war. For the Vulcans, the disintegration of the Soviet Union represented only a middle chapter in the narrative, not the end or the beginning.

Hundreds of books have been written about America's role in the cold war. Most of these works end in 1989, with the fall of the Berlin Wall, or in 1991, with the Soviet collapse. There is an entire school of study that is now called cold war history. Meanwhile, over the past decade, many other books have been devoted to what is commonly called the post–cold war world, and these works tend to begin in 1989–1991. All these books tend to assume that the end of the cold war marked a break so fundamental that historical narratives must either start or stop there.

The story of the Vulcans serves as a reminder that this bifurcation of history into cold war and post–cold war is ultimately artificial. In their careers, the Vulcans worked on both sides of the arbitrary divide. While working in government, they confronted firsthand both the world of the Berlin Wall and the world without it.

If we can reach beyond our continuing preoccupation with the end of the cold war, then we can begin to detect, through the lives of these Vulcans, a coherent narrative. It is the story of the gradual rise of an America whose strength is without precedent in the history of the world. Indeed, we can look at the time span covered in this book as itself a distinct historical period. Between the early 1970s and 2003 American power rose gradually from its nadir, at the end of the war in Vietnam, to a position of incontestable military power.

At the beginning of this era the United States was reeling from its defeat in Southeast Asia. A common view, both overseas and at home, was that the United States was in decline. The American military was in disrepute and was beset by racial tensions; in Congress, defense budgets were regularly under attack. The United States was eager for a new series of understandings overseas: détente with the Soviet Union and, meanwhile, a new relationship with China to help keep the Soviets in check.

Then America reversed course. Over the following decades the United States elected repeatedly to augment its power and to wield its economic and military might in such a way that it could overwhelm any potential rival. The Vulcans were at the center of these events and these choices. They were among those who were convinced America was not in decline, that it was and should be the world's most powerful nation and should advance its values and ideals overseas. Through the Vulcans and their careers we can see the transformation of America and the emergence of its role as the world's reigning superpower.

The purpose of this book is to examine the beliefs and the worldview of the Vulcans, Bush's foreign policy team, by tracing the histories of six of its leading members: Cheney, Rumsfeld, Powell, Armitage, Wolfowitz and Rice. The aim is to try to understand how and why America came to deal with the rest of the world in the ways that it did during the George W. Bush administration. Where did the ideas of the Vulcans come from? Why did these six Vulcans, in particular, rise to the top of the Republican foreign policy apparatus? What was it in their backgrounds and experiences that caused them to make the choices they made after taking office in 2001 and after the terrorist attacks of September 11?

An explanation may be in order about the terminology *Vulcans.* I am using the word symbolically to refer to anyone who worked on foreign policy in previous Republican administrations and then returned to office under George W. Bush.

The six people covered in this book were not all direct participants in the campaign advisory unit where the word *Vulcans* was first used. Cheney, Rumsfeld and Powell weren't members of this campaign group because they were above it; they were too senior for the day-to-day activities of electoral politics. All three, however, played crucial roles in the Bush campaign.

There were many other foreign policy hands from past Republican administrations who were not part of the campaign advisory group but who came back to power in 2001: men and women such as Scooter Libby, Deputy National Security Adviser Stephen Hadley, Undersecretary of Defense Douglas Feith and Undersecretary of State Paula Dobriansky. All of them qualify as Vulcans. I have chosen to concentrate on the careers and the views of six individuals because they were the most prominent and powerful of all the Vulcans.

In calling the Vulcans a generation, I do not mean to suggest that they all thought alike. Quite obviously, they did not. For example, the differences in outlook that often emerged between Powell and Armitage at the State Department, and Rumsfeld and Wolfowitz at the Pentagon—differences over Iraq, over the Middle East, over North Korea and other issues—were genuine and serious. They took up considerable energy within the administration, and they certainly dominated the daily press coverage of the administration.

Nevertheless, these disagreements tended to obscure the larger agreements in outlook among the Vulcans. All of them believed in the importance of American military power. Powell had been famously cautious about the use of force, but his aim was to avoid another Vietnam and to shepherd and preserve the U.S. armed forces; Powell supported the overall goal of military strength, as did other leaders, such as Wolfowitz, who were less hesitant about American military action. During the 1989–1991 period, when the Pentagon was trying to limit congressional efforts to cut back the defense budget, Powell and Wolfowitz were allies.

Moreover, as befitted their Pentagon backgrounds, all the Vulcans tended to concentrate on traditional national security issues, leaving America's role in the international economy largely in the hands of private businesses. Their approach differed from the economic-oriented focus of the Clinton administration, when the National Economic Council was for a time more powerful than the National Security Council and when the Treasury Department and the International Monetary Fund became prime instruments of American foreign policy.

All the Vulcans believed that American power and ideals are, on the whole, a force for good in the world. In that sense, they all differed from liberal Democrats, such as those in the Carter administration and in Congress, who worried about America's abuses of power and sought to create rules and an international order that might help curb such abuses.

Finally, throughout their careers, the Vulcans' view also tended to be optimistic about America's capabilities and its future. In this sense, the Vulcans' view differed from the gloomy outlook of Henry Kissinger, who had reigned over foreign policy in the Republican administrations of the early 1970s; it also differed from the perspective of Ross Perot, who warned in the late 1980s of the rise of Japan and of America's impending decline. Kissinger and his followers thought a weakened America needed détente; Perot and his followers believed that an unwitting United States was being made ever weaker. The Vulcans, by contrast, assumed that America was strong and getting stronger.

Characterizations of the Bush administration as divided overlook these commonalities. One way to illustrate this point is to look at the history of Powell and Armitage, the two State Department officials commonly depicted as the doves or liberals within the George W. Bush administration.

In 1981 Ronald Reagan became the most conservative American president since Calvin Coolidge. Within his administration the leading hardliner was Defense Secretary Caspar Weinberger. Powell and Armitage emerged as Weinberger's two key aides; in other words, they were loyal followers of the most hawkish cabinet member in the most hawkish administration in a half century. Armitage was one of the officials implementing the Reagan doctrine, the effort to provide military and financial support for armed rebellions against regimes supported by the Soviet Union. A few years later Powell was sounded out about the possibility of joining the Democratic party as vice presidential nominee or as secretary of state. He declined because on foreign policy issues he felt much more at home with the Republicans.

Powell and Armitage, in short, may have been doves in comparison with some of their colleagues at the Pentagon in the George W. Bush administration, but within the broad spectrum of American foreign policy over the past three decades, they were hardly doves and in fact shared much in common with the other Vulcans. Their relationship with hawks like Cheney, Rumsfeld and Wolfowitz was akin to that of a feuding family. They bickered; but they seemed to need one another, and they all kept on coming back to the dinner table.

And what of George W. Bush himself? Why not include the president of the United States in this book along with these six individuals who served under him? I have left Bush out for several reasons.

Bush himself had not worked directly on foreign policy before 2001. He had not been obliged to develop his beliefs or to execute policy during the cold war, the Gulf War or any other of the crises that dominated America's relations with the world over the previous decades. Bush's father had possessed his own base of prior knowledge with which to make presidential decisions. For example, the joke was that the senior Bush, the former American envoy to Beijing, was the day-to-day "desk officer" for China. The same could not be said for his son. What he did after 2001 cannot really be viewed as an evolution or judged against the backdrop of his own past because when it came to foreign policy, George W. Bush had no past. He was not, in that sense, a Vulcan.

Because Bush's prior experience was so limited, he was obliged to rely to an extraordinary extent on his advisers for ideas and for information. He could not have made decisions if the Vulcans had not laid out the choices; he could not have formulated policy without the words and ideas they brought to him. That reality too increased the importance of the Vulcans.

To say this is not to denigrate George W. Bush or to minimize his importance. Bush's inexperience in foreign policy was not necessarily a crippling defect. Those who complained that Bush had rarely traveled abroad before becoming president overlooked the fact that neither had Harry Truman. Before coming to the White House, Truman had never left the United States except for a one-year tour of duty in Europe as a soldier during World War I; he nonetheless became one of America's greatest presidents in the field of foreign policy.

Bush was the manager, the decision maker, the ultimate arbiter whenever, as happened frequently, those below him disagreed on foreign policy. This authority in itself represented awesome power. He also set the overall political direction for his administration, and that role too was of critical importance for foreign policy.

Nevertheless, the subject of this book is America's evolving relationship with the world over the past thirty years. For that, one must look to the members of Bush's foreign policy team and to the ways their views developed over time.

Americans often tend to overpersonalize the role of the president of the United States. The president's press aides and personal advisers, for their own reasons, foster the perception that the president is not merely at the center of everything but is in fact the driving force for every action taken by the U.S. government. Journalists and scholars scour the childhoods, the educations and the earlier careers of American presidents on the assumption that every triumph, every trauma, every Rosebud in the life of a president is significant. In reality, of course, the actions and words issued in the name of the president generally reflect the views of the officials working beneath him.

In many books about modern American history, the president is the central character. Here, in the story of the Vulcans and a changing America, he plays only a supporting role.

Rise of the Vulcans

CHAPTER ONE

A Rising Politician
Amid War and Dirty Tricks

DURING THE MIDDAY HOURS of Wednesday, April 7, 1971, Richard Nixon was sitting in his hideaway office in the Executive Office Building, next door to the White House, attempting to prepare himself for that night's prime-time presidential address to the nation. The subject, as usual, was Vietnam. And yet, as Nixon went over his speech with his two top aides, National Security Adviser Henry Kissinger and Chief of Staff H. R. (Bob) Haldeman, the conversation kept returning to a different topic—namely, what the president, with growing irritation, called "the Rumsfeld problem." Nixon was thinking of getting rid of Donald H. Rumsfeld, the former congressman then serving on the White House staff. "I think Rumsfeld may be not too long for this world," he said, adding, a few minutes later, "Let's dump him."[1]

The problem was that Rumsfeld was becoming, from Nixon and Kissinger's perspective, a troublesome antiwar advocate. Increasingly, Rumsfeld had emerged at the center of a small group of administration officials, all of them involved with domestic policy, who were privately questioning in staff meetings why the administration could not move more quickly to end the war. The internal opponents also included George Shultz, director of the Office of Management and Budget; Clark MacGregor, the counselor for congressional relations; and John Ehrlichman, who was in charge of domestic policy.

"They don't know a goddamn thing about foreign policy!" Nixon had exploded over the telephone to Kissinger a day earlier. "They're only concerned about, frankly, peace at any price, really. Because all they're concerned with is, well, revenue-sharing and the environment and all that crap—which doesn't amount to anything in my opinion." Kissinger had concurred, saying, "They don't know what we'll be hit with if this whole thing comes apart."[2]

The Vietnam War had reached a milestone the previous week: It had now claimed more American lives than had the Korean War. Vietnam had thus become the fourth most lethal conflict in American history, after the Civil War and the two world wars. At home it had created ever-greater upheavals on college campuses, in the streets of major cities and also in American politics. That spring a new round of antiwar protests was building. A Democratic challenger, Senator Edmund Muskie, was gearing up to run against Nixon in 1972; Muskie was challenging Nixon on the war, and polls showed that he was even with or ahead of the president. Even Republicans in Congress were becoming restive; in early April, nine Republican senators had met with Defense Secretary Melvin Laird at the home of Senator Jacob Javits of New York to plead for Nixon to end the war.[3]

For nearly two months Rumsfeld had been seeking some new role in the administration through which he could influence the administration's policy on Vietnam. In the process, he had become a particular annoyance to Kissinger. Rumsfeld's first attempt, in a memo to Nixon dated February 27, 1971, was to propose the appointment of "a high-level Presidential aide to review and report on postwar Southeast Asia during the winding down of hostilities." The detailed paper left no doubt Rumsfeld had himself in mind for this job. The special envoy could lay the groundwork for postwar reconstruction of Southeast Asia, Rumsfeld argued; he insisted such an envoy would not intrude on Kissinger's turf as national security adviser. Rumsfeld told Nixon that such an appointment "would focus attention and emphasis on Indo-China *peace* instead of Indo-China war."[4] In bureaucratic language, Rumsfeld was asking Nixon to give peace a chance.

Henry Kissinger was not about to yield any authority over Vietnam policy to this pushy politician. Kissinger's deputy, Alexander Haig, at first postponed any response to Rumsfeld's memo for weeks, then sent a reply saying that introducing a special envoy "would confuse our allies as to who was doing what."[5] Undaunted, Rumsfeld broached this idea in a one-on-one Oval Office meeting with Nixon. The president brushed him off. Nixon offered instead a diversion, suggesting that Rumsfeld broaden his foreign policy experience with a brief mission overseas. "It might be better from your standpoint—I think you want to take a trip to Europe," he told Rumsfeld. The trip, for the ostensible purpose of exchanging ideas with European officials about drug abuse, was scheduled for later that spring.[6]

Yet Rumsfeld still did not let go of Vietnam. On the morning of April 7 he pressed Kissinger in the presence of other White House staff members for an explanation of why the administration couldn't move more quickly to bring the war to a close. Afterward Kissinger grumbled to the president that Rumsfeld had never quite said exactly what he wanted Nixon to do. He had never called specifically for Nixon to set a "date certain" for the end of the war (as Nixon's critics were requesting) but had only spoken more vaguely of setting a date by which the United States would reduce its presence to a "residual force" in Vietnam. It was this staff meeting, and Rumsfeld's overall stance on Vietnam, that prompted Nixon to talk about firing him. The president also worried that Rumsfeld might quit first.

"He's ready to jump the ship, Rummy," Nixon said during his later meeting with Haldeman and Kissinger.[7]

"No, I don't think he's ready to jump," said Haldeman. "And I doubt if he ever would, just because [staying on in the administration] serves his interests more than not. But I don't think he's ever going to be a solid member of the ship."

"He's just positioning himself to be close to the *Washington Post* and the *New York Times,*" Kissinger interjected.

Nixon returned to business. "Well, then, let's dump him right after this," he said. "Good God, we're sending him and [the White House adviser Robert] Finch on a two-month holiday to Europe. Shit. For what purpose?"

"To get him out of town," said Kissinger, gently reminding his boss that Rumsfeld's "holiday" in Europe had originally been a Nixon-Kissinger idea.

Nixon tried to go back to the task of rehearsing that night's speech, in which he would announce that he planned to withdraw a hundred thousand Americans from Vietnam by the end of the year, but in which he also would explicitly refuse to set a date for the end of the war. Still, Nixon couldn't put Rumsfeld out of his mind.

"Coming back to the Rumsfeld problem—I'm disappointed in Don, Bob," he told Haldeman a few minutes later. "Understand, I don't want to be disappointed, just because—I don't want somebody who's just with us, God damn it, when things are going good, you know what I mean? If he thinks we're going down the tubes, and he's just going to ride with us, maybe he's going to take a trip to Europe occasionally—then screw him, you know?"

What galled Nixon especially was that Rumsfeld, who was viewed as one of the administration's most effective public speakers, refused to go out and defend the Nixon administration to the American people. "He won't step up to anything," Nixon grumbled. "We have given him time and time again, opportunities to step up, and he will not step up and kick the ball."

Haldeman agreed. "I used to think at one point he was a potential presidential contender, but he isn't," he told the president.

"He's like Finch," Nixon said. "They both have the charisma for national office, but neither has got the backbone."

Nixon's irritation with Rumsfeld eventually subsided. He was one of several aides Nixon talked about dumping but never did; Rumsfeld remained in the administration until its premature end. Yet the Vietnam episode provides a glimpse at how Rumsfeld's work in the Nixon administration contradicted some of the simplistic perceptions Americans came to have of Rumsfeld many years later.

During the following three decades Rumsfeld came to be viewed as an ardent hawk, a champion of American military power. Those perceptions do not fit the early phases of his career, when, as a fervent proponent of domestic reform, he was a moderate to liberal force within the Nixon administration. His dovish views matched his political ambitions: The war was unpopular, and Rumsfeld, as an adviser on domestic policy, had no personal or professional stake in winning it. Indeed, Rumsfeld, who throughout his government career seemed to relish bureaucratic combat, may have viewed Vietnam as an issue on which he could challenge Kissinger's primacy within the government (something Rumsfeld once again did with greater success in his more hawkish guise during the Ford administration).

Over the years another assumption about Rumsfeld has taken hold:

that he had no connection at all to the seamier side of the Nixon administration, the bare-knuckled political apparatus that waged combat with Nixon's political enemies. This idea was based in part on the fact that Rumsfeld was appointed ambassador to NATO and was thus thousands of miles away in Europe in 1973 and 1974, as the Watergate scandal crested and Nixon resigned. Gerald Ford, the old friend who brought Rumsfeld back to Washington to take charge of the White House staff after Nixon's resignation, helped foster this perception. "He [Rumsfeld] wouldn't tolerate political shenanigans and the men around Nixon knew he wouldn't, so to protect themselves, they kept him out of the loop," Ford wrote.[8]

However, Nixon's secret White House tape recordings portray a more complex reality. Rumsfeld was not entirely divorced from Nixon's political operations. There is no sign that Rumsfeld was involved in any of the illegalities of Watergate, but he was willing to offer Nixon other low-level help of a not particularly exalted nature—some dirt on political enemies, some covert ties with a prominent pollster. The Nixon tapes show that Rumsfeld was often working with and was a special favorite of John Mitchell and Charles Colson, Nixon's two roughest political operators, who viewed Rumsfeld as more savvy than other White House aides. Indeed, when Nixon first considered naming Rumsfeld NATO ambassador in the summer of 1971, Mitchell urged the president to delay the appointment until after the presidential election, and Nixon decided Mitchell was right. "Let me say this—he has done some good political stuff for Mitchell. He'll cooperate. NATO's fine, but it pulls him out of politics," Nixon told Haldeman about Rumsfeld at one point. ". . . He's an operator."[9] In short, the secret White House tape recordings demonstrate that Rumsfeld was not nearly so marginal a figure in Nixon's political apparatus as he was later portrayed.

Nixon and Rumsfeld seem to have formed a curious but strong bond early on. Rumsfeld saw Nixon as a mentor. In a series of lengthy one-on-one conversations in the White House, Rumsfeld repeatedly sought to advance to a cabinet job inside the administration and, at the same time, to obtain Nixon's advice on his political career. Rumsfeld was of course gaining private tutelage from America's most skilled political infighter.

Nixon valued Rumsfeld too. From Nixon's perspective, Rumsfeld stood in a different category from aides like Haldeman, Ehrlichman and Kissinger; as a former congressman Rumsfeld was the only senior White House staff member who had repeatedly subjected himself, as Nixon had, to the hazards and potential public humiliations of running for elective office. Nixon's political defeats in 1960 and 1962 and his long, acrimony-filled career had left the president not only with a strain of self-pity but also with a strong sense of a personal identification with other politicians. Top White House aides like Haldeman and Ehrlichman loathed Rumsfeld for his ambition and his self-promotion, but for Richard Nixon, these qualities did not count against Rumsfeld. Moreover, Nixon thought Rumsfeld was a good public face for the administration, and Nixon hoped to make use of him, especially in courting voters on college campuses and in America's suburbs. "He's young, he's thirty-nine years old, he's a hell of a spokesman," Nixon said.[10]

Yet their relationship remained largely private. In public Rumsfeld never seemed as though he were a central part of the Nixon administration. Nixon discovered, to his frustration, that Rumsfeld was too often willing to challenge existing policy inside the White House and not willing enough to defend it in public. For Rumsfeld's part, he never managed to obtain from Nixon the central role or the cabinet appointment he wanted. As things turned out after Watergate, Rumsfeld was fortunate that he was never identified too closely with Nixon.

Donald Henry Rumsfeld's father, a Chicago real estate broker named George Rumsfeld, had moved his family around the country during a stint in the Navy in World War II and then returned to settle on Chicago's North Shore. Donald went to New Trier High School, where he was the star of the school's state championship wrestling team. He went on to Princeton, where he became the captain of the wrestling team. One teammate, two years ahead of him, was Frank Carlucci, who, like Rumsfeld, was to rise to the top of America's national security apparatus.[11]

After college Rumsfeld spent three years in the Navy, where he became a pilot and flight instructor and, yet again, a wrestling champion; he hoped for a chance at the 1956 Olympics but gave up because of a shoulder injury. In the late 1950s he worked as a congressional aide in Washington. Eventually he decided to run for Congress himself. He entered the 1962 Republican primary for a congressional seat in Chicago's northern suburbs. His main rival was an Evanston insurance executive whose company had been under state investigation. One of Rumsfeld's campaign aides, the young Republican Jeb Stuart Magruder (later convicted of perjury in the Watergate scandal), made sure Rumsfeld's rival was asked repeatedly about the insurance investigation. Rumsfeld won the primary and captured the seat.[12]

In Congress, Rumsfeld first began to display some of the distinctive style that would mark his career for decades. Fellow representatives found that he hated clichés and enjoyed embarrassing in public those who lapsed into jargon-filled speech. He served on the House Committee on Science and Astronautics and took a special interest in the space program. Once an official of the National Aeronautics and Space Administration began telling the committee how NASA would do this project "in-house" and that project "in-house" and another project "in-house." Exasperated, Rumsfeld finally interjected, "What about the out-house?"[13]

Rumsfeld's voting record was not unlike that of other Republicans from the northern suburbs; he was economically conservative but socially moderate.[14] He supported civil rights legislation; he was a leader in the drive to replace the military draft with a volunteer army. (Four decades later, when Rumsfeld was secretary of defense, two members of Congress who were opposed to military action against Iraq introduced legislation to reinstate the draft. Rumsfeld, drawing on his old arguments from the 1960s, said that draftees had added "no value, no advantage, really" to the armed services. He was quickly obliged to apologize to veterans' groups.[15])

Rumsfeld also took a modest interest in foreign policy. In 1962, Richard Allen, the conservative Republican who later became Ronald Reagan's national security adviser, set up a think tank called the Center for Strategic Studies at Georgetown University. Rumsfeld was one of the organization's earliest congressional allies. "We organized a little salon back when the members of Congress still had time to think and breathe," said Allen. "Rumsfeld would come over along with a little coterie of Republican and Democratic congressmen. And Rumsfeld and I formed a friendship. We didn't have any money; we drove Volkswagens and went to each other's houses and drank jug wine and ate spaghetti."[16]

Rumsfeld's main achievement during this period was his role in a successful challenge to the existing political order on Capitol Hill. Following Barry Goldwater's humiliating defeat in the 1964 presidential election, some Republicans in the House of Representatives decided to push for new party leadership. The Republican minority leader at the time was Charles Halleck, of Indiana. Rumsfeld emerged at the head of this group of insurgents, which also included Representatives Charles Goodell of New York, Robert Griffin of Michigan, Albert Quie of Minnesota and Robert Ellsworth of Kansas. The group moved to dump Halleck and replace him with Representative Gerald Ford of Michigan.[17] The effort succeeded, and Rumsfeld became one of Ford's closest advisers.

For a generally conservative Republican congressman, Rumsfeld maintained some surprising friendships among the Democrats. One of his closest associates in the House of Representatives was Allard K. Lowenstein, a leader of the antiwar movement and perhaps the most liberal member of Congress at the time, who in 1967 led the fight within the Democratic party to drop Lyndon Johnson as the party's presidential nominee. Rumsfeld and Lowenstein had served as congressional aides together in the late 1950s and once dreamed of buying a country newspaper together.[18]

During the 1968 campaign Rumsfeld performed one noteworthy bit of service for the Republican presidential nominee Richard Nixon. Knowing that Rumsfeld came from Chicago, Nixon had asked him to help run a small Republican operation inside the Conrad Hilton Hotel during the Democratic National Convention there in August. The twenty-eight-story Hilton was serving as the headquarters for Vice President Hubert Humphrey, the leading Democrat, and for Eugene McCarthy, the antiwar candidate; many other Democratic delegates were staying there too. Working with several other Nixon supporters, Rumsfeld was supposed to serve as a public spokesman for the Republican candidate, providing reporters with on-the-spot responses to Democratic accusations. In addition, Nixon, a voracious, lifelong consumer of political intelligence, asked Rumsfeld to report back on what he saw and heard that week, from both the participants at the convention and the protesters expected outside it. When violence erupted, Rumsfeld served as Nixon's lookout man.[19]

In the afternoon and evening hours of August 28, 1968, Chicago police chased antiwar demonstrators through downtown streets and attacked them with their nightsticks. Some of the worst beatings took place along Michigan Avenue, directly in front of the Hilton. As he watched the bloodshed from his window inside the hotel, Rumsfeld provided quick eyewitness accounts for Nixon and his aides, who were relaxing and preparing their fall campaign in Key Biscayne, Florida.

"He would call up and say, 'They're breaking bones! Omigosh, look at that!' " recalled Robert Ellsworth, then serving as Nixon's national political director, who was on the other end of the phone when Rumsfeld called in from Chicago. "The information wasn't that politically useful, but it was titillating to the candidate. Nixon loved those details," Ellsworth added.

By 1968 Rumsfeld had been serving in Congress for nearly six years. He was ready for a change. After campaigning for Nixon throughout the country that fall, he hoped to be named Republican national chairman if Nixon won the election. He didn't get the job. As happened on other occasions throughout his career, Rumsfeld's driving, combative style had pleased the top man, Nixon, but had made powerful enemies among others near the top, particularly Haldeman, Nixon's chief of staff. According to Ellsworth, Haldeman blocked Rumsfeld both from the party chairmanship (which eventually went to a more easygoing congressman, Rogers Morton) and from various top jobs in the administration. Rumsfeld then sought a new position in the House Republican leadership as head of the party's Research and Planning Committee but lost out on that post too to Ohio Representative Robert A. Taft, Jr. In the process of leading the movement for Ford, Rumsfeld had antagonized some other party leaders in the House. By the early months of 1969 Rumsfeld seemed stuck, an up-and-coming congressman looking for a next rung to climb.

Three months after Nixon's inauguration, a job finally opened up. Two Republican governors had turned down Nixon's invitations to head the Office of Economic Opportunity, the agency established during the Johnson administration to run new programs aimed at eliminating poverty. Nixon offered the job to Rumsfeld, who had voted in Congress against many of these antipoverty programs. The job "was less than what he wanted but more than Haldeman wanted him to get," said Ellsworth.

Before taking the job, Rumsfeld bargained hard. At a meeting with Nixon in Key Biscayne, he won assurances that he would be named not only head of the antipoverty agency but also an assistant to the president, with cabinet-level status and an office in the White House. The concurrent White House appointment turned out to be important because it helped overcome a legal obstacle: The Constitution bars a member of Congress from accepting any job in the federal government if the salary for that job has been increased during the representative's time in office. While Rumsfeld was in Congress, it had increased the salary of the OEO director from $30,000 to $42,500. However, the Nixon administration obtained a memorandum from its bright new assistant attorney general, William H. Rehnquist, explaining that Rumsfeld's constitutional problem could be circumvented if Nixon agreed to pay him no salary for his work as OEO director and $42,500 for his work as a White House adviser. Rumsfeld thus got his first job in the Nixon administration partly through the convoluted legal reasoning of the future chief justice of the United States.[20]

One of Rumsfeld's first actions in the Nixon administration was a seemingly minor personnel decision the impact of which reverberated for decades. Rumsfeld was looking for a right-hand man to help run his office. He found and hired a twenty-eight-year-old Capitol Hill staff aide and graduate student named Richard Cheney.

Richard Cheney had grown up in Casper, Wyoming, the son of a career civil servant with the Department of Agriculture. He had been a football star and class president at Natrona County High School, where he dated the Wyoming state champion baton twirler, Lynne Vincent. He won a rare scholarship to Yale University but dropped out within two years. "I didn't relate to Yale at all," he later explained. ". . . I had some romantic notions about wanting to get out and see the world—or at least traveling all around the West."[21]

Cheney moved back west as what he later called a "lineman for the county," building power lines on construction crews in Wyoming, Colorado and Utah. Eventually he returned to college, at the University of Wyoming, married Lynne Vincent and went off with her to graduate school at the University of Wisconsin, where he became a doctoral candidate in political science. He was eligible for the military draft during the Vietnam War but obtained deferments, first as a student and then as a parent after his and Lynne's first daughter, Elizabeth, was born in 1966. (More than two decades later, when he was questioned by the Senate Armed Services Committee about these draft deferments, Cheney offered a memorable reply: "I had other priorities in the '60s than military service." He said that he would have been happy to serve if he had been called and that he believed the U.S. involvement in Vietnam had been a noble cause.)[22]

In 1968 Cheney had come to Washington on a fellowship from the American Political Science Association that enabled him to work for a member of Congress. One of the representatives with whom he interviewed for a job was Rumsfeld, but Cheney, the future vice president, failed to impress Rumsfeld, the future defense secretary. The applicant was neither particularly eloquent nor dynamic. "It was one of the more unpleasant experiences of my life," Cheney recalled in a 1986 speech. ". . . The truth is I flunked the interview. After half an hour, it was clear to both of us that there was no possibility that I could work for him."[23]

Cheney landed in the office of Representative William Steiger of Wisconsin. He was working there in the spring of 1969 when he noticed a note on Steiger's desk from Rumsfeld, looking for advice and help in his new OEO job. Cheney spotted an opportunity. Over a weekend he wrote an unsolicited memo for Steiger on how to staff and run a federal agency. The following week Steiger passed on the memo to Rumsfeld. A few weeks after reading it, Rumsfeld called up Cheney and offered him a position as his special assistant.[24]

It was the beginning of Cheney's long apprenticeship with Rumsfeld. Over most of the next seven years in the Nixon and Ford administrations, Cheney served as Rumsfeld's doorkeeper and top administrator in Washington. He proved to be quiet, discreet and efficient. Those working for Rumsfeld soon discovered that the way to get things done was to go to Cheney. Rumsfeld's style was to run day-to-day operations by remote control, issuing edicts and obtaining information through a special assistant. Cheney, as that assistant, gradually took on importance of his own. "When you gave something to Dick," one OEO veteran recalled, "it happened. It got done."[25]

They were a complementary pair, each offering traits the other didn't possess. Rumsfeld was full of energy; Cheney was low-keyed. Rumsfeld was overflowing with words and ideas; Cheney, the laconic westerner, never used a word beyond what the situation required. Rumsfeld always seemed to want more: more turf, expanded missions, a bigger job; Cheney appeared to the world as unfailingly modest and patient. Rumsfeld challenged people head-on and, in the process, made many others nervous or resentful; the self-effacing Cheney, by contrast, usually managed to leave adversaries thinking that whatever happened to them was merely the business of government and nothing personal. Rumsfeld loved to shake up the established order; Cheney conveyed an air of reassurance and stability.

Yet despite their contrasting styles, the two men tended to think alike. They were to work together, on and off, over a course of more than three decades without any strong differences of opinion emerging between them.

Cheney was merely one of several future leaders working at the OEO in those years, at a time when the eradication of poverty was given much higher priority than it would be later on. Rumsfeld also recruited Frank Carlucci, his friend and wrestling teammate from Princeton, to serve as one of his top aides. Thus, curiously, during the Nixon administration three of America's future secretaries of defense—Rumsfeld, Carlucci and Cheney—all were working alongside one another in an agency dedicated to social change. The OEO's employees in the late 1960s and early 1970s also included Bill Bradley, the future senator and presidential candidate; Christine Todd Whitman, the future governor of New Jersey and EPA administrator; Mickey Kantor, the future U.S. trade representative; Jim Leach, the future congressman; and Terry Lenzner, the future investigator and staff member for the Senate Watergate Committee. John D. Rockefeller IV had served as one of the earliest recruits of VISTA (Volunteers in Service to America), the OEO agency that served as the domestic version of the Peace Corps; VISTA assigned Rockefeller to West Virginia, where he later settled down and was elected first governor and then U.S. senator.

Many of them had been attracted by the idealism of the agency's mission. When Lyndon Johnson established the Office of Economic Opportunity in 1964, he had told Congress that "for the first time in our history, it is possible to conquer poverty."[26] The programs the agency had started in its early years included not only VISTA but the Job Corps for disadvantaged youth, legal services for the poor and Head Start, the education program for preschool children.

In its first three years under the Democrats, as OEO personnel began to organize and speak up for the poor, the agency aroused intense opposition from governors, local officials and the business community. In the most contentious of these disputes, lawyers for the antipoverty program in California had helped represent migrant farm workers in disputes against agricultural interests. In response, Governor Ronald Reagan tried to cut off OEO funding for the legal aid program.

During the 1968 campaign Nixon had promised to bring the antipoverty program to heel. According to Leonard Garment, Nixon's White House counselor and former law partner, Nixon's main objective for the OEO was "getting control of all the *meshuggenehs* who were driving governors and other people crazy."[27]

Rumsfeld was thus stepping into a potentially poisonous situation, taking over an agency that had been created by the Democrats and filled with enthusiastic young employees, but that was despised by the president for whom he worked. He quickly moved to curb some of the OEO's excesses. He drafted new rules that restricted the hiring of individuals with "recent convictions of serious crimes." He also directed that the VISTA program begin to hire older volunteers, who were better educated and had more skills to offer.[28]

Nevertheless, within a few months Rumsfeld also quickly became a staunch and surprisingly tough advocate for the antipoverty agency. This was Rumsfeld's first job in the executive branch of government, and from the very start he demonstrated a particular talent for defending his bureaucratic turf. To get what his organization needed, he quietly pushed the White House and the budget officers, and he also learned to go outside the administration to Congress and the press to counter resistance from within the administration.[29] He was trying to do his best for the agency, hoping to make it succeed.

In a speech to the National Press Club seven months after taking charge of the OEO, Rumsfeld even defended the concept of federally funded legal services, saying that "justice for the poor" was part of his agency's mission. By this point Rumsfeld was beginning to be viewed as a rare moderate, even progressive voice within the Nixon administration and was becoming a target of conservatives. At the press conference that followed this speech, the very first questioner asked Rumsfeld about reports that he was viewed "with open hostility" in the Nixon White House.[30]

Over the following year Rumsfeld sponsored one notable new initiative that eventually became a cherished cause of American conservatives, tuition tax credits. It was the first salvo in an educational controversy that has persisted for decades. Rumsfeld argued that with tax credits or vouchers, "poor parents would be able to exercise some opportunity to choose, similar to that now enjoyed by wealthier parents, who can move to a 'better' public school district or send their children to private schools."[31]

In a memo to Nixon about the tax credit idea, Rumsfeld said he thought he could convince Jewish groups that their fears about a violation of the principle of separation of church and state were "groundless." However, Rumsfeld went on, "The education lobby . . . is clearly correct in perceiving the potential threat that these experiments pose to their comfortable world." That memo encapsulated Rumsfeld's brash style, his overconfidence in his persuasive powers and his eagerness to upset the existing order.[32]

By late 1970 Rumsfeld had decided it was time to move on. He had managed to keep the OEO from being gutted by the Nixon administration, but his conservative friends were telling him that he had already stayed in the job for too long and it was becoming a political liability.[33] He also had hopes for a bigger job in the administration.

Soon after the 1970 congressional elections, in which the Republicans had done poorly, Nixon and his team began talking about an administration shake-up. Rumsfeld figured prominently in the maneuvering. Haldeman wrote in his diary on November 7, 1970: "Decided major personnel changes. [George] Romney out [as secretary of housing and urban development], Rumsfeld to replace him."[34] But Romney refused to leave, and although Nixon and his aides talked about firing him, the president couldn't bring himself to do so. Instead Nixon and Haldeman moved Rumsfeld to the White House full-time, as a senior adviser, leaving him on hold for a future cabinet-level post and postponing the question of exactly what he would do while he waited.

Throughout 1971 and 1972, while Rumsfeld was serving as a full-time White House adviser, he had a series of intermittent private talks with the president about his own future, about American politics, foreign policy and the state of the world. Those long, meandering one-on-one conversations, preserved on the Nixon tape recordings, provide a remarkable insight into the two men.

Rumsfeld continued to speak up for moderate to liberal causes that ran against the generally conservative drift of the administration. His work at the antipoverty agency had given him a constituency and, for a time, a sense of purpose. "We need to be able to communicate with the young and the black and the people who are out, even though we don't get their vote," he told Nixon in one private conversation in March 1971.[35]

Nixon decided Rumsfeld's liberalism could be put to good use, winning support in places where the administration was weak. "I think Rumsfeld doing, frankly, two [kinds of] people, suburbia and young, sounds awfully good," he told Haldeman. ". . . Forget the environment, farting around with the old folks, the Negroes and everything, right now there has to be organized, I want to get something done on college youth."[36]

Nevertheless, Rumsfeld's political positions were hard to separate from his intense ambition. He appeared to hope that his progressive views would work to his advantage in an administration that was struggling to attract voters in the political center. His plea on behalf of "the young and the black and the people who are out" was made immediately after the president asked Rumsfeld for his opinion about Vice President Spiro Agnew. Nixon wondered why Agnew was so unpopular.

RUMSFELD: The vice president's demeanor . . . tends to tell people that he's not communicating with them. Look at his background. He came to this straight out of Maryland.
NIXON: Pretty hard to go straight out of Maryland to the top.
RUMSFELD: You better believe it! My goodness. I mean, I had three times as much experience in government as he did.[37]

It is hard to escape the conclusion that Rumsfeld would have liked the president to dump Agnew and run on a Nixon-Rumsfeld ticket in 1972.

The principal item on the agenda in these conversations was Rumsfeld's career. Nixon was engaging in one of his favorite pastimes, dispensing political advice. At the time of their talks both men assumed that eventually Rumsfeld would run for the U.S. Senate from his home state of Illinois. The main question was what jobs or experience would help him win a Senate seat. Nixon encouraged Rumsfeld to do something in foreign policy.

"Believe me, in any big sophisticated state, and yours is a big sophisticated state, it's about the world. It's not about their miserable little subjects," the president told Rumsfeld. He recounted his own experience as a representative from California, becoming active in the House Un-American Affairs Committee and in the investigation of Alger Hiss, so that when he ran for the Senate from California in 1950, he was considered a foreign policy "expert" and voters looked up to him.

Rumsfeld agreed that he'd like to be involved in foreign affairs because "that'd give me a credential." Nixon suggested Rumsfeld might consider a job in the Defense Department but warned him away from becoming a secretary of the Army, Navy or Air Force. "The service secretaries, well, they're just warts," the president said. "I like them as individuals, but they do not do important things."

Nixon also outlined for Rumsfeld which countries and regions of the world might help further the career of an aspiring politician and which wouldn't. "The only things that matter in the world are Japan and China, Russia and Europe," Nixon explained. "Latin America doesn't matter. Long as we've been in it, people don't give one damn about Latin America, Don." Stay away from Africa too, Nixon warned. As for the Middle East, he went on, getting involved there carried too many potential hazards for a politician. "People think it's for the purpose of catering to the Jewish vote," Nixon told Rumsfeld. "And anyway, there's nothing you can do about the Middle East."[38]

But while repeatedly dangling the possibility of an assignment overseas or some big new domestic post, Nixon offered nothing specific. "We always expected you to go to a cabinet spot—I still expect you to, but yet the damn thing just hasn't opened up," he had told Rumsfeld in March 1971. Four months later he apologized again. "What we talked about is not going to materialize," he told Rumsfeld. Romney was going to stay on in the cabinet, and so was Transportation Secretary John Volpe, who occupied another job to which Rumsfeld might have been appointed.[39]

While he waited, Rumsfeld did what he could to please the president, and that meant helping out the White House political operations. He worked with Mitchell and Colson, the key figures in Nixon's political apparatus. One secret bit of help Rumsfeld volunteered was to use his old Princeton ties for secret contacts with the Gallup Poll, which Colson believed had "dovish" instincts. "We have decided that we'll try Rumsfeld working with Gallup. He went to school with George [Gallup] Jr. at Princeton," Colson told the president in July 1971. Nixon and Colson were eager to try to influence the results of major pollsters, notably Gallup and Harris, perhaps getting them to phrase their questions or to present their results in ways that were helpful to Nixon. "I mean, if the figures aren't up there, we don't want them to lie about it," Nixon explained to Colson at one point. "They can trim them a little one way or another."[40]

There is no evidence in the Nixon tapes that Rumsfeld tried to sway the outcome of Gallup's polling results. Rumsfeld did, however, manage to glean some advance information about what Gallup's upcoming poll results would show, giving Nixon an edge of a few days to prepare. Rumsfeld appeared to realize that in these contacts he was asking Gallup to go beyond the traditional independent role of a pollster. At a White House session in October 1971, Rumsfeld urged Nixon to keep these contacts with the Gallup Poll top secret:

RUMSFELD: Say, I want to just report, sir, about my conversation with George Gallup [Jr.].
NIXON: Oh yeah, you went to school with him, didn't you?
RUMSFELD: I did. And I kind of want to be awful careful about telling people around the building that I'm talking to him. Because all he's got in his business is his integrity.

Rumsfeld then informed Nixon an upcoming Gallup Poll would show that the president's popularity had recently gone up.[41]

Nixon and Haldeman seemed to believe that these secret contacts through Rumfeld to and from the Gallup organization were paying off in subtle ways. On the eve of Nixon's trip to China, Haldeman told the president that the Gallup Poll would be timed in a way that would help Nixon. "I can't believe that Gallup would tell Rumsfeld that he would *hold* a poll," Nixon exclaimed. "Because Gallup was always, 'Jesus Christ, I call them as I see them.' " Haldeman explained that Gallup wasn't rescheduling the poll itself, but merely altering when the results would be made public. "He would wait and release it next month, after you got back," he explained.

When Rumsfeld and Robert Finch went on their tour of ten European countries in the spring of 1971, they focused primarily on the issue of drugs, but Rumsfeld also brought home to Nixon a bit of political dirt. One U.S. ambassador "gave us a pile of bad stuff about Muskie and his extracurricular activities," Rumsfeld said.

Nixon immediately perked up. "What kind of extracurricular activities?" he asked. "Business? Women?"

Rumsfeld apparently hadn't thought to be quite as inquisitive as Nixon. "I took it to be business or women," he replied vaguely. Thus he had carefully passed on the ambassador's message, without getting involved in the details, leaving it for the president to pursue on his own if he wished.[42] (Nothing ever came of the allegation, which, it appears, was without substance.)

For Rumsfeld, the amorphous job of White House counselor was frustrating. He had no agency or department to run and no particular mission. He kept pushing Nixon for some specific task. "You once told me I should do something in a line area, and I agree. I like that," he told the president. "There is a problem, potentially, with a guy floating around the White House."[43] If he was going to stay in the White House, he suggested, he should have a specific title or portfolio.

Nixon's top aides had disliked Rumsfeld since the start of the administration and especially resented him after he became a full-time White House aide. "The senior staff grew to realize that the ambitious Rumsfeld would decline every assignment that did not enhance his personal goals," John Ehrlichman later wrote.[44]

At one time or another Rumsfeld tossed out to Nixon the possibility of becoming the envoy for postwar reconstruction in Vietnam, the secretary of commerce, an emissary to Latin America or "something in the trade area." He also appears to have asked friends to put in a good word for him with the president when the job of U.S. ambassador to Japan opened up. Nixon groused to Haldeman that someone had suggested "maybe I could talk him [Rumsfeld] into" the Tokyo job. "I'm not going to talk him into doing *anything*," Nixon said. "If Rumsfeld wants to be an ambassador, let him say so! But Jesus Christ, Bob, what the hell—I don't think Rumsfeld can do Japan, you know, because I don't think he'd be tough enough [for] our side, the side of business, you know what I mean?"[45]

Finally, in the summer of 1971, Nixon settled on what he could offer. He suggested the possibility of Rumsfeld's becoming U.S. ambassador to NATO. Rumsfeld was interested. "It would certainly fill a gap in my background," he told the president.

Yet Rumsfeld was wary. Nixon's first appointee as NATO ambassador had been Ellsworth, who had been handed the job after a brief stint in the Nixon White House in which he had run afoul of others in the administration. Rumsfeld told the president that when Ellsworth became NATO ambassador, "it looked as if he was being dumped." Rumsfeld didn't want his own appointment to NATO to be handled "in a way that it looked like I was being kicked upstairs." Don't worry, Nixon replied.[46]

Nixon, it turned out, was even more hesitant. Six days after the president broached the NATO job with Rumsfeld, his top aides urged him to delay the appointment until after the reelection campaign. Haldeman relayed to the president the advice from Mitchell. "He said he'd strongly urge, don't let him [Rumsfeld] go to NATO, he is a very valuable property here," Haldeman told the president. ". . . John thinks it's ridiculous to send him on foreign missions."[47]

The solution was to postpone the NATO appointment for more than a year, until Nixon's second term. In the meantime the president found other work for his restless young adviser. That fall Nixon named Rumsfeld to run the new Cost of Living Council, which kept him busy temporarily. Meanwhile Rumsfeld kept on serving as the go-between with the Gallup Poll, giving speeches for the administration and doing other political chores.

Nothing was finalized until after Nixon's reelection. By that time the White House aides with whom Rumsfeld was regularly at odds would have been happy to get him out of the administration entirely. Haldeman recorded in his diary that in a meeting with Ehrlichman on November 20, 1972, Rumsfeld had appeared to agree to go back to Illinois and run for the Senate. "But then when he [Rumsfeld] got in the meeting with the president, he said no, that just wouldn't do, that he had to have an Administration job for a year, which was a complete shock to the President and Ehrlichman," wrote Haldeman. "Typical Rumsfeld, rather slimy maneuver."[48] Rumsfeld finally prevailed upon Nixon to give him the NATO ambassadorship that had been first offered more than a year earlier.

The following year both Haldeman and Ehrlichman lost their own White House jobs as the Watergate scandal grew ever wider. Meanwhile Rumsfeld was safely off in Europe, far removed from the taint of the Nixon White House.

CHAPTER TWO

The Intellectual as Protégé

AMERICANS USUALLY THINK of the 1960s as the time when the United States turned to the intellectual left. The images still persist: At the nation's leading universities, it was the era of antiwar demonstrations, of Marxist professors and of students seizing the offices of university presidents. On some elite campuses, it seemed, the most conservative students joined the Young Democrats, while the true leftists became revolutionaries. Popular campus books, such as Charles Reich's *Greening of America*, Herbert Marcuse's *One Dimensional Man* and Frantz Fanon's *Wretched of the Earth*, preached messages of the need for limits on a malevolent American power.

Amid this campus tumult, attracting remarkably little notice, there arose a separate strand of intellectual development. It was conservative in the literal sense of the word; it embraced (indeed worshiped) traditional values and the philosophers and political theorists of the past. At the time this movement seemed to have little impact upon American government and policy, at least in comparison with the currents of the political left that were pushing powerfully—and ultimately successfully—for an American withdrawal from Vietnam.

Nevertheless, over a thirty-year period, this seemingly tiny, contrapuntal campus movement has had, arguably, a more significant and enduring effect on American policy than did the antiwar movement. By the beginning of the twenty-first century the New Left of the Vietnam era had long ago been buried. By contrast, the conservative campus movement of the 1960s was flourishing. Its adherents occupied high places in the administration of George W. Bush. At the vortex of these intellectual crosscurrents, where conservative theory meets the practice of American foreign policy, was Paul D. Wolfowitz, George W. Bush's deputy secretary of defense.

If any public official could be said to be a habitual protégé, it was Wolfowitz. By nature, he was bright, intellectually creative and diligent. He was the one Republican foreign policy official whose intelligence even some leading Democrats privately conceded they admired, though they disagreed intensely with his conclusions. At the same time, Wolfowitz was also loyal and unthreatening to those superiors with whom he worked. Throughout his long career he was carefully groomed as a protégé by one academic or governmental leader after another. Over the years Wolfowitz's mentors ranged from academic theorist Allan Bloom (himself a disciple of the philosopher Leo Strauss) to the nuclear strategist Albert Wohlstetter to the scholar-bureaucrat Fred Iklé to the senior cabinet members George Shultz, Dick Cheney and Donald Rumsfeld. After a time Wolfowitz began nurturing his own group of protégés, young conservatives whom he brought into government, such as Cheney's chief of staff, Scooter Libby, and the scholar Francis Fukuyama. In a sense, Wolfowitz's career fitted into the intellectual traditions of a European professor; his most important relationships were not so much with his peers as with his tutors and then, later on, with his students.

He served as a bridge between academia and government. To his academic mentors, Wolfowitz represented a link to the practical world of government and public policy. For mentors in government, he supplied the theoretical framework and rationale for decision making. Remarkably, never once did Wolfowitz rebel against or abandon any of these mentors. He did not push hard for and was not enlisted for a position of leadership at the very top. Although Wolfowitz's low-keyed personality and reflective, unpretentious style made him the perfect candidate for an academic dean, they did not fit easily into Washington's standards for how a cabinet secretary should look and behave; Wolfowitz was not as tough and decisive as Rumsfeld, or as skilled a manager as Colin Powell, or as politically attuned as Condoleezza Rice. As a result, even as Wolfowitz neared the age of sixty and his once-black hair faded to gray, he was still an underling—yet, given his innovative intellect, the most influential underling in Washington.

Wolfowitz's father, Jacob Wolfowitz, came from a Jewish family in Poland. Born in Warsaw, he settled with his parents in New York City when he was ten years old. He graduated from City College of New York, taught in high schools to earn money during the Depression, obtained a doctorate in mathematics from New York University and eventually became one of America's leading experts in the theory of statistics. He was a committed Zionist throughout his life and, in later years, was also active in organizing protests against Soviet repression of dissidents and minorities.[1]

During the early 1940s, while teaching at Columbia, the senior Wolfowitz was part of the university's statistical research group, which did wartime studies for the U.S. military. During this period, in 1943, Paul Wolfowitz was born, the second of two children.

Jacob Wolfowitz joined the faculty of Cornell in 1951, moving his wife and children from New York City to the pleasant, quiet university town of Ithaca, New York. Paul Wolfowitz spent most of his teenage years there, although he moved around as his father taught sabbatical semesters at UCLA and the University of Illinois. When he was fourteen, his father took a job as a visiting professor at Technion University in Israel and brought his family along with him. (Many years later Paul's older sister, Laura, a biologist, married an Israeli and settled down to live in Israel.)

He at first wanted to go to Harvard, but he had won a full scholarship to Cornell, and his father made it plain that this was too good a bargain to turn down. As an undergraduate he started to follow the path his father had taken; he majored in mathematics and chemistry. By his senior year, however, he had begun to stray from the sciences into other fields. He noticed that he was spending his spare time reading history and politics, while his fellow math majors were spending their spare time doing extra math problems.[2]

On campus, Wolfowitz had become a member of the Telluride Association. The group, set up in 1910 by a Colorado businessman named L. L. Nunn, selected an elite group of Cornell students with strong academic records to receive free room and board. The students had been all male, until Wolfowitz's older sister became the first woman member in 1962. The chosen students lived together in a large campus residence, Telluride House, where they learned democracy by actually practicing it; the students ran the house, hired the help, supervised the maintenance and organized speakers, seminars and other intellectual exchanges.[3]

The ideas behind the Telluride Association were not inherently polit-ical or ideological. But in 1963, a new faculty member, a professor of po-litical philosophy named Allan Bloom, arrived at Cornell and served for a time as a faculty member living at Telluride House. Bloom preached the importance of traditional values, great books and the classics; he later wrote *The Closing of the American Mind,* the 1987 best-selling book that crystallized the conservative movement's unhappiness with changes in American higher education. Bloom was also a charismatic figure, ques-tioning, Socratic, hedonistic and intensely intellectual, who served as the undisguised model for the title character in the novel *Ravelstein* by Saul Bellow, a close friend of Bloom's.

"For him, Jerusalem and Athens were the twin sources of civiliza-tion. . . . In his classroom, and the lectures were always packed, he coughed, stammered, he smoked, bawled, laughed, he brought his stu-dents to their feet and debated, provoked them to single combat, exam-ined, hammered them," wrote novelist Bellow about his character, Professor Ravelstein. "He didn't ask, 'Where will you spend eternity?' as religious the-end-is-near picketers did but rather 'With what, in this modern democracy, will you meet the demands of your soul?' . . . He would tell you about your soul, already thin and shrinking fast—faster and faster."[4]

Bloom quickly developed a network of students at Cornell, centered at Telluride. Wolfowitz was one of them. Others in this Telluride group included, at one time or another, political scientist Francis Fukuyama, presidential candidate Alan Keyes, intelligence specialist Abram Shulsky, Soviet expert Stephen Sestanovich and Central Asian specialist Charles Fairbanks. Many years later, in the Reagan administration, Wolfowitz hired several members of the Cornell-Telluride network onto his State Department staff. Some of the Cornell alumni, including Wolfowitz, continued to call Bloom from time to time to try to make sense of the dilemmas of Washington within the framework of traditional values and ideals.

The relationship between Bloom and Wolfowitz's father, who was still teaching mathematics at Cornell, was an awkward one. In *Ravelstein,* Bel-low portrayed a fictional character named Philip Gorman, a former stu-dent of Ravelstein's who later went on to become a senior Defense Department official, just like Paul Wolfowitz. In the novel, Gorman's father had been a professor teaching statistics on the same campus as Ravelstein, not unlike the real-life Jacob Wolfowitz and Bloom.

"Gorman's academic father had strongly objected to the Ravelstein seminars in which Philip was enrolled," wrote Bellow. "Respectable professors of political theory had told old Gorman that Ravelstein was off the wall, that he seduced and corrupted his students. 'The paterfamilias was warned against the bugger-familias,' Ravelstein said."[5] (Bloom was homosexual, a fact first publicly disclosed in Bellow's book. Some of his students simply considered his sexuality a mystery. "It was sort of 'don't ask, don't tell,'" Paul Wolfowitz later told an interviewer about Bloom.[6])

Wolfowitz thought that the novelist's portrait was simply inaccurate or possibly a composite based in part on some other Bloom students and their fathers. Looking back many years later, he reflected that his father and Bloom regarded each other with a mixture of wariness and admiration. Bloom, who believed that the life of the mind was the greatest activity, was impressed with the way Jacob Wolfowitz used to pace around the Cornell quadrangle for hours deep in thought, without even a pencil or paper to aid him. Yet the elder Wolfowitz was in mathematics and Bloom in political theory; the gulf between them was insuperable. Jacob Wolfowitz simply didn't think much of the social sciences and humanities or of the people engaged in them. Bloom was just one member of this subset.[7]

Most of Bloom's ideas and his intellectual framework were not his own. He was himself a disciple and popularizer of a philosopher named Leo Strauss, a German Jewish refugee who had left Europe in the midst of Nazi repression and was teaching in the political science department of the University of Chicago. Many of Bloom's themes—above all, his rejection of the mood of relativism that he thought pervaded modern intellectual life—had come directly from Strauss. Bloom had studied under Strauss at Chicago, dedicated his first book to him and once referred to his first encounter with him as the "decisive moment" in his life.[8]

In his senior year at Cornell, Paul Wolfowitz decided to apply to graduate schools, not in math or the sciences but in political science and international relations. His father made one last attempt to dissuade him, arguing that if he was determined to leave the pure sciences, he should at least study economics, more closely related to mathematics than any other social science. His plea was quickly rebuffed. Paul Wolfowitz was admitted to graduate school at Harvard and the University of Chicago. He chose Chicago. One of the key factors was that Leo Strauss was still teaching there. Wolfowitz thought Strauss was a unique figure, an irreplaceable asset. He wanted to know more about him.[9]

Leo Strauss is one of the icons of the modern conservative movement. His influence today is particularly strong among conservatives working on issues of public policy, including foreign affairs. His intellectual heirs include William Kristol, editor of the neoconservative magazine *The Weekly Standard,* former Education Secretary William Bennett and scholars such as Fukuyama and Harvard University Professor Harvey Mansfield, as well as quite a few officials in the Pentagon and national security community. Not all the Straussians have been conservative Republicans. William Galston, for a time one of President Bill Clinton's White House intellectuals, was also a student of Strauss's; like Wolfowitz, Galston first studied with Bloom at Cornell and then went on to study political science at the University of Chicago.[10]

Strauss's influence is surprising because his voluminous, often esoteric writings say virtually nothing specific about issues of policy, foreign or domestic. Like Bloom, he wrote mainly about the importance of understanding the classics, especially Plato and Aristotle, along with European philosophers from Locke and Rousseau to Nietzsche and Heidegger. One core idea in Strauss's work was a denunciation of the spirit of moral tolerance that, he argued, had come to dominate intellectual life in Europe and the United States. He described what he called "the crisis of liberalism— . . . a crisis due to the fact that liberalism has abandoned its absolutist basis and is trying to become entirely relativistic."[11] The problem with relativism and with liberalism, Strauss argued, was that they can degenerate into "the easygoing belief that all points of view are equal (hence, none really worth passionate argument, deep analysis or stalwart defense) and then into the strident belief that anyone who argues for the superiority of a distinctive moral insight, way of life, or human type is somehow elitist or antidemocratic—and hence immoral."[12] Strauss spoke of the need for an elite group of advisers, as in Plato's *Republic,* who could impress upon a political leader and upon the masses the need for virtue and for strong moral judgments about good and evil.

For America's relations with the world, Strauss's ideas carried a number of implications. First, his ideas stressed the importance of a leader who was especially strong in his actions, firm in his beliefs and willing to go against the grain to combat "tyranny" (Strauss frequently used the older word *tyranny*, rather than the more modern word *dictatorship*). In particular, Strauss and his followers revered Winston Churchill; during the Reagan administration and for years afterward, Straussians in Washington convened on Churchill's birthday to sip brandy and smoke cigars.[13] What attracted them to Churchill was his willingness to stand up to Hitler. In a eulogy of Churchill, Strauss wrote, "The tyrant stood at the pinnacle of his power. The contrast between the indomitable and magnanimous statesman and the insane tyrant—this spectacle in its clear simplicity was one of the greatest lessons which man can learn, at any time."[14]

Second, during the cold war, Strauss's thought provided some of the intellectual underpinnings for strong, unqualified anticommunism. The Straussians were not constrained, as many liberals often were, by the need to suspend moral judgments and to take into account differing cultural values and sensitivities. If a third world country was trying to choose its form of government, liberals might argue that communism was inefficient, that it didn't work; the Straussians, by contrast, would argue that communism was tyranny and inherently evil.

One of the great political milestones for the Straussians was President Ronald Reagan's denunciation of the Soviet Union as an "evil empire." In *The Closing of the American Mind*, Allan Bloom took specific note of Reagan's remark and acknowledged that many liberals had recoiled at Reagan's rhetoric. "What was offensive to contemporary ears in President Reagan's use of the word 'evil' was its cultural arrogance, the presumption that he, and America, know what is good; its closedness to the dignity of other ways of life; its implicit contempt for those who do not share our ways," he explained. Yet Reagan's rejection of cultural relativism was precisely what the Straussians applauded; it was the point of the exercise.[15]

A few of the Straussians believed that the philosopher's ideas carried with them a strong doubt about the value of the United Nations and other international organizations. "Such institutions were either steps on the way to the universal homogenization of human beings, or foolish examples of our loss of confidence in our justice and power," wrote one disciple of Strauss's in an essay on the political implications of his philosophy.[16]

These ideas were not in Strauss's writings, but they indicated what some of the Straussians thought his ideas implied for American foreign policy.

Finally, other Straussians, including Wolfowitz's close associate Abram Shulsky, carried the implications of Strauss's theories into the field of intelligence gathering. The Straussians argued that the analytic style of the CIA, developed under the Yale history professor Sherman Kent, had been intrinsically linked to the academic tradition of liberalism. Intelligence officials tended to assume that all leaders followed the same underlying processes and patterns of behavior (for example, trying to stay in power, furthering national interests, maintaining access to economic resources). Thus the best way for the CIA to predict how another government would behave in the future was to study objective criteria, such as economic outputs; planting spies and stealing secrets didn't matter so much. But in the Straussians' contrary view of intelligence gathering, what counted above all was the nature of the regime; tyrannies behaved in fundamentally different ways from democracies. As a result, the Straussians argued, American intelligence should pay much more attention to the phenomenon of deception. A totalitarian regime had the ability to deceive the world about what was happening inside its borders; to discover the reality that a dictator covered up, spies were important.[17]

After arriving at the University of Chicago, Wolfowitz did not become especially close to Strauss. The professor was near the end of his career at the university and left before Wolfowitz completed graduate school. Wolfowitz took two of Strauss's courses on political theory, one on Plato and the other on Montesquieu. He briefly explored the idea of writing a dissertation with another professor, Herbert Storing, who was applying some of Strauss's ideas to American politics. Yet according to Peter Wilson, one of Wolfowitz's friends from that time, Wolfowitz didn't talk much about Strauss in those days; moreover, Wolfowitz wasn't politically active and did not even identify himself as a conservative. At the time Wolfowitz seemed to Wilson to be a centrist, someone who would have fitted easily into the traditions of moderate Republicanism.[18]

In subsequent years colleagues both in government and in academia came to view Wolfowitz as one of the heirs to Leo Strauss's intellectual traditions. "Wolfowitz is still a leading Straussian," remarked the former ambassador to the United Nations Jeane Kirkpatrick in a 2002 interview.[19] Some of the themes Wolfowitz sounded when he talked about foreign policy carried clear overtones of Straussian thinking: his emphasis on stopping tyranny and condemning evil; the notion that dictatorships operate in fundamentally different ways from democracies; the belief that the liberal democracies and their intelligence agencies can be fooled by a dictator's elaborate deceptions. Wolfowitz applied these ideas first to the Soviet Union in the cold war and then, years later, to Saddam Hussein's Iraq.

However, as his own career progressed, Wolfowitz came to distance himself from any identification with Strauss. "I don't particularly like the label [Straussian], because I don't like labels all that much," he said in an interview.[20] In fact, from his earliest days in graduate school, Wolfowitz began gravitating toward a new field, nuclear strategy, and a new mentor, another University of Chicago professor named Albert Wohlstetter.

At the first faculty tea for new graduate students in the fall of 1965, Wohlstetter had asked him whether he knew someone named "Jack Wolfowitz." That's my father, Paul Wolfowitz replied. "I studied math with him at Columbia," said Wohlstetter. After his brief rebellion at Cornell, Paul Wolfowitz was on his way back into the fold.

Albert Wohlstetter was the sort of scholar of whom the mathematician Jacob Wolfowitz would have approved, if he might somehow have allowed himself to approve of anyone in political science. Wohlstetter's career demonstrated that one could usefully combine mathematics, science and public policy. He had grown up in New York City, gone to the City College of New York and to graduate school at Columbia. By the early 1950s he had settled at the Rand Corporation, the independent think tank in Santa Monica that did contract work for the U.S. Air Force. In that position Wohlstetter emerged as one of the nation's leading experts on the theory and strategy of nuclear war. His pioneering work in the early 1950s demonstrated that the United States' Strategic Air Command bases overseas, then the linchpin of American strategy in a nuclear war, were vulnerable to a surprise Soviet attack comparable to the Japanese raid on Pearl Harbor. From then on Wohlstetter concentrated on the concept of American vulnerability, becoming in the process the center of a conservative-oriented group of defense intellectuals that also included Herman Kahn, the man thought to be the model for the character Dr. Strangelove in the movie of that name.[21]

During the late 1960s Wohlstetter began teaching political science at the University of Chicago, attracting a number of students, like Paul Wolfowitz, who were interested in theory but also were eager to do something with practical applications. One of Wohlstetter's main causes was to prevent the spread of nuclear weapons. At one point in the late 1960s Wohlstetter returned from a trip to Israel in a state of agitation about what he believed was the danger of nuclear programs' spreading into the Middle East.

Since the 1950s the U.S. government had been talking about building nuclear-powered desalination stations near Israel's borders with Egypt and Jordan as a way of fostering a spirit of cooperation between Israelis and Arabs on issues such as water and irrigation. These desalting plants would have had a noble purpose but would have also produced plutonium as a by-product, and Wohlstetter feared that the plutonium could someday be used in nuclear weapons programs. By the mid-1960s an American firm, Kaiser Engineers, Inc., was specifically proposing a major project for nuclear desalination in Israel. Wohlstetter had brought back a collection of written material on the subject. He asked Wolfowitz if he could read Hebrew. Wolfowitz said he could. Those materials became the start of Wolfowitz's doctoral dissertation.[22]

Wolfowitz's doctoral thesis amounted to an extended argument against the idea of the nuclear-powered desalting stations, on grounds that the benefits were exaggerated and the risks of nuclear proliferation were too great. He wrote about the difficulties of conducting effective international nuclear inspections, the risks of clandestine diversion of nuclear materials and the dangers of helping a nation improve its technological and scientific capability in the nuclear sciences, all problems that came up again and again over the following decades.

What seems especially noteworthy, in retrospect, is that Wolfowitz's warnings about nuclear proliferation applied at the time to Israel as much as to the Arab states. Wolfowitz specifically argued against an Israeli nuclear weapon. "The fundamental point is that any Israeli nuclear force would have to depend on relatively simply delivery systems, which would be vulnerable even to conventional attack," Wolfowitz wrote in his dissertation. ". . . An Israeli nuclear threat against Arab cities would weaken Israel's conventional military position by cutting her off from friendly countries in the West, and by encouraging, if not forcing, the Soviet Union to intervene more actively on behalf of the Arabs. . . . Israeli nuclear weapons would push the Arabs into a desperate attempt to acquire nuclear weapons, if not from the Soviet Union, then at a later date from China or on their own."[23] Of course, in the early 1970s, after Wolfowitz's dissertation was written, Israel did develop nuclear weapons. Its Arab neighbors began to think of following suit, and one Arab government, Iraq, began a concerted drive to develop its own nuclear program, much as Wolfowitz had predicted. In public, at least, Wolfowitz in later years rarely, if ever, acknowledged his opposition to the Israeli nuclear program or the role that it had played in spurring on other countries in the Middle East to match it.

His doctoral dissertation became another important step in the evolution of Wolfowitz's thinking. At the earliest stage in his professional career he had focused upon the dangers of nuclear weapons programs in the Middle East. At the time this was a relatively obscure subject, but it was one that was to bedevil American foreign policy and to consume much of Wolfowitz's own time and energy for the next three decades.

Summer after summer eager young students flock to the nation's capital from university campuses to work at minuscule wages for various causes of the moment. The focal point of all this activity is Washington's Dupont Circle neighborhood, where a host of nongovernment organizations with vague names and even vaguer budgets set up shop in run-down low-rise office buildings. It was there in the summer of 1969 that the Committee to Maintain a Prudent Defense Policy opened its doors.

The group existed for only a few months. Yet during the summer of 1969 its office served as the setting for an extraordinary tutelage. In it, two of the principal American architects of the cold war, Dean Acheson and Paul Nitze, both in the latter stages of their careers, passed along some of their sophisticated knowledge of Washington and their tough-minded views of American foreign policy to two eager young graduate students, Paul Wolfowitz and Richard Perle.[24]

Acheson had been secretary of state and Nitze the State Department's director of policy planning in the Truman administration at the beginning of the cold war. Ever since the two men had been among the nation's principal advocates of uncompromising policies toward the Soviet Union.

Acheson and Nitze had created the Committee to Maintain a Prudent Defense Policy to lobby Congress on behalf of providing continued support for antiballistic missile systems. Amid the growing unpopularity of the Vietnam War, Congress was beginning to look more critically at the U.S. defense budget, and the antiballistic missile (ABM) system was the most expensive single item coming up for Senate consideration. Senate liberals from both parties—such political leaders as Edward M. Kennedy, William Fulbright, Albert Gore, Sr., Charles Percy and Jacob Javits—had joined together in opposition to the ABM. These opponents did something that was new in congressional battles over national defense: They enlisted on their side scientists, including famous experts from Harvard and MIT, who raised questions about whether the new weapons system would or could ever work.[25]

Acheson and Nitze were trying to counter these scientific opponents, whom they caustically dubbed the "Charles River crowd." Their principal ally was Albert Wohlstetter, and it was he who recruited the young, unsalaried graduate students who worked in the Washington office. From the University of Chicago, Wohlstetter dispatched Wolfowitz and another of his students, Peter Wilson. Separately, Wohlstetter also recruited Perle, then a graduate student at Princeton, whom he had known ever since Perle had dated Wohlstetter's daughter as a teenager in Los Angeles. Perle was nominally in charge of the office, although the organization had no rigid hierarchy.

Throughout the summer Acheson and Nitze regularly dropped by the office, dispensing advice. Acheson was by this point nearly deaf, but the young students were happy to have the chance to listen to him. Under the supervision of the two elder statesmen, Perle, Wolfowitz and Wilson wrote research papers and distributed fact sheets to the Senate in support of the ABM system. They also organized testimony before the Senate Armed Services Committee and drafted materials for a key senator, Henry M. (Scoop) Jackson, who was leading the fight to provide money for the system. When Senator Stuart Symington drew up an eye-catching chart that claimed the ABM system wouldn't work, Wolfowitz came up with an equally splashy chart for Jackson in rebuttal.[26]

By the end of the summer, in a significant victory for the hawks, the Senate approved the ABM system by a single vote, 51 to 50. "The papers they [Wolfowitz, Perle and Wilson] helped us produce ran rings around the misinformed papers produced by [the] polemical and pompous scientists," Nitze wrote in his memoirs.[27]

The Senate vote gave the president a bargaining chip to use in negotiations with the Soviet Union: The United States could now offer to limit the development of its ABM system in exchange for similar concessions from Moscow. Nixon eventually signed the Anti-Ballistic Missile Treaty, restricting antiballistic missile systems for the next several decades. The treaty endured until December 2001, when the George W. Bush administration announced it would withdraw from the pact.

That 1969 showdown marked an important turning point in Congress. It was the closest vote on a major national defense program since 1941, when the House of Representatives narrowly agreed to extend the peacetime draft.[28] The vote set the stage for decades of battles in Congress over arms control and the development of weapons systems; in these showdowns, both proponents and opponents recruited scientists and other academic experts to support their arguments.[29] The ABM debate was also the forerunner of the subsequent political struggles over the Strategic Defense Initiative; in all these cases, the key issues were whether an antimissile system was too expensive and whether it would work.

The summer of 1969 also proved to be a turning point for Paul Wolfowitz and Richard Perle. Both discovered that they enjoyed involvement in public policy more than the abstractions of academia. Through their contact with Acheson and Nitze, the two grad students learned the excitement of a Washington political battle and the possibilities of a future career in government. Eventually Perle and Wolfowitz became two of the leading hawks in the American foreign policy establishment in the last decades of the twentieth century, just as Acheson and Nitze had been among the leaders of the cold war in the middle of the century.

Above all, the two older men passed along to Wolfowitz and Perle an intense skepticism toward arms control with the Soviet Union. Such efforts might be well intentioned, they believed, but could also be harmful to American interests and could even psychologically undermine the United States.[30]

At the end of the summer Perle stayed on in Washington to work in the Senate as a staff aide to Henry Jackson, the senator who had led the campaign for the antimissile system. He never returned to graduate school. During the 1970s, with Jackson's considerable support, Perle emerged as the driving force behind congressional opposition to arms control with the Soviet Union. Henry Kissinger later wrote that Perle "proved as steadfast as he was ingenious in pursuing his larger aim: to stymie the administration's arms control policies."[31]

Wolfowitz did not abandon academic life as quickly as did Perle. He returned to Chicago, completed his dissertation for Wohlstetter and landed a teaching job at Yale. Then, in 1973, when he was offered a job in government for the Arms Control and Disarmament Agency, he accepted it and spent virtually all of his next twenty years in the State Department or Pentagon.

Wolfowitz owed his first government job, indirectly, to the efforts of Henry Jackson. In 1972 Nixon and Kissinger pursued their policy of détente with the Soviet Union—an effort aimed at easing tensions, backing away from confrontation and constructing agreements on arms control. After negotiating the Strategic Arms Limitation agreement in Moscow, Nixon and Kissinger came under intense pressure from critics of the deal. As a result, Nixon, seeking to shore up his fragile support in Congress, began to make political concessions that he hoped would ensure Senate ratification of this arms control treaty. In early 1973, under pressure from Jackson, Nixon agreed to replace most of the senior staff members of the U.S. Arms Control and Disarmament Agency; within months thirteen senior officials lost their jobs. Jackson believed that the arms control team in Nixon's first term had been too eager for agreements with the Soviet Union. Nixon and Kissinger were in any event happy to be rid of their first team of arms control negotiators, who had been unhappy when Kissinger began to exclude them from negotiations with Moscow and who knew too much about the concessions Nixon and Kissinger had made to the Soviets.[32]

Nixon selected Fred Iklé, a Rand strategist who had worked alongside Wohlstetter and other hawks, as the new head of the arms control agency. Iklé was considerably less enthusiastic about the wisdom and benefits of arms control than his predecessors had been. In effect, Jackson was installing someone sympathetic to his own point of view within the agency responsible for conducting arms control negotiations.

In turn, Iklé then brought a more conservative team to the arms control agency. One of his new recruits was Wolfowitz, who had been teaching at Yale. "Wohlstetter recommended him to me," recalled Iklé many years later.[33] Wolfowitz was barely thirty years old, yet he soon became one of Iklé's most trusted advisers. He wrote papers on problems of missile launches and early warning; he worked on strategic arms talks and other arms control negotiations; he traveled with Iklé to Paris and other European capitals. In 1974 and 1975 the young Wolfowitz was closely involved in a successful American campaign to dissuade South Korea from reprocessing plutonium, a program that could have produced fuel for nuclear weapons. Ironically, decades later the United States found itself engaged in a similar campaign with North Korea.

Wolfowitz clearly enjoyed his work inside the government. Everyone thought of him as a scholar and an intellectual, as indeed he was, but he was also by nature an insider, happy to write policy papers and to wage bureaucratic struggle on behalf of the ideas he espoused. Over the years Wolfowitz returned to government jobs again and again, sometimes surprising his friends, who occasionally wondered why he joined the government so often and stayed so long.

In this respect Wolfowitz differed radically from his friend Perle, whose combative style was more suited to work in Congress than inside the executive branch of government. In his job as a Senate staff member Perle enjoyed the freedom to oppose the Nixon-Kissinger arms control negotiations with the Soviet Union. In contrast, Wolfowitz was a member of the Nixon administration and therefore obligated to support the president's policies. Nevertheless, from his position on the inside, Wolfowitz was in a position to influence the administration's decisions before they became final; he could seek to narrow the scope of government actions or challenge the rationale underlying them.

Officially Perle and Wolfowitz were often on opposite sides of many of the arms control debates in the Nixon administration, yet in practice their views were similar. In fact, their talents were complementary. Perle's style was to challenge his opponents' motives and virtue through broadsides in the press and in Congress. Wolfowitz, by contrast, attacked his opponents' logic by writing carefully argued policy papers inside the U.S. government.

This team of Wolfowitz on the inside and Perle on the outside emerged on other occasions over the next three decades. To be sure, occasionally Perle was capable of working in the federal bureaucracy; he served for a time as a senior Defense Department official in the Reagan administration, displaying there the same confrontational style he had exhibited as a Senate aide. On the whole, though, Perle did not have the same stamina for long-term government service as Wolfowitz; Perle left the Pentagon before the end of the Reagan era and never returned to full-time work in any later Republican administration.[34]

Still, Perle remained active. In the George W. Bush administration, as senior officials tried to decide whether or not to go to war against Iraq, it was no surprise that two of the leading proponents of military action were once again Perle on the outside and Wolfowitz on the inside.

Indeed, some of the ideas that Perle and Wolfowitz raised in the debates over Iraq in 2002 and 2003 were vaguely similar to those they had first learned from their mentors Wohlstetter, Acheson and Nitze. There was the recurrent theme of a window of vulnerability. The United States was said to face a sudden threat from a rapidly advancing opponent: the Soviet Union's advancing military power in the cold war or Iraq's programs for weapons of mass destruction in 2002 and 2003. Under this line of reasoning, the United States had only a short time frame in which to confront the threat, and thus it was important to galvanize the nation into rapid action before it was too late.

In the 1960s Soviet military power had seemed so awesome that no one was thinking about the possibility of American supremacy. By the time of the George W. Bush administration, in a world where the United States had no military rival, Wolfowitz and Perle took these early ideas about vulnerability and updated them in such a way that they came out with prescriptions directly the opposite of those of their mentors from the 1960s. Acheson and Nitze had been architects of the policy of containment. But when it came to Iraq, Wolfowitz and Perle were no longer in favor of the old approaches of containment or deterrence. They argued in favor of direct military action, of preventive war.

A Soldier and a Sailor

RICHARD ARMITAGE was serving on a six-gun U.S. Navy destroyer off the coast of Vietnam in January 1968, when the North Vietnamese launched the Tet offensive, the short-lived campaign that surprised the Americans and changed the course of the war. Aboard the ship Armitage was restless and unhappy. He could hear the sounds of combat on the radio: the U.S. Army rushing back and forth; the Marines engaging in firefights; the urgent calls for reinforcements. There was too much water, too much separation, between Armitage and the action.

Armitage had graduated from the U.S. Naval Academy the previous year. He had grown up in Atlanta as a sandy-haired, barrel-chested teenager, garrulous and unusually strong, who had played four sports and served as copresident of his high school class at Pius X Academy. He had been planning to attend the University of Kentucky or the University of Tennessee at Chattanooga on a football scholarship when his father succeeded in persuading the Navy football coach to recruit him.[1]

Upon his arrival in Annapolis, it turned out that Armitage, despite his powerful physique, was too slow to play varsity football. Instead, as an upperclassman he coached the freshman football team. He also took up weight lifting, spending many hours each week on what became a lifelong avocation. His classmates nicknamed him Rach or sometimes Mule. Upon his graduation, the *Lucky Bag,* the academy's class yearbook, summarized Armitage's college years with these words: "Never one to hold a book open for more than an hour, Rach always managed to stay in front of academics. Due to an outstanding personality, Rach is known throughout the Brigade."[2]

At the time of his graduation Armitage had planned on joining the Marines. He switched plans after his best friend, the center on the football team, introduced him to his fiancée's roommate, a woman named Laura Samford. She was the daughter of an insurance executive, one of the most prominent and prosperous businessmen in Birmingham, Alabama. After falling in love, Armitage decided to forsake the Marines, to do a single tour of duty aboard a Navy destroyer and then come home to get married. Those plans lasted until the Tet offensive brought home to him the immediacy of the war nearby. "I just couldn't have these major events of our time going on without me participating more actively," Armitage explained many years later.[3]

Eager to get off the ship, he volunteered for duty inside South Vietnam as an adviser to South Vietnam's "brown-water navy," the sailors in small boats who patrolled the muddy rivers through the country's jungles and interior. He was given four weeks of Vietnamese-language training and then hurriedly sent off to fight the war. Armitage was freely choosing combat duty over the safety of the ship. Over the next few years he volunteered for action again and again, opting for danger rather than security, taking part in some of the grittiest, most secretive operations of the war.

For Colin Powell, combat duty in Vietnam was less a choice than an obligation. Powell had decided to make his career in the U.S. Army, and you went where the Army sent you. In 1962, in the earliest days of the Kennedy administration's involvement in Vietnam, the Army dispatched Powell to serve as an adviser to a South Vietnamese infantry battalion near the Laotian border. He was part of a contingent that raised the American presence in Vietnam from thirty-two hundred advisers to eleven thousand.

Powell, the son of Jamaican parents who settled in the South Bronx, had attended the City College of New York and, while there, signed up for the school's Reserve Officers Training Corps (ROTC). Finding that he loved the discipline, structure and camaraderie, he made the ROTC program the centerpiece of his college years, rising to become the cadet colonel, the leader of the thousand-student regiment.[4] After his graduation in 1958, he served the three years of active duty that were required of him after ROTC and then without hesitation elected to make the

Army his life's work. "I was a young black. I did not know anything but soldiering," Powell explained in his memoirs. "What was I going to do, work with my father in the garment district? . . . And for a black, no other avenue in American society offered so much opportunity."[5]

He studied for five weeks at Fort Bragg's Unconventional Warfare Center and then landed in Saigon on Christmas Day in 1962. He was excited to go to war. It was an assignment, not a choice, but a good one and a symbol that the Army valued him. "I became the envy of my fellow career officers, since those picked to go to South Vietnam were regarded as comers, walk-on-water types being groomed for bright futures," he later wrote.[6]

Their combat experiences in Vietnam eventually set Powell and Armitage apart from most of the other Americans at the seniormost levels of America's foreign policy elite. Quite a few Vietnam veterans went on to serve in the U.S. Senate, including, most prominently, John McCain. A handful had served along with Powell and Armitage in the Reagan administration. Generally, however, during the 1980s and early 1990s the top posts in foreign policy in Republican administrations were occupied by members of an older generation, men such as George Shultz, Caspar Weinberger, Brent Scowcroft and James Baker. Some within this older generation had fought in World War II. None of them had had the experience of Vietnam veterans, the intense frustration of fighting a war America hadn't won, the agony of having watched Americans be killed for a cause that Americans hadn't wholeheartedly supported.

By the beginning of the twenty-first century the members of this older generation had passed into retirement. The Vulcans of George W. Bush represented a successor generation of foreign policy officials; most of them had come of age in the late 1950s and the 1960s. Yet among this successor generation, the influence of Vietnam veterans was not particularly strong; in fact, Powell and Armitage were in the minority. Within the second Bush administration a few officials, like Secretary of Defense Donald Rumsfeld and National Security Adviser Condoleezza Rice, were either too old or too young to have served in Vietnam. Others, including Vice President Dick Cheney and Deputy Secretary of Defense Paul Wolfowitz, were of the right age but had not fought in the Vietnam War; along with many thousands of other Americans, they had obtained deferments from the draft that enabled them to continue their studies and their careers.[7] The best illustration of this generational change was at the very top. Whereas President George H. W. Bush had fought overseas in World War II, his son, President George W. Bush, had served in the Texas National Guard during Vietnam.

In his book *The Nightingale's Song*, a study of how combat service in Vietnam affected officials in the Reagan administration, Robert Timberg quoted one Vietnam veteran as saying, "There's a wall ten miles high and fifty miles thick between those of us who went and those who didn't, and that wall is never going to come down."[8] Fifteen years later, in the second Bush administration, that wall may not have been quite so high or so thick, but it was certainly still there.

During the summer of 2002, when Powell and Armitage were in charge of the State Department and America was contemplating whether to go to war with Iraq, the old, poisonous divisions within the Vietnam generation burst forth anew. Vietnam veterans argued that some of the most prominent proponents of military action against Iraq, including Cheney and Wolfowitz, could not understand war because they had not taken part in it themselves. "They come at it from an intellectual perspective, versus having sat in jungles or foxholes and watched their friends get their heads blown off," said Senator Chuck Hagel, a Vietnam veteran.[9]

In response, defenders of Cheney and Wolfowitz argued with equal passion that Vietnam veterans had no monopoly on wisdom. "Over and over again during the '90s, the generals with first-shand battlefield experience guessed wrong—and the civilians without it guessed right—about what would happen when the United States went to war," wrote a *New Republic* columnist, Peter Beinart, arguing that leaders such as Powell had been too cautious about the Gulf War and about U.S. military interventions in the Balkans.[10]

What, then, were the combat experiences of Powell and Armitage in Vietnam? And what lessons had they learned there? In fact, although their Vietnam service formed one part of the strong bond between the two men, their experiences were not at all similar.

Powell served in the Army, Armitage in the Navy. Powell was assigned to combat duty, while Armitage chose it. Powell's tours of duty amounted to stepping-stones in his long military service; Armitage's service in Vietnam, on the other hand, was the turning point that led him to abandon his military career. Powell's involvement with Vietnam was cool, detached and professional; Armitage formed an intense personal and emotional attachment to the country and its people. By the time the Vietnam War ended in 1975, Powell had already moved on, with new jobs and promotions elsewhere. The last days of the war brought for Armitage first a few days of heroism, followed by several years of rootless uncertainty.

Powell went to Vietnam for two one-year tours of duty, the first time in 1962–63 and the second in 1968–69. In his first tour, Powell was brought in by helicopter to South Vietnam's remote A Shau Valley, where he lived as an American adviser among South Vietnamese soldiers, Montagnard civilians, chickens, pigs, leeches and the Vietcong, who ambushed his unit almost daily. He experienced the terror of enemy fire. He had to depend on the irregular mail delivery (and, when it didn't work, the radio) to find out that his wife had given birth to their first child and that it was a boy. After six months in combat, Powell was wounded when he stepped on a punji trap, a bamboo spike hidden in the ground that pierced his foot. He served the remaining months at division headquarters in Hue.[11]

Powell finished his first tour with more than a touch of cynicism about civilian leaders in Washington. His memoirs are full of epithets— "McNamara's slide rule commandos," "slide-rule prodigies," "high-tech warriors back at the Pentagon"—that convey a soldier's distrust for those decision makers who are distant from the combat. Powell also came home with a sense of the seeming absurdity of many aspects of the war, epitomized when the South Vietnamese captain alongside whom he was working informed him that the A Shau base was important to protect the airfield and that the airfield was there to resupply the base. "I often wondered if we were achieving anything," Powell later reflected. "How did we fight foes who blended in with local peasants who were frightened or too sympathetic to betray them?" Nevertheless, he came home still believing "that it was right to help South Vietnam remain independent, and right to draw the line against communism anywhere in the world." The Americans simply needed to send more troops to Vietnam, Powell believed.[12]

By the time of Powell's second year in Vietnam, which began in July 1968, he had risen from lieutenant to major, and the American troop presence in the country had increased from eleven thousand to five hundred thousand. Powell began the year as executive officer of a battalion in the American Division, responsible for providing supplies and other support to the troops. This time he was not in a frontline fighting unit in the countryside, yet his battalion was regularly ambushed and subjected to rocket and mortar fire.

Two months after Powell started his tour, Major General Charles M. Gettys, the commanding officer of the American Division, noticed Powell's picture in the *Army Times* alongside a story that mentioned him as the second-ranking officer in a command and staff class from Fort Leavenworth. He brought Powell to the American Division's headquarters at Chu Lai and made him the unit's staff officer in charge of operations and planning.[13]

The new assignment brought out Powell's talents, his blend of organizational and political skills and personal charm. Over the following years Powell was asked to serve as a staff or administrative officer again and again. But Powell's new job also brought him his first brush with controversy—namely, the American Division's attempts to brush off complaints about what was later known as the My Lai massacre.

In March 1969, while Powell was at American headquarters, an official from the inspector general's office at U.S. military headquarters in Saigon visited his office and asked him to search the unit's archives to find the account of a day with an unusually high body count. Powell read through the journals and found for the investigator the entry from March 16, 1968, when an American platoon recorded 128 enemy dead on the Batangan Peninsula. According to Powell's account, he didn't know what the inspector general's inquiries were about until many months later, when news stories by independent journalist Seymour Hersh disclosed the details of the My Lai massacre. A platoon within the American Division headed by Lieutenant William Calley had shot and killed 347 unarmed Vietnamese, mostly older men, women and children.[14]

Powell had not arrived in Vietnam until three months after the My Lai massacre. Evidence suggests, however, that allegations of brutality in the American Division's treatment of civilians may not have been quite as far out of his consciousness as his account implies. In November 1968, Specialist Fourth Class Tom Glen, who had been serving in a separate platoon in the same brigade as Calley's unit and was on his way home, wrote a letter to General Creighton Abrams, the commander of American forces in Vietnam, claiming that American troops had murdered civilians and prisoners. Some units, he said, "fire indiscriminately into Vietnamese homes and without provocation or justification shoot at the people them-selves. . . . [These acts] are carried on at entire unit levels and therefore acquire the aspect of sanctioned policy." Glen's letter did not specifically mention My Lai or Calley's platoon.[15]

The letter was sent down to Americal headquarters, where Powell was assigned to investigate it and come up with a response. Powell gave the letter a quick brushoff. Four days later, after talking to Glen's com-mander, Powell drafted a reply saying that the charges were false. There might have been "isolated instances" of abuses by American troops, Pow-ell said, but these were punished. ". . . Relations between Americal sol-diers and the Vietnamese people are excellent," he added. Glen soon received a letter from an American general making these same points.[16]

That was the end of Glen's complaint, which suffered from a lack of detail. Powell, as a rising young staff officer, was not eager to pursue vague but troubling allegations of misconduct by American forces. The details of the My Lai massacre did not make their way out of the Americal Divi-sion until another soldier, Specialist Fourth Class Ron Ridenhour, later wrote his congressman, triggering an Army inquiry.

Powell was awarded a Legion of Merit during this second tour of duty for rescuing his commander, General Gettys, dragging the general and two other Americans to safety after the helicopter in which they were rid-ing hit a tree and crashed to the ground. Powell, who was riding in the same chopper, suffered a broken ankle. He finished out his tour and de-parted in the summer of 1969.

Powell still retained the infantryman's traditional resentment at the way civilians fail to appreciate their own freedom and security. When Lyndon Johnson announced he would not run for reelection in 1968, Powell noted that it was a "statesmanlike gesture" but that "packing it in and going home to the ranch was [sic] not an option available to career of-ficers, or to American draftees, for that matter."[17]

Yet after his second tour Powell also came away from Vietnam with much broader, considerably harder judgments about the war itself and the way America had gone about fighting it. Some of Powell's conclusions became well known to later generations of Americans because they were eventually enshrined in Pentagon guidelines known first as the Wein-berger doctrine (when Powell was serving as the military aide to Secretary of Defense Caspar Weinberger) and then later as the Powell doctrine (af-ter he had become chairman of the Joint Chiefs of Staff). The principal themes were the need for clear goals, the backing of the American public and the application of overwhelming force. "War should be the politics of last resort," Powell decided after his second Vietnam tour. "And when we go to war, we should have a purpose that our people understand and support; we should mobilize the country's resources to fulfill that mission, and then go in to win."[18]

Powell drew some secondary lessons from Vietnam. America's military leadership needed to be reinvigorated and its culture to be changed; senior officers were too obsessed with medals, promotions and phony statistics, such as body counts. Military leaders needed to speak the truth to civilian leaders and not merely go along with "halfhearted warfare for half-baked reasons." Two decades later Powell put these ideas for a strong, independent military leadership into effect as the most powerful chairman of the Joint Chiefs of Staff in American history.

Finally, Powell departed from Vietnam with a deep sense of injustice at the way poorer, less educated Americans did most of the fighting and dying. "I am angry that so many of the sons of the powerful and well-placed and so many professional athletes . . . managed to wangle slots in Reserve and National Guard units," he wrote.[19]

Out in the backwaters of South Vietnam, among the South Vietnamese soldiers with whom he was fighting, Richard Armitage went by the Vietnamese name Tran Van Phu.[20] The name made sense, in its way. *Phu* was a word that meant "prosperous" or "rich," an idea linked to Armitage's first name. *Van* signified a male. *Tran* was the surname of the great hero of the Vietnamese Navy, Tran Hung Dao, who defeated a Mongol invasion in 1287. So Armitage's Vietnamese name meant something like "rich Navy guy."

After volunteering to move from his Navy destroyer to combat duty, Armitage served inside Vietnam with the riverine forces that patrolled the Mekong River and other inland and coastal waterways. By his own and official accounts, in his first tour of duty, Armitage was an adviser to a South Vietnamese ambush team in a coastal area. He left the country after a year to serve as a counterinsurgency instructor at the military base in Coronado, California, teaching techniques of ambush and interrogation. He then elected to return for a second one-year tour starting in May 1971, as the adviser to another group in Tay Ninh near the Cambodian border. When that ended, he immediately volunteered for a third one-year tour starting in May 1972 as adviser to an ambush team along the coastline. He had married his college girlfriend, but that didn't stop him from going back again and again to the war.

These official accounts of Armitage's Vietnam record don't tell the full story. Several of his old friends and associates volunteered in interviews that Armitage had been an intelligence operative in Vietnam. "He was doing some black stuff there," said Richard Allen, who first met Armitage in 1980. Fred Iklé, who helped recruit Armitage to the Reagan administration and served as his Pentagon boss, said he believed that Armitage had been working for the CIA.[21] What sorts of covert operations? Others familiar with Armitage's activities during that era say he was associated with the infamous, intensely controversial Phoenix program, the American operation, directed by the CIA, that aimed to neutralize the Vietcong by eradicating its political apparatus in the countryside.

"He wound up in the Phoenix program, the most high-risk, nastiest, most vicious program in the Vietnam War. They weren't assassination teams; they were counterguerrilla teams," said Larry Ropka, an Air Force officer who worked alongside Armitage in Vietnam and Iran in the 1970s and later served as his assistant in the Pentagon. Asked if he was sure Armitage was in Phoenix, Ropka replied: " I know that for a fact. We spent a lot of time together in subsequent years. He told me of some of the gunfights. They were right out of *Rambo*. . . . They would sneak out in a boat at night, go upriver, crawl into a Vietcong village, find the hut where the head man was, take it out and then go back to the boat and get out of there."[22]

Critics charged that Phoenix amounted to a program of assassination, usually by South Vietnamese agents; defenders viewed it as a legitimate part of a dirty war. William Colby, who ran the program for the CIA, later testified in Congress that there had been some "excesses" in carrying out Phoenix. The program was remarkably successful; Colby claimed that the Phoenix had eliminated 60,000 Vietcong agents, in many cases by killing them. In a single year, 1969, the American mission in Saigon claimed that the Phoenix program had "neutralized" 19,534 agents, killing 6,187 of them.[23]

Asked if Armitage was associated with the Phoenix program, Ted Shackley, the veteran intelligence official who helped run Phoenix as the CIA's chief of station in Saigon, replied, "Yeah, he may have been on the fringes of it." Shackley said that he hadn't personally known Armitage in

Vietnam, but that there was a "connection" between Armitage and the U.S. intelligence operation.[24]

Armitage himself has maintained he was not in the Phoenix program. "I was never in Phoenix," he said in an interview for this book. "I was an ambush team adviser to a Vietnamese ambush team." He explained that sometimes, when his unit collected information, it would be passed along to a naval intelligence liaison officer, who would in turn pass it along to officials in Phoenix; as a result, Phoenix officers occasionally came to Armitage's area in the Vietnamese countryside for advice or help, and he might lead them somewhere. "But I never worked for Phoenix," he said. As for carrying out nighttime raids, Armitage said, "That's why I was an ambush team adviser. That's what I did. That was my life!"[25]

Armitage wasn't merely doing his military duty by fighting in Vietnam as Powell was; Armitage fell in love with the country and relished the opportunity it presented, coming back again and again. Speaking fluent Vietnamese, he particularly enjoyed being out in the countryside. Once, when he was sounded out about coming to work as an aide to an American admiral in Saigon, he asked if he would be obliged to wear socks. When told he probably would, Armitage turned down the job.[26]

"After my first tour, my wife will tell you, I came back so pumped up," Armitage told an interviewer many years later. "I loved the culture. The second time I got frustrated. I wanted the South Vietnamese to go out and fight. By the third tour, I was balanced. There were some days you wanted to go fight and there were some days you would take a bye."[27]

Armitage's military career reached a crisis in early 1973, after several months of wild swings in the Nixon administration's policy toward Vietnam. From Armitage's perspective on the ground, he believed that Richard Nixon's intensive bombing of Hanoi and Haiphong at the end of 1972 had finally given the United States the upper hand in the war. "I was aware in December, 1972, . . . how close we had come to victory," he later claimed. ". . . We had the sons-of-bitches on their asses and we let them go. I think Henry Kissinger lost his nerve and the president lost his nerve."[28] Instead, only a few weeks later the Nixon administration signed the Paris Peace Accords, accepting a settlement in which the United States agreed to withdraw its forces from Vietnam.

The Paris deal left Armitage embittered and adrift. "He was disgusted at the end of the war," said one friend, Richard Childress. "I don't think any of us imagined the Army and the United States just walking away." Years later Armitage gave vent to his anger over the Paris peace settlement by employing a revealing metaphor, one that left no doubt about his intense personal involvement with South Vietnam, its troops and its people.

"I found it [the withdrawal of American troops from Vietnam] very akin to getting a lady pregnant and leaving town," Armitage asserted. "It's not a pretty image, but I thought we were a runaway dad."[29]

Armitage's third tour inside Vietnam was nearing an end, but he still didn't want to leave the country. Under the Paris settlement after the withdrawal of American troops the United States was permitted to maintain only fifty military personnel inside South Vietnam. Armitage applied to his superiors in the Navy to be one of the fifty, thus volunteering to work in Saigon, the city he had earlier avoided. His request was turned down. Navy officials suggested to Armitage that he had had enough time in Vietnam and that it would be better for his military career to show he could do other things elsewhere in the world.

"The Navy assignment people said something to the effect that 'we feel you're starting to fall behind your contemporaries,'" said Armitage's friend James Kelly. "And when they said that, he told the Navy people what he thought of a system in which you fell behind your contemporaries by actively participating in a war, which was supposedly the highest priority going on, and if that was their view, they had a place where they could take their U.S. Navy. And he resigned on the spot."[30]

Armitage elected to abandon his career in the Navy and to stay on in South Vietnam. He became a civilian employee of the U.S. defense attaché's office in Saigon, where he continued to serve as an adviser to the South Vietnamese armed forces. Working out of Navy headquarters, he served as the operations adviser for South Vietnam's navy, marine corps and special operations forces. He would go out across the country, keeping track of how South Vietnamese forces were conducting the war and monitoring how they used American military equipment.[31]

Armitage brought his wife, Laura, to South Vietnam with him for a time. They stood out from many of the other Americans because Armitage spoke fluent Vietnamese and spent much of his time among Vietnamese. "Rich did not think that the people who hung around the PX compound in Saigon were worthy people to be seen around with, and so he didn't go there," said Kelly. "They lived around Vietnamese and went to Vietnamese markets."[32]

During this period Armitage was asked to serve as local host and guide for a visiting Pentagon official named Erich von Marbod, who came to play a major role in his life. Von Marbod, a civilian, was the Defense Department official responsible for managing logistics, money and weaponry for Vietnam. Inside the Pentagon he was a legendary figure, renowned for his ability to get things done and to do them efficiently and quickly, finding ways to circumvent cumbersome rules and regulations. If you wanted to steer arms to a foreign government, von Marbod was the man to see.[33] "He was the comptroller of what was called the Defense Security Assistance Agency, which basically made him the owner of all kinds of off-the-books material in Southeast Asia," explained Kelly, who worked as a naval assistant to von Marbod. Kelly believed von Marbod was the best bureaucrat he had ever seen, wielding the sort of power that generals and admirals rarely accorded to civilians other than the secretary of defense. Once von Marbod and Kelly were walking down a hallway in the Pentagon when a four-star admiral passed by and gave von Marbod a warm, effusive greeting. After the admiral had left, von Marbod, who liked to coin aphorisms, told Kelly, "Never mistake fear for love."[34]

In 1973 Senator John Stennis, chairman of the Senate Armed Services Committee, complained that the Pentagon was giving him too many conflicting reports about how much money and American military equipment South Vietnam needed to keep fighting the war. He asked that the Pentagon speak through a single voice. Secretary of Defense James Schlesinger responded by appointing von Marbod his principal deputy for South Vietnam. The following year von Marbod paid a visit to see firsthand how the war was going.[35]

In Saigon, Armitage was assigned the job of taking von Marbod around. He was less than pleased. "One day I got a call from [U.S. military officials in Saigon], saying we've got a big shot coming in, and he wants you to take him around and show him where the combat is," recalled Armitage. "I was annoyed and also hung over. And went over to the appointed place at Tan Son Nhut [airport] and I met Erich von Marbod and Jim Kelly. . . . And von Marbod wanted to go see some action. So I took them to one place where firing was heavy and we couldn't get in by helicopter, and then I took them to some other places. And he [von Marbod] just loved it. He was a real gun-loving, cordite-smelling freak. He loved that stuff, and he never forgot it."[36] Von Marbod was duly impressed. "He was very brave," he said of Armitage. "I wasn't used to taking fire, but he was very relaxed. We had difficulty getting people to take us to certain [dangerous] areas, but he arranged that through Air America and certain Vietnamese organizations. . . . He didn't seem to be concerned about his own safety."[37]

It was not the first time, or the last, that Armitage put his combat experience to good use by charming important officials in Washington who had not served in Vietnam as he had. Over the next few years Armitage was to rely upon von Marbod for work and help as he sought to establish a career outside the Navy.

In December 1974 Armitage quit his job in Saigon and returned to the United States. He thought the war effort was going poorly. He went to Washington and tried to raise alarms about the deteriorating situation in South Vietnam, but without success. No one seemed to be listening. Armitage went home briefly to his wife and family in San Diego. Then, restless, he flew back to Vietnam in March 1975 to visit Da Nang and travel up and down South Vietnam. He maintained then and afterward that he was merely traveling on his own, although it seems likely he was also on a mission to assess the military situation, possibly reporting to von Marbod, who was still charged with giving Congress a sense of how the war was going. Armitage found that South Vietnam seemed to be imploding. Upon his return, Armitage tried once again to arouse interest in helping to prevent a collapse. "I didn't know what to do," he recalled. "I just couldn't find anybody who would understand that the country was falling in on itself."[38]

At this juncture Armitage knew considerably more about conditions in South Vietnam than about the mood in the United States. Americans had no desire for a renewed effort to salvage the South Vietnamese regime, two years after the peace settlement that had removed U.S. troops and ended the American military involvement in the war. A last-ditch request by the Ford administration for another $722 million in aid to South Vietnam went nowhere in Congress.

In late April, Armitage was sitting at his home in San Diego when the phone rang. It was Erich von Marbod. "Ricky, get your ass to Washington," von Marbod said. "I got a job for you." He instructed Armitage to bring his wife and two children, because he was not going to be seeing them again for a while. Armitage flew to Washington with his family, checked in to a room at the Twin Bridges Marriott and the next morning walked over to the Pentagon. In von Marbod's office, Kelly noticed that Armitage was wearing the only sports jacket he owned, and probably one of the only neckties too.[39]

Von Marbod explained what he wanted Armitage to do. By now the Pentagon realized that South Vietnam was collapsing. The U.S. government wanted to prevent South Vietnam's military assets—its planes, ships and other valuable military hardware—from falling into the hands of North Vietnam. Von Marbod was flying to Saigon the following day and taking Armitage along with him. Their mission was to try to get as much matériel as possible out of South Vietnam and to try to destroy the rest.

Von Marbod, Armitage and two U.S. Air Force officers landed in Saigon on April 24, 1975, on Pan Am's last commercial flight there. Armitage was assigned to help get American ships and riverboats out of Vietnam, while von Marbod and the Air Force officers concentrated on the planes. The following day von Marbod and Armitage visited South Vietnam's naval commander, Vice Admiral Chung Tan Cang, and told him how quickly North Vietnamese forces were advancing. They presented Cang with their plan for evacuation: First, all Vietnamese navy personnel were to be instructed to bring their vessels to their bases, along with their families. Then, on signal, the Vietnamese would sail out to sea to a rendezvous point off Con Son Island, where American warships would pick them up and protect them.[40]

The plan was to be put into effect approximately a week later, on May 1 or May 2. The timing was chosen on the basis of CIA estimates of how long it would take the North Vietnamese to reach Saigon. The North Vietnamese, however, did not go by the CIA's timetables; they came much more quickly, hampering the American operations and limiting the numbers of planes, boats and South Vietnamese personnel the United States could save. Even after a quarter century Armitage spoke bitterly of "that son of a bitch" Thomas Polgar, the CIA station chief in Saigon, accusing him of relying too heavily on Polish and Hungarian sources for his intelligence about the North Vietnamese intentions.[41]

On April 28, von Marbod dispatched Armitage to the large American base at Bien Hoa, northwest of Saigon, with instructions to pack up and remove military stockpiles. Flying in by helicopter, Armitage found a mostly empty base occupied by only three or four dozen South Vietnamese maintenance workers. He made a deal with them: If they helped with the packing and agreed to shoot anyone who tried to come over the wall, Armitage would take them with him to Saigon. Within an hour they had packed up fifteen pallets, at which time Armitage got a call from von Marbod. "Get out," he said. "I can't tell you why." In Saigon, American defense officials had overheard a North Vietnamese radio message that said they had the base at Bien Hoa surrounded and that the enemy should not be allowed to escape. Armitage said he couldn't leave without the South Vietnamese he had promised to take with him. As Bien Hoa came under increasingly heavy rocket and mortar fire, a CIA-owned airplane sent by von Marbod landed, took Armitage and his South Vietnamese maintenance workers on board and shuttled them to safety in the capital.[42]

Within a couple of days, as North Vietnamese troops closed in on Saigon, the American evacuation began. Von Marbod and Armitage flew by Air America chopper to the USS *Blue Ridge*. Armitage had lost his identification papers in the tumult, but he persuaded the ship's commander, Admiral Don Whitmire, to let him board an American destroyer and take it south to Con Son Island.

What followed over the following week amounted to an epic denouement to Armitage's service in South Vietnam. Near Con Son, the South Vietnamese navy had assembled about ninety ships. They were occupied by at least twenty thousand South Vietnamese fleeing their country, most of them naval personnel and their families, including Vice Admiral Cang. The ships had little food or water, and some of them were barely seaworthy. Armitage was the U.S. Navy's sole representative to the Vietnamese in the flotilla.[43]

Armitage decided to try to sail the ships and the refugees to the Philippines, a distance of about a thousand miles. Most of the ships weren't seaworthy enough to make the voyage. At least sixty of the vessels were scuttled, in some cases with the help of gunfire. The 20,000 Vietnamese were packed into thirty-two boats; three boats originally used by the U.S. Coast Guard, each of which usually carried a crew of 170, were loaded with 1,500 Vietnamese apiece. Armitage sent urgent cables to the Defense Department, which succeeded in getting food and water brought to the boats. From May 2 to May 7 Armitage's Vietnamese convoy, protected by three American ships, sailed to Subic Bay in the Philippines. Amid the overcrowding, fights and even gunfire broke out on board.

When the ships approached Subic Bay, President Ferdinand Marcos and his Philippine government tried to stop the vessels, still carrying South Vietnamese flags, from entering Philippine waters. Once again Armitage played intermediary and translator in a flurry of negotiations involving American and Philippine officials and the Vietnamese refugees. Finally, on May 8, a solution was reached: In formal ceremonies that Armitage helped arrange, the ships took down their Vietnamese flags and hoisted American ones. They then sailed into Subic Bay. For Armitage, after more than seven years, the Vietnam War was finally over.

In the broadest sense, the impact of the Vietnam debacle was similar for all the Vulcans, both those who had fought in the war and those who had not. The defeat in Vietnam led to a preoccupation with first regaining and then maintaining American military power. This was as true for the careers of Richard Cheney, Donald Rumsfeld and Paul Wolfowitz as it was for Colin Powell and Richard Armitage. The pronounced emphasis upon military perspectives to foreign policy problems was the principal distinguishing characteristic of the team that came to power in the second Bush administration.

The Wise Men who ran American foreign policy at the beginning of the cold war had not been lacking in experience with military issues. For example, two of them, John McCloy and Robert Lovett, had served during World War II as top aides to Secretary of War Henry Stimson. But for this earlier generation, experience in military issues was secondary to the more extensive experience in diplomacy, international law and business.[44] Not surprisingly, then, the leaders of the post–World War II generation were more interested in creating lasting new international economic, legal and diplomatic institutions that would further American interests (the United Nations, the International Monetary Fund and World Bank, the Marshall Plan) than in creating new military institutions (NATO). In contrast, the Vulcans were energetic and innovative when it came to American military power, but far less eager to create new diplomatic or economic institutions.

However, while the Vulcans shared a common interest in military power, there were disagreements within their ranks about when to wield that power and about how best to preserve it. Those disagreements stemmed from their different experiences at the time of Vietnam.

Three decades after the American departure from Vietnam, Paul Wolfowitz remained uncharacteristically ambivalent about that war and the wisdom of fighting it. In a 2002 interview, he noted that Vietnam had seemed at the time like a noble cause; he pointed out that leaders such as Singapore's Lee Kuan Yew believed the United States had managed to save Southeast Asia by delaying and postponing a Communist advance throughout the region. On the other hand, Wolfowitz went on, it was a fair question whether the war had been worth the cost in American lives and the divisions it caused within American society; it had seemed like an "overexpenditure" of American power.[45]

Wolfowitz's detachment from the passions of Vietnam reflected his own background. During the Vietnam War years he had spent most of his time in academia. His graduate school mentor, the nuclear strategist Albert Wohlstetter, had not been a strong supporter of the Vietnam War. Although politically conservative, Wohlstetter tended to view Vietnam as a distraction, a misguided venture that sapped America's energies and diverted its attention away from its far more important, long-term competition with the Soviet Union.[46]

Powell and Armitage did not share Wolfowitz's sense of detachment. The war they had helped fight in Southeast Asia became the central factor in their views of U.S. foreign policy and America's relations with the world.

Vietnam left Powell with an enduring wariness about military missions that could diminish the power, prestige and fighting ability of the U.S. armed forces. For Powell, in other words, the main way to preserve American military power was to use it sparingly and with caution. Hence the Weinberger and Powell doctrines, prompted by Vietnam: Don't go to war until you have narrowly defined goals and strong public support, and once you do start a war, bring overwhelming force to achieve a quick victory. Powell tended to mistrust those officials whose main experience with defense issues was in Washington, not in the field. When civilian leaders pressed for military intervention overseas, Powell sometimes saw them as latter-day versions of Vietnam's Robert McNamara.

When Powell was dealing with civilian leaders in the Pentagon, their Vietnam record or lack of it was rarely far from his mind. Discussing his seemingly amicable partnership with Secretary of Defense Dick Cheney during the first Bush administration. Powell wrote in his autobiography: "This man, who had never spent a day in uniform, who, during the Vietnam War, had gotten a student deferment and later a parent deferment, had taken instant control of the Pentagon."[47]

Armitage took away from Vietnam many of the same lessons as did Powell. He too was committed to the principles of caution and overwhelming force embodied in the Weinberger-Powell doctrine.

Armitage learned some other lessons from Vietnam. One was the importance of America's alliances and commitments, particularly in Asia. Infuriated by the American pullout from South Vietnam, he was eager to make sure that the United States would never again behave like a "runaway dad." Over the following decades Armitage became one of Washington's leading proponents of strong alliances and an enduring American troop presence in Asia. With the exception of Ambassador Mike Mansfield, no other American official of the past thirty years had closer relations with Japan than did Armitage.

Other Vulcans had a more negative view of the value of alliances and were more willing to have America act on its own where necessary. Rumsfeld, in particular, who served as U.S. ambassador to NATO in the early 1970s, came away with a jaundiced view of the tedious, laborious consultative process by which America and its European allies reached their decisions. "Rumsfeld didn't seem to like NATO, where you had to be nice and say nice things to the Italian defense minister and had to deal with the misguided European thinking about the Soviet Union," said a former official who worked with Rumsfeld in the Nixon and Ford administrations.[48]

Armitage's Vietnam days also taught him some lessons about how the U.S. government and the Washington bureaucracy worked. What counted above all were personal connections and networks, not the formal workings of the bureaucracy. Armitage's first civilian boss, Erich von Marbod, had risen to power by developing an extensive informal network of friends throughout Washington he could call upon for favors. Armitage built a similar Washington network, and with his Vietnam experience in small-unit combat, he put the strongest emphasis on the personal values of trust, loyalty and friendship. Other top-level officials, such as Cheney, maintained a reserve and a professional distance from staff aides. Cheney usually won their considerable respect, but the relationship was not intensely personal, and his aides changed bosses from administration to administration. Armitage, by contrast, developed a small cadre of loyal aides who moved with him from one job to the next. Armitage in turn displayed extraordinary personal loyalty to top-level friends—above all to Powell.

Finally, the chaos of Vietnam taught Armitage that often events happen far more quickly than anyone can possibly control from Washington. At the end of the war Armitage had managed to sail to the Philippines with at least twenty thousand Vietnamese, even though the Philippine president didn't want the refugees and the U.S. government didn't know what to do with them.

Thinking back to that moment, Armitage said, "I learned one lesson that never served me wrong: that forgiveness is easier to get than permission."[49]

CHAPTER FOUR

Combating the Soviets, Détente and Henry Kissinger

DONALD RUMSFELD glided effortlessly from the Nixon administration to the Ford administration. Once, in the midst of the Watergate furor, he had privately informed Nixon that he was willing to resign from his NATO post and come back to Washington to help fight against impeachment in Congress. It is not clear whether or not he was serious. Fortunately for Rumsfeld, Nixon did not take him up on the offer.[1]

On the day before Nixon relinquished the presidency on August 9, 1974, Gerald Ford appointed a temporary transition team to help him take over the White House. One of the three members of that team was Rumsfeld, Ford's old friend from their days together in Congress. From NATO headquarters in Brussels, Rumsfeld quickly telephoned his former deputy Dick Cheney, asking that Cheney meet him at Dulles International Airport and help out with staff work for the transition. During Rumsfeld's time in Europe, Cheney had been working in Washington for a private company that advised investment banks.

Ford's instructions to his transition team were clear: Figure out how he should reorganize the White House staff and what he should do about domestic policy, but leave Henry Kissinger's foreign policy alone. "The marching orders were to go and view the Office of Management and Budget and the White House domestic operations and relations between the White House and the Cabinet and report back to me," recalled Cheney in an interview many years later. "But stay out of the national security area." Ford's message, Cheney said, was that "the National Security Council, State, Defense, they're off limits."[2]

The new president had no intention of interfering with Kissinger. At that time Kissinger was at the apex of his power. He held the titles of both secretary of state and national security adviser. Inside the government he chaired virtually all the interagency meetings on foreign policy and defense programs; he and his staff controlled the flows of information and intelligence; they drafted the options papers that went to the president. Outside, in the press and around the nation, Kissinger was celebrated as the Nobel Peace Prize winner who had worked out the 1973 peace accord paving the way for the withdrawal of U.S. troops from Vietnam and (so Americans then believed) the end of the war. With Nixon in disgrace, Kissinger was widely viewed as the architect of both the American opening to China and the policy of détente with the Soviet Union. So great was Kissinger's public standing that during Watergate, Nixon had sought to shore up his political standing through association with his secretary of state. As Ford took over the White House, he too sought to win public support by promising that Kissinger would stay.

For his own part, Kissinger wasted no time in ensuring he would possess at least as much power under Ford as he had enjoyed in the later years of Nixon's presidency. The day after Ford was sworn in, Kissinger drafted a memo for Ford to sign that extended his sweeping authority. Under it, Kissinger's National Security Council was put in charge of all decision making on foreign policy, and Kissinger continued to chair virtually all meetings among top-level government officials on foreign policy.[3] Whenever Secretary of Defense James Schlesinger wanted to give the president his views, which were considerably more hawkish than those of *Secretary of State* Kissinger, he had to go through the National Security Council, presided over by *National Security Adviser* Kissinger.

On Ford's first day as president, Kissinger sat down with Soviet Ambassador Anatoly Dobrynin to assure him that all would be well, both for Kissinger himself and for the policy of détente that he had been pursuing. Kissinger's message was that "Ford had asked him to stay on and pay special attention to relations with the Soviet Union," Dobrynin later wrote. ". . . Frankly speaking, at the beginning of the Ford administration my principal hopes were set on Henry Kissinger and his views."[4]

Over the two and a half years of Ford's presidency, there was a remarkable transformation within the top ranks of his administration. Henry Kissinger lost his preeminence over American foreign policy. His authority eroded to an extent that would have seemed unimaginable in the summer of 1974. Moreover, the touchstone of all of Kissinger's policies, his attempt to forge a new relationship with the Soviet Union, was increasingly challenged, to the point where Ford even avoided using the word *détente.* A new strain emerged in America's relations with the rest of the world, a line of thinking that questioned why or whether the United States should make deals or accommodations with Moscow. At the center of these changes were Donald Rumsfeld and his protégé Dick Cheney.

The month after Ford was sworn in, he brought Rumsfeld back from NATO as the White House chief of staff, replacing Alexander Haig. Rumsfeld quickly installed Cheney as his deputy, the same aide-de-camp role that Cheney had played under Rumsfeld in the Nixon administration. The two men held these positions for more than a year, until Ford appointed Rumsfeld his secretary of defense and named Cheney to be Rumsfeld's successor as White House chief of staff. Throughout the entire Ford administration the Rumsfeld-Cheney duo worked closely together, establishing mastery over the internal workings of government. There was never any doubt that Rumsfeld was the senior figure. Cheney was only thirty-three years old when he joined the Ford administration, and as one colleague put it at the time, "Cheney's adult life had been devoted to the study of political science and the service of Donald Rumsfeld."[5]

According to Robert Ellsworth, who served in Congress alongside Rumsfeld in the 1960s and then worked with him in the Nixon and Ford administrations, there is an old bit of folk wisdom that has been quietly passed around among Republicans for decades. The saying is short and simple: "Donald Rumsfeld does not lose."[6]

That is, to be sure, a slight overstatement. Over his long career Rumsfeld has occasionally lost out on a few things, big and small—not least his desire to become president of the United States. Yet Ellsworth's slogan is largely true as a description of Rumsfeld's record when it comes to bureaucratic skirmishes; rarely has anyone bested Rumsfeld in a power struggle or a test of wills inside the government. Ellsworth's slogan was regularly borne out in the Ford administration, when Rumsfeld overcame one rival after another inside the Ford White House and within the foreign policy apparatus.

First, during late 1974 and early 1975 Rumsfeld and Cheney established their dominance over the White House staff and domestic policy, pushing to the side the president's staff aides from his days as House minority leader and vice president. Next, in 1975 they began to undercut the power of Kissinger and of Kissinger's ally and friend Vice President Nelson Rockefeller. Finally, in late 1975 and 1976 Rumsfeld posed a frontal challenge to Kissinger's policies of détente and arms control with the Soviet Union. Each time the consequences were larger, the battles more intense. In these intra-administration battles, Rumsfeld never lost, and Cheney was regularly at his side.

The early struggles were for primacy within the Ford entourage. Rumsfeld's principal rival was Robert Hartmann, Ford's former congressional aide and vice presidential chief of staff, who had come up with the memorable words the new president had uttered on the day of Nixon's resignation: "Our long national nightmare is over."[7] Ford had appointed Hartmann to be White House counselor. In that role, Hartmann repeatedly urged Ford to put his own stamp on the presidency and to install his own team of loyal assistants; he viewed Rumsfeld as a Nixon holdover and as a front for the perpetuation of the Nixon administration. Hartmann moved into the only office in the West Wing directly connected to the Oval Office, enabling him to wander in and talk to the president whenever he wanted. Rumsfeld dealt with Hartmann through a housekeeping maneuver: He argued successfully that Hartmann's office should be turned into a private presidential study. Hartmann moved out, lost his proximity to Ford and was gradually marginalized.[8]

During the Ford years the Secret Service gave Richard Cheney perhaps the most apt code name it had ever devised, Backseat.[9] That was a perfect description of Cheney's role as an anonymous White House functionary.

Cheney's ascent in the Ford White House served as an illustration of how an individual can rise to the top by virtue of his willingness to take care of the mundane chores that persons with larger egos avoid, thereby establishing reliability and learning all the inner workings of an organization. Cheney was akin to the clerk who becomes chief executive, the copy editor who rises to become editor in chief, the accountant who takes over the film studio.

The archives of the period show how Cheney, as deputy chief of staff, started out in the Ford administration by supervising such lowly matters as plumbing and toilets:

> Memorandum for: Dick Cheney
> From: Jerry Jones
> Oct. 12, 1974
> We will be unable in the short term to fix the drainage problem in the sink in the first floor bathroom. The White House plumbing is very old, and we have had GSA [the General Services Administration] working for some time to figure out how to improve this problem. Hopefully, [sic] it will be done soon. . . .[10]

It was Cheney who oversaw the sending out of White House Christmas cards and gifts. When Betty Ford was uncomfortable on a White House helicopter, it fell to Cheney to try to get a headrest installed at her seat. Cheney even took care of the White House table settings.

> Memorandum for: Jerry Jones
> From: Dick Cheney
> Feb. 19, 1975
> It seems that there are salt shakers in the Residence which are used for the Congressional meals (little dishes of salt with funny little spoons). Is there some reason that regular salt shakers are not used for small breakfasts and small stag dinners?[11]

Others soon discovered, as Rumsfeld already knew, that when you gave something to Cheney, it got done—not flashily but competently. He was the perfect staff man. He worked longer hours than almost anyone else. "The individual who'll join the staff and who'll want to work nine-to-five and maybe see a little cocktail party circuit isn't there when you need him," Cheney told one interviewer.[12]

It wasn't long before Cheney was taking over larger, more important assignments, standing in as Rumsfeld's alter ego when the chief of staff was occupied elsewhere. One natural area for Cheney was intelligence: He was trustworthy, faceless and unfailingly discreet. During the Ford years the CIA was trying to fend off an unending series of press and congressional investigations and, with them, efforts by the Justice Department to establish new rules and guidelines to govern intelligence collection. In May 1975 the *New York Times* published a story by Seymour Hersh describing the U.S. intelligence community's secret effort to lift a sunken Soviet submarine off the seabed in the Pacific Ocean. Cheney was in charge of the meetings aimed at trying to figure out if the Ford administration should take legal action against the newspaper. Cheney's handwritten notes show that he actively considered a number of countermeasures, such as seeking an indictment of Hersh and the *Times* or even obtaining a warrant to search Hersh's apartment. The aim, Cheney wrote, was "to discourage the NYT and other publications from similar action." In the end Cheney and the White House decided to back off after the intelligence community decided its work had not been significantly damaged.[13]

In the early months of 1975 the luster that had attached to Kissinger began to fade. Rumsfeld began to challenge his control over foreign policy.

To some extent, Kissinger's decline was inevitable. By early 1975 Ford was fully established in the White House and beginning to think about the 1976 campaign. If he were to leave foreign policy entirely in Kissinger's hands, Ford risked giving the impression that he was less than presidential and that he was merely perpetuating the policies of the disgraced Richard Nixon. Others in the administration complained regularly about how much authority Kissinger had, and increasingly, outsiders remarked upon it. When novelist John Hersey spent a week in the Ford White House in early 1975, he reported that the president regularly discussed the economy, energy and domestic policy with large, diverse groups of advisers but talked about foreign policy only with Kissinger. "This president, who had a minimum exposure to foreign affairs before he came to office, hears, I am told, only one voice, and a mercurial voice it is, Henry Kissinger's," Hersey wrote. "Yes, this is the most alarming thought I have had all week. . . . Diplomacy, security, foreign intelligence—one daily voice for all?"[14]

If Kissinger was headed for a fall, Rumsfeld was ready to push. When White House press secretary Ron Nessen had a minor skirmish with a lower-level Kissinger aide, he was surprised to find that Rumsfeld raised the episode directly with the president. "I had the uneasy feeling that Rumsfeld was using the incident to drag me into a behind-the-scenes struggle to curb the power of Kissinger and the National Security Council," Nessen wrote.[15] That spring articles began appearing in the press about the efforts inside the White House to cut down Kissinger. "Gunning for Henry," proclaimed the *New Republic*.[16]

On April 23, 1975, as North Vietnamese troops were pushing south in their final assault to capture Saigon, Ford was traveling outside Washington. His speechwriters drafted a passage for him that was intended to acknowledge to the American people that the war was finally over. At first the president balked, saying Kissinger might not approve, but he then went ahead with the speech. "Today, America can regain the sense of pride that existed before Vietnam," Ford told an audience at Tulane University. "But it cannot be achieved by refighting a war that is finished as far as America is concerned." The speech attracted considerable praise, but no one had cleared the text with Kissinger, who was furious. He maintained that the speech had helped to shorten the time for the United States to evacuate refugees from Vietnam.[17]

Kissinger later wrote that by cutting him out from the Vietnam speech, the White House staff "masterminded a typical inside-the-Beltway bureaucratic victory." That was a curious charge from Kissinger, who had masterminded more than his own share of inside-the-Beltway bureaucratic maneuvers. Yet with Rumsfeld consolidating control of the Ford White House, the tide was clearly turning against Kissinger.

At the time of the final American withdrawal from Vietnam, it was Rumsfeld who, inside the Ford White House, delivered an epitaph for the war.

The administration botched its handling of the last, tumultuous moments. The White House announced to the press that all Americans had been flown out from Saigon only to discover a few minutes afterward that more than a hundred Marine security guards were still inside the American Embassy waiting for helicopters. The Marines were rescued within hours, but the question was how to tell the press the evacuation hadn't been completed the first time. "Kissinger wanted to blame the Pentagon's military communications center, although the false announcement resulted from his own incorrect assumption that [the American ambassador's] departure meant the end of the evacuation," wrote White House press secretary Ron Nessen.[18]

Nessen wanted to forget the whole thing and act as though the evacuation had really been finished at the time the administration originally said it was. But Rumsfeld, as White House chief of staff, refused to go along.

"This war has been marked by so many lies and evasions that it is not right to have the war end with one last lie," Rumsfeld said. He ordered the press secretary to be "perfectly honest" about the administration's mistake. Many years later, when Rumsfeld was the defense secretary at the time of America's war with Iraq, he was not always so forthcoming.

The American defeat in Vietnam had profound, long-term effects on politics, foreign policy and public attitudes toward the country and its relations with the rest of the world, effects that were not easy to grasp at the time. Kissinger later acknowledged he had failed to comprehend these changes and that Rumsfeld, by contrast, had been more perceptive.

Kissinger was preoccupied with the threats to his foreign policy from the political left—that is, the forces rising out of the Vietnam antiwar movement and the 1972 Democratic campaign of George McGovern, which sought to cut back on American power and troop deployments overseas. In Kissinger's view, détente with the Soviet Union was aimed in part at outmaneuvering the left; the United States, he hoped, would be able to withdraw from Vietnam but to preserve America's other overseas commitments by seizing "the high ground of the peace issue" through arms control agreements with the Soviet Union.[19] Kissinger was far less worried about challenges from the political right; he believed, wrongly, that Republican conservatives like Ronald Reagan and the Democratic neoconservatives such as Senator Henry Jackson shared the same general goals as the Nixon and Ford administrations and that their disagreements were merely over tactics. Kissinger thought that the principal mistake of the right wing lay in its failure to understand the power and the danger of the liberal Democrats. "Nixon and I believed that refusing to negotiate with the Kremlin would spread the virulence of the anti-Vietnam protest movement into every aspect of American foreign policy, and deeply, perhaps, into our alliances," he explained.[20]

In the short term, Kissinger's fears about the power of the liberal Democrats were borne out. The end of the Vietnam War did lead to further efforts in Congress to reduce America's overseas commitments, cut the defense budget and restrict U.S. intelligence. However, the American retreat from Vietnam also led more gradually to a rise in sentiments that

Kissinger had failed to anticipate: a sense that America should not suffer any similar defeats in the future, that it should more vigorously promote American values overseas and that it should not be so willing to compromise with Communist regimes.

The right wing, whose strength Kissinger had underestimated, became markedly more powerful. Within the Republican party, Reagan's challenge to the Ford administration began to take shape. In Congress, Jackson's challenge to the policy of détente grew stronger. By the summer of 1975 Ford was in retreat. He decided to postpone the idea of establishing diplomatic relations with the People's Republic of China until after the 1976 election, and he slowed down negotiations over the return of the Panama Canal to Panama.

Decades later Kissinger admitted that he had failed to sense where America was headed after Vietnam and that Rumsfeld had been in closer touch with the nation's mood. "As a veteran of the political wars, Rumsfeld understood far better than I that Watergate and Vietnam were likely to evoke a conservative backlash, and that what looked like a liberal tide after the election of the McGovernite Congress [in November 1974] in fact marked the radical apogee," he wrote.[21]

The stage was being set for a Rumsfeld-Cheney challenge to Kissinger's policy of détente.

In late June 1975 the exiled Soviet writer and Nobel Prize winner Aleksandr Solzhenitsyn visited Washington to address an AFL-CIO dinner in his honor. Republican senators tried to arrange for him to meet with Ford at the White House. The administration said no, insisting there was no time on the president's schedule. Kissinger viewed the dinner and the request for Solzhenitsyn to visit the White House as an attempt to undercut détente by irritating the Soviet leadership.

Cheney was evidently outraged. Others in the White House had long recognized that Cheney was deeply conservative. "Whenever his private ideology was exposed, he appeared somewhat to the right of Ford, Rumsfeld, or, for that matter, Genghis Khan," wrote Hartmann, no friend of Cheney.[22] Still, at this point Cheney was still merely the deputy chief of staff at the White House, and he had rarely ventured his opinions on foreign policy issues. This time Cheney decided to make his views known. Within the White House, he sent off a private memo that amounted to a withering attack on Kissinger's approach to the Soviet Union:

Memorandum for: Don Rumsfeld
From: Dick Cheney
July 8, 1975
Subject: Solzhenitsyn

. . . My own strong feeling is that the President should see Solzhenitsyn for any one of the following reasons:

1. I think the decision not to see him is based upon a misreading of détente. . . . It does not mean that all of a sudden our relationship with the Soviets is all sweetness and light.

2. Seeing him is a nice counter-balance to all of the publicity and coverage that's given to meetings between American Presidents and Soviet Leaders. Meetings with Soviet Leaders are very important, but it is also important that we not contribute any more to the illusion that all of a sudden we're bosom buddies with the Russians.

. . . [The Soviets] have been perfectly free to criticize us for our actions and policies in Southeast Asia over the years, to call us imperialists, war-mongers, and various and sundry other endearing terms, and I can't believe they don't understand why the President might want to see Solzhenitsyn.[23]

Cheney's effort failed. Solzhenitsyn never got his meeting with the president. The incident proved politically costly for Ford and for Kissinger.

That fall Ford suddenly unveiled the most extensive cabinet shake-up by any president in modern American history, one that affected virtually all the top officials in foreign policy and at the White House. The principal beneficiaries were Rumsfeld and Cheney.

Ford decided to fire Schlesinger as defense secretary and replace him with Rumsfeld. The president required Kissinger to give up the title of national security adviser and to serve exclusively as secretary of state; Kissinger's former deputy, Brent Scowcroft, became national security adviser. Ford informed Vice President Rockefeller he could be a political liability as a running mate in the 1976 campaign and obtained a public statement from Rockefeller taking himself out of the running for the vice presidential nomination. The president replaced William Colby as director of central intelligence with George H. W. Bush, who had been head of the U.S. liaison office in Beijing. Elliot Richardson was appointed secretary of commerce. Cheney was named to succeed Rumsfeld as White House chief of staff.

At first the shake-up was misconstrued by the press and others in politics as a victory for Kissinger and détente. By this interpretation (which was also accepted by Schlesinger), the secretary of state had succeeded in getting rid of a secretary of defense who had openly opposed Kissinger's policies toward the Soviet Union. After talking to Republican party leaders, Howard Callaway, the chairman of Ford's presidential campaign, reported to the White House: "The initial reaction is that Kissinger won over Schlesinger. This appeared as a defeat for a man who understood Soviet strength and spoke for a strong defense."[24]

Kissinger himself knew better. He had lost his dominating two-job role in the administration, his chairmanship of the principal interagency committees on foreign policy, his base in the White House and his proximity to the president. Moreover, Rockefeller, Kissinger's closest friend and his most senior ally and protector in Republican politics, had been transformed into a lame duck. The secretary of state perceived, rightly, that Rumsfeld, with his political ties and ambitions and his considerable bureaucratic skill, would be a far tougher adversary as secretary of defense than Schlesinger. To be sure, Kissinger had succeeded in installing Scowcroft as national security adviser, but Rumsfeld's ally, Cheney, had won the job of White House chief of staff. Kissinger was so upset with the series of changes that he summoned aides and friends for several evening meetings to decide if he should quit. He even drafted a letter of resignation before finally deciding to stay on.[25]

Over the years this Ford shake-up, sometimes known as the Halloween massacre, became part of the Rumsfeld legend. Many other Republicans believed (and continued to argue for decades) that Rumsfeld had engineered the changes as a way of enhancing his own political prospects. Rockefeller later claimed, on the record, that Rumsfeld hoped to become Ford's choice for vice president on the 1976 ticket.[26] Those close to Bush advanced an even more detailed and Machiavellian interpretation. They believed that Rumsfeld had managed to have Bush named CIA head in order to eliminate Bush as a rival for the vice presidential nomination; under this theory, Rumsfeld knew that any nominee for the CIA would have to promise the Senate at his confirmation hearings that he would not be involved in politics in 1976.

The reality was more prosaic than these conspiracy theories. By all accounts, notably including Ford's, the driving motivation behind the cabinet shake-up was the president's own intense antagonism toward Schlesinger. Ford felt his defense secretary was arrogant and condescending to him. When the president first outlined the series of changes, Rumsfeld balked at the idea of becoming secretary of defense, asking to think about it overnight. He wasn't sure he wanted to leave the White House.[27]

Indeed, by Cheney's subsequent account, the president had to enlist him to persuade Rumsfeld to take the job at Defense. "Frankly, I had to talk [Rumsfeld] into it—long distance," Cheney said in a late-1970s interview. ". . . It was a strange situation. I went from a position where on Saturday I was Rumsfeld's deputy, to a place where on Sunday I was working for Ford trying to get Rumsfeld to do something the President wanted him to do."[28]

The Bush entourage's suspicions about Rumsfeld seemed exaggerated. Rumsfeld was experienced enough with the custom of providing geographic balance to a presidential ticket to know it was unlikely that Ford, who came from Michigan, would choose a running mate from Illinois. If the administration shake-up had been designed to sideline Rumsfeld's rivals for the vice presidency, then why was Elliot Richardson, who was also a potential candidate, given a choice job? Ford's removal of Rockefeller from the vice presidential nomination had little to do with Rumsfeld; rather, it was part of Ford's much broader effort to placate the right wing of the Republican party. So far as is known, Rumsfeld never made any subsequent move toward the 1976 vice presidential nomination; the following summer Ford chose Bob Dole as his running mate.

Nevertheless, Rumsfeld's hand could be detected behind some aspects of the cabinet upheaval. Rumsfeld had been arguing for some time that Kissinger had too much power and that Ford deserved to get a wider range of views on foreign policy. Inside the White House, Rumsfeld had been at odds with Rockefeller for more than a year over issues such as control of domestic policy. While Rumsfeld may have resisted becoming secretary of defense at the last minute, he had let it be known at the start of the Ford administration that he would rather have a cabinet job like defense secretary than serve as White House chief of staff.[29]

The "Halloween massacre" left a legacy of animosity toward Rumsfeld inside the Ford administration, one that took years to heal. After the 1976 election the *New Republic*'s White House correspondent John Osborne interviewed many of the leading officials of the administration. He found that "Kissinger, Schlesinger and Secretary of the Treasury William Simon . . . detested the White House staff under Rumsfeld and his successor, Richard Cheney, as thoroughly as Rockefeller did." The administration's top ranks had been beset by a "welter of suspicion and hatred—the word hatred is justified," Osborne concluded.[30]

Although in the Nixon administration Rumsfeld had been a dove on Vietnam, during the Ford years he gradually emerged as the administration's leading hawk. As secretary of defense he did more than anyone else to block détente and to stiffen American policy toward the Soviet Union. "I remember very vividly, he beat the pants off of Kissinger," recalled Morton Abramowitz, who had worked as an assistant secretary of defense for Schlesinger and stayed on with Rumsfeld.[31]

Rumsfeld's motivation in these endeavors was open to question. Was he deeply committed to the conservative views he espoused in this 1975 to 1976 period, or was he simply courting the support of the political right? Kissinger and his aides believed that Rumsfeld's views were mostly a reflection of political opportunism. "Rumsfeld was thinking about eventually running for the presidency," asserted Brent Scowcroft in an interview decades later. "And I think he was positioning himself. He wanted to be on the conservative side. To me, it was a tactical and political shift, not an ideological shift."[32] Under this interpretation, Rumsfeld's Nixon-era pleas for a rapid end to the Vietnam War had been similarly based on political considerations: Rumsfeld was temporarily aligning himself with popular antiwar sentiments. The Kissinger team figured that opposing détente was another short-term maneuver by Rumsfeld.

However, there are signs that the positions Rumsfeld took as Ford's defense secretary reflected a broader, more enduring change in outlook. At least from the time Rumsfeld served as NATO ambassador in 1973–74, he was moving toward a more hawkish view of American policy toward the Soviet Union. Fred Iklé, then the head of the Arms Control and Disarmament Agency, visited Brussels while Rumsfeld was ambassador and found that Rumsfeld didn't want to do much business with him, simply because of Iklé's job title. "He was pretty rude," Iklé recalled. "I was the arms control director, and he didn't like arms control, even then." Iklé was no fan of détente himself, and he and Rumsfeld later worked closely together in Washington against Kissinger's arms control policies.[33]

Whatever Rumsfeld's original motivations, the hawkish views he espoused as secretary of defense in the late Ford administration turned out to be long-lasting. In that sense the Kissingerites were wrong; for Rumsfeld, opposition to détente in 1975 and 1976 was something more than a passing phase. Rumsfeld remained for decades an advocate of American military strength and a strong skeptic about the value of arms control treaties and other forms of accommodation with the Soviet Union. The period when Rumsfeld veered back and forth, from left to right, hawk to dove, had ended.

The archives of the Ford administration contain evidence that Rumsfeld worked skillfully to enhance his power at the Defense Department and to undermine Kissinger's control of American foreign policy.

During Rumsfeld's confirmation hearings he was interrogated at length about his views by Jackson, the leading Democratic critic of Kissinger's Strategic Arms Limitation Talks (SALT) with the Soviet Union. Conservative Republican senators also asked tough questions about détente. Rumsfeld carefully fended off the senators' queries and won confirmation.

For most nominees, that would have been the end of the story, but not for Rumsfeld. When the hearings ended, he sent a copy of the transcript of the proceedings directly to Ford with a private note, pointing the president specifically to certain passages. These passages involved complaints that previous secretaries of defense had been frozen out of arms control negotiations by Kissinger and had been denied the right to present their views to the president in person. Why, Jackson had asked, were the secretaries of defense reduced to playing second fiddle to Kissinger within the national security apparatus? Why were they just filing memos for Kissinger to rewrite in his "options papers"? Rumsfeld told Ford that the questions raised by the senators "reflect a concern about the operation of the National Security Council. . . . I think it is going to take the best efforts of all of us to see that it works in practice." Rumsfeld's subtext was clear: The president shouldn't let Kissinger or Scowcroft block the secretary of defense from the meetings where decisions were made.

Within weeks after Rumsfeld was sworn in, he succeeded in bringing Kissinger's attempts to negotiate a new SALT agreement with the Soviet Union to a standstill. Kissinger tried to obtain agreement to take a new arms control proposal to Moscow. Rumsfeld managed to win a few weeks' delay, demanding a more thorough review. "He [Rumsfeld] in effect permitted and encouraged the bureaucratic process to run into the sand," said Kissinger.[34]

In January 1976, Ford permitted Kissinger to take a new negotiating proposal to Soviet leader Leonid Brezhnev in Moscow. Rumsfeld made sure that for the first time a civilian representative of the Pentagon, someone who could report back to Rumsfeld, was included in Kissinger's traveling entourage. After Kissinger returned believing he had made progress toward a deal, he ran into resistance in Washington. "The opposition came from Secretary of Defense Don Rumsfeld and the Joint Chiefs of Staff, and I recognized that they held the trump card," wrote Ford in his memoirs. "The Senate would have to ratify the new accord. If Rumsfeld or the Joint Chiefs testified against it, there was no way that the Senate would ever go along with it." The Ford administration came up with a new proposal more acceptable to the Pentagon, but Brezhnev rejected it, ending the chances for an agreement that year.[35]

In public, Rumsfeld began to warn about the growing strength of the Soviet military, which he said necessitated significant increases in the U.S. defense budget. "There has been a massive shift of power in the world," he warned in one paper. "To fail to arrest trends adverse to our interests would mean that we could find ourselves, in the future, confronted by an adversary who does not share our most fundamental beliefs and who is able to threaten or intimidate much of the world."[36]

Kissinger objected to Rumsfeld's open discussion of a Soviet buildup, and Ford himself sought to smooth over the differences with euphemisms. Rumsfeld, however, held his ground. The declassified transcript of one Oval Office session on March 29, 1976, includes this testy exchange about the military balance between the United States and the Soviet Union:

KISSINGER: If we say the trend is going against us, that is bad enough. The impression that we are slipping is creating a bad impression around the world.

RUMSFELD: But it's true!

KISSINGER: Then we have to define our goals. It is inevitable that our margin since '60 has slipped. Are we trying to maintain the same margin as we had in 1960 or to maintain adequate forces?

RUMSFELD: But it is true! We have been slipping since the '60s from superiority to equivalence, and if we don't stop it, we'll be behind.

PRESIDENT: I don't think the President should say we are slipping. I can say we need to redouble our efforts. I don't want to say we are getting behind. I'll say we have a challenge, we have rough equivalence and we've got to keep up.[37]

Rumsfeld's departure from the White House meant that Cheney, as the new chief of staff, was effectively in charge of Ford's presidential campaign. What Cheney was hearing from Republican pollsters and politicians around the country matched his own deeply conservative instincts: He was even less inclined than Rumsfeld to support Kissinger's Soviet policy.

"Détente is a particularly unpopular idea with most Republican voters, and the word is worse," wrote pollster Robert Teeter in a private memo to Cheney less than two weeks after Cheney became chief of staff. "We ought to stop using the word wherever possible." When Ford's speechwriter Robert Hartmann submitted a draft of the State of the Union speech in early January, Cheney shipped it back with the notation "Bob—the foreign-policy section is too tough on the Congress and not tough enough on Russia."[38]

For a brief time Ford fought back against the critics. "I think détente is in the best interest of the country. It is in the best interest of world stability, world peace," he said in a January 1976 television interview. However, Ronald Reagan stepped up his attacks in the Republican primaries, claiming that détente allowed the Soviet Union to take advantage of the United States, to pull ahead of the United States militarily and to undermine American security. Within less than two months Ford was in full-scale retreat. "We are going to forget the use of the word détente," he told an audience in Peoria. ". . . What happens in the negotiations . . . are the things that are of consequence."[39]

That spring both Cheney and Ford's political advisers told the president not to contest Reagan's challenge to his foreign policy. To Kissinger's dismay, they argued that tangling with Reagan over foreign policy wasn't worth it; Ford would need the support of conservatives in the fall elections.[40]

Cheney was now, for the first time in his government career, no longer an aide to Rumsfeld but in a position of authority himself. Aides had joked to Ford that one of the big press questions about his cabinet shake-up would be: "Who in the hell is Richard Cheney?" But Cheney had quickly

consolidated his control over the White House staff. White House reporters soon gave him the name the Grand Teuton, a play both on the
Grand Tetons in Cheney's home state of Wyoming and on the Prussian
style of the Nixon White House staff under H. R. Haldeman.[41]

When Ford landed in Beijing for a summit meeting with Mao Zedong in December 1975, Henry Kissinger, who had visited Beijing often
in the previous four years, found a surprise waiting for him. "The [presi-
dential] advance team, who worked for me, had given me a bigger bed-
room, a bigger suite, than Henry had gotten," recalled Cheney in an
interview two decades later. "It was closer to the president. Henry didn't
like that." At the time Cheney was thirty-four years old.[42]

Reagan's challenge proved considerably tougher than Ford or Kissinger
had expected. When Reagan defeated Ford in North Carolina, it was the
first time any incumbent Republican president had ever lost a primary
election. Reagan stepped up his attacks on Ford's foreign policy throughout the spring. Still, as the primaries ended and the Republican National
Convention approached, Ford appeared to have enough delegates to win
the nomination.

On the first day of the convention in Kansas City, Reagan's forces
mounted a final challenge. They introduced for inclusion in the party
platform a plank on the subject of "Morality in Foreign Policy." It
amounted to a frontal attack on Ford and Kissinger's Soviet policies.

The goal of Republican foreign policy was "the achievement of liberty
under law," the morality plank said. It specifically commended Aleksandr
Solzhenitsyn "for his compelling message that we must face the world
with no illusions about the nature of tyranny." It also pledged a foreign
policy "in which secret agreements, hidden from our people, will have no
part."[43]

Ford later claimed he was furious. Kissinger, Scowcroft and Vice President Rockefeller were even angrier; they insisted that Ford should fight
to defeat the morality plank as a matter of principle because it amounted
to a condemnation of the administration. At first Ford served notice he
intended to do just that. Ford's negotiators meanwhile sought to draft
amendments that would weaken the plank by, among other things, eliminating the references to Solzhenitsyn.

But Cheney turned Ford around. The White House chief of staff,
backed up by Ford's political advisers, argued that if Ford fought the

"Morality in Foreign Policy" plank and lost in a symbolic test of strength with Reagan, it could jeopardize his chances of winning the presidential nomination. "Principle is okay up to a certain point," Cheney told other Ford aides. "But principle doesn't do any good if you lose the nomination . . . Platforms don't mean anything."[44]

Ford yielded. Avoiding a fight, he accepted the "Morality in Foreign Policy" plank. He went on to win the nomination, but the Republican platform on which he ran that fall represented the views of Reagan and other critics of the administration. It represented a crushing defeat for Kissinger and for détente.

To be sure, Cheney's action in pressing for acceptance of the Reagan language was an act of political realism. As a loyal and dedicated White House chief of staff Cheney was helping ensure that Ford would win the Republican nomination. Yet another interpretation also suggests itself: It seems likely that the conservative Cheney quietly agreed with the Reagan foreign policy plank far more than did Ford, Kissinger or Scowcroft. Cheney had himself privately challenged Ford and Kissinger's treatment of Solzhenitsyn. When it came to personal relationships, Cheney was a trustworthy Ford aide. When it came to abstract principles of foreign policy, however, he seems to have been closer to Reagan, the Republican challenger, than to Ford and Kissinger.

While Rumsfeld and Cheney were eviscerating Kissinger's Soviet policies at the top levels of the Ford administration and the Republican party, Paul Wolfowitz was engaged in a parallel effort inside the U.S. intelligence community.

At the end of each year, at a time when new defense budgets were being drafted, the CIA and other American intelligence agencies produced a secret National Intelligence Estimate on the intentions and capabilities of the Soviet Union. By the mid-1970s this process had become increasingly contentious; congressional critics complained that the intelligence community was offering too benign and too optimistic a view of the Soviet leadership and military. The underlying issue was whether the CIA and other agencies were underestimating the threat from the Soviet Union, either by intentionally tailoring intelligence to support Kissinger's policy of détente or by simply failing to give enough weight to darker interpretations of Soviet intentions.

In 1976 Bush, the CIA's new director, moved to counter the criticism.

He appointed a team of outside experts, called Team B, to review the classified data and to draw up its own separate report on the Soviet Union
and its intentions. Team B was headed by Richard Pipes, a professor of
Russian history from Harvard University. Wolfowitz, still working at the
U.S. Arms Control and Disarmament Agency, was one of the ten members.

The report, delivered at the end of 1976, presented an analysis of Soviet motivations profoundly different from the one U.S. intelligence had
been offering. The team concluded it was possible to interpret the available intelligence data as showing that the Soviet Union was striving for
military superiority over the United States and that it viewed détente as a
means of achieving this goal. "All the evidence points to an undeviating
Soviet commitment to what is euphemistically called the 'worldwide triumph of socialism,' but in fact connotes global Soviet hegemony," the report said. It criticized the CIA for relying too much on satellites and other
technology and for failing to give enough weight to what Soviet leaders
were saying.[45]

This Team B exercise represented an important step in Wolfowitz's career. For the first time he was focusing on the underpinnings of American
foreign policy, on the hidden assumptions and leaps of logic that lay beneath the dry, purportedly unbiased studies of the intelligence community. Many years later, in a retrospective interview with the CIA's own
internal historians, Wolfowitz said he came to the conclusion that U.S. intelligence analysts had been operating in the fashion of a priesthood, issuing conclusions as if they were commandments written on tablets. "The
B-Team demonstrated that it was possible to construct a sharply different
view of Soviet motivation from the consensus view of the analysts, and one
that provided a much closer fit to the Soviets' observed behavior (and also
provided a much closer fit to the Soviets' observed behavior up to and
through the invasion of Afghanistan)," Wolfowitz said.[46]

The Team B exercise created an important precedent. From that point
onward, whenever members of Congress believed that the CIA was min-
imizing the seriousness of a foreign policy problem, there were calls for a
Team B to review the intelligence and make its own independent evalua-
tion. During the mid-1990s the Republican majority in Congress set up
a special commission, modeled upon Team B, to study the threat to the
United States from ballistic missiles. After reviewing the intelligence, an
independent commission concluded that the danger of a missile attack

was considerably greater than the U.S. intelligence community had reported. That missile defense commission was headed by Donald Rumsfeld, and one of its leading members was Paul Wolfowitz.

Wolfowitz's work on Team B seems to have had a particularly strong influence on his own thinking. From then on the inadequacies of American intelligence became a frequent Wolfowitz theme. From his own perspective, the intelligence community simply wasn't being skeptical enough; it was too satisfied with information that confirmed its preconceptions. Critics made the reverse accusation against him; there were complaints that Wolfowitz was too eager to obtain intelligence reports that fitted in with his own conservative views.

After the terrorist attacks of 2001, as America gradually moved toward war against Saddam Hussein's Iraq, Wolfowitz was among the Bush administration officials pushing hard for the U.S. intelligence community to come up with stronger information about Iraq's ties to terrorism and its programs for weapons of mass destruction. Inside the Pentagon, Wolfowitz set up a special team to carry out independent analyses and draw its own conclusions from the intelligence on Iraq; the team was headed by Abram Shulsky, a veteran intelligence specialist who had been Wolfowitz's classmate and friend both at Cornell and at the University of Chicago.[47] In a way, Wolfowitz was creating his own in-house Team B.

By the mid-1970s Wolfowitz was questioning not only Kissinger's policy toward the Soviet Union but his broader assumptions, his worldview and his interpretations of history. Wolfowitz was young, and his opinions attracted little attention at the time, but they were representative of the developing intellectual challenge to Kissinger from the political right.

During the summer of 1976, while still working at the arms control agency, Wolfowitz invited two Harvard graduate students to work for him as interns. One of them was Francis Fukuyama. Over dinner in his home one night, Wolfowitz gave the interns a critique of Kissinger's academic work *A World Restored*, an admiring portrait of how the Austrian statesman Metternich had established a durable balance of power in Europe in the early nineteenth century. It was a good book, Kissinger's best, Wolfowitz told the students, yet Kissinger had missed the point: The hero of this history was not Metternich, the realist. It was Tsar Alexander I of Russia, who had pushed for stronger action against Napoleon, because Alexander I had stood for moral and religious principles.[48]

Kissinger had clearly identified himself with Metternich and with Metternich's aim of creating a stable equilibrium among major powers. Kissinger's pursuit of détente with the Soviet Union seemed to be based on this model. In *A World Restored,* he had written with distaste of moral concerns. "Moral claims involve a quest for absolutes, a denial of nuance, a rejection of history," Kissinger argued.[49]

By contrast, for Wolfowitz, moral principles were more important than stability or national interest. "I remember him saying the thing that's wrong with Kissinger is that he does not understand the country he's living in, that this is a country that is dedicated to certain universalistic principles," recalled Fukuyama.

Wolfowitz placed a higher value on political freedom than on preserving the existing balance of power. He would have happily embraced the Reaganites' "Morality in Foreign Policy" plank. Many years later, in the second Bush administration, Wolfowitz applied this same preference for moral values over political stability to the issue of American policy toward Iraq. If the overthrow of Saddam Hussein upset the existing balance of power in the Middle East, so be it, he reasoned. What mattered above all was the pursuit of what he considered moral values.

In his memoir of the Ford years, Kissinger disparaged those Americans who, in the fashion of Woodrow Wilson, see American foreign policy "as a struggle between good and evil, in each phase of which it is America's mission to help defeat the evil foes challenging a peaceful order. . . . Wilsonianism rejects peace through balance of power in favor of peace through moral consensus."[50] Those words were an apt description of Wolfowitz's views, beginning in the Ford administration and continuing through the second Bush administration. More than any other single figure in the Republican foreign policy hierarchy, Wolfowitz viewed himself as Kissinger's opposite, his adversary in the realm of ideas.

The evisceration of Henry Kissinger and détente represented a turning point for America's relations with the world. Inside the United States the issues and the very focus of debate over American foreign policy were undergoing rapid and fundamental transformation. Rumsfeld, Cheney and Wolfowitz all played key roles in these changes, and the changes in turn affected them later in their careers.

In the late 1960s and early 1970s, during the war in Vietnam, the principal underlying issue had been whether the United States—particularly the U.S. military—was a force for good or evil in the world. The American antiwar movement and the liberal wing of the Democratic party emphasized the harmful effects of America's overseas presence. Politically, the main struggle had been between the forces of Nixon and of George McGovern.

During the Ford years the debate over American foreign policy shifted to new questions, raised by different political forces. The underlying issue was the extent of American power—that is, how the Vietnam War had affected the country's overall military and economic strength. Was the United States in decline after its military defeat? Would it be forced to trim back on its overseas involvements? Were the American people ready to abandon efforts against communism and to accept, out of necessity, a working relationship with the Soviet Union?

Kissinger's foreign policy was based on one set of answers to these questions. He thought it inevitable that after Vietnam, the United States would have to scale back and to make accommodations with Moscow. "He felt that the United States was weakened by Vietnam and that the mood of the country was in favor of arms control and détente," said Fred Iklé. Critics complained that Kissinger had too dark a view of the United States and its future; some compared him with the pessimistic German philosopher Oswald Spengler. "Kissinger was a Spenglerian," said Zbigniew Brzezinski, who became national security adviser in the Carter administration. "He believed the United States was in decline, that the Soviet Union was going to prevail and that the best we could do was to cut a deal with them that would limit their ascendancy."[51]

Kissinger rejected such accusations, but in some respects the criticism was fair. He may not have believed that the Soviet Union was actually going to prevail, but he did seem to accept the inevitability of America's decline. In one interview conducted in 1977, one of Kissinger's closest aides, Winston Lord, said that Kissinger believed the era of global predominance for the United States was over. Another Kissinger deputy, Brent Scowcroft, said Kissinger thought that the United States had overestimated its ability to manage the affairs of the world on its own.[52] Kissinger himself argued that after Vietnam and Watergate, the American public simply would not support a confrontation with the Soviet Union.[53]

Such views seemed to fit the political climate of the mid-1970s, when Congress was seeking to slash U.S. defense budgets and was subjecting

U.S. intelligence operations to unprecedented scrutiny. Yet Rumsfeld, Cheney, Wolfowitz, the conservative wing of the Republican party and the neoconservative wing of the Democratic party rejected Kissinger's dark vision. They all were moving toward a different outlook, one that differed both from the Kissinger forces and from the McGovern wing of the Democratic party. Under this perspective the United States was *not* in decline; it need not adopt a more limited vision of American power or enter a new accommodation with the Soviet Union.

The philosophical cleavages that emerged during the Ford years were to persist through the end of the century and beyond. In 2002, as the second Bush administration was trying to decide whether to invade Iraq, a group of Republican critics warned that the United States should be careful to recognize the limits of its own power. The leader among these critics was Scowcroft, Kissinger's former deputy. The leading proponents of military action were Cheney, Rumsfeld and Wolfowitz.

CHAPTER FIVE

Enter the Persian Gulf

WHEN JIMMY CARTER and the Democrats took control of the White House in 1977, Paul Wolfowitz stayed on in the government. Although he had worked in the Nixon and Ford administrations, Wolfowitz was not himself a Republican. Two of his closest political allies, Senator Henry Jackson and Jackson's aide Richard Perle, were Democrats. As Carter took office, the Jackson forces still harbored hopes that the new administration might adopt their own hawkish views on foreign policy; during the 1976 campaign Carter had portrayed himself as a moderate to conservative candidate, carefully distancing himself from the liberal Democrats in Congress.

Wolfowitz had sought to work in the Defense Department for several years. He was hoping to branch out from nuclear weaponry, his original field of expertise, and to gain experience in conventional military issues in the Middle East and Persian Gulf. The key to preventing nuclear wars was to stop conventional wars, he figured.[1] At the start of the Carter administration he took a job in the Pentagon, an obscure midlevel position as the deputy assistant secretary of defense for regional programs. Wolfowitz was responsible for thinking beyond the Pentagon's day-to-day crises to the problems it might have to confront in the future. Soon he was at work on a new project, one that would play a groundbreaking role in changing American military policy toward the Persian Gulf over the coming decades. It was called the Limited Contingency Study.[2]

Secretary of Defense Harold Brown had asked Wolfowitz to examine the possible threats that the U.S. military might have to confront in the third world. Where else outside Europe, where the allies were poised to stop a Soviet invasion, might American troops be required to fight? Wolfowitz soon focused upon the oil resources of the Persian Gulf. By the mid-1970s the United States had already been subject to an Arab oil embargo and to unprecedented increases in the price of oil. In response, some American policy makers had vaguely suggested the possibility that the United States might have to resort to force to break a future embargo. To Wolfowitz, that prospect raised a number of questions. Could U.S. forces defend the oil fields of Saudi Arabia, the world's largest producer? Would the United States be able to get its troops into the region?

During his early months on the new job Wolfowitz attended a seminar given by Geoffrey Kemp, a young professor at the Fletcher School of Law and Diplomacy. Kemp, a specialist on the Middle East, argued that the American military was overly obsessed with defending Europe and wasn't paying enough attention to the possibility that Soviet forces might move southward, into the Persian Gulf. This warning struck a chord with Wolfowitz. It fit well with the conclusion he had just reached in the Team B intelligence review: that the United States was underestimating the military threat from the Soviet Union. Wolfowitz soon hired Kemp to work on the Limited Contingency Study. He also recruited a young Soviet specialist from the University of California, Dennis Ross. It was the first job in government for Ross, later to become famous as the Middle East peace negotiator for the Clinton administration.

The Limited Contingency Study was the Pentagon's first extensive examination of the need for the United States to defend the Persian Gulf. "We and our major industrialized allies have a vital and growing stake in the Persian Gulf region because of our need for Persian Gulf oil and because events in the Persian Gulf affect the Arab-Israeli conflict," the study began. "The importance of Persian Gulf oil cannot easily be exaggerated." If the Soviet Union were to control Persian Gulf oil, the impact would "probably destroy NATO and the U.S.-Japanese alliance without recourse to war by the Soviets."[3]

The Pentagon team studied the history of the military strategies and war plans of major powers in Iran and Iraq. In World War II the British government had worried that the German Wehrmacht, following its invasion of the Soviet Union, might swing south to invade the Persian Gulf and thus deny the oil fields of the Middle East to British forces, strangling the British economy. Might the Soviet forces of the 1970s drive through the Caucasus into the Middle East, following the path the World War II allies had once feared the Germans might take?

For the Pentagon, worrying about a Soviet invasion of the Persian Gulf represented a considerable change. Throughout the early years of the cold war, the focus of American defense planning was to worry about a Soviet invasion of Western Europe through the Fulda Gap in Germany, along NATO's northern flank in Norway or across its southern flank in Greece and Turkey.

Wolfowitz not only examined the possibility of a Soviet seizure of Persian Gulf oil fields, but then took the Limited Contingency Study one step further. He asked a question American policy makers generally hadn't addressed: What if *another country*, such as another national within the Persian Gulf itself, were to threaten the oil fields of the region? Specifically, what if Iraq were to invade its neighbors Saudi Arabia or Kuwait? The study concluded:

> . . . Iraq has become militarily pre-eminent in the Persian Gulf, a worrisome development because of Iraq's radical-Arab stance, its anti-Western attitudes, its dependence on Soviet arms sales, and its willingness to foment trouble in other local nations.
>
> . . . The emerging Iraqi threat has two dimensions. On the one hand, Iraq may in the future use her military forces against such states as Kuwait or Saudi Arabia (as in the 1961 Kuwait crisis that was resolved by timely British intervention with force). On the other hand, the more serious problem may be that Iraq's *implicit* power will cause currently moderate local powers to accommodate themselves to Iraq without being overtly coerced. The latter problem suggests that we must not only be able to defend the interests of Kuwait, Saudi Arabia and ourselves against an Iraqi invasion or show of force, we should also make manifest our capabilities and commitments to balance Iraq's power—and this may require an increased visibility for U.S. power.[4]

According to Ross, who wrote the sections about Iraq under Wolfowitz's direction, no one believed that Iraq posed a serious or imminent threat to the Saudis. However, Wolfowitz told Ross, "When you look at contingencies, you don't focus only on the likelihood of the contingency but also on the severity of its consequences." In other words, probabilities aren't everything; even if something seems unlikely to happen, you still have to worry about it if the impact would be disastrous for the United States.[5]

Raising the possibility of an Iraqi invasion was too much for Brown, the defense secretary. He thought that an Iraqi attack was not something that should be discussed in any study that could conceivably become public. If the study leaked, the United States might have to explain to the Iraqi government (increasingly controlled by the young leader Saddam Hussein, who was then vice chairman of the Revolutionary Council) why the United States considered Iraq a threat. Moreover, if the study became public, it could also unsettle Saudi Arabia—since inevitably, given the proclivity for conspiratorial thinking in the Middle East, the Iraqis would believe that the United States had done the study at the instigation of the Saudis.[6] These worries proved unjustified; the study never leaked out.

Overall, the military implications of the Limited Contingency Study were clear. The United States needed to take steps to develop the infrastructure for bringing its own military forces into the Persian Gulf. The report recommended new American bases in the region, better runways, improved capabilities for airlift and sealift of American troops and the development of storage locations where the United States could keep large supplies of military equipment. "The whole thrust of the study was to say that we [Americans] had a big problem, that it would take us a long time to get any significant military force into the area," explained Ross.

Overall, Wolfowitz and Ross's study broke new ground by studying seriously the possibility of an Iraqi invasion of Saudi Arabia or Kuwait and how the United States might respond to it. More than a decade later, in August 1990, on the day after Saddam Hussein's forces invaded Kuwait, Ross was traveling overseas on a plane with Secretary of State James Baker. A general aboard Baker's plane gave him a briefing on how Iraq might build up its forces in order to attack Saudi Arabia. Ross looked at the general's charts and realized to his surprise that they were an updated version of the work he had done in the Limited Contingency Study.

Iraq was a subject to which Wolfowitz would return over and over again during his career. Much later he emphasized again and again the theme of Saddam Hussein's tyrannical rule. But it is important to note that at this juncture in the late 1970s, when Wolfowitz first began to focus his attention upon Iraq, Saddam Hussein had not yet had time to consolidate his control over the leadership, to repress all dissent in the country or to use chemical weapons against Iraq's Kurdish population. Wolfowitz's earliest interest in Iraq, then, arose from concerns about oil, geopolitics and the balance of power in the Persian Gulf, not from concerns about Saddam Hussein's behavior.

Because of the intense U.S. military involvement in the Persian Gulf over the past quarter century, it is difficult today for anyone to imagine or recall how different the situation was in the 1970s. At the time the region seemed almost off the map in the Pentagon's worldwide military planning.

In that era the United States had no military command specifically for the Persian Gulf. The U.S. Central Command (CENTCOM)—the U.S. military command that became familiar to Americans when it directed the Gulf War under General Norman Schwarzkopf in 1991 and the wars in Afghanistan and Iraq under General Tommy Franks from 2001 to 2003—did not exist.

The responsibility for bringing American land forces into the Persian Gulf lay with the U.S. military commander in Europe, whose turf extended as far as Iran's border with Pakistan. The waters of the Persian Gulf and the Red Sea, on the other hand, were under the jurisdiction of the commander of U.S. forces in the Pacific, who also had responsibility for Pakistan and Afghanistan. Not surprisingly, the European command, based in Stuttgart, was preoccupied with defending Western Europe against a Soviet invasion, while the Pacific command, based in Honolulu, spent most of its time worrying about the problems of East Asia.[7] If the United States were suddenly obliged to fight a war in the Persian Gulf, it would find no detailed war plans on the shelf.

In fact, throughout most of the 1970s America's strategy for protecting its interests in the Persian Gulf depended largely on a single country and its moody, mercurial leader, the shah of Iran.

On their way home from a trip to Moscow in May 1972 Richard Nixon and Henry Kissinger had stopped briefly in Iran and had taken a momentous step, one whose implications were little noticed at the time.

They opened the way for an extensive new American relationship with Shah Mohammad Reza Pahlavi. The United States agreed to increase American military advisers in Iran and to let Iran buy advanced new U.S. military hardware and technology. In exchange, the shah agreed to take the lead in defending Western interests in the Persian Gulf. As their meeting came to a close, Nixon looked plaintively at the shah and said, "Protect me."[8]

Nixon's action was, like détente, an attempt to recalibrate American foreign policy to take account of the impact of the war in Vietnam. Nixon and Kissinger had decided that since the United States seemed unable to police the world on its own, the best alternative would be to build up strong regional powers that were closely tied to the United States and could help provide security in nearby areas. Iran seemed to be the perfect candidate for this new policy. It was the biggest, most populous nation in the Persian Gulf. The shah, with his grandiose ambitions and his dedication to Westernization, was exactly the sort of regional leader for whom Nixon and Kissinger yearned.

The Nixon administration was also reacting to the changing balance of military power in the Middle East. In 1971, as part of its retreat from areas east of Suez, Britain had withdrawn its forces from the Persian Gulf. In April 1972, a few weeks before Nixon's visit to Iran, the Soviet Union had signed a friendship treaty under which it was to supply new military hardware to Iraq, Iran's neighbor and rival for influence in the region.

Encouraged by the strong support from Nixon and Kissinger, the shah went on a protracted shopping binge in which he bought virtually anything that U.S. defense manufacturers offered him. His special preference was for the latest and most sophisticated military hardware. Over the six years from 1972 to 1978, Iran ordered at least twelve billion dollars of advanced American weaponry, including at least 160 F-16 jet fighters, 7 AWACS command and control planes, 4 *Spruance*-class destroyers, 3 submarines and 14,000 missiles.[9] The shah helped finance these purchases by pushing oil-producing nations for unprecedented increases in petroleum prices; in December 1973, following the Yom Kippur War and the Arab oil boycott, he persuaded the Organization of Petroleum Exporting Countries (OPEC) to raise the price for a barrel of oil to four times what it had been only three months earlier. When others in Washington, including Treasury Secretary William Simon, urged

Kissinger to hold up arms deliveries to Iran as a way of pressuring the shah to hold down oil prices, Kissinger refused.[10] America's relationship with the shah was too important, he argued.

From the outset Pentagon officials were uneasy with these arms sales to Iran, and on several occasions they voiced strong opposition within the U.S. government. Defense Department studies had regularly shown that Iran needed training for its armed forces far more than it needed advanced weaponry. Pentagon officials worried that Iran couldn't absorb all the new technology it was buying and that it was unclear how the new weapons would be used. Kissinger dismissed such concerns, claiming that the Defense Department merely preferred to sell Iran outdated equipment and to keep the newest hardware for the United States alone.

Commenting on one set of Pentagon objections, Kissinger reminded Nixon that following the 1972 visit to Iran, "We adopted a policy which provides, in effect, that we will accede to any of the shah's requests for arms purchases from us (other than some sophisticated advanced technology armaments and with the very important exception, of course, of any nuclear weapons capability . . .)."[11] While Kissinger insisted otherwise, those words appeared to tell the Pentagon that decisions on arms sales were largely a matter of giving the shah what he wanted.

During the Nixon and Ford administrations Washington relied upon the shah for insight and intelligence about the other governments in the Middle East. In an Oval Office conversation in 1975, for example, the shah warned President Ford and Kissinger that the monarchy in Saudi Arabia might not be too stable.

"The Bedouins are not easy to rule," he said. "Religion is important. We have to be prepared for anything." As it turned out, the Saudi monarchy was more stable than the shah himself.[12]

Among the many working-level U.S. officials passing through Iran during this era were Richard Armitage and Colin Powell. Their experiences were separate and not comparable; Armitage lived in Tehran for several months, while Powell merely stopped in Iran for a few days on a visit from Washington. Yet each was on a similar mission, one that stemmed from the Pentagon's desperate attempt to straighten out the arms sales to the shah. Both were able to witness firsthand the problems inherent in Nixon and Kissinger's policy of building up Iran as a regional power.

By the mid-1970s Defense Secretary James Schlesinger was becoming ever more disturbed by what he considered the irrationality and excesses of the shah's weapons purchases. Iran, for example, was trying to buy F-14, F-15 and F-16 warplanes, raising the prospect of a nightmare in logistics and spare parts. In a 1975 memo to President Ford, Schlesinger questioned "whether our policy of supporting an apparently open-ended Iranian military buildup will continue to serve our long-term interests."[13]

That September Schlesinger dispatched his civilian problem fixer, Erich von Marbod, to live in Tehran and serve as his representative there. Von Marbod's job in the Defense Security Assistance Agency included responsibility for arms sales. His main assignment was to try to instill some coherence and restraint in Iran's purchases of American weaponry.

Von Marbod brought his own entourage with him to Tehran, and Armitage was part of it. Armitage had already worked closely with von Marbod over the previous year, first in Vietnam during the frantic American withdrawal from Saigon and then in helping resettle Vietnamese refugees in the United States after the end of the war. In Tehran, Armitage helped out in dealing with Iran's navy and its special operations units. "He had no particular portfolio. He did kind of piecework out there," recalled Larry Ropka, the Air Force officer who was also in von Marbod's entourage. Armitage was a relatively junior member of the team. When U.S. Ambassador Richard Helms hosted ceremonies to honor the promotion of Air Force General Richard Secord, Armitage was present, handing out champagne and sprinkling water to keep down the Tehran dust.[14]

The stint in Tehran represented Armitage's first opportunity to become involved in some other region besides Southeast Asia. Yet the exposure was relatively superficial, by comparison with Vietnam; Armitage never had the chance to learn the language or to form the sorts of attachments he had developed in Southeast Asia. According to James Kelly, another von Marbod aide who served alongside Armitage in Tehran and later worked under him in the Reagan and George W. Bush administrations, there was little contact between the Americans in von Marbod's mission and ordinary Iranians. In fact, Savak, the shah's secret police, kept close watch over the Americans. In Vietnam, Armitage had lived alongside the Vietnamese. In Iran, by contrast, he lived comfortably with

Americans, impressing his roommate, Kelly, with his ability to do hundreds of push-ups and sit-ups each morning.

Armitage came to the conclusion that the shah "had no idea what was going on" inside his own country. The Iranian ruler would fly over the problems without experiencing them. More than a quarter century later Armitage also recalled discovering that "the Iranians had a huge sense of themselves." They seemed to be far more suspicious of foreigners than the Vietnamese were. "I've never met a more ethnocentric people in my life," he observed.[15]

Colin Powell visited Tehran much later, in October 1978, as a military aide in a traveling delegation headed by Carter's deputy secretary of defense, Charles Duncan. The Americans were once again trying to ascertain how well Iran was absorbing American arms. But by this time the U.S. team was also quietly checking on the country's political stability.

In Powell's autobiography, written more than a decade later, his memories of this trip are tinged with sarcasm. During the visit, he wrote, the Americans were informed that Iran's crack troops, known as the Immortals, would "fight to the last man to protect the shah." The shah, he said, was "beloved by his people, so we believed."[16]

During a sumptuous banquet in the city of Isfahan, Powell heard what sounded like machine-gun fire in the streets. The Iranian military leaders behaved as though nothing were happening. In Shiraz, Powell's delegation was supposed to go to a formal dinner hosted by a commandant in the Iranian Air Force. However, a "beautifully uniformed escort officer" showed up at the Americans' hotel to tell them they couldn't go outside. The streets were unsafe because of fighting between the police and fundamentalist mobs.

Powell couldn't have known at the time that he was witnessing a country in the early stages of revolution.

Wolfowitz's Limited Contingency Study had little immediate impact. The authors of the study were midlevel Pentagon civilians. Senior uniformed military leaders continued to resist suggestions that they alter the structure and organization of the U.S. armed forces to reflect the growing importance of the Persian Gulf. Indeed, even President Carter and the National Security Council had difficulty getting the military services to change their operations and their command structure. Carter had issued a directive in 1977 formally asking the Defense Department to set up a "rapid deployment force" that might move into the Persian Gulf, yet for two years the Pentagon did little to respond. The bureaucratic inertia was strong. "The military services didn't want to do anything to build up the military in the region of the world where, since that time, they have fought two major wars," said General William Odom, who served as the military adviser to Carter's National Security Council.[17]

Change finally came with the sudden collapse of the Nixon-Kissinger strategy for the Persian Gulf. On January 16, 1979, the shah of Iran fled the country amid a series of riots and demonstrations against his regime, and two weeks later Ayatollah Khomeini flew back to Iran from exile in Paris as the country's new leader. Near the end of 1979 Iranian students seized the U.S. Embassy in Tehran and took sixty-six Americans as hostages; Khomeini called America the great Satan. The Carter administration attempted to launch a rescue operation, called Desert One, to free the hostages in April 1980, but the mission had to be aborted when two American helicopters went down in the Iranian desert.

These upheavals in Iran, coupled with the Soviet Union's invasion of Afghanistan at the end of 1979, prompted the Carter administration to push through a series of steps aimed at increasing America's military presence in the Persian Gulf. The resistance of the military services began to ease, and the Pentagon began to set up a rapid deployment force. The president formally announced what became the Carter doctrine: that "any attempt by an outside force to gain control of the Persian Gulf region will be regarded as an assault on the vital interests of the United States of America, and such an assault will be repelled by any means necessary, including military force."[18]

U.S. officials began seeking air and naval bases near the Persian Gulf in such countries as Oman, Kenya and Somalia. They encouraged friendly governments in the Middle East to build larger airfields and storage facilities that American forces could use. In 1980 American and Egyptian troops carried out a joint exercise called Bright Star, in which U.S. military personnel got their first training in the desert conditions of the Middle East. U.S. forces began to develop new technology to produce drinking water in war-fighting conditions, and the Pentagon began to develop speedy "roll-on, roll-off" transport ships that could carry U.S. troops from the East Coast of the United States to the Suez Canal within ten days. The year after Carter left office, the Reagan administration formally created CENTCOM, the new military command for the Middle East.[19] Gradually, the United States began shifting to give the Persian Gulf the same sort of attention and emphasis it had long given to Europe and East Asia.

The revolution in Iran carried several lessons, ones that were to affect American thinking for decades. For those who were serving or had served in the U.S. armed forces, such as Powell and Armitage, Iran underscored once again the political lessons of Vietnam. One was that the U.S. armed forces should not rely too heavily on a leader or a regime that might not enjoy the support of its own people. "When the Shah fell, our Iran policy fell with him," reflected Powell in his memoirs. "All the billions we had spent there only exacerbated conditions and contributed to the rise of a fundamentalist regime implacably opposed to us to this day."[20]

The failure of Desert One added to the military's sense of defeat that was left over from Vietnam. Powell, who was not involved in the operation to rescue the hostages, was angry that the mission had nowhere near enough helicopters and was poorly planned, relying on a pickup team thrown together from various services. You have to "go in with everything you need—and then some—and not count on wishful thinking," wrote Powell. "I would have rated Desert One's chances of success at a hundred to one, foolhardy odds for a military operation."[21] A few years later Congress created a new Special Operations Command to take responsibility for future missions like the one that had failed in Iran. In the George W. Bush administration, this command took on ever-greater responsibility in overseas military operations.

The Iranian Revolution also carried other, broader implications for America's global strategy. It marked the end of the Nixon doctrine, the idea put forward during the Vietnam War that the United States would not serve as the world's policeman but would rely on other countries to defend themselves. The United States couldn't depend on the shah of Iran to protect the Persian Gulf—not merely because the shah proved to be unstable but because American interests in the gulf and its oil supplies were deemed too important to be left in the hands of a single leader or army in the region.

The United States would instead have to develop its own capabilities to protect the gulf and its oil resources. This was a crucial decision for the United States, one whose implications extended beyond the Persian Gulf. America was deciding to rely above all on its military resources. One might conceivably envision other strategies for ensuring the continuing flow of oil from the region: the use of diplomacy to ensure the cooperation of governments in the Middle East or economic power to buy or trade for the oil. Governments in Europe and Japan secured their Mideast oil without recourse to military strategies. Yet each of these other strategies carried high costs, and in the end none of them would guarantee the continuing flow of oil. (Indeed, governments like Japan's often relied in the end on U.S. military power to keep the oil flowing.)

In the late 1970s American military thinking about the gulf was focused, not surprisingly, on the Soviet Union. When Carter warned about any "outside force" trying to gain control of the Persian Gulf, he was of course referring to the Soviets. Yet once the president declared the Persian Gulf vital to America's strategic interests, the logic of his doctrine applied not only to nations outside the region but also to those inside the Middle East, that might try to dominate the oil supplies, such as Iraq or Iran.

And so the Persian Gulf remained at the center of American strategic thinking after the breakup of the Soviet Union. Wolfowitz, in warning about the dangers of Iraq in the Limited Contingency Study, was pointing the way to where Washington didn't know it was heading.

The Iranian Revolution had an impact too on American politics and in the realm of ideas. In particular, the fall of the shah widened the rift between the mainstream of the Democratic party and its hawkish neoconservative wing. The events prompted the neoconservatives to begin to adopt some curious ideas about democracy, ones from which they, many years later, quietly retreated.

The neoconservative movement that arose within the Democratic party was made up of intellectuals, scholars and party stalwarts who had originally been strong supporters of the party's New Deal traditions. Irving Kristol, one of the original neoconservatives and the editor of the magazine *Public Interest*, recalled: "We were all children of the depression, most of us from lower-middle-class or working-class families, a significant number of us urban Jews for whom the 1930s had been years of desperation, and we felt a measure of loyalty to the spirit of the New Deal if not to all its programs and policies."[22] In the late 1960s and 1970s these Democrats grew increasingly unhappy with the party's drift toward the political left. They were uneasy with Lyndon Johnson's anti-poverty program; they then were enraged when Democratic leaders embraced many of the causes of the youth counterculture of the 1960s, including opposition to the Vietnam War and support for affirmative action. In the 1970s the neoconservatives lined up behind Democratic leaders, such as Henry Jackson, Hubert Humphrey and Daniel Patrick Moynihan; the older intellectuals in the movement were joined by rising young foreign policy hawks such as Richard Perle and Paul Wolfowitz. All of them believed in the importance of American power; all hoped to revive the assertive, internationalist traditions under which the Roosevelt and Truman administrations had fought World War II and the cold war.

One of the most prominent of the neoconservatives was Jeane Kirkpatrick. By 1979 Kirkpatrick, a Georgetown University political scientist and longtime Democrat, who had been a longtime Humphrey supporter, was, like many other neoconservatives, thoroughly disenchanted with the Carter administration. Carter had given most of the key jobs in his administration to liberals, had continued to pursue détente with the Soviet Union and had, in the neoconservatives' view, remained largely passive as the Soviet Union made strategic gains around the world.

A few months after the Iranian Revolution, Kirkpatrick published an article in *Commentary* magazine that looked back on U.S. foreign policy and on the attitudes of American liberals toward the shah and other authoritarian rulers in the third world. The article was titled "Dictatorships and Double Standards."

In essence, the article argued that the Carter administration had been wrong in trying to push too many democratic reforms too quickly on autocratic leaders who had been strong supporters of the United States, such as the shah or Anastasio Somoza of Nicaragua. The United States had imposed expectations upon these dictators that it did not apply to leaders of Communist regimes in the third world, Kirkpatrick wrote. By pressing leaders like the shah for greater political liberalization, she contended, the Carter administration had perversely accomplished the reverse result. American policy weakened the dictators but paved the way

for their overthrow by new leaders, such as Khomeini's Islamic fundamentalists or Nicaragua's Sandinistas, who were far less committed to
democratic reforms or individual freedoms than the dictators they replaced. The governments in which the Carter administration pressed for
changes "turn out to be mainly those in which non-Communist autocracies are under pressure from revolutionary guerrillas," Kirkpatrick wrote.
". . . We seem to accept the status quo in Communist nations (in the
name of 'diversity' and national autonomy) but not in nations ruled by
'right-wing' dictators or white oligarchies."[23]

In theory, at least, Kirkpatrick might have argued that the antidote to
this "double standard" was for the Carter administration to be just as fervent in pressing for democracy in Communist nations or other hostile
regimes as it had been with friendly dictators like the shah. In practice,
Kirkpatrick's article suggested precisely the opposite solution: that the
United States should end this double standard by becoming more toler-
ant of the status quo in dictatorships that support American policy.

Some of Kirkpatrick's language was hostile to the entire concept of
promoting democracy in third world countries. "Although most governments in the world are, as they always have been, autocracies of one kind
or another, no idea holds greater sway in the mind of educated Americans
than the belief that it is possible to democratize governments, anytime,
anywhere, under any circumstances," she asserted. Americans sought
democratic changes at much too speedy a pace. ". . . Decades, if not centuries, are normally required for people to acquire the necessary disci-
plines and habits [of democracy]."[24]

Kirkpatrick never said specifically that she was opposed to the cause of
democracy in the third world. The essence of her argument was America
should apply its belief in democracy to all countries equally and that the
United States should make sure that in seeking political liberalization, it
didn't unintentionally bring about the opposite result, such as a Khomeini-
led Iran. Nevertheless, her argument could easily be oversimplified as a
plea for American support of dictatorships, and in fact, it was widely
misinterpreted in this fashion. (A few years later Kirkpatrick, on a trip to
Manila, was embarrassed when Philippine President Ferdinand Marcos
offered a dinner toast to her in which he glowingly quoted some of her
words in "Dictatorships and Double Standards," clearly believing that
the article conveyed support for his authoritarian regime. Kirkpatrick

felt compelled to respond by preaching the virtues of republican government.[25])

The ideas expressed in "Dictatorships and Double Standards" became part of the litany of neoconservative complaints about the Carter administration. Few noticed at the time, but Kirkpatrick's article also created an underlying tension that neoconservatives would have to confront in the future. They all were anti-Communists—that was the cause that brought the movement together—but was their goal a *geopolitical* struggle against the Soviet Union, or was their aim the spread of democratic government? If the neoconservative movement was motivated mostly by the desire for an anti-Soviet foreign policy, then friendly right-wing dictators might be viewed as helpful to the cause, but if the goals were political liberalization and individual freedom, then the judgment about dictators would be different. In "Dictatorships and Double Standards," Kirkpatrick had denigrated the wisdom and the benefits of trying to promote democracy. Yet quite a few neoconservatives, like Wolfowitz, believed strongly in democratic ideals; they had taken from the philosopher Leo Strauss the notion that there is a moral duty to oppose a leader who is a "tyrant."

Over the following decades the neoconservatives struggled to come to grips with the antidemocratic implications of Kirkpatrick's article, sometimes defending it, sometimes ignoring it. By the beginning of the twenty-first century, the neoconservative movement had come to espouse ideas directly contrary to those in "Dictatorships and Double Standards." Whereas Kirkpatrick had ridiculed the notion that it is possible to establish democracy "anytime, anywhere, under any circumstances," during the George W. Bush administration neoconservatives argued that the United States should seek democratic reforms wherever possible, from Saudi Arabia and Egypt to Pakistan and Uzbekistan.[26] Kirkpatrick had suggested that democratizing third world countries might take decades or centuries, but by 2002 neoconservatives were seeking democratic change among the Palestinians and in Iraq within no more than a couple of years.

Kirkpatrick's "Dictatorships and Double Standards" was published in November 1979. Among its readers was Ronald Reagan, the former governor of California, who was in the process of running for the 1980 Republican presidential nomination. Not long afterward, he sent a note to

Kirkpatrick telling her how much he had enjoyed her article. Reagan, himself a former Democrat, followed up by asking his foreign policy adviser Richard Allen to set up a meeting with Kirkpatrick.[27] For American politics and foreign policy, it was the beginning of an epochal shift. The neoconservatives were about to abandon the Democratic party and to throw their support to the Republicans.

CHAPTER SIX

Transitions

AT THE BEGINNING of 1977, Dave Gribben helped his friend Dick Cheney pack a rented Ryder truck. The Cheneys were moving from Bethesda, Maryland, back to Casper, Wyoming. After serving as the youngest White House chief of staff in history, Cheney was leaving in humble fashion, a *Mr. Smith Goes to Washington* in reverse. As it turned out, he was not gone for long. Two years later, in January 1979, he returned, and Gribben, in his own old Volkswagen, drove him up Pennsylvania Avenue to the Capitol, where Cheney moved into his new offices as a freshman congressman.

Gribben and his wife, Laurie, had grown up in Wyoming with Dick and Lynne Cheney; the four had attended Casper's Natrona City High School together. They had lost touch with one another for a time, until one day, in the early 1970s, Gribben's wife went canvassing door to door for baby-sitters in Bethesda. She ran into Lynne, living only a block away. From then on, while Cheney was working six and a half days per week in the Ford White House, the two families shared an occasional Sunday barbecue, which sometimes came to an abrupt end when Cheney was called back to work.

Back in Wyoming, Cheney had rejoined Bradley, Woods & Company, the same private investment firm at which he had worked in the early 1970s after his patron Donald Rumsfeld had left the Nixon White House to become ambassador to NATO. But Cheney could manage to keep himself away from public life for only less than nine months. In September 1977 Wyoming's sole representative, the Democrat Teno Roncalio, decided to retire. A few weeks later Cheney announced he was running for the seat.

On June 18, 1978, in the midst of his first campaign for Congress, Cheney suffered his first heart attack. He was forced to stay at home for six weeks, and it appeared as though concerns about his health might jeopardize his candidacy. Cheney rushed to respond. Before the primaries he sent every Republican in Wyoming a two-page letter, saying that he had given up smoking. He also made light of his condition, joking that he had formed a fictitious group called Cardiacs for Cheney. Democrats accused Cheney of being an outsider, someone who came home to Wyoming only when he got into trouble (at Yale) or when he was out of a job (after Ford's defeat in 1976).[1] This carpetbagger strategy didn't work. Cheney was still only thirty-seven years old, and there were too many people in Wyoming who remembered him as a local high school football star. That November the Republicans picked up twelve seats in the House of Representatives, and one of the seats they gained was in Wyoming.

Cheney came back to Washington in a considerably less exalted status than in his previous job. As White House chief of staff he had commanded limousines and advance men, decided which cabinet members would meet the president and supervised State of the Union speeches. In his new life Cheney was a freshman congressman in the minority party. The Republicans had not controlled the House for twenty-four years and had little hope of doing so anytime soon. Among the thirty-six new Republican members of Congress in Cheney's class of 1978 was a college teacher from Georgia named Newt Gingrich, who became Cheney's good friend.

Cheney asked Gribben to serve as his administrative assistant. When the two of them attempted for the first time to enter Cheney's new congressional office, they had to wait outside in the vacant, cavernous hallway because they couldn't find a key. Once inside, they found piles of constituent mail from Wyoming and a chaotic tableau of unplugged typewriters, chairless desks and faded couches.[2] These obstacles, however, were quickly overcome. Cheney stood out from other freshmen because of his familiarity with Washington, with the federal government and with national Republican leaders. He rose through the ranks quickly and became chairman of the Republican Policy Committee after only two years.

From the very start, Cheney displayed the characteristics that made his congressional career different from most others. In a legislative institution whose members thrive on headlines, Cheney preferred to operate largely in the shadows. His stock-in-trade was not persuasion but discretion. He didn't bother to hire a speechwriter, and he probably gave fewer floor speeches than any other prominent member of Congress. His choice of committee assignments showed a similar disdain for the limelight. Predictably, Cheney at first grabbed a seat on the Interior Committee, a spot that representatives from western states often seek in order to influence federal decisions on the land, water and mining issues important to their states. He subsequently elected to join the House Ethics Committee and the House Intelligence Committee, both of which conduct many of their proceedings in secret. Whenever there was a closed-door meeting on Capitol Hill where congressional Republicans were working out their policies or strategy, Cheney was probably inside.

He was determinedly conservative and proud of it. Cheney was occasionally mischaracterized as a centrist Republican, perhaps because he had worked for Ford against Ronald Reagan in 1976 and perhaps because of his subdued, nonconfrontational style, a marked contrast with the fervor of Gingrich and some other Republicans. Nevertheless, Cheney's voting record and his views on issues of both domestic and foreign policy put him solidly on the political right. In his first year Cheney voted against implementation of the Panama Canal treaties negotiated by the Carter administration, thus effectively aligning himself with the antitreaty position Reagan had embraced against Ford in the 1976 Republican primaries. Over the years, he regularly supported hefty increases in defense spending and the development of new weapons systems, such as the MX missile.[3]

Indeed, Cheney became annoyed when his political views were misinterpreted. Once, when an article in the *Washington Post* referred to him as a "moderate" (a designation many politicians of both left and right avidly seek), Cheney summoned his aide Gribben to push for a correction. "Will you please call the *Post* and tell them I'm a conservative?" Cheney grumbled. "Don't they ever check my voting record? I've got a voting record, and they ought to look at it."[4] That was vintage Cheney, choosing substance over style, policy over flash, and always proving more conservative than he appeared.

In late 1979, about a year before the next presidential election, Fred Iklé telephoned Paul Wolfowitz at the Pentagon with a warning. Iklé had been Wolfowitz's boss during the Nixon administration. Now Iklé was preparing to help out in Ronald Reagan's campaign. Wolfowitz was still working under Harold Brown, Jimmy Carter's secretary of defense.

"Paul," said Iklé, "you've got to get out of there. We want you in the new administration."[5] Iklé's meaning was clear: It was time for Wolfowitz to choose which team he was on. If Reagan were to win the election, there would be a housecleaning. Anyone associated with the Carter administration was unlikely to get a job with the Reagan team, no matter what his own views might be.

Wolfowitz was not making this choice in a vacuum. Many of his neoconservative soul mates, the Democratic opponents of détente who during the 1970s had aligned themselves with Senator Henry Jackson or Hubert Humphrey, had by this juncture given up on Carter and, indeed, had all but abandoned the Democratic party. Some of them were already gravitating toward the Reagan campaign.

In the early stages of the 1980 campaign Reagan's advisers John Sears and Richard Allen were especially skillful in detecting and exploiting the possibilities for a new political coalition that would combine these neoconservative Democrats with more traditional conservative Republicans. Reagan himself joined that effort when he sent his note to Jeane Kirkpatrick, praising her article "Dictatorships and Double Standards."

"I didn't know that Ronald Reagan, first, would ever read *Commentary,* and second would ever read 'Dictatorships and Double Standards,' and third would even be interested at all if he did," admitted Kirkpatrick. "But he did, and he then pursued me, and he called me; he did that a couple of times. It was sort of like being courted. . . . "[6] In the spring of 1980, after a meeting with Reagan, Kirkpatrick, who, over the years, had attended one Democratic National Convention after another, took the first step toward the Republicans. She agreed to have her name included on a list of people advising Reagan on foreign policy.

Kirkpatrick's odyssey was merely one symbol of a far-reaching political realignment. The conservative wing of the Democratic party was in the process of disintegrating. The Carter administration had already proved too liberal for many of the older Democrats, who had come of age in the Roosevelt and Truman administrations. Moreover, Carter's main rival for the Democratic presidential nomination in 1980, Senator Edward Kennedy, was challenging Carter from even further on the left. Hubert Humphrey had died in 1978. Henry Jackson, who had made an unsuccessful run for the presidency himself in 1976, was becoming increasingly detached. Jackson made some perfunctory campaign appearances at Carter's side in 1980, but he eventually told some of his neoconservative staff members and associates that he would not object or stand in their way if they wanted to work for Reagan.[7]

At the Pentagon, Wolfowitz heeded Iklé's admonition. He was getting discouraged by the lack of response to his warnings about possible Soviet or Iraqi attacks on the oil fields of the Persian Gulf. Undersecretary of Defense Robert Komer told him to hang on, that there would be a bigger job for him in the Pentagon after Carter won reelection.[8] But at the beginning of 1980 Wolfowitz quietly resigned from the Carter administration to become a visiting associate professor at the Johns Hopkins University School of Advanced International Studies. He got out just in time; Wolfowitz had worked for a Democratic president for so long that he later was viewed by some Republicans with a certain amount of wariness.

No one was urging Colin Powell to get out of the Pentagon. His problem was the reverse. By the late 1970s everyone wanted him to stay there. Even though Powell was a Regular Army officer, expected to move regularly from post to post around the nation and the world, both military officers and civilians, each for their own reasons, repeatedly pressed him to take assignments in Washington.

Powell's transformation had begun modestly enough. One Saturday morning in 1969, during his second Vietnam tour of duty, he went to a Quonset hut in Da Nang and took the Graduate Record Examination (GRE), the standard test for admission to graduate school. He did well and won acceptance to the business school at George Washington University in Washington. At the time he hoped to learn computer skills and management, not only to help his Army career but also to help land a job afterward.[9]

After receiving his MBA, Powell reported to the Pentagon, aiming to become a specialist in installing computer systems. From there events took over. First Powell was recruited by the Army's vice chief of staff. Then, one day in 1972, an Army official told him to apply for a White House fellowship, an elite, highly selective program for young Americans thought to have leadership potential. At the time Powell didn't even know what the program was, but on the application form, he came up with answers that were, as usual, both straightforward and perfectly attuned to the times. Asked why he hoped to take part in the program, Powell said that amid the nation's divisions over Vietnam, he wanted to show civilians that military officers did not have horns.[10]

Out of fifteen hundred applicants, Powell was one of seventeen who won a fellowship. Drawing on his business training, he elected to serve his fellowship year in the Office of Management and Budget. At the time that agency was headed by Caspar Weinberger and his deputy Frank Carlucci, who had first joined the Nixon administration to help run the nation's antipoverty programs under Donald Rumsfeld. Carlucci thought Powell was a comer, a rising star; he was a quick study, worked hard and was forceful when he needed to be.[11]

In 1973, Powell went back to Asia to command an infantry battalion in South Korea. After studying for a year at the National War College, he moved up to a brigade command at the 101st Airborne Division at Fort Campbell. He seemed to be rising up the ladder of a traditional Army career. Then, as the Carter administration took office, Washington took hold of Powell and refused to let go.

By this time Powell had an extremely attractive résumé. He was young, had held military commands, had fought in Vietnam, had been a White House fellow and had studied at the War College. At the beginning of 1977 Zbigniew Brzezinski, Carter's national security adviser, brought Powell to Washington and tried to recruit him for a job as a military aide on the National Security Council staff, but Powell turned him down. General William Odom, who was working under Brzezinski, later remembered Powell's voicing skepticism about his own abilities. "He said, 'I know I can't do that kind of analytic work,'" Odom said.[12] Powell may well have been downgrading his own abilities in order to get out of a job he didn't want; at the time he was hoping for a promotion within the 101st Airborne.

A few months later Brzezinski tried again. This time Powell also had a second offer, an invitation to work in the Pentagon for one of the top aides to Defense Secretary Harold Brown. At Fort Campbell, Powell's commanding officer, General John Wickham, told him to take either of these jobs. The Army thought it was a great opportunity to have one of its own people working for a well-placed civilian in Washington.[13]

These were the dynamics that propelled Powell's career. He was the perfect intermediary between the Army and its civilian overseers. Army leaders were pushing Powell to Washington because they saw him as a superb representative of their institutional interests, a smart, affable, articulate African-American, barely forty years old, who would give civilian leaders the sense that the Army was changing and was no longer stuck in the Vietnam-era rigidities embodied by General William Westmoreland. Meanwhile civilian leaders saw in Powell an easygoing, sophisticated officer who could talk their language, wasn't threatening or adversarial and could accurately convey their concerns and interests back to the military.

Powell turned down Brzezinski and chose the Pentagon job, working first as an aide to John Kester, a special assistant to the secretary of defense. Following a promotion from colonel to brigadier general, Powell served as the military aide to Deputy Secretary of Defense Charles Duncan and then, after moving for a few months with Duncan to the new Energy Department, became the military assistant to Duncan's successor, Graham Claytor.

Four straight assignments, three bosses, four years stretching out over an entire administration: Powell became a Washington professional. He knew how the paper moved and why it didn't, how deals were cut within the Pentagon and with Capitol Hill, how promotions were made. He learned how the bureaucracy operated, not merely at the top but at the working levels too. His skills in negotiating between Washington's military and civilian leaders were so obvious that no one wanted to let him go back out into the field. Powell at first thought of this period as a diversion from his career in the Army, but in fact, he was blazing a new career path.

Donald Rumsfeld stood in a different position from either Wolfowitz or Powell. No one needed to warn him to get out of the Pentagon, and no one was begging him to stay either. As defense secretary in the Ford administration he had simply run out of time on January 20, 1977.

Rumsfeld soon embarked upon a new career in business. After a few months of study and reflection at Princeton University, he accepted an offer to become president and chief executive officer of G. D. Searle & Company, one of the nation's most prominent pharmaceutical companies, whose products included Dramamine for motion sickness, the antidiarrheal drug Lomotil and Enovid, an early birth control pill. The company, run for nearly a century by members of the Searle family, was based in Rumsfeld's old congressional district in Chicago; indeed, the Searle family had helped provide the money for Rumsfeld's first congressional campaign.

In 1977 Searle and the Searle family were in trouble. The stock price had fallen from $110 a share to $12, earnings had dropped 23 percent the previous year and the Food and Drug Administration was investigating if the company had misreported the results of testing for new drugs. It was having difficulty obtaining FDA approval to market a new artificial sweetener called aspartame.[14]

Rumsfeld quickly showed he could transfer his uncompromising management style from the federal government to business. Within nine months he divested Searle of twenty unprofitable businesses. It took only slightly longer for him to cut Searle's corporate staff from 800 employees to 350. Stories made the rounds of employees who were paged at airports, asked to come home and then fired. An executive who hurriedly returned from vacation to make a presentation to Rumsfeld was astonished to be cut off after a few minutes and barraged with questions. Describing the atmosphere at the company, a former Searle executive said, "You could almost hear people's knees knocking when he walked down the hall." In 1980 *Fortune* magazine published a story on the "ten toughest bosses" in American business. Rumsfeld made the list.[15]

Amid these upheavals, Searle's fortunes improved. The FDA ended its investigation of the firm's testing procedures and, after many delays, opened the way for the company to sell aspartame. Searle's earnings on operations averaged 17 percent per year in the five years after Rumsfeld was brought in, and the stock price rose to about thirty dollars a share. The turnaround was good not only for the Searle family but for Rumsfeld himself. His salary had started at two hundred thousand dollars a year in 1977 and had climbed to five hundred thousand by 1982. He was also given stock options that at 1982 prices were worth at least four million dollars. Reflecting on the changes in his life in moving from government to business, Rumsfeld told a *Fortune* magazine interviewer, "At forty-seven, I would rather have the movers move me than do the U-Haul bit. I did the U-Haul bit every time before I came to Searle."[16]

Still, it was clear Rumsfeld was never entirely content as a business executive. At the White House and the Pentagon, he had been involved in the cold war and the future of the nation. At Searle the issues included whether to market Metamucil, the company's popular fiber laxative, in the same old way or in a new version, with NutraSweet, in flavors of lemon and orange.

From a distance, Rumsfeld occasionally kept his hand in defense issues. When the Carter administration sent a new Strategic Arms Limitation Talks (SALT) Treaty to the Senate in 1979, Rumsfeld testified against it and called for a forty-billion-dollar increase in defense spending. "Our nation's situation is much more dangerous today than it has been at any time since Neville Chamberlain left Munich, setting the stage for World War II," he said.[17]

He made it clear to everyone he expected to come back to Washington. From the outset of his time at Searle there were rumors his mandate was to accomplish a quick turnaround so that the company could be sold. "I expect that at some point, the odds favor my being involved in government again," Rumsfeld told the visitor from *Fortune*. "One, I enjoyed it. Two, I think I did a good job. Three, I'm interested in our country and the world."[18]

He was right. He would return, although at first only for short-term assignments. Rumsfeld had no idea he was starting what became nearly a quarter century of life as a private citizen, away from the daily flow of the White House, the National Security Council, the cabinet and the other institutions of power that he had known so intimately as a young man.

The presidency of Ronald Reagan is now remembered as a time of heady confidence and, indeed, triumphalism. As a result, it is difficult to convey just how insecure Reagan and his conservative forces were as they prepared to run against Jimmy Carter in the 1980 campaign.

Reagan was the most conservative candidate the Republicans had nominated since Barry Goldwater, and Goldwater had lost the 1964 election in a landslide. For many years the conservatives had taken it for granted that their own views were hopelessly out of touch with those of a majority of American voters. In 1977 the longtime conservative Richard Allen had confided to one scholar that he personally favored Reagan for the presidency and thought Reagan deserved to be president, but that the possibility of the conservatives' gaining control of the White House was so remote he didn't even think about it.[19]

Even after Reagan had easily defeated George H. W. Bush and several other challengers for the 1980 Republican nomination, the Reagan forces were still uncertain how they would fare in a general election. Thus, at the 1980 Republican National Convention in Detroit, Reagan and his advisers were eager for a vice presidential candidate who might broaden Reagan's appeal to middle-of-the-road voters and the business community. That July it appeared they had found the candidate for a "dream ticket,"

Gerald Ford. No former president had ever subsequently run for vice president, but Reagan decided to try to recruit Ford as his running mate.

On the night the Republican convention approved Reagan's nomination for president, Reagan's advisers held a series of intense negotiations with some of the leading officials of the Ford administration, led by Henry Kissinger and Alan Greenspan. The Ford team was seeking an agreement under which Ford would become in effect a copresident with responsibility for certain issues, including foreign policy. In the early negotiations the deal was specifically to include the appointment of Kissinger as secretary of state. That specific provision was subsequently dropped, but in later talks Ford, as vice president, was to be chairman of the National Security Council and to have veto power over the president's choice for secretary of state; the vice president would also have the power to choose the national security adviser, subject to Reagan's veto. Kissinger would have directed American diplomacy and national security from a position in the vice president's office.[20]

It was a fateful moment for U.S. foreign policy. The underlying question was whether Reagan and his supporters were willing to abandon their challenge to Henry Kissinger and his policies in hopes of attracting moderate Republicans and improving their overall chances in the fall election. The Reaganites had chosen to make détente one of the main issues during Reagan's 1976 primary challenge to Ford. In the 1980 campaign they had repeatedly argued that the Carter administration was weak in foreign policy, principally because they claimed he too had supported détente for too long. Yet now, at the conservatives' moment of victory within the Republican party, the Reagan forces were still so unsure of their chances of defeating Carter that they were on the verge of handing the control of foreign policy back to Kissinger, their bête noire, the architect of détente. Some of Reagan's foreign policy advisers were horrified. One, Richard Allen, lobbied against the Ford deal.

Finally, late at night, the negotiations broke down. The Reagan advisers began to balk at the requests of the Ford team for power sharing, which would have amounted to an unprecedented—and, some said, unconstitutional—delegation of presidential authority. Meanwhile Ford, never so enthusiastic about running for vice president as his own advisers or the Reagan entourage, concluded that the arrangement under consideration was a bad idea. Finally he paid a visit to Reagan's hotel suite and told the Republican nominee, "Look, this isn't going to work."[21]

The sudden collapse of these negotiations left the Reagan team in crisis. It was nearly eleven o'clock Wednesday evening, and by that time the Republican convention and the nation were waiting for Reagan to announce his vice presidential choice. "For several days, I had expected Ford to be on the ticket, and I hadn't given much thought to other candidates," Reagan later admitted. He needed to find someone else quickly. At that moment of uncertainty, Allen, who for several hours had been suggesting Bush as a possible alternative to Ford, again suggested Bush and found his phone number; Bush and his wife, Barbara, were at a nearby hotel, where they had been glumly watching television reports of the Reagan-Ford discussions. Reagan made the call, and a surprised Bush happily accepted the invitation to run for vice president.[22] In those few moments, almost by happenstance, the Bush family dynasty was given its start.

Reagan's belated offer to Bush was especially disappointing to one other Republican aspirant who thought he should have been chosen instead. Donald Rumsfeld was, as usual, attending the Republican convention. He had been among the handful of names mentioned as a vice presidential candidate, and he had given a speech to the convention supporting Reagan.

Afterward, Rumsfeld asked Allen, his friend of many years, why the Reagan team had decided to turn to Bush instead of him. "Because I didn't happen to have your phone number handy, and I did have Bush's," Allen answered.[23] That wasn't the full story; Allen had been pushing for Bush because he seemed like the Republican with the best chance of derailing the Ford-Kissinger deal.

Many years later Allen privately mused to friends that he had probably made a mistake, that instead of having had Reagan telephone Bush, he should have lobbied for Rumsfeld, who he thought would have become vice president and then made a great president.

As Reagan crisscrossed the country in the fall of 1980, his campaign headquarters attracted a new recruit, a hulking, gravelly voiced young man who was making political connections and trying to learn Washington as well as he had known Vietnam, Richard Armitage.

In the five years since his departure from Vietnam, Armitage had been trying to build a new life. He had worked briefly with Vietnamese refugees in the United States. He had gone to Iran hoping that his boss,

Erich von Marbod, might eventually help him move from temporary duty in Tehran to some sort of permanent government job in Washington, but in 1977 the incoming Carter administration imposed a hiring freeze.[24] At home, he and his wife, Laura, were not only raising their own children but also beginning to take in Vietnamese families and foster children.

For nearly a year Armitage moved back to Southeast Asia, believing his old military and intelligence connections might lead to commercial opportunities. Settling in Bangkok, Armitage went into business with Brigadier General Harry C. (Heinie) Aderholt, the legendary air commando. Aderholt had been a military officer with longstanding ties to the CIA and covert operations, somewhat like Armitage himself, except that Aderholt was considerably older and more experienced. He was also, like Armitage, a fun-loving, hard-drinking connoisseur of Southeast Asian nightlife.

Aderholt had for decades been a central player in many of the secret operations conducted by the U.S. Air Force. He had dropped agents behind enemy lines during the Korean War and had commanded the airlift operations in the CIA's campaign to support the Tibetans' revolt against Chinese rule in the late 1950s.[25] During the Vietnam War, Aderholt had conducted clandestine air combat operations as part of the CIA's secret war in Laos, using World War II warplanes from bases in Thailand to hit North Vietnamese tanks and trucks moving down the Ho Chi Minh Trail.[26] Aderholt was yet another friend and admirer of Armitage's patron von Marbod. During the final days of the Vietnam War, while Armitage was helping von Marbod to get ships and other naval assets out of South Vietnam, Aderholt was working similarly to evacuate American warplanes to Thailand. It was Aderholt who had dispatched a plane to save Armitage when he was trapped at the Bien Hoa Air Base.[27]

After retiring in 1976, Aderholt had stayed on in Bangkok to set up a business called the Southeast Asia Travel Agency. Two of his Air Force buddies, Richard Secord and Larry Ropka, both of whom had worked in Tehran alongside Armitage, recommended that Aderholt give Armitage a job. "Secord called up and said, 'Help the guy out,'" recalled Aderholt many years later. Through his connections in the Thai military, Aderholt obtained a fifteen-hundred-dollar-a-month retainer to try to help win contracts that would help Thai military leaders. Armitage drew on this retainer for his living expenses, while Aderholt lived off his own military pension.[28] The main client was Air Siam, a tiny airline with a single Boeing 747 that flew from Bangkok to Los Angeles. Aderholt and Armitage were trying to help the airline win permission to expand, but the competition from Thai International proved too difficult; Armitage later said he learned the lesson never to challenge a government-owned airline.[29] In 1977 Air Siam went out of business, and so did the Aderholt-Armitage partnership. "It was a small company, and we went broke," Aderholt explained. "I was the only one with any money coming in. Armitage was a good guy, and I liked to drink and do things with him."[30]

Once again unemployed, Armitage returned to the United States and moved his family to Washington, determined to find work there. He was eager to learn who made the kinds of foreign policy decisions he had spent many years executing in Vietnam and Iran. "I was tired of being on the pointy edge of the spear, and I wanted to see who was chucking the spear," reflected Armitage in an interview many years later.[31] Soon, through Republican friends, he was introduced to Senator Bob Dole, who agreed to hire him as an administrative assistant. "Dole had a particular appreciation for people with combat experience," recalled Armitage's friend James Kelly. "He had gone through various assistants with Washington experience who didn't work out, and so he figured, let's try a person who doesn't have Washington experience but does have combat experience."[32] In 1979, Armitage left Dole's office to work for the presidential campaign of George H. W. Bush, who, as a former director of central intelligence was an especially popular candidate within the U.S. intelligence community.

After Bush's campaign failed, Armitage went to Allen, seeking to sign on with the Reagan team. Initially cautious, Allen asked Armitage if he possessed any academic credentials. Had he written anything for publication? Undeterred, Armitage went home, wrote an op-ed piece and within days got it published in the *Christian Science Monitor.* In the article, titled "Hanoi's Crumbling Policy," Armitage concluded that "there is a new Asia, and it is anxious for our help."[33] As soon as it appeared, Armitage returned to Allen to show him that he had now been published. He was hired and put to work organizing papers, press contacts and other campaign tasks. Allen and Iklé both were impressed with his organizational skills.

That November the Reagan forces won an easy victory over Carter. The country was eager for a change, tired of high inflation and frustrated with Carter's inability to win freedom for American hostages in Tehran. A surprising number of traditional Democratic voters switched over to Reagan, following the earlier exodus of Kirkpatrick and other neoconservatives. The Republicans took control of the Senate along with the White House.

Within weeks Armitage began pressing for a job as an Asia specialist with the new administration. He still looked and sounded rough, as though he had just been brought into Washington from the battlefield, and some of the older Washington hands were at first taken aback by his manner and his bluntness. "I thought he was some kind of bouncer or that he ought to be in a gymnasium handing out towels," recalled James Lilley, the former intelligence official who had worked under George Bush as the CIA station chief in Beijing. Lilley was a representative of the Ivy League elite that had dominated the U.S. intelligence community in its early years; Armitage was something different. "He [Armitage] had this gruff voice. He'd come up to you and say, 'Argh, you're going to be on the NSC [National Security Council] Asia staff. I wouldn't mind being there too. Maybe we can work it out. You're older than I am, you can have the senior position, I don't give a shit.'"[34]

The top jobs for Asia at Reagan's National Security Council went to Lilley and another CIA veteran, Donald Gregg. Armitage was undaunted. He had been working with Iklé on the Reagan transition and obtained a temporary assignment to help the incoming defense secretary, Caspar Weinberger, in selecting a new Republican team at the Pentagon.

Weinberger was precisely the sort of person whom Armitage knew how to charm. In style, Armitage was everything Weinberger was not. The defense secretary was slight in build, formal in manner, cultivated and enamored of pomp and ceremony; Armitage was physically imposing, loose, brash, outgoing and informal. In military terms, the defense secretary could legitimately look upon Armitage as representing a successor generation; during World War II Weinberger had been an infantryman and an intelligence officer under General Douglas MacArthur in the Pacific theater.

As Weinberger toured the Pentagon before Reagan's inauguration, Armitage was there with him, helping him select new people for the Pentagon, including himself. "I don't want a big job that requires Senate confirmation, just an ordinary job," he told others at the time.[35] When Armitage submitted a list of prospective candidates for Pentagon jobs to Weinberger, he put down his own name as deputy assistant secretary of defense for Asia. Weinberger gave him the job.

Allen, who was Reagan's choice to be national security adviser, also headed the group in charge of deciding who should get jobs on Reagan's foreign policy team. When he first saw Paul Wolfowitz's name and credentials on a rundown of possible appointees, Allen quickly crossed him off the list. "He was a goner, as far as I was concerned," Allen later recalled. "He'd just been at the Pentagon. He had worked for Carter. I thought he was a Carter guy." Soon Allen's friend John Lehman, a fellow conservative who had worked with Wolfowitz in the Nixon administration, begged Allen to reconsider. Why not talk with Wolfowitz first? Allen agreed and, after a meeting, realized quickly that Wolfowitz was hardly a Jimmy Carter liberal. Wolfowitz was slotted for the position of director of policy planning at the State Department.

Yet Wolfowitz's political problems weren't quite over. Although his new job didn't require Senate confirmation, the whole lineup of new State Department appointees had to be cleared with Republicans on the Senate Foreign Relations Committee. The most conservative among them, Senator Jesse Helms, balked when he saw Wolfowitz's name. "He thought Wolfowitz might be a Democrat or a liberal, because he had worked in the Carter administration," recalled John Carbaugh, who was Helms's staff aide at the time.

Wolfowitz invited Carbaugh out to his home on a Sunday night and, with his family alongside, proceeded to establish his conservative beliefs and credentials. Carbaugh recalls that he was finally convinced Wolfowitz must be okay when Wolfowitz at one point promised to appoint Alan Keyes, whom Carbaugh was promoting as one of the nation's few black conservatives, to be part of the Wolfowitz team at the State Department.[36]

In retrospect, of course, this entire process was preposterous. At the time Wolfowitz was already a well-established hawk, and he subsequently developed into the leading conservative foreign policy thinker of his generation. Yet he nearly lost out on a job in the Reagan administration on the mistaken notion that he was a liberal Democrat. This was, however, how politics usually worked in Washington: When the White House changed hands, everyone who had worked for the previous administration was cast under suspicion.

Colin Powell was not registered for either political party. In 1976 he had voted for Jimmy Carter. But after serving for four years in the Carter Pentagon, he cast his New York absentee ballot for Ronald Reagan. Powell thought the Carter administration had been insensitive to the military, too heavy-handed in cutting the defense budget and at times naïve in dealing with the Soviet Union.[37]

Within weeks Reagan named Weinberger, who had been Powell's boss when he was a White House fellow, his defense secretary. Just as in the Nixon administration, Carlucci became Weinberger's deputy. Powell, it turned out, had as close connections to the top levels of the incoming administration as to the outgoing one.

For American foreign policy, the impact of the 1980 election was breathtaking. The Democratic party had fractured. Its hawkish activists had deserted the party for Reagan, followed by millions of ordinary moderate to conservative Democrats. The result was to eviscerate the political power of the liberals, who since the Vietnam War had been pressing for restrictions upon American power and a reduction in U.S. military commitments overseas.

Meanwhile, within the Republican party, Henry Kissinger and his allies had attempted a comeback at the Republican National Convention and had failed. Kissinger's foreign policy of realism and his belief in balance of power diplomacy had never been popular with the Republican rank and file, but they had held sway within the party's establishment. During the 1970s there had been enough opposition among Republicans, both in Congress and among executive branch officials like Rumsfeld and Cheney, to block Kissinger from having his way, especially on détente. Still, during the past two Republican administrations, foreign policy had been largely in the hands of Kissinger and his allies. With Reagan's election, the conservative Republicans now had the power not just to block policy but to initiate it. They controlled the executive branch of government.

Since the 1960s most of the domestic political struggles over American foreign policy had been waged between liberal Democrats and Republican pragmatists. Now both these forces were in decline. A new movement was in the ascendancy, one that accepted neither the liberal premise that America should scale back on its overseas role nor the Kissingerian notion that the United States needed to seek accommodations with other major powers. The conservatives were about to get their first opportunity to try out a different vision of America's role in the world.

CHAPTER SEVEN

Camelot
of the Conservatives

SCOOTER LIBBY was practicing law in Philadelphia when, one day in early 1981, he received a notice from the alumni records office of Yale University. Someone named Paul Wolfowitz was trying to reach him. Was Libby willing to allow Yale to give out his phone number? He was. Libby had graduated from Yale nine years earlier, and Wolfowitz had been one of his favorite professors. Within hours Wolfowitz called up and asked Libby to come work for him at the State Department. At the time Libby was reading William Stevenson's *A Man Called Intrepid*, an account of British and American intelligence operations before and during World War II. The book described people working secretly for a noble cause, trying to overcome American complacency and seeking to combat an evil dictator; the characters' lives seemed considerably more exciting and meaningful than Libby's work in Philadelphia. He signed on as one of Wolfowitz's new recruits.[1]

Wolfowitz's job was not really comparable to *Intrepid*; he was running memos, not spies. He had been put in charge of the State Department's policy planning staff. Although the title sounds vague and bureaucratic, this post is often at the center of an administration's attempt to define its relations with the rest of the world. While State Department specialists on countries like Russia or China address specific problems within their regions and deal with day-to-day events, the policy planning staff tries to work out the more generalized, longer-term goals; it was as head of policy planning that George Kennan had propounded his doctrine of containment of the Soviet Union in the late 1940s. With his academic interests in theory, ideas and political ideologies, Wolfowitz was well cast for the job.

During the early months of the Reagan administration Wolfowitz replaced virtually all of the twenty-five members of the policy planning staff. In their places, Wolfowitz installed a new team of people, some of whom became, over the following two decades, the heart of a new neoconservative network within the foreign policy bureaucracy.

Many of these recruits had come from the same schools as Wolfowitz himself. From Cornell, Wolfowitz brought in Francis Fukuyama, the political theorist and later the author of the famous essay *The End of History*, and Alan Keyes, the African-American conservative. From the University of Chicago, he brought in Zalmay Khalilzad, who had been (like Wolfowitz) a student of the nuclear theorist Albert Wohlstetter. From the Defense Department, he imported James Roche, who went on to serve as secretary of the Air Force and then secretary of the Army in the second Bush administration.

Not everyone on the staff was a neoconservative. Wolfowitz's aides included Dennis Ross, the Soviet and Middle East specialist who had worked with him at the Pentagon in the Carter years, and Stephen Sestanovich, a Russia scholar who had been at Cornell with Wolfowitz. The fact remained, however, that Wolfowitz's policy planning staff turned out to be the training ground for a new generation of national security specialists, many of whom shared Wolfowitz's ideas, assumptions and interests.

Within a relatively short time, Wolfowitz began to challenge some of the linchpins of American foreign policy. In the Middle East he raised questions about the wisdom of selling American-made airborne warning and control system (AWACS) aircraft to Saudi Arabia. He also sought to slow down the growing momentum within the U.S. government to try to talk and do business with the Palestine Liberation Organization.[2] In both instances, Wolfowitz demonstrated himself to be one of Israel's strongest supporters in the Reagan administration.

It was on China that Wolfowitz launched his boldest challenge to the established order. Ever since the pathbreaking visits to Beijing by Richard Nixon and Henry Kissinger in 1971 and 1972, American foreign policy had taken for granted that China was of surpassing strategic importance and that the United States needed cooperation from Beijing as part of its cold war struggle against the Soviet Union. As a result, American policy makers had gone to great lengths to accommodate China's Communist leadership.

During the first two years of the Reagan administration China insistently sought a promise that the United States would cut off all American arms sales to Taiwan. During the discussions within the Reagan administration over whether to go along with these demands, Secretary of State Alexander Haig, who had served as Kissinger's deputy during the opening to Beijing, as usual invoked China's strategic importance, warning that America simply could not afford to antagonize China.

In response, Wolfowitz not only questioned whether it was necessary to end arms sales to Taiwan but also launched a much broader attack on Washington's assumptions about China. The United States exaggerated China's strategic significance, Wolfowitz argued; although China was important within East Asia, America's defense buildup and the evident weakness of the Chinese People's Liberation Army meant that China would not be of any great help for the United States in the event of a war with the Soviet Union. In fact, Wolfowitz went on, China had far greater reason to fear a Soviet invasion than America did, and as a result, China needed help from the United States considerably more than America needed China's.[3]

Here, once again, Wolfowitz was taking American foreign policy several steps beyond the usual cold war thinking of the era. When he studied the Persian Gulf in the late 1970s, Wolfowitz had started out with the predictable cold war anxieties about a Soviet drive toward the oil fields of the Middle East, but he then had gone on to focus on a different possibility, the prospect that Iraq might try to dominate the oil fields by invading its neighbors. So too with Wolfowitz's China policy. Throughout the late 1970s most of Washington's hawks, including Senator Henry Jackson, the patron saint of the neoconservatives, had argued that in order to combat the Soviet Union, America needed to give the strongest possible support to China. Now Wolfowitz was urging that the United States begin to look at China in a different way, outside the usual anti-Soviet framework. In both instances, Iraq and China, Wolfowitz was beginning to think about foreign policy issues that were to arise a decade later, after the Soviet collapse. Wolfowitz was serving as, in effect, an advance scout for the neoconservatives; while others were still preoccupied with the Soviet Union, Wolfowitz was beginning to address questions that would preoccupy the neoconservative movement in the 1990s.

Above all, Wolfowitz's evolving perspective on China was significant because the approach was similar to his and other neoconservatives' view of détente with the Soviet Union in the 1970s. The underlying assumption was that the United States should not and need not reach an accommodation with any other of the world's major powers. Under Wolfowitz's view, America was strong enough that it did not require China's help in the cold war. In the same fashion, he and others had argued that the United States would be better off without an agreement with Moscow on arms control. In both cases Wolfowitz was striking at the underpinnings of Henry Kissinger's foreign policy: détente, the opening to Beijing and the pursuit of a stable balance of power.

Not surprisingly, Wolfowitz soon found himself at odds with Haig, Reagan's first secretary of state, who had risen to power in Washington as Kissinger's deputy. Wolfowitz's memos questioning the strategic importance of China infuriated Haig, and the secretary of state also spurned several other initiatives from Wolfowitz's policy planning staff. In an interview two decades later Libby reflected that never did so many talented people seem to accomplish so little as the team Wolfowitz had assembled at policy planning.[4]

On March 30, 1982, the *New York Times* carried a short item buried in a collection of random notes from Washington. The article reported that Secretary of State Haig "has notified Paul D. Wolfowitz, the director of policy planning, that he will be replaced. . . . Associates reported that Mr. Haig found Mr. Wolfowitz too theoretical."[5] Haig denied the story, which seemed to be a sign of the growing friction between the two men. It soon turned out, however, that Haig was out of step with the Reagan administration even more than Wolfowitz was at odds with the secretary of state. To Reagan's growing irritation, Haig had waged a series of battles with the White House staff centering on his authority over foreign policy. On June 25 Reagan announced that Haig was stepping down, even though, by Haig's candid account, "the President was accepting a letter of resignation that I had not submitted."[6]

Reagan appointed George Shultz to take Haig's place. The change marked one more step by the Reagan administration away from the vestiges of Nixon-Kissinger diplomacy. Even after rejecting the deal at the 1980 Republican convention that would have made Gerald Ford vice president and restored Kissinger to power, Reagan had still remained insecure enough about foreign policy that he appointed Kissinger's deputy as his first secretary of state. Yet Haig had never fit in with Reagan and his aides, who had different ideas about the world.

After nearly being fired, Wolfowitz was instead promoted. Shultz appointed him to be assistant secretary of state for East Asia and the Pacific. It was a big step for Wolfowitz's career, the first time he was put in charge of something that extended beyond ideas, theory and memo writing. Shultz checked to make sure he was ready for the change. "Paul, this is an administrative job," Shultz told Wolfowitz. "It's not just thinking. It's a big area. You've got to get around, get to see a lot of people."[7] Years later Shultz reflected that he had been right and that Wolfowitz had done extremely well in the Asia post. Yet Shultz's initial worries were revealing: Throughout his career Wolfowitz regularly had to overcome the perception that he was primarily a theorist, not a manager or an administrator.

For Wolfowitz, the Asia job represented something new and refreshing. At the time many of the countries in East Asia were in the midst of rapid economic growth. "When I went from policy planning, where I was mostly doing Middle East stuff, to East Asia, it was like walking out of some oppressive, stuffy room into sunlight and fresh air," he reflected in an interview twenty years later. "At the time I felt that I was going from a part of the world where people only know how to create problems to a part of the world where people solve problems."[8]

Shultz proceeded to embrace Wolfowitz's views about China policy, the same ones Haig had spurned. The new secretary of state agreed that Washington had been overvaluing the strategic importance of China and that as a result, the United States had been unnecessarily weakening its bargaining position in dealing with Beijing.[9] Shultz began to reorient American policy toward Asia to give greater weight to relations with Japan. It was neither the first time nor the last that Wolfowitz's ideas, after at first being rejected as heretical, came out on top.

In both symbolic and tangible ways, Ronald Reagan moved quickly to restore morale in the armed forces, attempting to overcome the legacy of Vietnam.

The previous year a retired army sergeant named Roy Benavidez had been belatedly awarded a Congressional Medal of Honor for his bravery in saving eight members of the Special Forces in Vietnam. The medal was actually an upgrade; Benavidez had earlier won a Distinguished Service Cross for the same event. During his final months in office, President

Carter had been asked by the Pentagon to award Benavidez his medal, but he delayed and finally left office without doing so. On February 24, 1981, Reagan presided over an elaborate White House ceremony for Benavidez, read the Medal of Honor citation himself and added some pointed words whose meaning could not be missed. "It is time to show our pride" for those who fought in Vietnam, Reagan declared. ". . . They came home without a victory not because they were defeated, but because they were denied a chance to win."[10]

The Army officer who quietly orchestrated this event was Brigadier General Colin Powell. At the beginning of the new administration Powell was serving as a military aide to his third consecutive deputy secretary of defense, Frank Carlucci. President Carter's failure to hold a ceremony for Benavidez "epitomized for me an insensitivity to the military during this time," Powell later wrote. Shortly after the new administration took office, Powell approached Carlucci to say that "it would mean a lot to us to see this hero get his due."[11] Powell was demonstrating his political skill, finding a way for Reagan and Weinberger to register their support for the military at no cost to themselves or anyone else.

It turned out that the new Reagan administration was also willing to spend money, indeed unprecedented sums, in its support for the military. Within a few weeks after the inauguration Weinberger took the Carter administration's defense budget for 1982 and asked for an increase of twenty-six billion dollars, or 11 percent. Weinberger also sought another seven billion dollars immediately for expenses in the last half of 1981.[12] These were the first steps by the Reagan team on behalf of a foreign policy that emphasized the importance of American military power.

With some difficulty, Powell managed to obtain permission from Carlucci and from his military superiors to leave the Pentagon for nearly two years in assignments at Fort Carson and Fort Leavenworth. He was hoping to win the command of an Army division afterward. Yet he was too experienced and too useful at the Pentagon to be allowed to stay out of Washington for long. In early 1983 Weinberger's senior military assistant was scheduled to leave. General John Wickham, the new Army chief of staff, eager to have someone from the Army in that job rather than from the Navy or Air Force, pushed Powell as the new military assistant. The secretary of defense too wanted Powell as his aide.[13] Once again, Powell was both the Army's chosen representative to top civilian leaders and the civilians' favorite intermediary with the military brass. Overall, between

1977 and 1986, Powell held five different jobs in the Pentagon front office, working as military aide to either secretaries or deputy secretaries of
defense. He was the man who kept the building running. "Weinberger
was remote and hard to talk to," recalled Lawrence Korb, an assistant secretary under Weinberger. "With Powell, he was down to earth, he was a
regular guy, he'd take care of things."[14]

It was Powell, then Weinberger's military aide, who received the late-
night phone call on October 23, 1983, to pass on the news that a truck
carrying a bomb had hit the U.S. Marine barracks in Beirut. The terrorist attack killed 241 American marines, who were in Lebanon as part of a
multinational force designed to stabilize the country in the midst of its
civil war. For more than a year Weinberger and the Joint Chiefs of Staff
had opposed the stationing of the Marines in Lebanon. "This night, each
of my calls was like a physical blow to the Secretary," Powell later wrote.
"Eighty bodies pulled out. A hundred. A hundred and fifty. . . ." Powell
admitted that he never forgot that night. In 1991, when others proposed
American military intervention in Bosnia, "the shattered bodies of
Marines at the Beirut airport were never far from my mind in arguing for
caution."[15]

For American foreign policy, Lebanon demonstrated another part of
the legacy of Vietnam, one for which the Reagan administration had no
easy answers. Reagan and his team had already provided money, rhetoric
and symbols in support of the armed forces. The administration was suc-
ceeding in its efforts to show that the military was being restored to a position of respect in America and to ease the Vietnam-era tensions between
military and civilian society. But it was far harder, particularly after Vietnam, to answer the question of when U.S. leaders should resort to the use
of force. Under what circumstances was it worthwhile to risk the lives of
American soldiers and sailors? The State Department and the National
Security Council, seeking the greatest possible options for an active, assertive American foreign policy, tended to favor military intervention
overseas far more often than the Pentagon, which was directly responsible
for the lives and well-being of U.S. service forces. For their part, Pentagon
leaders were concerned above all with maintaining the strength to win
major, protracted conflicts like World War II, and to them, missions like
the one in Beirut seemed like diversions.

Inside the Pentagon, Vietnam had been originally justified as part of
America's cold war struggle against the Soviet Union, and the cold war it-

self fit into the World War II framework of a worldwide struggle against a major military power. But the Vietnam War had been conducted, like the Korean War before it, as a limited war; America didn't want the hostilities to escalate into a direct, all-out conflict with the Soviet Union or China. In the end, many military leaders came to question the restrictions imposed by the policy of limited war and, more broadly, the wisdom of intervening in Vietnam under these restrictions. Now, following the dispatch of American forces to Lebanon, U.S. troops had been killed on a mission that was not directly related to the cold war, a mission in which the goal was not even winning a limited war but merely preserving order.

Weinberger, who revered the history and traditions of World War II, was especially outraged by the Beirut disaster. He ordered a review of American policy and goals in Lebanon and within months won approval from Reagan for the withdrawal of the American forces. Then Weinberger took much broader aim at American policy. He drafted a detailed series of rules and conditions for deciding when American combat forces should be sent abroad.

Weinberger at first wanted to announce these new rules the summer after the Beirut bombing. But the 1984 presidential campaign was under way, and Reagan's White House advisers blocked the defense secretary from discussing these issues in public; doing so might have suggested to voters that Reagan had been wrong to send the troops to Beirut in the first place. Finally, in late November, Weinberger unveiled his new guidelines in a speech at the National Press Club titled "The Uses of Military Power."

America should not send its combat forces on overseas missions unless doing so was vital to U.S. national interests, Weinberger said, and it should do so only in cases in which the United States had the clear intent of winning. Moreover, the United States should have "clearly defined political and military objectives" for a combat mission and regularly reassess the situation to make sure it still met these objectives. American leaders should have some reasonable assurance that the mission would have the support of the American public. Finally, the use of American combat troops should be a last resort, after other options had failed.[16]

At the time Powell, serving as Weinberger's military aide, was uncertain about the wisdom of issuing these guidelines. "I was concerned that the Weinberger tests, publicly proclaimed, were too explicit and would lead potential enemies to look for loopholes," he later wrote.[17] Over the next few years, as Powell rose to become chairman of the Joint Chiefs of Staff, he came to identify with them so thoroughly that they became known not as the Weinberger guidelines but as the Powell doctrine. The rules were, in effect, a compendium of the Pentagon's considerable caution about the use of force; they were an attempt to put down in writing the ways to avoid another long, unsuccessful, unpopular war like Vietnam.

Throughout this period Powell was working closely with another of Weinberger's top aides, Richard Armitage. Brought into the administration as a regional specialist, a deputy assistant secretary for East Asia, Armitage had been promoted in early 1983 to assistant secretary for international security affairs, one of the most important policy jobs in the Pentagon. Weinberger had installed Richard Perle, Washington's most determined opponent of détente, as assistant secretary in charge of dealing with the Soviet Union and Europe; Armitage was, in effect, given the rest of the world, including the Middle East and East Asia, two regions of profound importance for American security. "You had in Armitage and Perle probably two of the most powerful assistant secretaries in history," recalled Dov Zakheim, who worked for Perle during this period. "Weinberger was comfortable with these guys, so they had tremendous clout." When Weinberger pushed for a review of Mideast policy after the Beirut bombing, he placed Armitage in charge of it. Armitage served as Weinberger's right-hand man too when the Reagan administration decided to bomb Libya in 1986 in retaliation for Libyan involvement in a terrorist attack on a Berlin discotheque.[18]

Powell and Armitage had become close friends in the earliest days of the Reagan administration. When Powell was brought back to Washington in 1983 as Weinberger's military aide, he and Armitage became a two-man team running most of the day-to-day operations of the Defense Department. The biggest decisions went up to Weinberger, and Soviet policy was up to Perle. Otherwise Armitage and Powell were the people to see at the Pentagon; it almost didn't matter which one, because the two friends swapped notes, information and stories several times a day. They had their own network of loyal friends and aides. Those few inside the Defense Department who crossed one or the other of the two men found themselves at odds with both; although both men were charming, the

combined power of the Armitage-Powell partnership was also occasionally a source of resentment within the Pentagon.

Powell and Armitage shared a common outlook on events and people.
Both men had served in Vietnam, and both were interested in restoring
America's military strength. More generally, however, when it came to
foreign policy, both Armitage and Powell were mistrustful of people with
strong views or ideologies. They had taken from Vietnam the lesson that
events often outran everyone's preconceptions. Moreover, having an ideology might entail pushing for ideas or principles; in the process, one
might incur enemies who could damage the chances for career advancement.

Both men viewed themselves as poor boys, up from the streets and
more in tune with ordinary Americans than the well-bred civilians with
whom they worked (although Armitage, by virtue of his marriage to the
daughter of a wealthy business executive, was anything but poor). Both
men loved working in Washington, were talented at it and, despite occasional disavowals, hoped to stay on in public life; neither had a second
profession, such as academia or law, upon which he could fall back if he
didn't rise to the top in government. Once, when the former deputy secretary of defense Robert Ellsworth met Armitage in the Pentagon, Armitage told him, "You're an inspiration to me; you prove that there's life
after this shit." But Armitage always kept coming back for more, and so
did Powell.[19]

Powell and Armitage were determinedly moderate to liberal in their
views on domestic issues, particularly about the importance of overcoming America's legacy of racial discrimination. Both men sent their children to public schools; Armitage and his wife, Laura, adopted six
children, including three African-Americans, and as foster parents cared
for approximately forty other children in their home. For some others
working on foreign policy in the Reagan administration, America's domestic and social policies didn't matter. Jeane Kirkpatrick, for example,
acknowledged that she had switched to the Republican party in 1980 after reaching the point where foreign policy utterly dominated her thinking and interests.[20] In this respect, Powell and Armitage were different
from many of their colleagues on Reagan's foreign policy team.

Because of his responsibility for the third world and his own experience
in covert operations, Armitage became heavily involved in what was

called the Reagan doctrine. Director of Central Intelligence William Casey was the driving force behind the doctrine, under which the United States provided large-scale financial and military help for armed rebellions against regimes that were supported by the Soviet Union. The key battlegrounds were Afghanistan, Cambodia, Nicaragua and Angola.

"Support for freedom fighters is self-defense," Reagan had declared in his State of the Union speech in 1985. The choice of the term *freedom fighters* was an inspired oversimplification, glossing over the fact that the policy was based above all on opposition to the Soviet Union. In fact, in Afghanistan the United States supported some Islamic fundamentalists with curious notions of freedom, and in Cambodia it supported a coalition of opposition groups whose main fighting force was the murderous Khmer Rouge. Nevertheless, Reagan's new doctrine represented another far-reaching step in the reassertion of American military power after Vietnam. First, the United States in the late 1970s had begun to develop the forces and infrastructure to wage war in the Persian Gulf; second, the Reagan administration had pushed through unprecedented increases in the defense budget; now it was moving to engage in proxy wars around the world. "The United States today is not the United States of a decade ago, one that is full of self-doubts," asserted Armitage at one congressional hearing. "We're a different nation now."[21]

Armitage traveled around the world, organizing support for various anti-Soviet and anti-Communist insurgencies. Approximately every three months he would visit Islamabad to talk with the leaders of Pakistan's Interservices Intelligence Directorate (ISI), the country's powerful intelligence service, which was channeling American support to Afghanistan's mujahideen rebels in their battle against Soviet forces. Often Armitage traveled on to Pakistan's border town of Peshawar to meet with mujahideen leaders themselves. One of the Afghans whom Armitage saw regularly in the mid-1980s, Burhanuddin Rabbani, went on to become the president of Afghanistan in the early 1990s and then the political leader of Afghanistan's Northern Alliance in the war against the Taliban in 2001.[22]

Still, Armitage's support for the Reagan doctrine seemed to be subtly qualified by practical concerns. "If a group is fighting a repressive regime and shares our values and concerns, then *we have very little choice* but to support them," he told Congress in one revealing policy formulation (emphasis added). "For us, the issue is not whether freedom fighters deserve our support; the real question is what support should be offered."[23] When some conservative Republicans pressed the Pentagon to provide Stinger antiaircraft missiles to the Afghan rebels, Armitage stayed in the background, and his boss, Weinberger, unsuccessfully opposed the idea, fearing that missiles might be lost and the technology might find its way to the Soviet Union. The Reagan doctrine had its limits.

Moreover, Armitage's Vietnam experience meant that there were some causes advanced by DCI Casey for which he had little enthusiasm. In theory, Armitage was responsible for Latin American policy, yet he left Nicaragua and El Salvador almost entirely in the hands of a superior, Fred Iklé. The defense intellectual Edward Luttwak was working in the Pentagon during that period, and Armitage asked him why he was spending so much time on Central America. "He figured it was a guerrilla war, and so we'd lose, " Luttwak recalled.[24]

Two weeks after the deadly attack on the Marines in Beirut, Reagan decided to seek a negotiated settlement to Lebanon's civil war. He announced that he was naming a new special envoy as his personal representative to the Middle East, Donald Rumsfeld, the president of Searle. "I can't think of a better individual in whom to entrust the coordination of our role in the Middle East peace process," Reagan told a White House news conference.

Rumsfeld had been largely shut out of foreign policy during the Reagan administration's first two years, despite his work as secretary of defense in the previous Republican administration. He did not get along well with Haig or Weinberger, neither of whom had been allies in the Nixon administration;[25] Haig in particular tended to view Rumsfeld with suspicion. However, the path finally cleared for Rumsfeld after George Shultz became secretary of state. Rumsfeld and Shultz had been allies working on the Cost of Living Council in the Nixon years. Shultz first tried without success to win Rumsfeld the job of national security adviser and, when that attempt failed, to get him appointed Middle East envoy.[26] Rumsfeld quickly began to fly from one Middle Eastern capital to another, looking for openings for new American diplomacy.

One unusual place Rumsfeld tried was Iraq, with which the United States had had no diplomatic relations since the 1967 war between Israel and its Arab neighbors. On December 19 and 20, 1983, Rumsfeld held friendly talks in Baghdad, first for more than two hours with Deputy

Prime Minister Tariq Aziz and then the following day for another ninety minutes with President Saddam Hussein. He was the first senior American official to visit Iraq in six years. So enthusiastic was he about the session with Hussein that he cabled Washington the meeting "marked [a] positive milestone in development of U.S.-Iraqi relations and will prove to be of wider benefit to U.S. posture in the region."[27]

At the time Iraq was in the midst of its war with Iran, which had begun in 1980 and lasted for eight years. Ever since the downfall of the shah, U.S. policy in the region had been devoted above all to containing Iran and preventing it from trying to spread its brand of Islamic fundamentalism throughout the rest of the Middle East. Rumsfeld's trip to Baghdad was a reflection of that policy. Many years later, when Rumsfeld was questioned in Congress about his amicable 1983 meeting with Saddam Hussein, he emphasized that he had been a private citizen at the time and that his goal had been to eliminate terrorism in Lebanon.[28] The answer was misleading. He was in Baghdad as the representative of President Reagan, and the declassified cables show he was seeking not just Iraq's help in Lebanon but broader cooperation between the United States and Iraq to offset the power of Iran and Syria in the Middle East. As Rumsfeld explained in his meeting with Tariq Aziz, the United States was interested in "security and stability in the [Persian] Gulf, which had been jeopardized as a result of the Iranian revolution."[29]

Saddam welcomed Rumsfeld in military dress, with a pistol on his hip. Rumsfeld gave the Iraqi leader a letter with greetings from Reagan and then, getting down to business, said that "our [American] understanding of the importance of balance in the world and the region was similar to Iraq's," according to Rumsfeld's account of the conversation. The day before, Rumsfeld had told Tariq Aziz he thought it would be a shame if "a whole generation of Iraqis and Americans grew up without understanding each other." Saddam Hussein echoed this thought back to Rumsfeld.[30]

For their part, Hussein and Aziz kept bringing the conversation with Rumsfeld back to their pressing wartime concern: that the United States should tell its allies and friends around the world to stop selling arms to Iran. Aziz even handed Rumsfeld a list of countries that were shipping weaponry to Iran. Rumsfeld told the Iraqi president not to worry; the United States was already encouraging other governments not to provide weapons to Iran and would continue to do so. Rumsfeld could not have known then he was making a promise to Iraq that the United States would soon violate. Within eighteen months others in the Reagan administration began discussing the possibility of secret American arms shipments to Iran.

Back in Washington, Rumsfeld made the rounds, arguing that the Pentagon wasn't doing its job in the Middle East. Never one to shrink from personal and bureaucratic combat, he was taking direct aim at Weinberger and the military leadership. "He was disturbed by the timidity that had characterized Pentagon officials in Lebanon," Shultz later said. And Lebanon, Rumsfeld argued, was merely a sideshow. The real danger was that Iran seemed to be winning its war against Iraq and could threaten Kuwait and Saudi Arabia. "The Gulf could cave in to Iran—a collapse," Rumsfeld warned. He argued that the U.S. military wasn't prepared to deal with such a crisis. The Carter administration had declared that the Persian Gulf was vital to American interests, but the Pentagon still wasn't ready to back up this commitment.[31] By attacking Weinberger, Rumsfeld was also implicitly putting himself at odds with Armitage, the secretary of defense's adviser for the Middle East, and with Powell, Weinberger's loyal military assistant. It was an early precursor of the frictions between Rumsfeld and the Powell-Armitage team in the second Bush administration.

The disagreements were more than personal. At the heart of the dispute was Weinberger's caution in sending American troops on the mission to Lebanon. The same post-Vietnam tensions over the use of force emerged again and again during the next two decades as America contemplated military intervention in Bosnia, Haiti, Somalia, Rwanda, Kosovo and, above all, Iraq. Powell, Weinberger's disciple, was at the center of many of these debates.

By the time of Rumsfeld's session with Saddam Hussein, the U.S. government already had intelligence information, to which Rumsfeld had access, that Iraq was using chemical weapons in the war against Iran. Shultz asserted in his memoirs that "something sinister seemed to be going on in Iraq" and that reports of its use of chemical weapons dated back to "late 1983." By other accounts, Iraq began using nerve gas as early as February 1983, in an attempt to stop a major Iranian offensive.[32]

Nearly two decades later this Iraqi use of chemical weapons against

Iran became part of the justification regularly advanced by Rumsfeld and others in the second Bush administration for seeking the overthrow of Saddam Hussein. "They have killed thousands of their own people with chemical weapons and they have used them to get the Iranians," declared Rumsfeld in one interview in 2002. "So we know we have a leader who's a dictator, who's got the programs, who has a perfect willingness to use them."[33]

At the time of Rumsfeld's 1983 meeting, however, the United States had other interests in the Middle East, and Saddam Hussein's use of chemical weapons was not viewed as something that should stand in the way of doing business with him. Rumsfeld's trip proved to be the groundbreaking step in the American drive to upgrade its ties with Iraq. In formal ceremonies at the White House on November 26, 1984, less than a year after Rumsfeld's visit to Baghdad, the Reagan administration restored full diplomatic relations with Iraq.

But by then Rumsfeld was no longer Reagan's Middle East envoy. He was not the sort of person to waste time or to be associated with a losing cause, and negotiations in the Middle East are time-consuming and frequently unsuccessful. "He'd come back and shake his head at me and say, 'A just and lasting peace? Are you kidding?'" recalled Shultz.[34] On May 18, 1984, after only six months on the job, Rumsfeld resigned and went back to Searle, a deus ex machina leaving the scene in the middle of the act.

CHAPTER EIGHT

Of Dictatorships and Democracy

THE CLUE THAT Richard Armitage's Pentagon aides knew to watch for was the occasional notation on his daily schedule that said "haircut." Since Armitage was nearly bald, they knew he had little need for a barber. In fact, "haircut" meant that there was some interagency battle within the Reagan administration and that Armitage was going off for a quiet, unannounced meeting with Paul Wolfowitz and Gaston Sigur to try to straighten things out.

Throughout the mid-1980s, Wolfowitz, Armitage and Sigur formed a cohesive troika in charge of the Reagan administration's policy toward Asia. Wolfowitz represented the State Department, Armitage the Pentagon and Sigur the National Security Council. They gathered once a week on Monday afternoons in Wolfowitz's State Department office. Those sessions were not secret. But then, whenever touchy issues came up, such as proposals for American arms sales to either China or Taiwan, the troika gathered again in a more clandestine fashion.[1]

Sigur was by far the oldest of the three. A pale-faced, ruddy World War II veteran who bore a slight resemblance to W. C. Fields, he had come to the Reagan administration after a semiacademic career with the Asia Foundation and as head of George Washington University's Institute of Sino-Soviet Studies. Sigur was also, more covertly, an alumnus of the U.S. intelligence community. Like some other officials of the Asia Foundation in its early years, he had worked under contract for the CIA while overseas; stationed in Afghanistan, he had helped recruit agents, had reported on meetings with officials of foreign governments and had done other assorted intelligence chores. He had also been posted in Japan.[2]

Years later many in Washington looked back and were astonished that Wolfowitz and Armitage had collaborated so closely and amicably in the Reagan era. The styles of the two men could not possibly have been more different. Wolfowitz was a cerebral conceptualizer, Armitage a hands-on operator; Wolfowitz was full of conservative passion, Armitage determinedly nonideological; Wolfowitz's training ground was in the world of academia, while Armitage's was in the mud of Vietnam. Years later, as the George W. Bush administration pursued its war on terrorism, the two men became frequent antagonists. (Once in 2001, when Armitage was irate at some of the criticisms of Colin Powell by conservatives within the Pentagon, he told Wolfowitz, "If you pick on my friends, you pick on me."[3]) In retrospect, many in Washington came to believe that Sigur, the third man, deserved credit for bridging the gulf between Armitage and Wolfowitz and, for a time, bringing them together.

The work of this triumvirate represented a rare instance in which the lower and midlevels of the Washington bureaucracy overcame differences at the top. Armitage's and Wolfowitz's bosses, Secretary of Defense Caspar Weinberger and Secretary of State George Shultz, were regularly at loggerheads; the two men didn't like each other personally, and they disagreed over issues ranging from Soviet policy to the use of military force, terrorism and Lebanon. None of Reagan's national security advisers stayed on the job for long; six men served as national security adviser over the course of Reagan's eight years. The theory behind the work of Sigur's troika was that if an issue was allowed to go up to the level of the cabinet, then the Weinberger-Shultz frictions and the weakness of the national security advisers meant that there was likely to be a battle over policy even when one was unnecessary, so why not try to work things out at lower levels?

Armitage, Wolfowitz and Sigur were at the center of what was in many ways the most surprising change in the Reagan administration's foreign policy, the decision to encourage Philippine President Ferdinand Marcos to give up power in 1986. The administration's actions in the Philippines ran contrary to the views expressed at the time Reagan took office. America's encouragement of democracy in the Philippines soon influenced events in other Asian countries as well—especially South Korea and Taiwan and, less happily, Burma and China.

Over the long term the Reagan administration's conduct in the

Philippines ushered in a new era for American conservatives and neoconservatives. Until the late 1980s the causes of democracy and self-determination overseas had been espoused mostly by liberals and Democrats; Woodrow Wilson, America's most ardent proponent of an idealistic foreign policy, had been a liberal Democrat. After the Philippines, promoting democracy abroad gradually turned into a cause of the political right more than of the left. When in 2002 and 2003 the George W. Bush administration began to call for democratic government for the Palestinians, in Iraq and elsewhere in the Middle East, it was following a line of policy and doctrine that first took root when the Reagan administration dealt with the Philippines.

At the time Reagan was sworn in, pressing for democracy in third world countries was among the last things on his mind. The Reagan team was convinced that the Carter administration had been wrong to push for political liberalization in Iran under the shah and in Nicaragua under Anastasio Somoza, opening the way for revolutions that harmed America's interests. Human rights had been primarily a Democratic issue, pushed forward by members of Congress like Representative Donald Fraser and Senator Edward Kennedy. Elliott Abrams, who for a time served as Reagan's assistant secretary for human rights, admitted many years later that when the Republicans took office in 1981, they had no human rights policy of their own, only a critique of the Democrats.[4]

One of the first foreign leaders welcomed to the Reagan White House was South Korean President Chun Doo Hwan, the military leader who had seized power in a coup in May 1980. The Carter administration had frozen U.S. relations with South Korea because of Chun's imposition of martial law there. The Reagan administration quickly restored those ties.

Before agreeing to Chun's trip, Reagan's new foreign policy team had joined with the outgoing Carter team to obtain a commitment that the imprisoned dissident Kim Dae Jung would not be executed. Despite that significant victory, Reagan's invitation to Chun served as a symbol of where the new administration stood: It was not going to criticize dictators allied with the United States, as Carter had. If Carter's policy was to condemn repression by right-wing rulers while glossing over the abuses of Communist regimes, then Reagan's initial policy would be precisely the opposite: to denounce Communist oppression while remaining mostly silent about the repressive behavior of America's allies. Thinking back to the beginning of the Reagan era, William Kristol, the editor of the neoconservative *Weekly Standard,* reflected, "I don't think that neoconservatives at that time were particularly strong supporters of democracy."[5]

Vice President George H. W. Bush visited Manila in mid-1981 and, at a banquet, told Marcos, "We love your adherence to democratic principles and democratic processes," ignoring the clear evidence that Marcos's regime was anything but democratic. The following year Marcos and his wife, Imelda, were permitted to visit Washington for the first time in sixteen years. The Reagans treated them like royalty, granting them a lavish welcome and a state dinner in the White House. The Marcos visit represented the nadir of Reagan's human rights policy; by that time some members of the team were starting to have second thoughts about the wisdom and the morality of embracing dictators.[6]

One important impetus for change came from Eastern Europe. In 1980 and 1981, Lech Wałesa's Solidarity movement had burst forth with its challenge to Poland's Communist regime. The startling success of the movement seemed to show that there were possibilities for political change in Eastern Europe and that non-Communist institutions might be emerging. In talking about the Soviet Union during the 1970s, American conservatives had primarily emphasized security issues; they had argued that the Soviets represented a threat to the United States and that America should build up its military power. But the 1981 upheavals in Poland brought the issue of political freedom back to the top of the conservative agenda once again.

In a speech to the British House of Commons in 1982, Reagan proclaimed that one of the central goals of American foreign policy would be the promotion of democracy, particularly in Eastern Europe and the Soviet Union. He said he rejected the idea "that once countries achieve a nuclear capability, they should be allowed an undisturbed reign of terror over their own citizens." He proposed new efforts to foster "the infrastructure of democracy," including a free press, labor unions, political parties and academic freedom. Reagan's speech soon led to the creation of the National Endowment for Democracy, which provided American funds to help build democratic institutions overseas.[7]

Initially, the espousal of democracy seemed to be intrinsically linked to the Reagan team's anticommunism. Yet there were also occasional hints that this new belief in democracy might extend beyond the borders of Communist countries. In the State Department, Secretary of State

Shultz and Abrams began pushing Chile's General Augusto Pinochet to open up his dictatorship to democratic change, thereby incurring the wrath of right-wing Senator Jesse Helms. Still, their actions did not seem to be representative of the Reagan White House. "I was not really on the wavelength of the president and many of his advisers," Shultz later admitted. "To them, Pinochet was a friend of the United States and a bulwark against communism. Pinochet made everyone uneasy, but he was on our side."[8]

The initial impetus for changing policy in the Philippines was not an abstract commitment to democracy. Rather, it was the U.S. government's desire to preserve Clark Air Force Base and the Subic Bay Naval Station, the two huge military bases in the Philippines that were at the center of U.S. strategy for maintaining the American presence in Asia. Marcos, who had become president in 1965 and had held unchallenged power since imposing martial law in 1972, was confronting a growing challenge from a Communist insurgency, the New People's Army. American officials worried that a revolution in the Philippines would jeopardize America's continuing access to the military facilities.

At first, the Reagan approach was simply to support and strengthen the Marcos government. That approach was increasingly called into question, however, after the assassination of the opposition leader Benigno Aquino in 1983 as he landed at the Manila airport to return from exile; Marcos's top military commander, General Fabian Ver, was soon linked to the murder.

The following year the administration approved a new policy aimed at goading Marcos to reform. The United States began to push Marcos to open the way for fair elections and a free press, to break up the monopolies granted to Marcos's friends and to bring in new leadership for the military. The administration wasn't abandoning Marcos; rather, it believed the reforms should be made under his leadership. Although Marcos was "part of the problem, he is also necessarily part of the solution," the administration's new policy specified.[9]

Wolfowitz and Armitage each made trips to the Philippines to deliver the message that it was time for Marcos to change his dictatorial regime. In January 1985 Wolfowitz and his aide Scooter Libby pointedly chose to meet in Manila with some of Marcos's leading opponents.[10] In Washington, meanwhile, Armitage and Wolfowitz testified side by side in Congress on behalf of the new policy of pushing Marcos to open up. The two men were viewed as close partners. "I remember Wolfowitz and Armitage joined at the hip in dealing with us on the Philippines," recalled Stanley O. Roth, then the staff aide to Congressman Stephen Solarz, the chairman of the House Foreign Affairs Subcommittee on Asia.[11]

While pressing Marcos for change, the two men were at the same time struggling to prevent the Democratic Congress, which was eager to put pressure on the Philippine leader, from freezing all military aid to Manila. In one session Armitage paced around Solarz's office, fuming that a cutoff of U.S. military aid could lead to upheaval in the Philippines and, ultimately, a Communist dictatorship.

For Armitage in particular, the Philippines raised the specter that America could become bogged down in another Vietnam and in another counterinsurgency campaign like the one in which he had fought. Armitage warned Congress that the Communist rebellion in the Philippines was growing ever stronger and that there could be a "strategic stalemate within three to four years."[12] In pushing for far-reaching reforms that would help the Philippine government win popular support, he was seeking to accomplish what the United States had never been able to do in South Vietnam.

Armitage and Wolfowitz were not working in a vacuum. Several other State Department and military officials were also active in trying to obtain changes from Marcos. They included Undersecretary of State Michael Armacost and U.S. Ambassador Stephen Bosworth in Manila. Yet Marcos didn't respond, largely because he believed that no matter what these lower-level officials said, Reagan would support him. During the 1984 presidential campaign Reagan had made it clear he thought the United States had no choice but to back Marcos. "What is the alternative?" asked Reagan during one televised debate. The only alternative to Marcos, the president continued, was "a large Communist movement to take over the Philippines." Reagan's answer seemed to treat the many non-Communist opponents of Marcos as though they didn't exist.

In late 1985 the Philippines began to career toward a crisis. Marcos, seeking to deflect American pressure, ordered a quick election he thought he could control. Opposition forces and the Roman Catholic Church lined up behind Corazon Aquino, the widow of the leader who had been assassinated. Election returns appeared to show that Aquino had won the election; but Marcos claimed victory, and the American embassy in

Manila reported that Marcos's allies were holding back on reporting votes.[13]

In Washington these events led to a series of testy exchanges between Reagan and Shultz. Their dialogue was of historic importance both for the future of U.S. foreign policy and for American conservatives. Shultz argued that it was time for the United States to separate itself from Marcos. Reagan balked. The president countered with the traditional anti-Communist view that the United States should support friends and allies, even if they were dictators, because withdrawing support from them could undercut America's struggle against the Soviet Union. But Shultz came back with a different formulation of anticommunism: By clinging to Marcos's dictatorship, Shultz argued, the United States might strengthen the insurgency against his regime and thus open the way for a Communist victory in the Philippines.

The secretary of state gradually brought the president over to his side. When Reagan at one point suggested that there might have been election fraud by both Marcos and Aquino forces, Shultz countered there was no factual evidence of fraud by the Aquino camp. Reagan began to give ground. After Aquino's supporters took to the streets and Marcos threatened to use force against them, Shultz persuaded the president to send two private messages to Marcos, the first threatening to cut off military aid to the Philippines and the second urging Marcos to give up power.

Finally, the Philippine president agreed to step down. He was flown out of the Philippines on an American Air Force plane. Immediately afterward Shultz pushed for a statement granting formal U.S. recognition to Aquino's government. Reagan was dubious. "The president objected. . . . We argued," Shultz wrote in his memoirs. The secretary of state warned that any equivocation by the United States "can turn a triumph of democracy into a catastrophe." In the end Reagan went along, although so reluctantly that Shultz said his relations with the president were badly strained as a result.[14] With American support, and as a result of Shultz's remarkable tenacity, the Philippines was transformed from dictatorship to democracy.

Overall, the Reagan administration's decision to support democratic government in the Philippines had been hesitant, messy, crisis-driven and skewed by the desire to do what was necessary to protect the American military installations. Yet the impact was profound. The Reagan administration demonstrated (above all to itself) that the United States could withdraw support from a dictator and support democratic change without producing another Iran or Nicaragua. Once the precedent had been set, the Reagan administration found it easier to embrace the same approach again. The following year, when South Koreans staged massive street demonstrations against the government of Chun Doo Hwan, the Reagan administration dispatched Gaston Sigur to Seoul to tell the South Korean president that he too should open the way for democratic elections and far-reaching political change.

Evaluating what had happened in the Philippines, Henry Kissinger and Wolfowitz emerged as representatives of opposing schools of foreign policy. Kissinger, as usual, was preoccupied with stability and the existing balance of power, while Wolfowitz was willing to forsake the status quo in pursuit of democratic ideals.

In his syndicated newspaper column, Kissinger denounced the Reagan administration for its withdrawal of support from Marcos and its new emphasis on promoting democracy. "Are there no other overriding American interests?" Kissinger mourned. ". . . Whatever else may be said about the Marcos regime, it contributed substantially to American security and had been extolled by American presidents for nearly two decades." Kissinger said he had "grave concerns" about the long-term implications of the Reagan policy in the Philippines, particularly for authoritarian regimes nearby, such as South Korea, Thailand and Indonesia. "Will they become the next targets of a new American strategy?"[15] Kissinger could not accept the proposition that democratic change overseas might, over the long run, result in greater stability and thus serve American interests.

For his part, Wolfowitz recognized that the Reagan administration's abandonment of Marcos was the logical consequence of its earlier decisions to press for democracy in Eastern Europe and to support the cause of freedom against Communist or Soviet-backed regimes around the world. "You can't use democracy, as you appropriately should, as a battle with the Soviet Union, and then turn around and be completely hypocritical about it when it's on your side of the line," Wolfowitz explained.[16]

Both men were being logically consistent in their views. In fact, Kissinger hadn't championed the cause of democracy against the Soviet Union either; instead, in his dealings with Moscow, his main concerns had been geopolitics and the balance of power. During the 1970s Kissinger had been distressed to discover that the neoconservatives wouldn't give greater support to his attempts to gain strategic advantage for the United States in such countries as Vietnam, Cambodia or Angola because the neoconservatives viewed these third world campaigns as diversions from the ultimate moral struggle against the Soviet Union.[17] To Kissinger, then, Marcos was above all an ally in America's worldwide struggle for geopolitical advantage; to Wolfowitz, Marcos was a liability in America's worldwide battle on behalf of democratic ideals.

And whatever happened to Kirkpatrick's warning against undermining dictators? Was her *Commentary* article "Dictatorships and Double Standards," which had guided the thinking of the Reagan administration when it first took office, ever openly repudiated? No. Long after Marcos's ouster, Wolfowitz continued to insist that Kirkpatrick's ideas were still valid. He refused to acknowledge that he and the neoconservatives had changed their views between the late 1970s and the late 1980s.

One argument Wolfowitz made was that the Reagan administration's sense of timing in the Philippines had been better than the Carter administration's in Iran. He maintained that the Reagan team, heeding Kirkpatrick's warnings about the dangers of destabilizing an authoritarian regime, had waited patiently in the Philippines. For several years it had encouraged Marcos to reform, avoiding far-reaching steps that would have undercut his government until there was a non-Communist alternative. "If we had said, 'We are enemies of the Marcos regime. We want to see its demise rather than reform,' we would have lost all influence in Manila and would have created a situation highly polarized between a regime that had hunkered down and was prepared to do anything to survive and a population at loose ends," Wolfowitz argued many years later.[18]

This timing argument raised more questions than it answered. How does the United States know when the timing is right to push for democracy? Some in the Reagan administration had been ready to lean on Marcos well before he called for an election, while others wanted to stick with him even after he fared poorly in the election. Perhaps in Iran, the Carter administration had been too late and timid—not too early and forceful, as Kirkpatrick had suggested—in pushing for democratic changes. Conceivably, if the United States had pressed the shah for reforms harder and over a longer period, there might have been no Islamic revolution in Iran.

Wolfowitz also contended there had been a fundamental difference between Marcos's Philippines and the shah's Iran, one that justified supporting democracy in the former and not in the latter. In contrast with Iran, Wolfowitz pointed out, the Philippines had in fact possessed well-established institutions of democracy before 1972, when Marcos declared martial law. "When we went to work on Marcos, it was not to dismantle the institutions of the Philippines; it was actually to get him to stop dismantling them himself," Wolfowitz argued. "Military reform, economic reform, getting rid of crony capitalism, relying on the church, political reform: It [the Reagan administration policy] was very institutionally oriented."[19]

This was a sophisticated argument. However, its implications were also more confining than Wolfowitz or the neoconservatives might have liked. Few other countries in Asia, Africa or the Middle East had a history of democracy comparable to that of the Philippines. If a country's traditions were the main factor in determining whether the United States should promote political liberalization, then there would be no reason to seek democracy in countries like China, which has a long history of authoritarian rule. In the second Bush administration, Wolfowitz and other neoconservatives proposed democratic change in the Middle East. Yet outside of Israel (and, to some extent, Iran) none of the countries in the Middle East possessed well-established democratic institutions or traditions.

In short, there was no good way to square the Reagan administration's policy in the Philippines with the Kirkpatrick article that had served as a guiding statement of neoconservative doctrine. "The best antidote to communism is democracy," wrote Wolfowitz during the Philippine crisis.[20] That was a pithy summary of the evolving neoconservative viewpoint of the late 1980s, and it represented a dramatic reversal from the 1970s.

Gradually the Vulcans were developing ideas they would later apply to a world in which there was no Soviet Union. In opposing détente, Donald Rumsfeld, Dick Cheney and Wolfowitz were looking ahead to the time when the United States need not make accommodations with other major powers. In warning that the oil fields of the Persian Gulf might be threatened not just by the Soviet Union but by Iraq, Wolfowitz was laying down the outlines of post–cold war American policy in the Middle East. In questioning the wisdom of Kissinger's China policy, Wolfowitz was foreseeing the time when the United States would view China as something other than a strategic ally against the Soviet Union. In Caspar Weinberger's Pentagon, Colin Powell and Richard Armitage worked to build up American military power in the aftermath of Vietnam. After the Beirut bombing, they also helped develop new rules aimed at describing the circumstances in which American troops could be sent abroad on combat missions. In the Philippines, Wolfowitz and Armitage helped establish the idea that the United States should support democracy in dealing not only with America's adversaries but also with its allies.

In all these instances, the Vulcans, during the last two decades of the cold war, were laying down the building blocks for the foreign policy they would establish in a new era, a post–cold war world.

CHAPTER NINE

In the Midst of Armageddon

AT LEAST ONCE A YEAR during the 1980s, Dick Cheney and Donald Rumsfeld vanished. Cheney was still working diligently on Capitol Hill, and Rumsfeld remained a hard-driving business executive in Chicago. Yet for three or four days at a time, no one in Congress knew where Cheney was, nor could anyone at Rumsfeld's offices locate him. Even their wives were in the dark; they were handed only a mysterious Washington phone number through which they might relay messages in case of emergencies.[1]

After leaving their day jobs, Cheney and Rumsfeld usually made their way to Andrews Air Force Base outside Washington. From there, in the middle of the night, each man, joined by a team of forty to sixty federal officials and a single member of Ronald Reagan's cabinet, separately slipped away to some remote location in the United States, such as a discarded military base or an underground bunker. A convoy of lead-lined trucks carrying sophisticated communications equipment and other gear made its way to the same location.

Rumsfeld and Cheney were principal figures in one of the most highly classified programs of the Reagan administration. Under it, the administration furtively carried out detailed planning exercises to establish a new American "president" and his staff, outside and beyond the specifications of the U.S. Constitution, in order to keep the federal government running during and after a nuclear war with the Soviet Union. Over the years a few details about the existence of this Reagan-era effort have come to light, but not the way it worked or the central roles played by Cheney and Rumsfeld.

This clandestine program of the 1980s served as the hidden backdrop to the operations of the second Bush administration in the hours, days and months after the terrorist attacks on the World Trade Center and the Pentagon on September 11, 2001. When Vice President Cheney urged President Bush to stay out of Washington that day, when Secretary of Defense Donald Rumsfeld ordered his deputy, Paul Wolfowitz, to get out of town and when other federal officials were later sent to work outside the capital to ensure the "continuity of government" in case of further attacks, these actions had their roots in the Reagan administration's classified program. When Cheney himself began to move from Washington to one or another "undisclosed location" after September 11, he never acknowledged that he had also regularly gone off to undisclosed locations in the 1980s.

In the early Reagan years the U.S. government gave more serious consideration to the possibility of a nuclear war with the Soviet Union than at any time since the Cuban missile crisis of 1962. Reagan had spoken in his 1980 campaign about the need for civil defense programs to help the United States survive a nuclear exchange. Once in office, the Reagan administration not only moved to boost civil defense but also approved a new defense policy document that included plans for waging a "protracted" nuclear war against the Soviet Union.[2] The continuity of government exercises in which Cheney and Rumsfeld participated were the hidden component of these more public efforts to prepare for nuclear war.

The underlying premise was that the United States needed to act swiftly to avoid "decapitation," a break in civilian leadership, in case of a nuclear attack on Washington. In fact, one core element of the Reagan administration's new strategy for fighting a nuclear war was an effort to decapitate the Soviet leadership by striking at top political and military officials and their communications lines.[3] The Reagan team wanted to make sure the Soviet Union couldn't do to America what its nuclear strategists were planning to do to the Soviets.

In the Truman and Eisenhower administrations the U.S. government had built large underground installations at Mount Weather in Virginia's Blue Ridge Mountains and near Camp David along the Pennsylvania–Maryland border that could serve as military command posts for an American president in time of war. Yet the construction of these facilities didn't settle the crucial problem of what might happen if an American

president couldn't make it to one of these bunkers in time. What if a nuclear attack killed *both* the president and the vice president? Who would
run the country? What civilian leader could give American military commanders the orders to respond to an attack, and how would that leader
communicate with the military? In a continuing nuclear exchange, who
would have the authority to reach an agreement with the Soviet leadership to bring war to an end?

The Reagan administration's secret continuity of government program was designed to resolve these questions. The concept was simple:
Once the United States was (or believed it was about to be) threatened by
a nuclear attack, three separate teams would be sent out from Washington to three different locations around the United States. Each team had
to be prepared to proclaim a new American "president" and to assume
command of the country. Then, if the Soviet Union was somehow to locate one of the teams and hit it with a nuclear weapon, a second team
could take over, and, if necessary, the third.

This was not some abstract textbook plan but was practiced in concrete, thorough and elaborate detail. The Reagan administration assigned
personnel to three teams, each named for a color, such as red and blue.
Each team included an experienced leader, who could operate as a new
White House chief of staff. The obvious candidates were people who had
already served at a high level in the executive branch, preferably with experience in the national security apparatus. This was where Cheney and
Rumsfeld came in since they had previously served as White House chief
of staff in the Ford administration. Besides Cheney and Rumsfeld, who
were regulars, other team leaders over the years included James Woolsey,
later the director of Central Intelligence, and Kenneth Duberstein, who
worked for a time as Reagan's real-life White House chief of staff.

Each time a team left Washington, it brought along a single member of
Reagan's cabinet, who was designated to serve as the next American "president." Some of these cabinet members had little experience in national security; at various times, for example, the participants in the secret exercises
included Reagan's first secretary of agriculture, John Block, and commerce
secretary Malcolm Baldrige. What counted was not experience in foreign
policy, but simply that the cabinet member was available to fly out of
Washington with the team. It seems fair to conclude that some of these
American "presidents" would have served as mere figureheads for their
more experienced chiefs of staff, such as Cheney or Rumsfeld. Still, the

cabinet members were the ones who would issue orders (or in whose name the orders would be issued).

The problem that this program was extralegal and extraconstitutional—that it established a process for designating a new American president that is nowhere authorized in the U.S. Constitution or federal law—is not merely a criticism manufactured by a law professor or an opponent of the Reagan administration. Rather, this problem was inherent in the Reagan-era program and was indeed part of the very rationale for the exercises.

One of the questions studied in these exercises was what concrete steps the team might take to establish its "credibility." What might be done to demonstrate to the American public, to U.S. allies and to the Soviet leadership that "President John Block" or "President Malcolm Baldrige" was now running the country and that he should be treated as the legitimate leader of the United States? One of the options the teams studied was to have the cabinet secretary order that an American submarine come from the depths to the surface of the ocean since the ability to surface a submarine would be a clear sign that someone like Block or Baldrige, previously thought to be merely the secretary of agriculture or commerce, was now in full control of U.S. military forces. (This standard, control of the military, is one of the same tests the U.S. government uses for deciding whether to deal with a foreign leader after a coup d'état.)

The Constitution and the Twenty-fifth Amendment make the vice president the successor if the president dies or is incapacitated, but they do not establish any order of succession beyond that. Federal law, most recently the Presidential Succession Act of 1947, establishes further details: If the vice president dies or cannot serve, then the Speaker of the House of Representatives becomes president. After him in line of succession are the president pro tempore of the Senate (typically the longest-serving member of the majority party) and the members of the cabinet in the order in which their cabinet posts were first created, starting first with the secretary of state, followed by the secretary of the treasury and then defense.

Reagan's secret program set aside these constitutional and statutory requirements under some circumstances; it established its own process for creating a new American president, ignoring the hierarchy of presidential succession established by law. In general, the idea was to concentrate on speed and continuity of government and to avoid cumbersome procedures.

"One of the awkward questions we faced was whether to reconstitute

Congress after a nuclear attack," explained one participant. "It was decided that no, it would be easier to operate without them." (The participant was referring to discussions among the officials who devised the program; there is no indication that Rumsfeld, Cheney or any other of the team leaders had any role in these deliberations.) In the first place, it was thought that reconstituting Congress would take too long. Moreover, there was another problem: If Congress did reconvene, then it might elect a new Speaker of the House, who would then conceivably have a rival claim to the presidency, one with greater legitimacy than a secretary of agriculture or commerce set up as "president" under Reagan's secret program. The election of a new House Speaker would not only take time but create potential confusion.

The Eisenhower administration had built a mammoth underground installation at the Greenbrier resort in White Sulphur Springs, West Virginia, in order to house members of Congress during and after a nuclear war.[4] Although the Reagan administration did not abandon this congressional facility, it elected to concentrate on plans for a new American presidency in the midst of nuclear crisis in which members of Congress, including even the Speaker of the House and president pro tempore of the Senate, played a greatly diminished role.

Reagan established his continuity of government program under a secret executive order. According to Robert McFarlane, who served for a time as Reagan's national security adviser, the president himself made the final decisions on who would head each of the special teams, such as Cheney and Rumsfeld. Within Reagan's National Security Council, the "action officer" for the secret program was Oliver North, later the central figure in the Iran-contra scandal.[5] Vice President George H. W. Bush was given authority to supervise some of these efforts, which were run by a new government agency with the bland name of the National Program Office. It had its own building in the Washington area, run by a two-star general, and a secret budget adding up to hundreds of millions of dollars per year. Much of this money was used to buy advanced communications equipment that would enable the new teams to have secure conversations with American military commanders. In fact, the few details that came to light about the secret program were the result of allegations of waste and abuses in awarding these communications contracts to private companies and of the malfunctioning of the equipment.[6]

The exercises were usually timed to take place during a congressional recess, so that Cheney, one of the three team leaders, would miss as little work on Capitol Hill as possible. Although Cheney, Rumsfeld and the other team leaders took part in each exercise, the Reagan cabinet members playing the new "president" changed, depending on which cabinet official was free at a particular time. Once Attorney General Ed Meese participated in an exercise that departed from Andrews Air Force Base in the pre-dawn hours of Wednesday, June 18, 1986, which, as it happened, was the morning after Chief Justice Warren Burger resigned. One official remembered looking at Meese and thinking, "First a Supreme Court resignation and now America's in a nuclear war—you're having a bad day."

In addition to the designated White House chief of staff and his "president," each team would include representatives of the State and Defense departments and the Central Intelligence Agency, as well as various domestic policy agencies. The idea was to practice running the entire federal government during a nuclear war. At one point there was talk of bringing in the governors of Virginia and Maryland and the mayor of the District of Columbia, but the idea was discarded because these officials didn't have the necessary security clearances.

The exercises were purposely designed to be stressful since presumably an America on the brink of a nuclear war would not be a tranquil place. The participants gathered in haste, worked and moved in the early-morning hours, lived in army base conditions and dined on the military's dry, mass-produced MRE (meals ready to eat). An entire continuity of government exercise lasted for about two weeks, but in fact, each team took part for only about three or four days. One team would leave Washington, run through its exercises and then hand off to the second team as if, under the scenario, it were on the verge of being "nuked." Then the members of the first team were excused from the exercise and could return home, healthy and radiation-free, while a second team went through its drills for running the country.

The exercises were carried out with elaborate measures of deception, aimed at making sure Soviet reconnaissance satellites could not detect where in the United States the three teams were going. That was why the three teams were sent out in the middle of the night and why they changed facilities from one exercise to another. In addition to the genuine convoys of trucks carrying the communications gear, sometimes decoy convoys were dispatched to different locations in a way that might confuse the Soviet satellites. The underlying logic was that in a nuclear war the Soviet Union might be able to launch missile strikes to hit the permanent bunkers at Mount Weather and near Camp David, but it could not possibly target all the various makeshift locations around the United States where the Reagan teams were operating.

As the capstone to all these other efforts to stay mobile, the program included a special airplane, the National Emergency Airborne Command Post, a Boeing 747 based at Andrews Air Force Base and specially outfitted with a conference room and special communications gear. In it, a president could remain in the air and run the country during a nuclear showdown. In one of the exercises run by the Reagan administration, a team of officials stayed aloft aboard this plane for three straight days, cruising up and down the coasts and across the country and back, with the help of periodic air-to-air refueling.

When George H. W. Bush was elected president in 1988, members of the secret Reagan program rejoiced, because the senior Bush had been closely involved with the effort from the start, wouldn't have to be initiated into the intricacies of the program and probably wouldn't reevaluate it. In fact, despite the dramatically improved climate in relations with Moscow, Bush continued these continuity of government exercises, with some minor modifications. Cheney dropped out as a team leader after he was appointed secretary of defense. And after the fall of the Berlin Wall and the Soviet collapse, the justification and underlying premise for the exercises changed. A Soviet nuclear attack was no longer plausible, but the exercises continued with a different nightmare scenario: What if terrorists carrying nuclear weapons attacked the United States and killed the president and vice president? Finally, during the early Clinton administration, it was decided that this scenario too seemed farfetched, so officials decided to abandon the program as an outdated legacy of the cold war.[7] There was, it seemed, no longer any enemy in the world capable of attacking Washington and "decapitating" America's leadership.

There things stood until September 11, 2001, when the George W. Bush administration was jolted into reexamining the confident assumption of safety that had held sway when the program was phased out. Cheney and Rumsfeld were familiar with the Armageddon exercises of the Reagan era. They themselves had practiced all the old drills.

It must be emphasized that the inspiration for this secret continuity of government program came from within the Reagan administration itself, not from Cheney, Rumsfeld or the other team leaders such as Woolsey or Duberstein who helped carry out the program. None of these team leaders bore the responsibility for the novel idea of setting up an American "president" in a way never envisioned by the Constitution or federal law. In fact, except for Rumsfeld's brief stint as Middle East envoy, neither he nor Cheney ever served in the Reagan administration. Nevertheless, as team leaders Cheney and Rumsfeld played important roles in this project.

Moreover, their participation in these Reagan-era exercises demonstrated a broader underlying truth about Cheney and Rumsfeld: Over three decades, from the Ford administration onward, even when they were out of the executive branch of government, they were never too far away; they stayed in touch with its defense, military and intelligence officials and were regularly called upon by those officials. Cheney and Rumsfeld were, in a sense, a part of the permanent, though hidden, national security apparatus of the United States, inhabitants of a world in which presidents may come and go, but America always keeps on fighting.

Amid these secret preparations for a nuclear war, Reagan waged a public campaign of condemnation and vilification of the Soviet Union, one that went well beyond the language of any of his predecessors. Reagan's most famous denunciation, his "evil empire" speech, was given to the National Association of Evangelicals in Orlando on March 8, 1983. At the time the president was responding to the budding movement at American universities calling for a nuclear freeze. Reagan urged his audience to avoid the temptation "to declare yourselves above it all and label both sides equally at fault, to ignore the facts of history and the aggressive impulses of an evil empire, to simply call the arms race a giant misunderstanding and thereby remove yourself from the struggle between right and wrong, good and evil."[8] Reagan's repeated invocation of the word *evil* served as a model for a later president, George W. Bush.

To many of America's leading experts on the Soviet Union, Reagan's rhetorical flourishes seemed excessive. They took it for granted that the Soviet Union was an unfortunate but permanent fixture of the international scene. Among these cool professionals was a Stanford University professor, a young, ambitious specialist on the Soviet military who, in the middle of the Reagan administration, came to the Pentagon for a year to work for the Joint Chiefs of Staff on technical issues of nuclear strategic planning. Her name was Condoleezza Rice.

Her views about the Soviet Union were not especially distinctive. They were similar to those of countless other Sovietologists at America's leading universities and within the U.S. government. In one book she pointed out that the liabilities for the Soviet Union in trying to maintain control of Eastern Europe were coming to outweigh the benefits and that if the Soviet Union were a business, its leader might decide to cut losses and pull out. However, she went on: "No one would suggest that this is in the cards for the Soviet Union, no matter how expensive Eastern Europe becomes. States, especially great powers, do not behave that way." Those words were published in 1986, only three years before Soviet leader Mikhail Gorbachev let the Berlin Wall come down and ended Soviet domination of Eastern Europe.[9]

If her views didn't stand out, Condoleezza Rice certainly did, by virtue of her background, her personality, her aristocratic bearing and her talent. At elite academic gatherings of Russia scholars or within Washington's arms control bureaucracy, she was usually the only black person, often the only woman and always the only black woman. She was as knowledgeable as other experts and often more articulate. She was cheerful and outgoing, yet also by nature extremely controlled and disciplined. To powerful people, those at the top ranks of America's foreign policy leadership, Rice was refreshingly different, and her potential seemed boundless.

"Somewhere in 1985 I was out at Livermore [National Laboratory, southeast of San Francisco], and then for dinner I went over to Stanford and met with their arms control group," recalled Brent Scowcroft, who had been Kissinger's deputy and President Ford's national security adviser. "There were about fifteen of them. And one of the people there, who looked like an undergraduate, was Condi Rice. And in this group of aficionados of arms control, which is a pretty esoteric subject, she spoke right up. She was thoughtful, she was good, she wasn't intimidated and I thought, This is somebody I really want to get to know."[10]

Rice had been raised in Birmingham, Alabama, the only child of the Reverend John Rice, a guidance counselor, and Angelena Rice, a schoolteacher. They were proud, educated members of the city's black middle class; they started their daughter on piano lessons at age three and also gave her lessons in dance, the flute, violin and French.

Birmingham itself was not so refined as the Rice family. Beneath the famous statue of Vulcan, the city was segregated, and some in the white community were willing to use violence to keep it that way. When a Baptist church was bombed in 1963 at the height of the city's racial turmoil, one of Rice's elementary school friends was among the four children who were killed. When the Civil Rights Act of 1964 was passed, Rice and her parents for the first time walked into and dined at an elegant Birmingham restaurant from which they had previously been excluded.[11]

When Condoleezza was eleven, she moved with her family first to Tuscaloosa, where her father was a college dean, and then two years later to Colorado, where John Rice began working as a University of Denver administrator. Condoleezza entered a private Catholic school, St. Mary's Academy, the first integrated school she ever attended. A guidance counselor tried to tell her she was not college material, but Rice ignored the advice.[12] She entered the University of Denver as a music major, hoping to become a concert pianist. In her sophomore year she decided she wasn't as good as some of the other prodigies and that if she persisted, she might be fated "to teach 13-year-old kids to murder Beethoven."

Rice was looking for another field when she met Professor Josef Korbel, the émigré Czech diplomat who had fled from both Nazism and communism. Korbel, the father of the future secretary of state Madeleine Albright, persuaded Rice to switch to international relations and, in particular, Soviet studies. "I was attracted to the Byzantine nature of Soviet politics, and by power, how it operates, how it's used," Rice later explained.[13]

She graduated at age nineteen, went to Notre Dame for a master's degree and then returned to the University of Denver to obtain her doctorate, writing her dissertation on the Czechoslovak Army and its relationships to the Soviet Union and Czechoslovakia's Soviet-backed civilian leaders. As soon as she finished, she began teaching at Stanford.

At the time Stanford was dominated by proponents of realism, the school of thought holding that the relationships among countries are governed by considerations of power, not morality. Rice adopted many of the beliefs and assumptions of this school and afterward regularly identified herself as a realist. "She believes in realpolitik, that the main driving force of international relations is balance of power politics and that what happens internally inside a country should not be a part of foreign policy," explained Michael McFaul, a fellow Russia scholar on the Stanford faculty.[14]

She had voted for Jimmy Carter for president in 1976, but in 1980 Rice abandoned the Democrats for Reagan after deciding that Carter's policy toward the Soviet Union was too weak. "Condi's always been fairly conservative," observed Coit Blacker, another Stanford colleague who was Rice's oldest and closest friend in academia. "She realized she wasn't a Democrat in response to Carter's handling of Afghanistan. That's when she began identifying as a Republican." Rice's own father had been a Republican, in part as a reaction to the Dixiecrats, the white Democrats who had ruled the South and had gone to great lengths to prevent blacks from voting.[15]

However, Rice was not an ideological conservative. Her espousal of realism distinguished her from a future colleague in government, Paul Wolfowitz, who argued that ideals and values were an important component of international relations. Her views were much closer to those of Henry Kissinger and Scowcroft than to the Reagan wing of the Republican party.

Indeed, at the time Rice was unmoved by the rhetorical denunciations of the Soviet Union in which Reagan specialized. "Like most Americans, I listened with some skepticism to the Cold War claim that America was a 'beacon of democracy,'" Rice later explained. "When American presidents said that, I chalked it up to bad speechwriting and hyperbole. Sometimes I was just plain embarrassed, because America is at best an imperfect democracy. . . . My ancestors were property—a fraction of a man. Women were not included in those immortal constitutional phrases concerning the right of the people 'in the course of human events' to choose who would rule." Yet, Rice acknowledged, when she traveled in Eastern Europe and the Soviet Union in 1989 and 1990, she concluded that the words that once seemed hackneyed to her had been true: that America, despite its imperfections, had served as a beacon of democracy.[16]

Trained by endless recitals, skilled in figure skating, she had a presence that attracted attention. "When I first met her in the early 1980s, she already had all the components that make charisma," said McFaul. "She's got it. It's like what Bill Clinton has when he walks into a room." She also seemed willing and able to take on endless amounts of work. In the mid-

1980s Kiron Skinner, one of Rice's graduate students, was astonished by how many time-consuming responsibilities Rice assumed. All at once, Rice was serving as her department's director of graduate studies, working as assistant director of Stanford's project on arms control, teaching and writing a book, while she was still grieving the recent death of her mother.[17]

To those contemporaries who worked alongside her, even in these early stages of her career, there was little doubt where she was headed. Francis Fukuyama, the political scientist and sometime Republican appointee who met Rice at the beginning of the 1980s, told a colleague, "You know, we're all going to be working for Condi some day."[18] When Rice went to Washington to work in the Pentagon in the Reagan administration, it was only for a year's fellowship sponsored by the Council on Foreign Relations. But everyone knew that year was only a first step.

CHAPTER TEN

A Scandal
and Its Aftermath

By the middle of the Reagan administration, Richard Armitage had managed not only to rise to the senior ranks of the Pentagon, as assistant secretary of defense, but also to make the recalcitrant and impersonal federal bureaucracy bend to his freewheeling style. He tended to hire people he knew personally, longtime associates who would be loyal to him and form part of his team. When he needed an assistant for Japan, he brought back his old friend James Kelly, a former Pentagon colleague whose specialty had been Iran, not Japan. On the road, outside of official meetings, Armitage could be sometimes be found relaxing in Hawaiian shirts, smoking a cigar. When he traveled overseas, as he regularly did, he often stayed not in big hotels or at the American ambassador's residence but at a military base or the home of one of his network of fun-loving friends, many of them military attachés, with whom he could enjoy the local nightlife. He sought to develop ties not only with leaders such as King Hussein of Jordan but also with less savory characters who might nevertheless be of consequence for American military relations. During an era when the United States was seeking close defense and intelligence ties to China, Armitage's staff cultivated some of China's "princelings," the grown children of military leaders, many of whom were arms dealers. The princelings were welcomed to the Pentagon, given grand tours of the United States, taken to bars and nightclubs and accorded what former U.S. Ambassador to China James Lilley later called the wet T-shirt treatment.[1]

On regular workdays in Washington, Armitage arrived at the Pentagon at 5 o'clock in the morning and walked to the cable office to pick up the half-foot-high collection of traffic on what was happening overseas. By 6:00 A.M. he was on the phone, calling friends, sources and military attachés around the world for information, gossip and ideas before he headed to his 7:00 A.M. workout in the Pentagon gym. After 1986, one of his regular overseas phone contacts was Paul Wolfowitz, who had left Washington at the end of the Philippine crisis to become the American ambassador to Indonesia. Another early-morning Armitage call invariably went to Colin Powell, wherever he was. Powell had stayed as Secretary of Defense Caspar Weinberger's top military aide until early 1986 and then managed to return to the field as commander of V Corps, composed of seventy-five thousand American troops in West Germany.[2]

Powell and Armitage didn't realize it at the time, but they soon came to look back upon this mid-1980s period as paradise lost. They were about to confront a prolonged series of investigations that caused them to spend parts of the next six years answering questions from investigators and the FBI, giving depositions and testifying at congressional hearings.

In late 1986 the Iran-contra scandal broke. Although Powell and Armitage were not targets of the investigation and had in fact been among the opponents of the Reagan administration's clandestine courtship of Iran, they had also been among the handful of insiders who were aware of the secret operation. Their names were swept up in the affair, and in a roundabout way, Armitage's career was seriously damaged.

Iran-contra represented an important way station not just for the education of Powell and Armitage personally but more broadly for the emerging foreign policy of the Vulcans' generation. The affair taught some enduring lessons. In America's first brush with international terrorism in the modern era, President Reagan had gone down the road of making secret deals and, in effect, paying ransom. Other countries, such as France, had tried a similar approach. But Iran-contra showed that this didn't work, at least not for the United States.

The broader reality underlying the secret deals was that the United States, still recovering from its defeat in Vietnam, was reluctant to use military force in the third world. The Reagan administration had intervened on a relatively small scale in Grenada and with airpower against Libya, but it was not yet prepared for the large-scale military operations that were launched from 1989 to 1991 in Panama and against Iraq. Later on, as America's confidence in its armed forces became stronger, it turned increasingly to the military for responses to terrorism.

Iran-contra also served as a case study in how *not* to deal with Congress. Several of the principal figures, including national security advisers Robert McFarlane and John Poindexter and their aide, Oliver North, had served in Vietnam.[3] The logic of Iran-contra seemed to be that the White House could overcome the Vietnam-era problem of congressional opposition to foreign policy by simply keeping secret what the executive branch was doing. This proved as disastrous as the idea of negotiating with terrorists. The lesson from Iran-contra was that one could co-opt Congress, intimidate it or win from it a sweeping grant of presidential authority, as President George W. Bush later did in the post-2001 war on terrorism—but that it was politically dangerous, not to mention illegal, to ignore Congress entirely. Even Representative Dick Cheney, who became one of the principal defenders of the Reagan administration's conduct in Iran-contra, concluded afterward, "No policy can be effective for long without the wholehearted support of the Congress and the American people."[4]

As witnesses and bit players in the Iran-contra affair, Powell and Armitage in particular became increasingly mistrustful of large-scale secret operations. In the aftermath they always seemed to worry about how their own actions might be perceived if they were subjected to future investigations like those they faced in the late 1980s.

The Reagan administration's clandestine overtures to Tehran took root in June 1985, when Robert McFarlane, the national security adviser, and his staff drafted a presidential directive for a new Iran policy and sent copies to Secretary of State Shultz and Secretary of Defense Weinberger. The memo proposed an initiative to cultivate moderate elements within Iran's leadership as a means of preventing the Soviet Union from gaining influence there; the memo specifically suggested opening the way for American allies and friends to supply "selected military equipment" to Iran.

Shultz and Weinberger, who rarely agreed upon anything else, both opposed the idea. Among other things, McFarlane's proposed policy would make a mockery of Operation Staunch, the policy under which the United States had repeatedly asked other countries not to provide arms to Iran. (This was the policy that Donald Rumsfeld had promised

Saddam Hussein would be strictly enforced.) When Powell showed Weinberger the NSC's top secret eyes only memo about supplying arms to Iran, the secretary of defense scrawled on it: *"This is almost too absurd to comment on. By all means pass it to Rich [Armitage], but the assumption here is: 1) that Iran is about to fall, and 2) that we can deal with that on a rational basis. It's like asking Qadhafi to Washington for a cozy chat."*[5] However, the Iran initiative won the support of Director of Central Intelligence William Casey and, ultimately, President Reagan, who was eager to win the freedom of seven American hostages seized in Lebanon by pro-Iranian Shiite groups. That summer Reagan approved the first arms deal for Iran, in which the United States allowed Israel to transfer five hundred American-made TOW (tube-launched, optically tracked, wire-guided) antitank missiles to Iran. Their hope was that all the American hostages in Lebanon would be set free; in fact, only one was.

That first transaction set the pattern for what was to follow. The NSC proceeded with a series of arms sales to Iran, at first using Israel as intermediary. Shultz and Weinberger objected to the arms sales and the whole policy. Inside the Defense Department, Weinberger's two aides, Powell and Armitage, were an integral part of this internal opposition. Powell had an aide draft a memo to be sent to the White House emphasizing that under the law Congress must be notified of the ultimate destination of American arms sales. Armitage worked with a State Department official to seek to stop the arms sales.

One part of their motivation was bureaucratic: This was an internal struggle with Reagan's National Security Council over the control of Persian Gulf policy, and Powell and Armitage, as Defense Department aides, were trying to protect their boss. At one point North kept the defense secretary off the distribution list for secret National Security Agency intercepts about Iran; Powell made sure his boss got copies of the secret intelligence. At another point Armitage invited the NSC's North to the Pentagon for a lunch and told him: "I don't think my boss knows anything about this. I doubt that Secretary of State Shultz knows anything about [this]. I think your ass is way out on a limb and you best get all the elephants together to discuss this issue."[6]

Nevertheless, Powell and Armitage also occasionally became involved on the fringes of the Iran operation. When Reagan ordered Weinberger to help arrange the sale of another four thousand TOW missiles to Iran in early 1986, the secretary of defense gave Powell the job of finding these missiles and transferring them to the CIA, a legal transaction that would keep the Defense Department at one remove from dealing directly with Iran.[7]

The Iran initiative suddenly fell apart on November 1, 1986, when a Beirut magazine broke the story of the Reagan administration's secret arms sales. Later that month came the additional disclosure that Poindexter and North had been overcharging Iran for the weaponry and using the extra money to help fund the Nicaraguan contra forces seeking to overthrow the Sandinista regime. In this latter operation, Reagan's NSC was circumventing a law passed by Congress that had prohibited American funding of the contras.

Amid the resulting furor, as Congress and a special prosecutor began investigating these transactions, Weinberger, Powell and Armitage found themselves in the curious position of being interrogated about a policy they had earlier complained was unwise and potentially illegal. Still, even though Iran-contra hadn't been their own policy, they were obliged to disclose to investigators what they knew about it. Armitage assigned one of his top aides, Lincoln Bloomfield, to monitor the congressional hearings and prepare Weinberger's responses. These efforts were not sufficient to keep Weinberger out of trouble. At the end of a six-year investigation Special Prosecutor Lawrence Walsh concluded that Weinberger had lied to investigators to hide his knowledge of the Iran arms sales. He accused Weinberger of concealing his daily diary notes, which would have served as important evidence both of the administration's actions and of the Pentagon team's involvement in arms transfers that were made before Reagan gave them formal legal authorization in January 1986. Weinberger was indicted on charges of obstructing an investigation and perjury. On December 24, 1992, a few weeks after he lost the presidential election and a month before he left the White House, President George H. W. Bush granted Weinberger a full pardon.

The special prosecutor judged Powell relatively favorably. "Most of Powell's early statements regarding the Iran initiative were forthright and consistent," Walsh said in his *Final Report*, which was produced while Powell was the chairman of the Joint Chiefs of Staff. "But some were questionable and seemed generally designed to protect Weinberger." The special prosecutor was more critical of Armitage, who was said to have given false testimony and to have failed to produce documents concerning some of the early arms shipments. Armitage was not charged. Walsh's report concluded: "Independent Counsel could not prove beyond a reasonable doubt that the initial nonproduction and Armitage's false testimony were deliberate."[8]

Iran-contra marked a turning point for Powell and Armitage. Although the two friends' careers ran along separate tracks, in the early Reagan years Armitage was at least arguably the more senior of the pair. Armitage, as an assistant secretary of defense, actually made policy; Powell was primarily a staff aide carrying out decisions made by his superiors.

However, in the aftermath of Iran-contra Powell's career took off while Armitage's stalled. What happened was to some extent a consequence of the different paths the two men had taken in the early 1970s. Powell had remained in the military and thus carried the respect and credibility of a uniformed officer. Armitage had left the regular military and had been associated with the more secretive world of special operations, intelligence and advising foreign military forces, a milieu that was viewed with suspicion in Washington.

When the Iran-contra scandal broke in November 1986, Reagan fired Poindexter as his national security adviser and named Frank Carlucci, the former deputy secretary of defense, to replace him. Carlucci immediately telephoned Powell, his former military aide, and, with Reagan's help, persuaded Powell to return from Germany as the deputy national security adviser.

Powell later claimed he tried to avoid the new Washington job and stay in the Army, telling Carlucci, "Frank, you're gonna ruin my career."[9] The prediction proved spectacularly wrong. In the fall of 1987 Weinberger stepped down as secretary of defense. Carlucci was named to replace him at the Pentagon, and Powell moved up to national security adviser. Over a period of eleven months, then, Powell had risen to the top ranks of the Reagan administration.

For Armitage, the problem was not that he had been a supporter of Iran-contra but that to conspiracy theorists, it seemed as if he *should* have been. He had close ties to the covert side of American foreign policy, both from his Vietnam days and in the Reagan administration. He also seemed to have connections to a few of the people involved in Iran-contra. General Richard Secord, the retired Air Force officer who was a central figure both in getting arms to Iran and in supplying the contras, had worked alongside Armitage in Tehran. Ted Shackley, the retired intelligence operative who had been one of the first Americans contacted by Iranian arms dealers, had served as CIA station chief during the time Armitage was in Vietnam.[10] An organization called the Christic Institute filed a lawsuit weaving an elaborate conspiracy theory in which a "Secret Team" of Americans with military and intelligence connections, including Armitage, was alleged to have carried out operations in Southeast Asia, Iran and Central America. There was no substantiation to justify the claims; eventually a federal judge dismissed the suit as frivolous and ordered the Christic Institute to pay $955,000 in penalties, leaving the organization bankrupt.[11] But for a time the Christic Institute allegations attracted nationwide press coverage.

The damage to Armitage from Iran-contra was not immediate. He kept on working as assistant secretary of defense for the remainder of the Reagan administration, his power undiminished. Yet Armitage also harbored higher ambitions. "He was angling for a big job in the [first] Bush administration," recalled Ropka, his Pentagon assistant.[12] The undercurrents from Iran-contra left him in a weakened position in which either further allegations or a powerful enemy could sidetrack his career. As it turned out, Armitage soon had to confront both.

By all accounts, Powell brought discipline and efficiency to a National Security Council staff that had been chaotic during Reagan's first six years in office, culminating in the Iran-contra scandal. When Powell started there, Fritz Ermarth was serving as the NSC's leading expert on Soviet affairs. One Saturday, Ermarth received alarming news. A Soviet dissident named Lev Albert was conducting a hunger strike to win a visa for emigration to Israel, and Ermarth was told that Albert's condition had become so weak that he was in danger of dying.

It was a quiet weekend. Ermarth figured that if he started trying to arouse the cumbersome Washington bureaucracy to decide what to do about Albert, he might not get an answer for several days. Even then the American response might be tepid. So Ermarth decided upon a different approach. He called the American Embassy in Moscow over an open phone line rather than the customary secure telephone. Then, knowing the KGB was likely to be monitoring the call, Ermarth mused aloud to a senior embassy official that it would be a disaster both for U.S.-Soviet relations and for Soviet leader Mikhail Gorbachev if Albert died. After all, Ermarth went on, Secretary of State Shultz had been emphasizing the importance of human rights issues, and the United States had already raised Albert's case with Soviet officials.

On Monday, Ermarth received the news from Moscow that Soviet officials had decided to grant Albert a visa and that as a result, Albert was ending his hunger strike. Ermarth, pleased at his success, sent a note to Powell, explaining what had transpired. Powell sent a note back. It said, "I'm glad your little stunt worked. But just remember, freelancing [by individual members of the National Security Council] went out with Ollie North."[13]

That episode was emblematic of Powell's tenure in the White House, first as the deputy to Carlucci and then as the national security adviser. Under Powell, paper moved, decisions were made and, for a change, the NSC worked in relative harmony with the State and Defense departments. Powell's NSC ran on time and on schedule. "Everyone knew that [a] meeting would last exactly one hour," Powell later recalled. No one but Powell was permitted to talk for the first five minutes (when he gave his overview of the issues at hand) or the last ten (his summary). No one could introduce items that weren't on the agenda.[14] A few years later, under the Clinton administration, when Powell was obliged to work as chairman of the Joint Chiefs of Staff in an atmosphere of endless unstructured meetings, he became outraged and disgusted.

Along with his passion for order, Powell brought to the Reagan White House his considerable political skills. He formed close alliances, especially with Shultz at State and with Kenneth Duberstein, Reagan's final White House chief of staff. Each morning Reagan was in Washington, the president met at 9:00 A.M. with his White House chief of staff and at 9:30 with his national security adviser. Powell and Duberstein began to meet regularly beforehand to plot out how they would present the issues to Reagan. Sometimes Duberstein would assist Powell by raising a foreign policy issue with the president and laying out the domestic political advantages. Other times Powell would reciprocate by mentioning, for example, how America's allies would welcome a free trade initiative that Duberstein knew the American business community was already supporting.[15]

Powell's actions at the Reagan NSC made it plain that he was not a liberal. He supported Reagan's Strategic Defense Initiative. He favored a continuation of congressional funding for the Nicaraguan contras. Indeed, by his own account, he served as "the chief administration advocate" in Congress for supplying the contras. When the Democrats balked, Powell put his Vietnam memories to the service of winning votes. "I've been where the contras are now, except that it was in Vietnam in 1963," he told them. Out in the jungle he and his troops had waited desperately for the helicopter to come with resupplies every two weeks, depending on it for their lives. "It's no different for the contras today," he said. The analogy may have been open to question, but the strategy worked; Congress decided to keep up the contras' supplies.[16]

Nevertheless, Powell's tenure at the NSC was noteworthy more for his managerial talent than for any new ideas about American foreign policy. Powell did not put himself forward as a visionary or even as the leading voice within the administration. During 1987–88, while Powell was at the NSC, Shultz emerged as clearly the dominant figure on Reagan's foreign policy team, the first time any secretary of state had played that role since Henry Kissinger had left office in 1976. Powell's role was to support Shultz.

Reagan still let Americans know he had not changed his fundamental views about communism or the "evil empire." In June 1987, on a trip to Europe, he delivered one of his most famous speeches, standing before the Berlin Wall and shouting, "Mr. Gorbachev, open this gate! Mr. Gorbachev, tear down this wall!" The drafting of that speech had touched off a struggle within the Reagan administration, in which the State Department argued that the language was too inflammatory and might harm the attempt to develop a relationship with Gorbachev. As Reagan began a trip to Europe, both Shultz and Powell joined the fray, seeking to have the "tear down this wall" passage deleted. But Duberstein, then the deputy White House chief of staff, noticed that the secretary of state didn't feel strongly enough to ask for five minutes of private time with the president. Informed of the internal wrangling, Reagan finally murmured, "I think we'll leave it in," and went ahead with the speech.[17]

Such rhetorical displays were symbolically important, but they did not stop the president from doing business with Moscow. With Shultz taking the lead and with Powell alongside, Reagan during his last two years held three summit meetings with Gorbachev and concluded a major arms control agreement, the Intermediate-Range Nuclear Forces Treaty, which limited the development of intermediate-range missiles. For Reagan, previously the leading opponent of détente, these steps toward easing the tensions of the cold war represented a dramatic reversal of the policies in the early years of his administration. "Ultimately, Reagan's achievements in dealing with the Soviet Union could certainly compare favorably with, and perhaps even surpass, those of Richard Nixon and Henry Kissinger," wrote Anatoly Dobrynin, the veteran Soviet ambassador to Washington.[18]

One result was that Reagan's standing soared in public opinion polls. After Iran-contra, Reagan's approval ratings dropped more than fifteen points, to about 50 percent, and approval of his handling of foreign policy declined to 33 percent. Both figures rose dramatically immediately after Reagan's Washington summit with Gorbachev in December 1987. By the time he left office, Reagan's approval numbers stood at 68 percent, the highest of any president at the end of his term since World War II.[19]

The lessons of the late Reagan years were not lost on Powell. In fact, the 1987–88 period served as an important precedent for Powell's operating style as secretary of state under George W. Bush. As Reagan's national security adviser Powell had come to the conclusion that American presidents never quite conform to ideological stereotype. When the politics are right and the situation overseas changes, a president can reverse his foreign policy dramatically and quickly.

As president George W. Bush was regularly compared to Reagan.[20] On the surface, the reasons are obvious. Both rose to the presidency with the strong support of the right wing of the Republican party; in that sense, both men differed from Bush's father, who had never managed to win over the Republican right. So, too, both Reagan and George W. Bush passed over complexities and reduced issues to simplistic terms: good and evil.

In reflecting upon his work as NSC adviser, Powell was remarkably blunt about Reagan's shortcomings. In their memoirs, both Powell and Shultz admitted their considerable embarrassment when, at the beginning of Reagan's Washington summit with Gorbachev, the Soviet leader gave a detailed presentation on arms control and the American president could offer only a joke about a cabdriver. Still, Powell also admired

Reagan. "The man had been elected president twice by knowing what the American people wanted and, even rarer, by giving it to them," Powell concluded.[21]

If George W. Bush was similar to Reagan, then, from Powell's perspective, it followed that Bush's views might eventually turn around as Reagan's had during the 1987–88 period. As national security adviser Powell had watched a conservative president reverse course, to the point where critics were complaining that he had become far too dovish. It wasn't surprising, then, that during the George W. Bush administration, Powell occasionally behaved as though he were expecting another conservative president to undergo an eventual transformation, in the fashion of Ronald Reagan.

At the end of 1987, as the Reagan administration entered its final year, a historian at Yale University named Paul Kennedy published a weighty treatise titled *The Rise and Fall of the Great Powers.* The book, its surprising popularity and the intellectual debate it engendered had a lasting influence on the Vulcans—not because they concurred with the book's arguments but because they disagreed so strongly.

Kennedy warned that America's power in the world was on the verge of decline. He traced through the history of the previous five centuries, examining how various other nations, such as Spain, the Netherlands, France and Britain, had first acquired the status of great powers and then eventually fallen back. Each of these countries, Kennedy wrote, had fallen victim to the syndrome he called imperial overstretch. Each had taken on more military commitments overseas than the country's economy could sustain. Now it seemed to be America's turn. The United States "like Imperial Spain around 1600 or the British Empire around 1900 is the inheritor of a vast array of strategical commitments which had been made decades earlier, when the nation's political, economic and military capacity to influence world affairs seemed so much more assured," wrote Kennedy.[22]

The Rise and Fall of the Great Powers came out at a time when daily newspaper headlines seemed to give some credence to its thesis. During the Reagan administration both the U.S. budget and trade deficits had risen to unprecedented highs, and the dollar declined to its lowest levels in decades against the Japanese yen and West German mark. On October 19, 1987, American investors were shaken by a stock market earthquake in which the Dow Jones industrial average suddenly fell by 508 points, or 22 percent, a bigger single-day drop than in the crash of 1929.

The American economy was faltering. At the same time the Soviet Union, confronting its own, considerably more dismal economic problems, seemed to be pressing for an end to the cold war. In the face of these two developments, *The Rise and Fall of the Great Powers* raised the question of why the United States was continuing to spend huge sums to maintain bases and troops overseas. While the American economy languished, Japan, which spent vastly less money on its military, instead depending on American troops for its security, was in the midst of a remarkable boom.

Kennedy's book struck a responsive chord with the American public. The book began appearing on best-seller lists soon after it was published and stayed on them throughout the year. Random House, the publisher, issued an initial 9,000 copies at the end of 1987; within a year it had sold more than 225,000.[23] The book became the focus of an entire school of intellectual thought in the United States; its adherents were called the declinists, those who believed that America's power and stature in the world were on the wane.

The popularity of these declinist views represented a direct threat to the interests of the Reagan administration's foreign policy apparatus and above all to the Pentagon. If Americans believed that their economic problems were the result of overly ambitious foreign and military policies, as Kennedy had suggested, then the logical response would be to reduce defense spending and to let other nations, such as Japan, assume more of the costs and responsibility for their own security.

As Kennedy's book took hold, the Reagan administration mounted a public campaign in response to it. In speeches, congressional testimony and interviews, several high-ranking officials brought up the subject of Kennedy's book and sought to rebut his arguments. The most active single participant in this campaign was Armitage, who, as assistant secretary of defense, bore primary responsibility for maintaining America's bases and its defense commitments throughout Asia and the Middle East and who also served as the Reagan administration's point man in maintaining its close alliance with Japan. "Paul Kennedy is wrong about the United States," asserted Armitage at one congressional hearing. Nevertheless, Armitage went on, Kennedy's book was being used "by many who want to roll back our defense commitments around the world."[24]

It is important to note that the debate over Kennedy's book was not fundamentally an ideological one. *The Rise and Fall of the Great Powers* did not argue that America exerted its power overseas in a way that was immoral or that U.S. foreign policy was wrong or harmful. The book merely contended that the United States couldn't afford the foreign policy it was conducting. In theory, at least, that message was compatible with the views of the political right as well as the left. Indeed, while Kennedy's arguments were popular with liberals, some conservatives began to echo his themes too.

The underlying disagreement was over how much power the United States actually possessed in comparison with other nations. Kennedy thought the trends showed that America was on the way down. "The only answer to the question . . . of whether the United States can preserve its existing position is 'no,'" Kennedy wrote. ". . . Even in the military realm, there are signs of a certain redistribution of the balances, away from a bipolar to more of a multipolar system."[25] Officials such as Armitage countered that the United States was much stronger than the declinists believed.

In retrospect, it seems clear that Kennedy's analysis was faulty. He overlooked some of the long-term advantages the American economy enjoyed in comparison with other nations, such as the continuing flow of immigration. He missed the impact of the revolution in computer technology, which was in its early stages when his book came out. He also overemphasized budget deficits that turned out to be reversible. "The deficits stem from the weaknesses not of the American economy but of Reagan economics," wrote Harvard University political scientist Samuel Huntington in a response to Kennedy.[26]

In the fifteen years after *The Rise and Fall of the Great Powers* was published, America's economy revived, and Japan's economy entered a prolonged period of stagnation. In the military sphere, the redistribution of power and the multipolar system Kennedy had predicted failed to materialize; instead, the gulf between American power and that of other nations increased. By the year 2002 the American defense budget of nearly four hundred billion dollars a year was larger than those of the next twenty-five nations combined.[27] Meanwhile, the question of whether the United States could afford such high levels of military spending had virtually vanished from American politics (until, in 2003, the war in Iraq and a new series of budget deficits threatened to raise the issue anew).

This debate over America's decline represented another defining moment in the evolution of the Vulcans' view of the world. The cold war was beginning to subside. Once again, just as after the Vietnam War, the United States was trying to redefine its international role. And once again, the Vulcans were opting for the most expansive, assertive view of American capabilities and American power.

In the mid-1970s, Donald Rumsfeld (joined by others, including Dick Cheney and Paul Wolfowitz) had rejected the Kissingerian argument that American military power was slipping and that, as a result, the United States needed détente with the Soviet Union. So too in the late 1980s Armitage rejected the view that America's economic power was in decline and that the United States should reduce its network of bases and troop deployments overseas. At each key juncture, the Vulcans rejected the idea of decline and went on to fashion a foreign policy that would maximize America's global strength. They were gradually trying to move toward a world in which the United States had no military rival.

The decisions the United States was making during this transition period were not inevitable. There were other choices and other strategies available. America's extensive network of bases and troop deployments had been established to protect against the Soviet Union, yet the Soviet threat was rapidly diminishing. In theory, at least, the United States might have responded by beginning to withdraw from its involvements overseas, as it had after World War I. American officials might have elected to strengthen the United Nations or to establish new multilateral organizations in which the United States would share a greater degree of responsibility with other countries for international security. America might have chosen to divert large sums of money from the defense budget to domestic priorities, such as health care, education and a reduction in poverty. The point here is not to argue that America's leaders should have chosen any one or another of these approaches but merely to note that there were alternatives.

The declinists had misjudged. Apostles of American power such as Armitage, it turned out, had a more accurate sense of just how strong America remained at the end of the 1980s, despite the economic problems of the Reagan era. From the perspective of the Vulcans, Kennedy's book was comparable to the forecasts in the 1780s that Britain would fall into decline because of its loss of the American colonies. Eventually, nearly two hundred years later, those predictions had come to pass—but only after Britain had risen to new heights and had remained, throughout the nineteenth century, the world's dominant power. The Vulcans harbored hopes that America could become even more dominant than Britain.

CHAPTER ELEVEN

A New Republican President, a New Foreign Policy Team

IN 1985 THE YOUNG neoconservative William Kristol moved to Washington as an aide to Secretary of Education William Bennett. Amid the right-wing ferment of the Reagan era, Kristol became part of a network of adherents of the philosopher Leo Strauss working within the federal bureaucracy, waging daily battle against relativism on the home front and tyranny overseas.

One day the following year Kristol was invited to breakfast at Washington's Madison Hotel by someone he barely knew, Donald Rumsfeld. The message was simple: Rumsfeld was planning to run for the 1988 Republican presidential nomination against Vice President George H. W. Bush and was looking for someone who might help run his campaign. Kristol later recalled that Rumsfeld portrayed himself as someone who was "hardheaded, a conservative type. . . . He didn't have a high opinion of Bush, I believe."[1]

Donald Rumsfeld had never discouraged others from thinking he might someday be president of the United States. His résumé and his limitless ambition were his calling cards. Party leaders, among them Rumsfeld's old boss Richard Nixon, made sure Rumsfeld was always on the list of Republican presidential candidates for the future.

Finally, in the mid-1980s, Rumsfeld decided the time seemed right, both politically and personally, to run for president. For eight years, as chief executive at G. D. Searle & Company, Rumsfeld had been spending his long workdays on the future of commercial products such as Nutra-Sweet, Equal and Metamucil; he rejoiced when Pepsi and Coke began using NutraSweet exclusively in their diet colas and again when Searle introduced sugar-free Metamucil in 1984.[2] These were important ventures for Searle, but Rumsfeld was eager to play on a larger public stage. In mid-1985 Searle's stock was acquired by the Monsanto Company, America's fourth-largest chemical firm. Rumsfeld's work with Searle came to an end. He was free to return to politics.

At the time, even though Vice President Bush was Reagan's heir apparent, Bush seemed to be vulnerable to a challenge for the 1988 Republican nomination, both because of uncertainty about his ability as a campaigner and because of his unpopularity with the right wing of the party.[3] Rumsfeld consulted with political leaders, business executives and old friends from the Nixon and Ford administrations, such as Frank Carlucci and George Shultz. Even though Shultz was then serving as secretary of state under Reagan and Bush, he gave Rumsfeld his quiet backing. "I've always been a Rumsfeld supporter," Shultz later explained.[4]

Rumsfeld started his campaign in late 1985. Over the next eighteen months he made the required pilgrimages to New Hampshire and Iowa, gave speeches across the country, talked to political reporters and editorial boards, formed his own political action committee to raise money and began appearing on panels of potential Republican candidates.

He sought to challenge Bush, his old political rival, from the right. "In the 1988 primaries, Rumsfeld could well emerge as a tough-minded conservative alternative to Vice President George Bush," wrote *Chicago Tribune* political reporter Steve Neal. Rumsfeld especially portrayed himself as a hawk on foreign policy. When Soviet officials imprisoned an American correspondent, Nicholas Daniloff, on spying charges, Rumsfeld called a press conference to say it would be a "grave error" and would amount to "ratifying Soviet extortion" to trade for Daniloff's freedom by releasing a Soviet official imprisoned in the United States (as the Reagan administration eventually did). "It would encourage the Soviet Union and other nations to seize U.S. citizens and to hold them hostage in exchange for exacting some concessions," Rumsfeld argued.[5]

From the outset, however, there were difficulties with Rumsfeld's conservative strategy. Although Reagan had managed to unify the right wing of the Republican party, by the late 1980s it was beginning to fragment in such a way that no single conservative challenger to Bush would emerge in 1988. Supporters of supply-side economics were lining up behind Jack Kemp, and so were neoconservatives like Kristol; meanwhile, Pat Robertson of the Christian Coalition was winning the support of social conservatives. Rumsfeld was loosely identified with the old Nixon-Ford wing of the Republican party, not with the newer, more populist Reagan wing, making his effort to emerge as the conservative candidate all the more difficult.

There were other problems as well. Despite Rumsfeld's impressive résumé, he hadn't run for political office since his last congressional campaign in 1968. "His campaign style is about as colorful as a CEO's wardrobe," observed one reporter.[6] Rumsfeld's work at Searle had taken him out of public life for too long; polls showed that not many people recognized his name. As vice president Bush had been in a position to dispense patronage and to acquire debts that could be called in at the time of a presidential campaign. Rumsfeld found that he was unable to raise as much money as he wanted.

On April 1, 1987, nearly a year before the first primaries, Rumsfeld suddenly withdrew. "I don't see any way to get there from here," he wrote in a memo to his contributors and supporters. Both publicly and in private conversations with his powerful friends, Rumsfeld blamed the ardors of fund-raising. "Why'd you stop?" Shultz asked him. "Because I concluded that I could either raise money or run for president. I couldn't do both," Rumsfeld answered.[7] "He told me the fund-raising was more than he could tolerate," recalled Carlucci, who was serving as national security adviser at the time.[8]

Yet Rumsfeld's inability to raise money was perhaps as much a reflection of his failed candidacy as its cause. He had failed to develop a strong constituency or base within the Republican party. He had been unable to seize upon any compelling issue that would set him apart from other candidates. The Rumsfeld campaign had been mostly a curiosity. By early 1987 his attempt to challenge Bush, a sitting vice president, enjoyed the quiet backing of both the secretary of state (Shultz) and the national security adviser (Carlucci), yet not nearly enough local party chairmen in New Hampshire. If Republican presidential nominees had been selected by the National Security Council, Rumsfeld might well have won.

After finally abandoning his campaign, Rumsfeld was asked what he would do next. He didn't know. "It's like turning a battleship around," he told one reporter. "You can't spend a year-and-a-half going in one direction and then spin on a dime."[9] To those who had ever worked for or engaged in bureaucratic combat with the strong-willed Rumsfeld, the "battleship" metaphor was a rare moment of self-revelation.

George Bush outlasted all his challengers for the Republican nomination and then defeated Democratic nominee Michael Dukakis in the fall election. The only semblance of a foreign policy issue was a symbolic one. After Dukakis put on a jumpsuit and a helmet several sizes too large to ride around in an M1A1 tank, the Bush campaign turned the event into its own campaign ad, warning that Dukakis wanted to be commander in chief and that "America can't take that risk." The Bush strategy seemed to work. Despite the easing of the cold war in the late Reagan administration, American voters, it seemed, still wanted a president who was comfortable with military power.

For foreign policy, the most significant change in 1988 was not the election but the transition from the Reagan administration to the first Bush administration. Ordinarily, when a sitting vice president rises to the presidency, the emphasis is on harmony and continuity, but at the start of the new Bush administration the change seemed more like a hostile takeover. Quite a few of Reagan's conservative followers were summarily ousted.

Suddenly, Kissinger and his philosophy of realism were back in vogue. Bush selected Brent Scowcroft, Kissinger's longtime deputy, to serve as his national security adviser, the same job Scowcroft had held during the last year of the Ford administration. Eleven days before the inauguration, when Bush held a long strategy session with his new team on how to deal with the Soviet Union, the participants included Scowcroft, the incoming secretary of state, James A. Baker III, the new White House chief of staff, John Sununu, and a single outsider, Henry Kissinger. At this session Kissinger urged the new administration to set up an informal channel with Soviet leader Mikhail Gorbachev and modestly suggested himself as the possible intermediary. The Bush team wasn't willing to give Kissinger quite so central a role.[10]

This Reagan-Bush transition has often been characterized as a change from hawks to doves, from conservatives to moderates. Yet the reality was far more complex. First, contrary to these images, in 1988 and 1989 the officials of the outgoing Reagan administration were the doves, and the new Bush team the hawks. In Reagan's final two years he had moved so rapidly to ease tensions with Moscow that skeptics claimed his administration was putting too much hope on the notion that the Soviet Union was changing. The incoming Bush administration reflected this attitude of wariness; the realists emphasized that despite the arrival of Gorbachev,

the cold war was not yet over. Scowcroft appointed as deputy national security adviser Robert M. Gates, the Soviet specialist and senior CIA official who in Reagan's final years had aroused Shultz's ire by arguing
forcefully that the Soviet Union remained a determined adversary of the
United States.

Second, every administration, Republican or Democratic, reaches
across ideological lines to embrace individuals with personal ties to one
another. When Scowcroft and Bush's secretary of state, James A. Baker III,
put together the new foreign policy team, old friendships counted at least
as much as whether an individual was conservative or centrist. Bush's first
choice for secretary of defense had been John Tower, but when the Senate
rejected Tower's nomination in March 1989 amid a series of allegations of
personal misconduct, the Bush team, in need of a quick replacement, immediately turned to a familiar face, Representative Dick Cheney.

On Capitol Hill, Cheney had been rising steadily in the House leadership throughout the 1980s. He had served on the Intelligence Committee, a post that perfectly suited both his interests in the details of
policy and his knack, indeed his reverence for preserving secrets. He had
also taken the leading role for the House Republicans in limiting the
scope of Congress's response to the Iran-contra affair. In 1988, when
Congress began moving toward a bill that would have required the White
House to notify Congress of any covert operation within forty-eight
hours of its start, Cheney argued vigorously against limiting the authority of the president. "On the scale of risks, there is more reason to be concerned about depriving the president of his ability to act than about
Congress's alleged inability to respond," he wrote in an op-ed piece. The
law didn't pass.[11]

After the 1988 election, in which Representative Trent Lott had won
election to the Senate, Cheney had become the House Republican whip, the
second-ranking Republican. He was also the heir apparent to succeed House
Minority Leader Robert Michel. Yet at the time there seemed to be no
prospect the Republicans would ever break the Democrats' three-decades-
old control of the House. By moving to the Bush administration, Cheney
cleared the way for Newt Gingrich to move up in the ranks of the House Republican leadership Cheney had abandoned.

Scowcroft played the leading role in recruiting Cheney. During the
Ford administration the two men had worked closely together. Cheney
had been promoted from Rumsfeld's deputy to White House chief of

staff when Rumsfeld became defense secretary, and Scowcroft had been elevated from Kissinger's deputy to national security adviser in the same shake-up. Inside the Ford White House, Scowcroft and Cheney were the low-keyed staff members who had tried to keep things running and to smooth over the frictions between their two less self-effacing mentors, Kissinger and Rumsfeld. Cheney had also collaborated in those years with Baker, who had been working on Ford's reelection campaign.

"We needed a secretary of defense very badly. This was already March [1989], and we just couldn't make policy with a big gap there," recalled Scowcroft in an interview. "So we needed somebody fast. That meant it had to be somebody from the Congress because otherwise, we'd go through long hearings. And then I automatically went to Cheney."[12] Even many years later, during the George W. Bush administration, as Cheney was beginning to press for a war against Iraq that Scowcroft opposed, Scowcroft still refused to think of Cheney as having a different outlook on foreign policy from his own. "He's not ideological, in my mind," Scowcroft said of Cheney. ". . . He's been very conservative, but I never had any trouble with him. I think the problem [within the George W. Bush administration] is at the second echelons."[13] After decades, through his nonconfrontational style, Cheney still managed to persuade establishment insiders like Scowcroft that he was a member of their team, despite his profoundly conservative views.

Tower had selected Paul Wolfowitz to be the undersecretary of defense for policy, the senior policy-making position in the Pentagon. After serving as U.S. ambassador to Indonesia in the late Reagan years, Wolfowitz had been unsure he wanted to return to the life of a Washington bureaucrat. "He hesitated a long time. He couldn't make up his mind. He talked about going back to academia," said Fred Iklé, his old boss from the Nixon administration.[14] Wolfowitz's friends finally persuaded him to take the post. It would mean that Wolfowitz, after six years specializing on Asia, would once again have responsibility for arms control, the Middle East and the Persian Gulf, the areas to which he had devoted the early years of his career.

Cheney, who had the power to select his own team of Pentagon aides, stuck with Tower's choice of Wolfowitz. Cheney's decision wasn't made immediately; aides recall that for a brief time he was wavering, and Wolfowitz had to get a high-level recommendation from Senator Richard Lugar, with whom Wolfowitz had worked closely during Ferdinand Marcos's

Don Rumsfeld as captain of the Princeton University wrestling team in 1954. The Princeton yearbook called him a "speedy take-down specialist." *(Princeton University Library)*

The young soldier Colin Powell relaxing in a hammock in Vietnam. *(From the papers of General Colin L. Powell, USA [Ret.], National Defense University Library)*

Colin Powell as an Army officer in Vietnam. He was injured in a helicopter crash during his second tour there. *(From the papers of General Colin L. Powell, USA [Ret.], National Defense University Library)*

Richard L. Armitage's 1967 yearbook photo at the U.S. Naval Academy. The text said: "Never one to hold a book open for more than an hour, Rach always managed to stay in front of academics. Due to an outstanding personality, Rach is known throughout the Brigade." *(Courtesy of the U.S. Naval Academy Alumni Association, Class of 1967, Lucky Bag)*

Richard Armitage as an ambush team adviser on the banks of the Co Chien River, Vinh Binh Province, South Vietnam, April 1969. *(Courtesy of Richard Armitage)*

President Nixon and Donald Rumsfeld in the Rose Garden, February 13, 1973. *(Nixon Presidential Materials Collection, National Archives)*

To Lieutenant Colonel Colin Powell
With appreciation and best wishes,

President Nixon greets Lieutenant Colonel Colin Powell, a member of the White House fellows program. Powell worked in the Office of Management and Budget under Caspar Weinberger and Frank Carlucci, who later became Ronald Reagan's two secretaries of defense. *(From the papers of General Colin L. Powell, USA [Ret.], National Defense University Library)*

Condoleezza Rice as a young college student at the University of Denver. She entered as a music major but switched to international relations after deciding that she might be obliged "to teach thirteen-year-old kids to murder Beethoven." *(University of Denver Special Collections & Archives)*

President Ford meets with Chief of Staff Donald Rumsfeld (left) and Deputy Chief of Staff Dick Cheney (right) in the Oval Office on April 28, 1975. *(Courtesy of the Gerald R. Ford Library)*

Secretary of Defense Donald Rumsfeld at Edwards Air Force Base in April 1976, after personally flying a B-1 bomber. *(© Bettmann/CORBIS)*

Assistant Secretary of State for East Asia and Pacific Paul Wolfowitz meeting with Cambodian refugees at the Thai border, spring 1983. Wolfowitz later said East Asia felt like "sunlight and fresh air" after his many years of dealing with the Middle East. *(Courtesy of Paul Wolfowitz)*

Condoleezza Rice, professor of political science at Stanford, with a map of
the Soviet Union in 1983. She had originally supported President Jimmy
Carter, but switched to the Republicans after deciding that he was too weak
in dealing with the Soviets. *(Chuck Painter/Stanford News Service)*

Colin Powell and his wife, Alma, with President and Mrs. Clinton as he retires as commander of the Joint Chiefs of Staff. *(From the papers of General Colin L. Powell, USA [Ret.], National Defense University Library)*

On September 2, 2000, Republican presidential nominee George W. Bush meets with his two top campaign advisers for foreign policy, Condoleezza Rice and Paul Wolfowitz, at Bush's ranch near Crawford, Texas, before the start of an intelligence briefing from the CIA. *(AP Photo/David J. Phillip)*

Condoleezza Rice, professor of political science at Stanford, with a map of the Soviet Union in 1983. She had originally supported President Jimmy Carter, but switched to the Republicans after deciding that he was too weak in dealing with the Soviets. *(Chuck Painter/Stanford News Service)*

Assistant Secretary of State for East Asia and Pacific Paul Wolfowitz (left) with Secretary of State George Shultz at the demilitarized zone (DMZ) between North and South Korea, 1983. Shultz became one of Wolfowitz's most important mentors and patrons. *(Courtesy of Paul Wolfowitz)*

Donald Rumsfeld, President Reagan's special envoy for the Middle East, meets with Iraq's President Saddam Hussein in December 1983. *(Photo by Getty Images)*

Pentagon colleagues Richard Armitage (left) and Richard Perle, both assistant secretaries of defense, at a March 25, 1986, dinner in honor of General Colin Powell. *(From the papers of General Colin L. Powell, USA [Ret.], National Defense University Library)*

Representative Lee Hamilton (left), D-Ind., chairman of the House select committee probing the Iran-contra affair, confers with Representative Dick Cheney, R-Wyo., vice chairman of the committee, as public hearings into the affair begin, May 5, 1987. *(© Bettmann/CORBIS)*

National Security Adviser Colin Powell meets with President Reagan at Reagan's ranch in Santa Barbara, California, November 1987. *(Courtesy of the Ronald Reagan Library)*

Secretary of Defense Dick Cheney looks on as President Bush announces the appointment of Colin Powell as chairman of the Joint Chiefs of Staff, August 10, 1989. Cheney had selected Powell over several more senior four-star generals. *(Courtesy of the George H. W. Bush Presidential Library)*

Colin Powell, chairman of the Joint Chiefs of Staff, briefing the press on Operation Desert Storm. *(From the papers of General Colin L. Powell, USA [Ret.], National Defense University Library)*

General Colin Powell (left) with Undersecretary of Defense for Policy Paul Wolfowitz (right) and CENTCOM commander in chief General Norman Schwarzkopf during Operation Desert Storm, 1991. *(© CORBIS)*

Secretary of Defense Dick Cheney and General Colin Powell, chairman of the Joint Chiefs of Staff, visit an Air Force base in Saudi Arabia on February 12, 1991. *(David Hume Kennerly/Getty Images)*

Undersecretary of Defense for Policy Paul Wolfowitz talks with President-elect Boris Yeltsin of the Soviet Republic of Russia, June 20, 1991, at the Pentagon. Standing next to Wolfowitz is his deputy, I. Lewis ("Scooter") Libby. *(Courtesy of Paul Wolfowitz)*

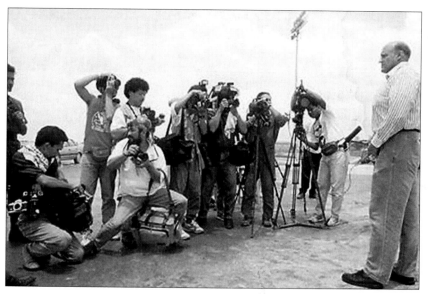

Richard Armitage, who led the U.S. team in negotiations to maintain America's military bases in the Philippines, talks to reporters at Clark Air Base after it has been severely damaged by the volcanic eruption of Mount Pinatubo. In the end the United States withdrew from both Clark and the Subic Bay Naval Station, its two largest military installations in Southeast Asia. *(DOD photograph, TSGT. Val Gempis, Clark Air Base, Philippines, 1991)*

Colin Powell and his wife, Alma, with President and Mrs. Clinton as he retires as commander of the Joint Chiefs of Staff. *(From the papers of General Colin L. Powell, USA [Ret.], National Defense University Library)*

On September 2, 2000, Republican presidential nominee George W. Bush meets with his two top campaign advisers for foreign policy, Condoleezza Rice and Paul Wolfowitz, at Bush's ranch near Crawford, Texas, before the start of an intelligence briefing from the CIA. *(AP Photo/David J. Phillip)*

Secretary of Defense Donald Rumsfeld (left), Deputy Secretary of Defense Paul Wolfowitz (center), and Vice President Richard B. Cheney (right) at Wolfowitz's swearing-in ceremony, March 2001. Inscription, by Cheney, reads: "Paul—Who is the best Secretary of Defense you ever worked for? Dick." *(Courtesy of the Department of Defense)*

Condoleezza Rice playing the piano to accompany cellist Yo-Yo Ma before an audience that included President George W. Bush, April 22, 2002.
(Reuters News Media Inc./CORBIS)

final days in the Philippines. Cheney talked at length to Wolfowitz, found that their ideas were compatible and proceeded with his nomination. It proved to be a lasting partnership. Between the two of them, Cheney and Wolfowitz often provided a hawkish counterweight to the more dovish impulses of Bush, Baker and Scowcroft. With Cheney and Wolfowitz at the Pentagon, it was difficult to argue that the transition from the Reagan administration to the first Bush administration represented a simple, one-directional change from a conservative foreign policy to a moderate one.

Bush was sworn in on a Friday. On the following Monday the Bush White House had its first internal crisis. An unmarked gray van pulled up to the northwest gate of the White House. The driver said he had a large package for the new president, one that had been received from the Soviet airline Aeroflot. The box had no note or card. Nervous Secret Service officials mobilized their bomb squad and hurriedly took the package to its offices in an impoverished section of Washington. When they finally opened the box, they found that it contained a five-hundred-pound cake.[15]

Where had the cake come from? The Soviet Embassy said it had no idea. Scowcroft and Gates assigned this bit of detective work to their new Russian-speaking National Security Council staff aide for Soviet affairs, Condoleezza Rice. She finally discovered that the cake had been sent by a bakers' collective in a small town inside the Soviet Union. After a few weeks in which rats in the Secret Service office nibbled away at the gift, Bush sent a thank-you note to the collective, along with a Bush family picture.

From the very start of the first Bush administration, at the age of thirty-four, Condoleezza Rice was an inside player. When it came to Bush presidencies, she was, in a sense, present at the creation. Scowcroft had kept in touch with her ever since first meeting her at Stanford three years earlier, making sure she was brought into elite groups, such as the Aspen Strategy Group, that serve as training grounds for future leaders. In assembling his National Security Council staff, he had quickly recruited Rice from the Stanford faculty—none too soon, because Dennis Ross, the new head of the State Department's policy planning team, was also trying to hire her.[16]

In the first weeks after the inauguration it was Rice who wrote for Scowcroft the memo that laid out the key elements of a cautious new Bush policy toward the Soviet Union. The emphasis was on shoring up relations with NATO allies, concentrating on arms control and trying to cultivate ties with Eastern Europe before seeking any broader accommodation with Gorbachev. Having studied under the Czech émigré Josef Korbel and written her dissertation on Czechoslovakia, Rice took a particular interest in the Warsaw Pact nations. When the Bush team began holding sessions to plan for various contingencies, Gates ran the meetings on the Soviet Union, but Rice chaired the sessions on Eastern Europe.[17] The NSC work not only was exciting but gave Rice a chance to demonstrate talents that were of lesser utility in the abstract academic world of international relations: She was down-to-earth, politically skilled and engaging, but also firm and decisive. Watching Rice's transition to government work, her Stanford friend Coit Blacker observed, "She took to it like a duck to water."[18]

She also seemed to develop, more than other White House staff members, a strong personal identification with the Bush administration and family. The month after Bush was inaugurated, Rice visited Kennebunkport, the Bush family compound in Maine, as part of a group of Soviet specialists assigned to brief the new president; she was to return there many times.[19] As an African-American woman in the overwhelmingly white male worlds of Soviet affairs and arms control, Rice had usually stood apart, a tough, independent subculture of one. "She did not come to Washington with a team," observed Stanford political scientist Michael McFaul. "She was not one of the boys, or one of the girls, or one of the academics, or one of the military guys, or one of the Brookings [think tank] crowd or one of the Rhodes scholars."[20] She was, however, a charter member of the Bush team.

Rice was not the only incoming Bush official trying to draft a new Soviet policy in the spring of 1989. At the Pentagon, Wolfowitz carried out a review of U.S. defense policy toward the Soviet Union, with the help of two of his former aides from the State Department, Scooter Libby and James Roche. This Pentagon study also concluded that the United States should proceed cautiously in dealing with Gorbachev because it was too soon to know the extent to which the Soviet Union was really changing.[21]

Still, Wolfowitz clearly was eager to shift the Pentagon away from too close a focus on the Soviet Union. In the fall of 1989 he ordered a review of American policy toward the Persian Gulf, with an emphasis on how to defend the oil fields of Saudi Arabia. It was a follow-up to the study he had carried out inside the Pentagon in the late 1970s. This time, however, the starting premise was not on how to defend the Persian Gulf against an invasion by the Soviet Union. Rather, the focus of the study was how to protect the oil fields from seizure by some nation inside the Persian Gulf itself—such as, perhaps, Iraq.

Among the Republicans who garnered high-level foreign policy jobs at the start of the new administration, one person was notably missing. Richard Armitage did not land a position. That failure was attributable in large part to the intense, determined opposition of a single powerful businessman, Ross Perot, who had been conducting an extraordinary personal campaign against Armitage for three years before 1989 and continued this effort for several years afterward.

Perot's vendetta against Armitage grew out of the issue of American prisoners of war in Vietnam. Since the end of the war Perot had been convinced that large numbers of Americans classified as missing in action had survived the conflict and were still alive in Southeast Asia. He also believed that the U.S. government was covering up the supposed existence of these POWs and was failing to do what it could to bring them home.[22]

By 1986 Perot was seeking to lead what he hoped would be a new Reagan administration initiative on the POWs. There was talk in Congress of creating a new Vietnam commission, with Perot as its chairman. Perot began talking to the Vietnamese government on his own and in early 1987 paid a visit to Hanoi. He returned to Washington with proposals for improving America's economic relations with Vietnam as part of an implicit deal that would lead to cooperation from Hanoi on prisoners of war. The Reagan administration had been insisting that before the United States eased its economic sanctions against Vietnam, Hanoi should first withdraw Vietnamese troops from Cambodia. Reagan's aides on the National Security Council were outraged at Perot's initiative; they believed he was being used by the Vietnamese government to undermine the administration's negotiating position. Moreover, amid the growing Iran-contra scandal, they also thought that Perot's proposal sounded suspiciously like a request for them to pay ransom for hostages once again (and this time for hostages whose existence was merely rumored).[23]

"I felt the Vietnamese were playing him like a kids' player piano," recalled James Kelly, then one of Reagan's NSC staff aides. Kelly had been prepared to resign from the administration if the president had gone along with Perot's proposal. The feud between the administration and Perot was particularly delicate because at the time Perot had pledged two and a half million dollars to the new Reagan presidential library. In the end, following a showdown meeting with Perot, Reagan backed his own aides and turned aside Perot's attempts to serve as America's intermediary with Vietnam. Furious at the administration's rebuff, Perot reneged on two million dollars of his pledge to the Reagan library.[24]

As these disputes were being waged over Vietnam policy, Perot began increasingly to focus upon Armitage as a target. Exactly why he did so remains unclear. As assistant secretary of defense and the Pentagon's top Asia official Armitage was generally responsible for Vietnam, and he had helped expose as fraudulent some of the sensational claims about live POWs in Vietnam.[25] However, there had been no specific confrontation between Perot and Armitage over Vietnam; indeed, at the time Perot began to attack Armitage, the two men had never met.

One factor may well have been that amid the swirl of amorphous, unprovable rumors concerning the POWs, Perot thought that Armitage was one individual about whom he had uncovered something definite. A local detective investigating Asian organized crime in the Virginia suburbs of Washington handed Perot a file that showed Armitage had written a letter on Pentagon letterhead to a local judge on behalf of a Vietnamese woman who was awaiting sentencing. The woman had pleaded guilty to conducting an illegal gambling operation that police said took in over fifty thousand dollars a day in bets on football pools. The policeman's file included a picture of Armitage posing with the woman, Nguyet Thi O'Rourke, whom he had first met in South Vietnam during the war.[26] Armitage admitted he should not have used the Pentagon stationery. From the starting point of this police file, Perot went on to develop a series of dark conspiracy theories involving Armitage, corruption, organized crime, drug trafficking and Vietnam. For these other speculations, he had neither pictures nor other evidence.[27]

Perot made the rounds of the Pentagon, looking for damaging information about Armitage. "He invited me to lunch and asked me what I knew about Armitage, about his personal life, why he was in Bangkok for a long time while his wife and kids were at home," recalled an Asia specialist who was serving as a Defense Department official at the time.[28] One day, discovering that Perot was inside the Pentagon yet again, Ar-

mitage introduced himself and asked, "What's your problem with me?"
When Perot said he thought Armitage had been compromised by his relationship with O'Rourke, Armitage answered, "I've been married for a
number of years. What I've done in good and bad is a matter of record
with my wife, and unfortunately that's my business and her business, and
certainly not your business."[29] Perot disagreed. He tried to get Armitage
fired, bringing his series of charges and speculations both to Carlucci and
to Vice President Bush. The campaign failed; Armitage kept his job.

After Bush won the 1988 election, Cheney asked Armitage to stay on
in the Pentagon as secretary of the Army. Once again Perot revived his
anti-Armitage crusade, offering his allegations about Armitage both to
the FBI, which was conducting the background checks for Armitage's
nomination, and to Congress. This time Perot was more successful. The
FBI compiled a report of several hundred pages, but found no evidence
that Armitage had been involved in drug running, organized crime, covering up the existence of POWs or any other of the broad allegations
about him beyond a relationship with O'Rourke. Perot found a more
receptive audience on Capitol Hill, not only among his allies on the
POW issues but also in the office of Senator Jesse Helms, who had been
unhappy with Armitage in the Reagan years because of Armitage's advocacy of a close American partnership with Japan. In order to win approval
for Armitage as secretary of the Army, it appeared, the Bush administration was going to have to go through another difficult nomination battle,
only two months after it had failed to win Senate approval for Tower.

In May 1989, with his nomination vote approaching, Armitage went
to see Cheney. By Armitage's account, he asked the new defense secretary,
"Are we going to win this thing? Are you ready for battle?" To Armitage's
surprise, he got a cool, noncommittal answer. "I don't know," Cheney
replied.

"It was the strangest thing I had ever heard," Armitage reflected many
years later. "Where I came from, with [Defense Secretary Caspar] Weinberger and Powell, if you're on the team, you're on the team. I just needed
him to say, 'Sure, we'll do whatever it takes to win it.' But he just said, 'I
don't know.' I realized then that Dick Cheney is a little different. I wasn't
his political equity. And he was going to be damned if he was going to
start off his career at Defense with what could have been a burdensome,
noisy debate."[30]

The strained conversation made plain the chasm in style between the two men. Armitage's approach was intensely personalized. He often treated even government work in Washington as an outgrowth of small-unit combat: You kept watch over your close friends, they kept watch over you and together you went out into the night. By contrast, Cheney was remote, impersonal and deliberate: You added up the costs and the benefits and made your calculations.

Stung by Cheney's seeming lack of enthusiasm, Armitage withdrew from the nomination. For the remainder of the Bush administration, Armitage served in special foreign policy assignments (such as heading the negotiations over the future of American bases in the Philippines) that required no Senate confirmation. Privately he told friends in Washington he blamed Cheney for not fighting hard enough for his nomination. One friend later acknowledged that some of Armitage's grumbling probably made its way back to Cheney. The two men remained on cordial terms, dealing with each other without rancor, but at a distance.[31]

Colin Powell fared much better with Cheney. After serving as Reagan's national security adviser, in early 1989 Powell had returned to military life as commander of the U.S. Forces Command, the organization in Atlanta that was responsible for the nearly one million Army troops, including reserves and National Guard, based inside the United States. The job meant that Powell became a four-star general.

He held the post for little more than six months. In the early summer Admiral William Crowe announced he intended to retire rather than seek reappointment as chairman of the Joint Chiefs of Staff when his term expired in September. Cheney soon decided Powell was his candidate to become the next chairman. The two men had met casually when Cheney was a member of Congress and Powell was a commander in Germany, they had done business with each other when Powell was national security adviser and Cheney a House Republican leader and they had talked again briefly when Cheney became defense secretary and Powell was head of the U.S. Forces Command.[32]

The president had some reservations about Cheney's choice. Bush liked Powell, but wondered whether it might cause problems with the military if he bypassed all the older candidates for the chairmanship. At the age of fifty-two Powell was the youngest of the fifteen four-star generals eligible to succeed Crowe. "He [Powell] was young enough to serve as chairman later," Bush wrote in his memoirs. However, he said, "Cheney was adamant—and persuasive." Powell got the job.[33]

Press stories about Powell's appointment concentrated on the fact that he was the first black chairman and that he was relatively young. The coverage tended to overlook two other factors that were equally significant. Powell was the first chairman of the Joint Chiefs who had already served in a cabinet-level post. As national security adviser he had gained broader experience in American foreign policy than most commanders of the Joint Chiefs are able to obtain. Even before starting his new job, Powell had spent more time in National Security Council meetings than Cheney and arguably more than Secretary of State Baker (who had served as Reagan's treasury secretary).

Even more important, Powell was becoming the first chairman of the Joint Chiefs to serve a full term with the powers granted by the Goldwater-Nichols Act of 1986. That legislation gave the chairman of the Joint Chiefs vastly greater power within the military than he had previously enjoyed. When the job was first created after World War II, the chairman was empowered only to give the president and the secretary of defense a consensus view from among the chiefs of the Army, Navy, Air Force and Marines. The 1986 legislation for the first time freed the chairman from the need to find a consensus among the service chiefs and instead gave the chairman the authority to speak, individually and on his own, on behalf of the entire military. It also gave the chairman sole authority over more than fifteen hundred personnel working for the Joint Chiefs of Staff, who previously had worked not for the chairman but for all five service chiefs collectively.

Powell thus took office as chairman of the Joint Chiefs in a far stronger position, both inside the armed forces and with civilian leaders, than any of his predecessors. Cheney knew it. He was careful and, indeed, somewhat testy about his relations with the military. When Cheney first took charge at the Pentagon, he had publicly reprimanded an Air Force chief of staff who had been negotiating in Congress without Cheney's approval. But the defense secretary showed considerable deference to Powell. Every afternoon that both men were in Washington, they held a five o'clock meeting in Cheney's office. Cheney's aides discovered that no matter whom else the defense secretary was seeing and no matter what other issues were pending, at a couple of minutes before five he would say, "Let's wrap this up. I don't want to keep the chairman waiting." Dave

Gribben, Cheney's old friend and longtime aide, thought to himself, "Powell works for Cheney, not vice versa." But he and other aides realized that this was Cheney's way of trying to demonstrate respect for the military. (In 1993, Cheney's successor Les Aspin sometimes failed to watch the clock and kept Powell waiting, a not inconsequential oversight.)[34]

Cheney and Powell had no more idea than anyone else in Washington of the unprecedented challenges the two of them were soon to confront. On November 10, 1989, after weeks of unrest, East Germans tore down the Berlin Wall. Over the following six weeks, with the acquiescence of Gorbachev and the Soviet leadership, democratic revolutions spread across Eastern Europe.

This time even the most skeptical in Washington did not contest the evidence that the Soviet Union was changing. Now Cheney and Powell faced the task of trying to decide what to do about the defense budget and the troops that had been stationed overseas to defend against the Soviet Union. Together they would have to define America's role in the new era, to work out how much military power the Pentagon should maintain and how and when that power should be exercised.

CHAPTER TWELVE

Use of Force

IN THE MEMOIR of the George H. W. Bush administration by the former president and his national security adviser Brent Scowcroft, Panama does not rate a chapter or a subchapter, only a passing mention. In a sense, that oversight is understandable. A history of those four years couldn't cover everything, and Bush and Scowcroft were far more preoccupied with their policies toward the Soviet Union, Europe and the Persian Gulf. Moreover, against the backdrop of American history, the overthrow and capture of Panamanian dictator Manuel Noriega in December 1989 were not even especially unusual. The United States has been conducting military operations and overthrowing governments in the Western Hemisphere since the nineteenth century, long before it sent American forces to fight land wars in Europe, Asia and the Middle East.

Nevertheless, for the Pentagon the Bush administration's intervention in Panama was of profound importance. It was by far the largest American military operation since the end of the Vietnam War. In all, more than twenty thousand U.S. troops went into battle against the Panamanian Defense Forces, an American force far larger than had been used in Grenada or any other operation of the 1980s. The Pentagon began to employ some of its newly developed high-tech weaponry, notably the F-117A stealth fighter. Less than two months after the fall of the Berlin Wall and the revolutions in Eastern Europe, the United States was putting its new military prowess on display, although, admittedly, in the relatively safe confines of its own hemisphere.

Panama was also the first military operation conducted with a post–cold war rationale. When the United States invaded Grenada six years earlier, the stated purpose had been to prevent the spread of communism or Marxism, the same rationale that had been offered in other military operations since the Korean War. With Panama, the principle was different: America sent its troops for the purpose of restoring democracy and overthrowing a leader whose behavior was abhorrent. In this respect, Panama was a forerunner of the later American effort against Saddam Hussein in Iraq.

American anger at Noriega had been steadily rising. He had been on the CIA and Defense Department payrolls for two decades, but by the mid-1980s he had been linked to drug trafficking and to the brutal murder of one of his political opponents. In December 1987 the Reagan administration had dispatched the Pentagon's Richard Armitage, who sometimes served as America's unofficial ambassador for the handling of thugs, to try to persuade Noriega to step aside. The Panamanian leader refused, and a few weeks later two federal grand juries in Florida indicted him on drug charges. Undeterred, Noriega's troops and partisans roughed up opponents, rigged an election and began to harass Americans in Panama. In October 1989 an attempted coup against Noriega by one of his subordinates failed, prompting a wave of criticism in Congress that the Bush administration should have given the attempt greater support. Finally, when Panamanian forces two months later shot and killed an American serviceman and detained another soldier and his wife, the Bush team decided to launch its invasion.

The main legacy of the Panama intervention was simply that it was a success, one that could be used to restore the confidence of the American public in the Pentagon's capabilities. Secretary of State James A. Baker III, the most politically oriented member of Bush's foreign policy team, later explained: "In breaking the mindset of the American people about the use of force in the post-Vietnam era, Panama established an emotional predicate that permitted us to build the public support so essential for the success of Operation Desert Storm some thirteen months later."[1] The Pentagon had begun the decade of the 1980s with the bungled rescue mission to free the hostages in Iran; it ended the decade with an operation that was well coordinated and achieved its mission.

The impact was not merely upon the American public. Panama also helped overcome resistance within the Pentagon itself to the use of force. During the final year of the Reagan administration and again in Bush's first months in office, the State Department had suggested the possibility of military action to overthrow Noriega. But under the leadership of Defense Secretary Frank Carlucci and William Crowe, the chairman of the Joint Chiefs of Staff, the Pentagon had opposed the idea.[2]

The Pentagon's resistance eased under the two men who succeeded Carlucci and Crowe: Defense Secretary Dick Cheney and Colin Powell, the new chairman of the Joint Chiefs. On Panama, Cheney and Powell were powerful collaborators, each in his own way contributing to a changing climate concerning America's willingness to send troops into military conflict. Using the new power granted to him by the Goldwater-Nichols Act, Powell won the support of the Joint Chiefs for the invasion, making plain that he no longer needed a consensus and was prepared to recommend military action to the president on his own, whether his fellow service chiefs agreed with him or not. Cheney, meanwhile, served as the bridge between the military leaders, on the one hand, and the Bush White House and Congress on the other.

In private, the two men remained wary toward each other. In the fall of 1989 Cheney had told Powell he was "off to a good start" in his new job but was holding back too much information that should be passed on to the defense secretary. Powell found that Cheney was "a conservative by nature and in his politics, a loner who would take your counsel but preferred to go off by himself to make up his mind."[3]

In public, none of this uneasiness showed, and the two men were a team. The day after the Panama invasion, the defense secretary and the chairman of the Joint Chiefs appeared together at a Pentagon press conference. After a brief introduction, Cheney stepped aside and allowed Powell to dominate the event. Powell, a talented briefer, was simultaneously low-keyed and swaggering. Asked whether Noriega might somehow escape and survive in the jungle, Powell replied, "He's used to a different kind of lifestyle, and I'm not quite sure he'd be up to being chased around in the countryside by Army Rangers. . . . He's not running anything, because we own all of the bases he owned eight hours ago."[4] Noriega was eventually captured, brought back to the United States, convicted of racketeering and cocaine smuggling charge, and sentenced to forty years in prison.

Powell's performance on Panama attracted attention and praise. "By all accounts, Powell has won the applause of his Pentagon colleagues," reported an Associated Press correspondent. "Clearly he was in charge. . . . In a brilliant if violent thrust, Powell had proved his military mettle," said *Newsday* in a long and flattering magazine profile.[5] When Powell appeared in public as Reagan's national security adviser, he had been a quiet, dark-suited, self-effacing staff aide. Now he took on a new role. Outspoken, assured, bedecked in green dress uniform, he was the symbol of and spokesman for the revived, newly triumphant American armed forces. Panama made him a celebrity.

In the years since the Panama invasion, Powell has become identified, more than any other American leader, with a reluctance to send troops into battle. It is worth noting, then, that the reality is not quite so simple. In Panama, his first crisis as chairman of the Joint Chiefs of Staff, Powell proved to be considerably more disposed to support military intervention than his predecessors—so long as the United States was willing to use overwhelming force for narrowly defined objectives, the same conditions his former boss Caspar Weinberger had set down.

In his willingness to send troops to Panama, Powell was defying predictions about himself and the American military. Less than three months before the Panama invasion, in a news analysis in the *New York Times,* correspondent R. W. Apple had written prematurely: "What is undisputed, indeed obvious, is that few senior officers in the executive branch have much appetite any more for small-scale wars involving American troops. That is as true of Gen. Colin L. Powell as it was of his predecessor as Chairman of the Joint Chiefs of Staff, Adm. William J. Crowe. The Vietnam War, a ranking officer said, 'has made us wary of places like Panama and Colombia.'"[6]

Panama proved the contrary. In this particular phase of his career, Powell not only supported military intervention but led the way. With the easing of the cold war and under the right conditions, America was in fact regaining an appetite for wars it could win.

On July 20, 1990, Israel's Defense Minister Moshe Arens landed in Washington on a clandestine mission, carrying along with him Shabtai Shavit, the director of the Mossad, Israel's intelligence service, and General Amnon Shahak, the head of military intelligence. They were escorted to secret meetings with Cheney and with Director of Central Intelligence William Webster. In each session, the Israelis delivered their warnings:

You'd better pay closer attention to Iraq. Its agents have been trying to buy nuclear weapons technology. Saddam Hussein poses a threat not merely to Israel but also to Saudi Arabia and Kuwait.[7]

The admonitions went unheeded, written off in Washington as yet another bit of alarmism from the Israelis. Ever since Donald Rumsfeld's groundbreaking 1983 meeting with Saddam Hussein, America had tried to build steadily stronger relations with Iraq. After the end of the Iran-Iraq War in 1988 the United States had operated on the assumption that Saddam Hussein would begin to demobilize his forces and give greater attention to the domestic economy. In its first eighteen months the Bush administration was preoccupied with changes in Eastern Europe, China and Central America and devoted little attention to Iraq. By the subsequent admission of Secretary of State Baker, policy toward Iraq was "not immune from domestic economic considerations." With the help of credits from the U.S. Commodity Credit Corporation, Iraq was buying more than one billion dollars a year in American grain, and, noted Baker, "these programs were immensely popular on Capitol Hill and with farm state politicians."[8]

In late July 1990 American intelligence officials at the CIA and the Pentagon began to sound their own warnings about Iraq, which was moving troops, tanks and other equipment toward its border with Kuwait. Finally, the Bush administration began to debate whether to take steps to deter Saddam Hussein. Some Pentagon and State Department officials recommended sending the aircraft carrier *Independence* or a squadron of warplanes, but these recommendations went nowhere.[9] Saudi and Egyptian officials were telling the Bush White House not to overreact; they thought the Iraqi would not invade Kuwait and would be amenable to diplomacy.

On August 1 Powell ordered General H. Norman Schwarzkopf, head of the U.S. Central Command, to give Cheney and the Joint Chiefs a briefing on Iraq. "What do you think they will do?" asked Cheney. Schwarzkopf predicted Iraq would launch a limited attack to seize one Kuwaiti island and an oil field, but not invade all of Kuwait.[10] The following day Iraqi forces invaded and took control of Kuwait in its entirety. The United States, it turned out, had been consistently wrong about Saddam Hussein.

Americans now tend to accept as foreordained the first Bush administration's decision to respond with force to Iraq's invasion of Kuwait. It is important to keep in mind that at the time the American military intervention came as a surprise. The United States had never done anything comparable, at least not in the Middle East. The accepted cliché about Saddam Hussein is that he had a tendency toward miscalculation and that he misjudged when he assumed the Bush administration wouldn't send its own troops to defend Kuwait. However, quite a few knowledgeable Americans made the same miscalculation, and Colin Powell was among them. On the day following the Iraqi invasion, the chairman of the Joint Chiefs was briefing Schwarzkopf as the two men were preparing for the Bush administration's first National Security Council meeting on the crisis. "I think we'd go to war over Saudi Arabia, but I doubt we'd go to war over Kuwait," Powell said.[11]

Powell, Cheney and Wolfowitz all were participants in the Bush administration's deliberations before, during and after the Gulf War. Although that administration was extremely skillful at maintaining a façade of unity, there were in fact internal disagreements, some of them intense, throughout this period. The ramifications of these Gulf War debates, and of the interactions among Powell, Cheney and Wolfowitz, lingered for years. This legacy of the Gulf War—an intellectual divide and a residue of mistrust between Cheney and Wolfowitz, on the one hand, and Powell, on the other—still hung in the air, unacknowledged but undeniable, when the George W. Bush administration took office a decade later.

In essence, the submerged Gulf War tensions within the first Bush administration can be reduced to four separate issues: Should America go to war? What should the war plan be? When should America end the war? And (once the war was over) should the United States prevent Saddam Hussein from using force to regain control of his country? Cheney, Powell and Wolfowitz took differing positions on these issues.

At the Bush administration's very first session to decide what to do about the Iraqi invasion, Powell asked the president and members of his cabinet if it was worth it to go to war to liberate Kuwait. "I detected a chill in the room," he later recalled. After the meeting Cheney rebuked Powell for exceeding his authority. "Colin," he said, "you're chairman of the Joint Chiefs. You're not secretary of state. You're not the national security adviser. And you're not secretary of defense. So stick to military matters."[12]

On the issue of going to war, Powell was the odd man out. His opposition put him into direct conflict with Cheney. At the same session in which Powell had questioned whether war was worth it, Cheney had argued that if Iraq were allowed to absorb Kuwait, it would become a major oil power overnight. Economic sanctions against Iraq wouldn't work, Cheney contended, because the rest of the world wouldn't stick to the sanctions; it needed oil and would eventually decide to accommodate Iraq.[13]

The president and Scowcroft agreed with Cheney. Scowcroft portrayed the issues raised by the Iraqi invasion in broad terms that extended beyond oil and the Middle East; he said he was worried about "the ramifications of the aggression on the emerging post–Cold War world." Within three days Bush made clear where he stood, declaring on television: "This will not stand, this aggression against Kuwait."

Nevertheless, over the following weeks Powell quietly campaigned to organize high-level opposition within the administration to the use of force. "He made an effort to try to enlist Baker at one point," recalled Dennis Ross, who was then the secretary of state's leading policy adviser. "Baker wasn't an enthusiast for war, but Baker was a complete loyalist to Bush. . . . He thought that Bush had boxed himself in [by pledging to reverse the Iraqi invasion], but it was a decision the president had made and that settled it, and therefore Baker's job was to make it work."[14] Still, Powell persisted, to the point where he finally argued directly to the president that the United States could accomplish his objectives without going to war through economic sanctions and a strategy of containment. Bush rejected the advice.

Here, as on other occasions in his career, Powell was reflecting the legacy of Vietnam. In this instance, he was attempting to assert the independence he believed America's senior military leaders should have shown during the Vietnam War. Seeking to explain why he had been so willing to question the use of force after the invasion of Kuwait, Powell later observed, "As a midlevel career officer, I had been appalled at the docility of the Joint Chiefs of Staff, fighting the war in Vietnam without ever pressing the political leaders to lay out clear objectives for them."[15]

Cheney was motivated by a desire to be loyal to the president. As defense secretary he believed his primary responsibility was to deliver whatever military capability Bush wanted. Moreover, Wolfowitz, Cheney's top civilian adviser, was warning repeatedly and forcefully to Cheney and others in the administration against a strategy of containment.

Wolfowitz too viewed the Iraqi invasion of Kuwait against the backdrop of his own career and intellectual history. Where Powell was preoccupied with the lessons of Vietnam, however, Wolfowitz had since the early days of his career been concerned with the balance of power in the Middle East and the Persian Gulf. He had written his doctoral dissertation on preventing the spread of nuclear weapons in the Middle East, and by 1990 Iraq was attempting to buy the technology to become a nuclear power. Wolfowitz had begun to warn in the late 1970s that Iraq could pose a threat to the oil fields of Saudi Arabia and Kuwait, and now Saddam Hussein's invasion of Kuwait had confirmed his fears. For Wolfowitz, it was clear the United States needed not only to undo the Iraqi invasion of Kuwait but also to leave Iraq in a weakened position where it could not pose a military threat to its neighbors.

"Paul's view was that containment would be a complete disaster," said Ross. "You'd have this huge Iraqi army which would be right on the Saudi border. Even if you got them out of Kuwait, they would still be on the Saudi border, and they'd still be able to use their forces for coercion. . . . So Paul was from the beginning strongly determined to say that we can't have an outcome where he [Saddam Hussein] simply pulls out of Kuwait and everything else is left intact. He took the view that we had to deal with this threat and now we had the opportunity to deal with this threat."[16]

By October this internal debate was over. The president was unmoved by Powell's arguments in favor of containment. The Bush administration was moving toward war.

Privately Cheney and Wolfowitz also were at odds with Powell over the details of the military strategy the United States should employ in a war against Iraq. Here too the Pentagon's top civilian leaders had some qualified support from the White House.

In theory, the job of working out a war plan was up to Schwarzkopf, the military commander in the field. He and his aides had at first been preoccupied with the need to defend Saudi Arabia against an Iraqi attack. But by October they were being pressed to come up with a plan for an offensive to dislodge the Iraqi troops from Kuwait. Schwarzkopf's initial effort called for a direct, head-on attack against the Iraqi forces. Although the CENTCOM commander protested that this plan had been hastily drafted and wasn't in final form, Powell and one of Schwarzkopf's aides presented it to Bush, Scowcroft and others at a White House meeting on October 11.

They hated it. "It was a terrible plan," Scowcroft recalled. "It called for a frontal assault, right up to the Iraqi strength." It ran the risk of substantial American casualties. "What role Powell played, I honestly don't know. He said it wasn't his plan, but he submitted it on behalf of Schwarzkopf."[17] At the Pentagon, Cheney and Wolfowitz had a similar reaction to Schwarzkopf's initial war plan.

Meanwhile, clandestinely, without telling Powell or anyone else on the Joint Chiefs of Staff, Cheney and Wolfowitz had begun to develop their own separate war plan. It was the brainchild of Henry S. Rowen, a scholar on leave from the Stanford Business School and the Hoover Institution who was then serving under Wolfowitz as the assistant secretary of defense for international security affairs.

In September, Rowen had gone off to his vacation home in the south of France with a stack of reading about warfare in the Middle East. He became especially interested in an episode during World War II in which there had been an Iraqi revolt against British occupation. The British had put down the rebellion by sending reinforcements quickly overland from what is now Jordan eastward across the desert to Baghdad. Since the British could accomplish this feat with Arab Legion troops in 1941, Rowen reasoned, then American forces, vastly better equipped and with the support of air power, could similarly invade Iraq from the west and move through the country's empty desert regions toward the Euphrates River. Upon his return to Washington, Rowen laid out his ideas to Wolfowitz and then to Cheney. "Set up a team, and don't tell Powell or anybody else," Cheney told him.[18]

Wolfowitz and Scooter Libby, his civilian aide for contingency planning, created a secret group to explore Rowen's idea. The team included some retired and active military officers with no connection to the Joint Chiefs. The result was called Operation Scorpion. American troops from Saudi Arabia would have gone into Iraq's western deserts and established a base there, as little as sixty miles from Baghdad. At that point, so the theory went, Saddam Hussein might have had to withdraw troops from Kuwait to defend Baghdad, and these forces would have been vulnerable to attack from the air. If he didn't move forces, then these allied troops inside Iraq would have been in a position to threaten the capital and thus to force a settlement on favorable terms.[19]

Rowen's idea also had another explicit aim: to help protect Israel from

Scud missiles. Even at this early stage of planning, American officials were worried that Iraq could succeed in breaking up America's Gulf War coalition by attacking Israel and bringing it into the war. Iraq's Scuds could reach Israel's cities only if the missiles were launched from western Iraq. If American forces had light forces on the ground in Iraq's western deserts, supported by airpower, they would be in position to hunt for the Scuds.[20]

"Cheney was hot on this [alternative war plan] for a long time," Rowen subsequently recalled. While Powell was out of town, visiting Saudi Arabia, Cheney—again, without telling Powell—took the civilian-drafted plan, Operation Scorpion, to the White House and presented it to the president and the national security adviser.

It is worth pausing here to underscore just how extraordinary this maneuvering was within the top ranks of the Bush administration. To the American public and the rest of the world, the administration seemed to be unified. But behind the scenes, during the three months after the Iraqi invasion of Kuwait, the chairman of the Joint Chiefs of Staff was quietly seeking to win support for a strategy of containment that the secretary of defense opposed. And the defense secretary was quietly campaigning for a war plan different from the one submitted by the chairman of the Joint Chiefs of Staff.

In the end, the Cheney-Wolfowitz-Rowen war plan was set aside. Schwarzkopf believed it would have been impossible to supply the troops in western Iraq, hundreds of miles away from friendly forces. Schwarzkopf was furious at the defense secretary. "I wondered whether Cheney had succumbed to the phenomenon I'd observed among some secretaries of the army," he later wrote. "Put a civilian in charge of professional military men and before long he's no longer satisfied with setting policy but wants to outgeneral the generals."[21]

Moreover, at the White House, Cheney's plan was viewed as too risky and politically disruptive. The fear was that if the plan succeeded, the result could have been chaos inside Iraq.[22] Going into western Iraq would raise the specter of an allied attack on Baghdad or even a possible breakup of Iraq, and that was precisely what America's closest partners in the Middle East, including Saudi Arabia and Turkey, most feared.

Nevertheless, the strong opposition of the White House and the secretary of defense to Schwarzkopf's initial war plan forced the military to come up with something different. At Powell's prodding, military planners working for the Joint Chiefs and for Schwarzkopf's command in

Saudi Arabia decided to embrace an idea they had earlier rejected. Instead of a frontal assault on Iraqi forces, the United States and its allies would carry out a flanking maneuver and move around the Iraqis to their west. This was the so-called left hook strategy that was eventually employed with success against the Iraqi forces. It represented at least a nod in the direction of the plan Cheney had advocated.

This new war plan required far more in the way of troops, equipment, aircraft and warships than the earlier plan. But the president was willing to support a huge operation, and it suited Powell too. The revised Iraq operation fitted in perfectly with the chairman's overall strategy to use overwhelming force, win in a short time and get out. Powell had begun to turn his ideas, stemming from the defeat in Vietnam and the success in Panama, into a sweeping statement of principles for the American Army: "We had learned a lesson in Panama. Go in big and end it quickly. We could not put the United States through another Vietnam. We could be so lavish with resources because the world had changed. We could now afford to pull divisions out of Germany that had been there for the past forty years to stop a Soviet offensive that was no longer coming."[23]

Thus, in Powell's view, the easing of the cold war made it easier for the United States to wage war in a way that met the standards Powell and his former boss Caspar Weinberger had set down, the ideas that eventually became known as the Powell doctrine. The Gulf War of early 1991 was carried out as a demonstration project for these principles.

Bush obtained a resolution from Congress authorizing the use of force. Beforehand, Cheney, who during Iran-contra had already argued that an American president has sweeping authority over foreign policy, tried to persuade Bush he could go to war without congressional approval and that the administration might lose on Capitol Hill. The president rejected Cheney's recommendation and won the vote.[24] America and its allies massed their troops, started the war with an intensive air campaign, carried out their left hook envelopment and defeated Iraq within a few short days. Then they rushed to get out.

Over the years a myth has developed about the end of the Gulf War and about Powell's relationship to it. According to this myth, during the final days of the war, Powell, as chairman of the Joint Chiefs, played the leading role in preventing America and its allies from moving forces on to Baghdad and overthrowing Saddam Hussein. In some versions of this myth, more hawkish officials, such as Wolfowitz, favored a move on the Iraqi capital but were blocked by Powell.

There is no evidence to support these claims. Indeed, so far as can be established, at the time of the Gulf War no one in any senior position in the Bush administration proposed going to Baghdad. Powell was not in favor of doing so, but neither were Bush and Scowcroft at the White House, nor Cheney and Wolfowitz, the more hawkish civilian leaders at the Pentagon. "Nobody, including Paul [Wolfowitz], argued for 'Let's go to Baghdad,'" said Dennis Ross, the State Department official who worked closely with Wolfowitz at the time.[25]

All these officials reflected the considerable caution and conservatism of American foreign policy during that era. No one in the first Bush administration was seeking to remake the political institutions of the Middle East. Merely dispatching American troops to reverse Iraq's invasion of Kuwait was considered as adventurous as anyone wanted to be. At the time marching on Baghdad was thought to be militarily risky and politically unwise since it would go beyond the original war aim of ousting Iraq from Kuwait.

The most articulate explanation of the first Bush administration's unwillingness to march to Baghdad has come from Wolfowitz himself. In an essay published in 1997, he asserted: "A new regime [in Iraq] would have become the United States' responsibility. Conceivably, this could have led the United States into a more or less permanent occupation of a country that could not govern itself, but where the rule of a foreign occupier would be increasingly resented.

". . . Officials in the Bush administration were very conscious of the bloody stalemate into which General MacArthur had dragged the country during the Korean War by his reckless pursuit north to the Yalu River following his stunning success at Inchon."[26]

Above all, going to Baghdad was also considered unnecessary, since most officials in Washington believed, erroneously, that Saddam Hussein would be overthrown after losing the war. Even Rowen, who had devised the more ambitious war plan that would have put American troops sixty miles from Baghdad, did not propose seizing the Iraqi capital.

In another article he wrote after the end of the war, Wolfowitz effectively endorsed the 1991 decision not to go to Baghdad. "Nothing could have insured Saddam Hussein's removal from power short of a full-scale occupation of Iraq," he asserted. ". . . Even if easy initially, it is unclear how or when it would have ended."[27]

At the time, in early 1991, Wolfowitz and some others in the Pentagon were unhappy about something different: the timing of the Bush administration's decision to call a cease-fire and end the ground war. On that decision Powell had indeed taken the lead, and thus his actions are fairly open to question.

The chairman of the Joint Chiefs had sought to create a climate within the Bush administration for a speedy end to the conflict. He had read a book titled *Every War Must End* by Fred Iklé, the veteran foreign policy hand who had served in the Nixon and Reagan administrations. Iklé argued that generals should think not only about military maneuvers and tactics but also about how a conflict can finally be terminated. The Japanese military, for example, had come up with a brilliant plan for attacking Pearl Harbor but had no idea how Japan could bring a war against the United States to a close. Powell liked this book so much that before and during Desert Storm, he distributed passages from it to Scowcroft, Cheney and the Joint Chiefs. "We were fighting a limited war under a limited mandate for a limited purpose, which was soon going to be achieved," he explained in his autobiography. "I thought that the people responsible ought to start thinking about how it would end."[28]

By the fourth day of the war the allied forces had taken tens of thousands of Iraqi prisoners and Iraqi forces were fleeing from Kuwait along a "highway of death," subjected to withering American attacks. Powell began pressing Schwarzkopf to think about a cease-fire. At a White House meeting Powell, citing the warrior's code against purposeless killing, told the president and other administration officials he thought the war could be brought to a close within hours. "I remember Colin Powell saying with a trace of emotion, 'We're killing literally *thousands* of people,'" wrote Baker in his memoirs.[29] As a result, the ground war was terminated after exactly one hundred hours, at a time when American and allied forces were in position to inflict considerably greater damage on the Iraqi forces.

Scooter Libby, who was serving as Wolfowitz's assistant, recalled that when informed of the decision to terminate the war, he and Wolfowitz were deeply disappointed. "We objected to it," Libby said. "I was floored by the decision. Neither of us liked it."[30] However, even if Wolfowitz had been prepared to take on the formidable task of persuading the rest of the Bush administration to keep on fighting, the decision concerning the cease-fire was made and executed before he had an opportunity to challenge it.

Cheney was present alongside Powell when the decision was made to stop the war, and he raised no objections. He, like others in the administration, was eager to have the Gulf War end quickly and in a way that would be pleasing to Iraq's neighbors. "As the war was coming to an end, I went to Cheney and said, 'You know, we could change the government and put in a democracy.'" Rowen recalled. "The answer he gave was that the Saudis wouldn't like it."[31]

Within days, U.S. intelligence reported that many of the Republican Guard troops, Saddam Hussein's best fighting forces, had managed to escape with equipment from Kuwait after the cease-fire. The conflict had ended before allied forces could finish closing off the Iraqis' line of retreat. According to the CIA's analysis, at least 365 of the Republican Guard's T-72 Soviet tanks, nearly half of the total, got away, as did the entire Hammurabi Division.[32] Powell had succeeded in his goal of working out a rapid ending to the war, but the hasty American cease-fire permitted Saddam Hussein's regime, in the final hours, to preserve some of the Iraqi Army's best troops and equipment.

Later in the 1990s Wolfowitz reflected that the Bush administration should have delayed announcing the end of the Gulf War in order to encourage an Iraqi coup d'état. "Simply by delaying the ceasefire agreement—without killing more Iraqi troops or destroying more Iraqi military assets—the United States might have bought time for opposition to Saddam Hussein to build and to act against him," he wrote. However, he admitted somewhat ruefully that he was making this argument in hindsight.[33]

A few days later the Bush administration unexpectedly found itself facing another fateful decision, this time involving the postwar power of the Iraqi armed forces. Saddam Hussein's control over his country hung in the balance. This time a serious, open debate erupted within the Bush administration. Wolfowitz sought to challenge the policies of the Bush White House and Powell. He lost.

At the time of the cease-fire Iraqi military officials had asked Schwarzkopf for permission to fly helicopters over their airspace, claiming they needed to be able to transport Iraqi officials from one location to another. The American commander had naïvely given his assent. Over the following days the Iraqis used their helicopter gunships to attack the Shiite and Kurdish forces that were seeking to rebel against Saddam Hussein. These Kurds and Shiites may well have been encouraged by President Bush's suggestions, before the start of the war, that the Iraqi people should overthrow Saddam Hussein.

In Washington, both Wolfowitz and Dennis Ross of the State Department were outraged at this turn of events. They argued that the United States should intervene with force to stop the Iraqi helicopter attacks. "There was a particular meeting where the two of us worked very hard to try to persuade Baker and Cheney on this," said Ross. "Neither one of us persuaded our bosses." Scowcroft later wrote that he too had talked to Cheney about rescinding the permission to fly the helicopters; however, both Cheney and Powell argued that doing so would undermine the authority of Schwarzkopf, who had granted the authority for the helicopter flights in the first place.[34]

In reality, Schwarzkopf's authority was not the main issue. In declining to prevent Saddam Hussein's attacks on the Shiites and Kurds, Bush administration officials were motivated by a number of factors—strategic, military and emotional. Taken together, these overcame Wolfowitz's and Ross's pleas for a new U.S. military intervention.

Above all, Bush administration officials were afraid any action in support of the Shiites and Kurds might lead to the disintegration of Iraq, the result that the Saudis and others in the Middle East were trying to prevent. They also believed, wrongly, that the Shiites in southern Iraq were allied with Iran, even though during more than eight years of the Iran-Iraq War the Iraqi Shiites had never tried to join with Iran.

The most succinct and Machiavellian description of the Bush administration's underlying strategy came from Powell. The United States wasn't merely neutral, he later admitted; in fact, it actually favored Saddam Hussein's armed forces over the Shiites and Kurds. "Our practical intention was to leave Baghdad enough power to survive as a threat to an Iran that remained bitterly hostile to the United States," Powell acknowledged.[35]

Meanwhile, Schwarzkopf and his officers were urging the Bush administration to get the American troops out as quickly as possible. A week after the war Schwarzkopf was arguing that that his soldiers in the theater faced miserable conditions, including minefields. In Washington the Bush administration's top officials had no more appetite than Schwarzkopf to intervene in Iraq once again, after what had seemed like a triumphal ending to the story. "Bear in mind, there was this kind of group thinking that was cemented by meeting almost daily over a six- or seven-month period of the president, Baker, Cheney, Scowcroft, [Deputy National Security Adviser Robert] Gates and Powell," explained Ross. "They had gone through a period of incredible emotional stress. You'd had experts predicting that America was going to lose fifty thousand dead. The group went through a period of high anxiety [before the war] and then exhilaration."[36]

In the end the Iraqi Army suppressed the rebellions without American interference. Although before the Gulf War, Bush had compared Saddam Hussein with Hitler, the Iraqi leader nonetheless was permitted to regain control of Iraq after the end of the conflict. As a result, over the following decade America had to commit itself to a huge presence in the Middle East and to engage in intermittent conflict to make sure that Saddam Hussein's power was contained.

At the time of the Gulf War President George H. W. Bush declared that it was being waged on behalf of what he called a new world order. His vague phrase carried several meanings. First, the United States was assuming a role as the world's preeminent leader. Second, America would be willing to use its military power in areas of the world where it had not previously intervened for fear of a cold war confrontation. Third, the United States would act, with force if necessary, to prevent aggression and to preserve the existing balance of power. Fourth, and most significant, the United States would work in concert with its old allies in Western Europe and East Asia and with its new partner, the Soviet Union. Explaining this new concept, Bush told a joint session of Congress before the Gulf War that "the crisis in the Persian Gulf . . . offers a rare opportunity to move toward an historic period of cooperation." A new partnership between the United States and the Soviet Union, he said, had "opened the way for the [U.N.] Security Council to operate as its founders had envisioned."[37] Bush implied that he was establishing a lasting new framework for international affairs.

Yet for the Vulcans and their generation, the Gulf War and the new world order came to represent only a moment in history, not something permanent. In the years after 1991 some elements of the new world order proved more enduring than others. America continued to assert its leadership role and its willingness to use military force (within limits that soon emerged in such places as Rwanda). However, the broad coalition that had joined together in the Gulf War soon fell apart. Other nations had different interests from the United States and were unwilling to follow its lead. In the late Clinton years, the United States was able to join together with its European allies, but not Russia, in military operations against Serbia's Slobodan Milosević. Clinton's Iraq policy of the late 1990s was supported by Britain but not by France, Russia and China.

After the terrorist attacks of 2001 the Vulcans of the George W. Bush administration chose to wage the war in Afghanistan with help only from Britain, spurning offers of help from European allies whose military abilities were far behind those of the United States. By the time of America's second war with Iraq in 2003 only Britain and Australia were willing to send troops in significant numbers to fight with the United States. The George W. Bush administration proclaimed that it had put together a "coalition of the willing," but the undeniable reality was that at least by the standards of 1991, most of its members weren't willing to do very much.

Beyond its broader implications for America's role in the world, the Gulf War carried personal significance for Powell, Cheney and Wolfowitz. The events influenced both their careers and their relationships with one another.

Powell and Cheney emerged from the Gulf War with even higher reputations than they had enjoyed after Panama. Cheney found himself being described as a possible presidential candidate. PRESIDENTIAL TIMBER? asked a headline in the *Los Angeles Times*. Powell, despite his private opposition to the war, managed again in press conferences to speak with the machismo of a professional soldier. "Our strategy for dealing with this [Iraqi] army is very simple," he said at one point. "First, we're going to cut it off, then we're going to kill it."[38]

Cheney, Powell, Schwarzkopf and their wives were honored in a ticker tape victory parade up Broadway in New York City. Riding in front of troops from the seventeen nations that had fought against Iraq, accompanied by marching bands, the three leaders received the sort of treatment once accorded to Charles Lindbergh and Douglas MacArthur.

Mayor David Dinkins gave them the keys to the city. "It's a great day to be back home in New York," declared Powell.[39]

Wolfowitz, as a lower-ranking official, was not the subject of such adulation, but he too had enhanced his career. He had played a key role in two of the most sensitive diplomatic missions of the nine-month crisis. In August 1990 Wolfowitz had flown with Cheney to Saudi Arabia in a successful effort to convince King Fahd that he should accept the deployment of American forces to his country. In January 1991, working with Deputy Secretary of State Lawrence Eagleburger, he had traveled to Jerusalem to persuade Israeli Prime Minister Yitzhak Shamir he should stay out of any war with Iraq and should instead let the United States respond on Israel's behalf to any Iraqi Scud missile attacks on Israeli territory. Through this diplomacy, and in the many policy deliberations up to and during the Gulf War, Wolfowitz had managed to establish an enduring bond with Cheney.

Temporarily forgotten amid the victory parades were the disagreements that the Iraq crisis had engendered. Intellectually Cheney and Wolfowitz had differed with Powell on many of the key strategic and foreign policy issues, starting with the need for military intervention. As defense secretary Cheney had found himself obliged to defer to Powell's extraordinary authority as chairman of the Joint Chiefs of Staff. Yet he had also chafed at Powell's exertions of power and warned him not to make the sorts of decisions that should be left to the civilian leadership.

For Cheney and Wolfowitz, the lesson for the future was clear: Keep a tight rein on the generals. A decade later, during the George W. Bush administration, Wolfowitz once again worked in the Pentagon, this time under Donald Rumsfeld, Cheney's former mentor. Rumsfeld took care not to let anyone in the military acquire as much power as Powell had once wielded. When Rumsfeld appeared at press conferences with the chairman of the Joint Chiefs of Staff, the defense secretary usually dominated the podium and let the chairman stand quietly alongside or behind him. It was a reversal of the way the Cheney-Powell briefings had been conducted.

In 2002 and 2003, as a new military crisis brewed with Iraq, the civilians of the George W. Bush administration, from the president on down, suddenly began to appear in public holding a book by a scholar named Eliot A. Cohen. The book, titled *Supreme Command,* argued that in time of war civilian leaders should make the key decisions on military strategy and should not show too much deference to their generals. Few recognized the symbolism and subtext of carrying Cohen's book, the determination not to let U.S. military leaders play the powerful political role Powell had exerted at the time of America's first war with Iraq. Cheney and Wolfowitz certainly understood.

CHAPTER THIRTEEN

Death of an Empire, Birth of a Vision

IN THE FALL OF 1991 the Pentagon stood at a crossroads. A few months earlier, party leaders and the Soviet Union's security apparatus had attempted to mount a clumsy coup d'état against President Mikhail Gorbachev. When it failed, the Soviet Communist party collapsed, and some Soviet republics, such as Ukraine, began quickly moving toward independence. By autumn the Soviet Union was in the process of disintegrating. For more than forty years American military strategy and planning had been premised upon the Soviet threat. Now that threat had disappeared, and the Pentagon needed to formulate a new strategy that would guide U.S. military thinking in a new era.

The primary responsibility for drafting a new strategy lay with Paul Wolfowitz, the undersecretary of defense for policy. In public appearances that fall, Wolfowitz fell into brooding about the lessons of American history. "We've never done it right in the past," Wolfowitz told one audience. America had demobilized too quickly, he asserted. After World War I the Western democracies had brought the troops home and slashed their military budgets; in the long run, that demobilization had paved the way for the rise of Hitler. After 1945, Wolfowitz went on, America repeated the error: "It only took us five short years to go from having the strongest military establishment in the world, with no challengers, to having a force that was barely able to hang on to the Korean Peninsula against the attack of a fourth-rate country."[1] After the two world wars America was under pressure to demobilize because its Army was made up of draftees who were eager to go home. This time, noted Wolfowitz, the United States possessed a volunteer force, whose soldiers had planned to make a career in the military. How much should it cut back on the size of this Army?

Preserving American military power was important, Wolfowitz argued. North Korea appeared to be committed to developing nuclear weapons. Then there was the problem of oil reserves in the Middle East. ". . . The combination of the enormous resources of the Persian Gulf, the power that those resources represent—it's power. It's not just that we need gas for our cars, it's that anyone who controls those resources has enormous capability to build up military forces." The danger, Wolfowitz said, could come either from Iran or from a rebuilt Iraq, perhaps by the end of the decade.[2]

The search for a new post–cold war rationale for American military power culminated a few months later in one of the most significant foreign policy documents of the past half century. It set forth a new vision for a world dominated by a lone American superpower, actively working to make sure that no rival or group of rivals would ever emerge. The document, written by Wolfowitz's assistant Zalmay Khalilzad, leaked out of the Pentagon in draft form. After it had become public, the administration, embarrassed, ordered it rewritten. Yet this document, both in its original form and in the sanitized version that was finally approved, had a lasting impact. It outlined many of the specific ideas and policies that the Vulcans were to pursue when they returned to office in the George W. Bush administration. In a more general way, the document set down some themes that even the Vulcans' Democratic opponents borrowed in the 1990s. As a guide to where American foreign policy was headed it had no peer.

The Pentagon document envisioned a future in which "the world order is ultimately backed by the U.S." The concept of collective security, on which the United States had relied during the cold war, was no longer at the heart of American strategic thinking. The United Nations was given short shrift. Alliances like NATO would also be of reduced importance, the document asserted. In the future the United States would deal with the world less with permanent, formal alliances and more through "coalitions" or "ad hoc assemblies, often not lasting beyond the crisis being confronted."[3] (This was an early rendition of what President George W. Bush meant when he said the United States would deal with crises by leading a "coalition of the willing.")

The proposed new strategy concentrated heavily on the potential threat to the United States posed by the spread of weapons of mass destruction. The document argued that in dealing with this threat, America should not simply rely upon the strategies of deterrence and containment that had worked against the Soviet Union but should contemplate the possibility of offensive military action. There might be a need, the draft statement said, for "preempting an impending attack with nuclear, chemical or biological weapons."[4] In this respect too the Pentagon's strategy of 1992 foreshadowed the policies of the George W. Bush administration after September 11, 2001.

This new Pentagon strategy served as the bridge that transported the Vulcans and their generation from the 1970s and 1980s into the world after the Soviet collapse. The underlying assumptions were once again roughly the same: America need not and should not reach an accommodation with any other country. Now, however, the United States was not combating a single, known rival, such as the Soviet Union or China. Rather, America was making sure no future adversary with whom anyone could suggest the need for détente would ever emerge. The vision was indeed breathtaking.

The ideas for America's role in a post–cold war world evolved over three years, from 1989 to 1992. During this period, as events in Eastern Europe and the Soviet Union unfolded and as the cold war doctrines of the past were rendered obsolete, the Pentagon reacted by gradually, progressively shifting its explanations of why America should preserve its military power. The central figures in this drama were Dick Cheney, Colin Powell and Paul Wolfowitz, usually working together.

All of them were seeking to come up with new principles and a new logic to govern American military planning. The process of drafting a new Pentagon strategy was inextricably linked to the annual defense budgets, which Cheney, Powell and Wolfowitz all were required to justify on Capitol Hill. You couldn't ask Congress to continue to spend large sums on defense without explaining why the United States needed to maintain its military strength.

As defense secretary Cheney was particularly resistant to change. Despite Wolfowitz's reputation as a hawk, there were times when Cheney took a harder line. One aide recalled how several Pentagon officials, including Wolfowitz, once tried to persuade Cheney to consider a different approach toward North Korea. After broaching the idea in writing, they went into the defense secretary's office to talk about it. He already had an amused grin on his face. "I want to see how you argue this," he said. He smiled throughout the meeting, signifying that he wasn't mad at them but that they had to realize this was just a game, an abstract debating exercise. There was just no way he was going to change the long-standing U.S. policy toward North Korea.[5]

Cheney once self-mockingly quipped that while in Congress, he had been "a self-described and proud-of-it hawk . . . who never met a weapons system he didn't vote for."[6] At the Pentagon in 1989, he dug in his heels as the Bush administration weighed what actions it should take to respond to Gorbachev's reforms. "Cheney was the most skeptical, holding the view that the changes [in Moscow] were primarily cosmetic and we should essentially do nothing," National Security Adviser Brent Scowcroft later wrote.[7]

By contrast, Powell, who had already dealt with Gorbachev as Reagan's national security adviser, was convinced that the Soviet Union was changing and that the implications for the American defense budgets would be profound. Within weeks after he became chairman of the Joint Chiefs that October 1989, Powell began contemplating far-reaching reductions, such as cutting the active-duty Army from 760,000 troops to 525,000. Nevertheless, Powell admitted, "Those levels would be tough to sell to Cheney."[8]

Despite these apparent differences, Cheney and Powell soon became collaborators. When it came to dealing with Congress, the two men were equally astute and had similar instincts. In November and early December 1989 the Berlin Wall came down, paving the way for the democratic revolutions in Eastern Europe. The Warsaw Pact was on its deathbed; Soviet troops were gradually going to be pulled back to Soviet territory. By the end of the year it was becoming clear that if the Pentagon didn't come up with its own new strategy and its own proposals for some budget cuts, Congress was going to do the job by itself in a far more drastic way.

America's leading newspapers were filled, day after day, with articles about the "peace dividend." Indeed, the focus of debate at the time was not over whether there would be money saved from the defense budget after the cold war but over how it should be used. Should it be devoted to domestic programs, to tax cuts or to reduction of the federal budget deficit? On Capitol Hill, Senator James Sasser, the Democratic chairman of the Senate Budget Committee, proclaimed "the dawn of the primacy of domestic economics." Representative Lee Hamilton, the chairman of the Joint Economic Committee, held hearings on America's economic adjustment after the cold war. Former Defense Secretary Robert McNamara and Lawrence Korb, an assistant secretary of defense in the Reagan administration, testified that the defense budget, then $300 billion a year, could be cut by half, to $150 billion (in constant dollars) in the year 2000.[9]

Cheney briefly sought to mock and defy his old congressional colleagues. He lashed out at "irresponsible" critics who suggested "there is some kind of big peace dividend here to be cashed in and to buy all the goodies everybody on Capitol Hill can think about buying."[10] Yet before too long he, like Powell, recognized the need to move before Congress did. In January 1990 Cheney announced that he was asking Wolfowitz to reassess America's overall defense strategy.

Powell and Wolfowitz began working closely together. At later times and on other issues the two men emerged as adversaries; in this instance, seeking to come up with modest defense reductions and a rationale that would forestall deeper cuts from Congress, they saw eye to eye. Over the first half of 1990 they and their staffs crafted what amounted to a first attempt at a post–cold war military strategy. Cheney unveiled parts of it in the spring, and the complete version was presented by President Bush in Aspen, Colorado, on August 2, 1990.

In this revised strategy, the Pentagon for the first time recognized the permanence of the changes in Eastern Europe and accepted that in response America could reduce the size of its own armed forces. Bush announced that America's active-duty armed forces would be cut by nearly 25 percent over five years, from 2.1 million to about 1.6 million. Yet he warned that the Soviet Union might still pose a future threat. "The Soviet Union remains a world-class military power," said the president.[11] Cheney went further, suggesting that because of the Soviet Union's amicable new relationship with the West, it might be able to acquire advanced military technology that could even make it more dangerous. "We may well find ourselves ten or fifteen years from now faced with a Soviet military that's smaller, but that is in fact more capable, more lethal than it is today in terms of its modern capabilities," the defense secretary warned.[12]

At the same time, both Bush and Cheney began to refocus the justification for American military power away from the Soviet threat. They pointed to different sorts of dangers. "Terrorism, hostage-taking, renegade regimes and unpredictable rulers, new sources of instability—all require a strong and an engaged America," said the president. Above all, he said, there was the danger posed by the spread of nuclear, biological and chemical weapons. Cheney expressed astonishment that anyone should have thought America's troops and weaponry had anything to do with anticommunism. "I don't think the notion of a military threat to the interests of the United States was invented by the Communist Party of the Soviet Union, and I think it will be there long after the Communist Party of the Soviet Union no longer wields the interest that it has in the past," asserted Cheney.[13]

Within a year the defense secretary shifted his rationale once again. By February 1991 he was warning about the opposite danger from the Soviet Union: not that it might someday regain its military strength but rather that it might weaken or fall apart. In justifying a new defense budget, he told Congress that he was worried about "the Soviet inability to control events inside the Soviet Union."[14]

Over this period, Powell too was advancing new justifications for maintaining America's military power. Powell and Wolfowitz together began arguing for what was called a base force, a minimum level of strength that the United States needed to preserve, even in the absence of any immediate threats. "We might not face the old threat from the Soviet Union . . . but we had to maintain certain fundamental capabilities," Powell explained.[15]

In fact, by the spring of 1991, after the end of the Gulf War, Powell had begun to suggest that there really was no serious military threat to the United States anymore. "I'm running out of demons. I'm running out of villains. I'm down to Castro and Kim Il Sung," he joked in an *Army Times* interview. With Saddam Hussein vanquished, said the chairman of the Joint Chiefs, "I would be very surprised if another Iraq occurred."[16]

Yet Powell contended that the United States needed to build and maintain its military strength, even if there were no other superpowers. "We no longer have the luxury of having a threat to plan for," he said in another interview that spring. "What we plan for is that we're a superpower. We are the major player on the world stage with responsibilities around the world, with interests around the world."[17]

At one point during the 1991 budget hearings, Senator John Glenn asked Powell a casual question—not about what he and Cheney had said but about what they had left out. "I don't know whether this is inadvertent or not," said Glenn. "It doesn't seem to me that in his [Cheney's] whole statement or in your statement that there really is any emphasis on the United Nations," the senator told Powell. ". . . Is this sort of inadvertent that we're reading the U.N. out of our future planning? Because I thought that was going to be one of the key elements of this new world order. . . ."

Powell deflected the query. "I think it's just premature at this point to make judgments about what the new security arrangement might be," he told Glenn.[18] In fact, the United Nations was not to be a central element in America's new vision.

From 1989 to 1991, as Cheney, Powell and Wolfowitz were revising their strategies and defense budgets, others in the Bush administration were struggling to come to grips with Gorbachev and the political changes in the Soviet Union. In these endeavors, Condoleezza Rice emerged as a central figure. Winning the trust of Bush and Scowcroft, she became their representative, both in resolving the numerous disputes within the Washington bureaucracy over Soviet policy and in preparing their meetings with Soviet leaders.

At first Rice worked at the lowest level of the National Security Council staff, serving under Robert Blackwill, the senior director for European and Soviet affairs. Before long, as Soviet policy became the preoccupying issue of the Bush administration, "I just moved her out and made her sort of independent," recalled Scowcroft. She was given the title of senior director in May 1990 and then promoted again to special assistant to the president three months later.[19]

It was Rice who was assigned the thankless task of handling Boris Yeltsin when he asked to visit the White House in September 1989. At the time Yeltsin, the former Communist party secretary for Moscow, had emerged as Gorbachev's leading critic; he complained that Gorbachev's reforms were too timid and that he should get rid of conservative leaders in the Politburo. Bush and Scowcroft didn't want to anger Gorbachev with a warm embrace of Yeltsin, but they didn't want to deny Yeltsin a White House meeting either. Scowcroft remembered all too well the furor when President Ford had refused to meet with the dissident Aleksandr Solzhenitsyn.

The president and his national security adviser decided Yeltsin would not be granted a presidential meeting in the Oval Office but would be permitted a talk with Scowcroft (at which Bush would casually "drop by" in a supposedly unplanned manner). When Yeltsin arrived at the White House's West Wing, Rice was there to greet him. Yeltsin demanded an assurance he would see the president. Rice coolly told him his appointment was with Scowcroft. Yeltsin countered that without the guarantee of a presidential audience, he wasn't taking a single step further. [20]

In hindsight, this Rice-Yeltsin confrontation was almost comic; it is difficult to imagine a greater contrast in styles and personalities. Rice's entire life was a testimonial to self-discipline. Yeltsin was prone to alcoholic binges; on the previous night he had consumed more than a quart of Jack Daniel's whiskey.[21] Rice was respectful of (and regularly rewarded by) elites. Yeltsin relished challenging the Soviet elites, or nomenklatura. When Yeltsin asked in Moscow for a White House meeting, he certainly didn't envision he'd be seeing a young African-American woman. When Rice was invited to leave Stanford and coordinate Soviet policy for the White House, she didn't imagine she'd be dealing with a beefy, thundering Russian populist.

Finally Rice ended their standoff with an implied threat. She told Yeltsin that if he didn't want to keep his appointment with the national security adviser, he should return to his hotel. Yeltsin gave in. Rice virtually pushed him up the stairs into Scowcroft's office, for a meeting that Bush eventually joined.

"He [Yeltsin] made a bad impression on Condi that visit, and I think that this had an effect later on," said Rice's longtime colleague Michael McFaul, a Russia scholar at Stanford University. During the 1990s, when the Clinton administration gave its strong support to Yeltsin as Russia's president, Rice became a leading critic of that policy. Only after Yeltsin had been succeeded by the tightly controlled personality of President Vladimir Putin did Rice once again support a close American identification with the president of Russia.

In this period the Bush administration was beset by a progressive series of internal disputes over Soviet policy. At first in 1989 the question was whether to work closely with Gorbachev, as the Reagan administration had in its final year. After initial caution the administration decided to proceed. By 1991, the issue was whether to back away from Gorbachev and begin to show greater support instead for Yeltsin and the anti-Communist opposition. In these debates Secretary of State James A. Baker usually took the pro-Gorbachev position; the skeptics were Cheney, Deputy National Security Adviser Robert M. Gates and the Soviet specialists at the CIA.

Rice offered few far-reaching ideas of her own. "She was not a conceptualizer," said Fritz Ermarth, one of the CIA's Soviet specialists. Instead, she managed to persuade virtually all the participants that she agreed with them. Even many years later both the hawks and the doves were still equally convinced that during these debates over Soviet policy, Rice had been in their corner. "I felt she was closer to us than to Gates," asserted Dennis Ross, Baker's principal adviser on Soviet policy. Yet the hawkish Gates, in his memoirs, repeatedly described Rice as a key ally and supporter in these same intra-administration arguments.[22] Navigating among these competing factions enabled Rice to practice the bureaucratic skills she needed more than a decade later when, as national security adviser in the George W. Bush administration, she was obliged to settle even nastier battles between Colin Powell's State Department and Donald Rumsfeld's Pentagon.

America's military strategy against the Soviet Union relied heavily upon a network of bases in allied countries around the world through which the United States could move its troops, ships and warplanes. Among the largest of these installations were the Subic Bay Naval Station and Clark Air Force Base in the Philippines. On April 10, 1990, President Bush named Richard Armitage to negotiate with the government of Philippine President Corazon Aquino a new agreement permitting the United States to continue using these bases.

Armitage's appointment made sense in several ways. He knew the Philippines well. At the end of the Vietnam War he had sailed into Subic Bay with his convoy of twenty thousand South Vietnamese refugees. In the 1980s he had been closely involved in the Reagan administration's decision to withdraw support from President Ferdinand Marcos. Armitage also knew the Pentagon well, a key requirement, since the U.S. negotiators were going to have to come up with a package of aid for the Philippines to help pay for the bases. "He knew all the programs and money at the Defense Department and where they were buried," recalled Matt Daley, a State Department official on the negotiating team. Armitage had strong ties to the military, starting with his friendship with Powell, the chairman of the Joint Chiefs of Staff.

Armitage quickly confronted an outpouring of Philippine sentiment to oust the American military from the bases. Subic Bay and Clark were portrayed as lingering symbols of America's colonial occupation of the Philippines after the Spanish-American War. Top Philippine officials, among them Foreign Secretary Raul Manglapus, joined in the nationalist opposition to any renewal of the American bases. At one point Manglapus had informed correspondents that Filipinos needed to "slay the American father image" in order to become a sovereign nation."[23]

In conducting the negotiations, Armitage was characteristically blunt. Ostensibly, the main issue was how much the Americans should pay. Aquino and her government sought $825 million annually for a seven-year renewal of the leases on the bases, far more than the Americans were willing to pay. At the outset of the talks Armitage announced that he hadn't come to the Philippines to engage in "cash-register diplomacy." Those words created an uproar in Manila. Cartoons began appearing in Manila's newspapers showing Armitage as a muscle-bound bully trying to intimidate the wiry, bespectacled Manglapus. Nevertheless, after insisting the talks weren't about money, Armitage came up with a package of $360 million annually for a ten-year renewal of the leases on the bases.

Ultimately the result of the negotiations was determined by an unexpected natural disaster. On June 9, 1991, the volcano Mount Pinatubo erupted in the Philippines, covering Clark with ash, and the U.S. Air Force soon decided that it no longer wanted to keep the base. Soon afterward Armitage worked out with the Aquino government a proposed treaty under which the United States would remain at Subic Bay for ten years but turn Clark over to the Philippines; the U.S. aid package was cut to $203 million a year, far below the earlier American offers of $360 million. On September 16, 1991, the Philippine Senate voted 12–11 to reject the treaty.

Within less than a year the American military pulled out of the Philippines entirely. In the case of Subic Bay, the U.S. Navy abandoned its best and largest ship repair facilities outside the United States, as well as a deepwater harbor that it had held since Commodore George Dewey vanquished the Spanish fleet in Manila Bay in 1898. On the surface it seemed a serious defeat for the Pentagon.

Yet over the long run the departure from the Philippines was also a reflection of America's growing, changing military power. U.S. military planners were in the process of adapting to a new environment, one in which they no longer had to worry about the Soviet Union. Two decades earlier the United States had been preoccupied with the fear of Communist expansion throughout Southeast Asia; by 1991 those fears had vanished. In military terms, the United States didn't need Clark and Subic as much as it had in the past. The Navy could find other countries to take over some of the functions of Subic Bay; indeed, within a short time the Navy transferred some of Subic's ship repair work to Singapore and Japan. As the range of American warplanes increased and as the United States developed the capacity for air-to-air refueling, Clark had become even less necessary. By 1991 the United States also no longer needed Subic Bay and Clark as tangible symbols of the continuing American military presence in Asia. By that time the United States had become the unchallenged military power in the region, with or without its bases in the Philippines.

As defense secretary, Cheney had warned in the midst of the talks that America's view of its need for the Philippine bases was changing. If the Philippines didn't want a new treaty for the bases, the defense secretary said in the summer of 1991, "We'll pack up and leave. That's it." In the end the United States made good on these threats. When the U.S. Navy withdrew from Subic Bay, it left little equipment behind. Over the following years American military aid to the Philippines evaporated. When presidents and other top-level American officials visited Asia, Manila was no longer an obligatory stopping point. The United States managed to demonstrate that American military power was so great that it no longer depended on any individual country or military base.[24]

At the end of 1991 the Soviet Union broke up and disappeared. That sent Pentagon planners back to the drawing boards once again. The strategies and budgets they had put forward over the previous two years had assumed that the Soviet Union would continue to exist, although the threat from it would be greatly diminished. Now the Soviet collapse altered the calculations once again.

In Congress the calls for a large peace dividend intensified. Senator Edward M. Kennedy proposed taking $210 billion from the defense budget over seven years and devoting the money to universal health insurance, education and job programs.[25] Amid the new climate of uncertainty, even Wolfowitz, who had heretofore regularly warned against exaggerating the degree of change in the Soviet Union, fell into unaccustomed optimism about the extent to which future Russian governments might help the United States. He raised the possibility that Russian troops might someday fight side by side with Americans. "We would even hope . . . if we were to face a crisis like the Persian Gulf ten years from now, that a democratic Russia would not just be a sort of passive political partner, but would be an active military participant in a coalition, if we had to put one together," Wolfowitz asserted.[26]

Wolfowitz's office was working intensively on the preparation of a new version of the Defense Planning Guidance. This classified document, rewritten every two years, describes America's overall military strategy and serves as the basis for coming defense budgets. The 1992 Defense Planning Guidance was to be the first since the Soviet collapse. It was an early draft of this document that leaked to the press in March 1992, making public the vision of the United States as the world's sole superpower, actively warding off potential rivals.

Ever since it first came to light, this document has been linked to Wolfowitz's name. He has received both the credit and the blame for it. That judgment is ultimately fair since the Defense Planning Guidance was drafted by Wolfowitz's office and reflected, in a general sense, many of his ideas. Yet attributing the document to Wolfowitz carries a triple irony. First, the ultimate sponsor of this now-famous document, the person who took primary responsibility for it, was Cheney, the defense secretary. Second, Wolfowitz didn't write the document himself and never saw it before it became public; indeed, for a few days afterward he nervously sought to distance himself from it. Third, Wolfowitz and his top aide Scooter Libby thought that in subtle but important ways, the early draft that leaked to the press was flawed, not because it was too radical but because in some ways it didn't go far enough.

Inside the Pentagon, Wolfowitz had delegated the job of coming up with the new Defense Planning Guidance to Libby, his protégé and top assistant, who held the title of principal deputy undersecretary of defense for strategy and resources. The document was due in early 1992 and was to serve as the basis for future defense budgets starting in fiscal year 1994. Libby, in turn, assigned the task of writing the new strategy to Khalilzad, a member of his staff and another longtime aide to Wolfowitz.

Khalilzad began holding meetings on what this new Defense Planning Guidance should say. Sometimes Wolfowitz and Libby participated, as well as other Pentagon insiders, such as Andrew Marshall, the head of the Office of Net Assessment, the Pentagon's internal think tank. Outsiders also invited to contribute ideas included Richard Perle and Wolfowitz's University of Chicago mentor, Albert Wohlstetter.[27]

Khalilzad set to work crafting the new vision and finished a draft at the beginning of March. He asked Libby for permission to circulate it to other officials inside the Pentagon for comment. Libby gave his okay without reading the draft. Within three days the draft sent out by Khalilzad was passed to the *New York Times* by someone described in the newspaper as "an official who believes this post-cold-war strategy debate should be carried out in the public domain."[28]

Khalilzad's draft echoed some of the ideas Wolfowitz had been putting forward in his speeches. "In the Middle East and Southwest Asia, our overall objective is to remain the predominant outside power in the region and preserve U.S. and Western access to the region's oil," the statement said. In Western Europe and East Asia as well as the Middle East, the goal of American policy should be "to prevent any hostile power from dominating a region whose resources would, under consolidated control, be sufficient to generate global power." The draft suggested the possibility of bringing the new states of Central and Eastern Europe into the European Union and of giving them new security commitments from the United States that would protect them from an attack by Russia.

The part of Khalilzad's draft that attracted the most notice was its suggestion that the United States should work actively to block the emergence of any potential competitor to American power. Vague as it was, this language seemed to apply to Japan, Germany or a united Europe, as well as to China and Russia. The draft said the United States should discourage the "advanced industrial nations" from challenging America's leadership, in part by taking these countries' interests into account but also through unmatchable military strength.[29]

At the time there was speculation that America's future competitors would be Germany and Japan. Germany had just reunified, and Japan was at the apogee of its economic power after decades of remarkable growth. During the early presidential primaries for the 1992 election Democratic candidate Paul Tsongas told voters the result of the cold war was that "Japan won." Henry Kissinger argued that the growing "German domination of Europe" was reducing American influence on the Continent. American bookstores in 1992 included new titles like Lester Thurow's *Head to Head: The Coming Economic Battle Among Japan, Europe and America*. Inside the White House, Scowcroft acknowledged he was increasingly worried about growing "West-West" conflict among the United States, Japan and Germany.[30] Khalilzad's draft suggested that that the competition with Japan and Germany should be confined to economics; the United States should make sure it had no military rivals.

The initial news stories about the Pentagon's proposed strategy provoked a deluge of criticism, both inside the United States and overseas. Bill Clinton, the leading Democratic presidential candidate, said through his campaign spokesman George Stephanopoulos that the document represented "one more attempt" by Pentagon officials "to find an excuse for big budgets instead of downsizing." Tsongas called for "a United Nations Security Force with real teeth" and for "a new internationalism truly based on the principle of collective security." In Germany one leading official called the Pentagon draft "a prescription for disaster." In response, columnist Charles Krauthammer defended the Pentagon's new vision. "What is the alternative?" he asked. "The alternative is Japanese carriers patrolling the Strait of Malacca, and a nuclear Germany dominating Europe."[31]

The Bush White House moved quickly to end the furor. The image of an America eager to keep its allies weak was not likely to win friends for the United States overseas. Nor was the debate over America's military strategy one that the administration wanted to conduct in public during an election year. The White House distanced itself from the leaked Pentagon document. So, for that matter, did Wolfowitz.

Khalilzad, who had written the draft, found that Wolfowitz was unhappy with the controversy it had engendered. "In the postleak environment, he [Wolfowitz] didn't want to be associated with it," Khalilzad explained. For a few days Khalilzad felt a bit insulted and ostracized. Then the atmosphere turned around—because Cheney read the leaked document and praised it. "He said to me, 'You've discovered a new rationale for our role in the world,'" recalled Khalilzad in an interview.[32]

Libby thought that Khalilzad's version of America's strategy had missed a key point.[33] In a subtle way it hadn't gone far enough. The draft suggested that the main purpose of American military power was to preserve America's role as a superpower and to block countries like Japan and Germany from equaling the United States. That sounded like a provocative idea, but in practical terms, it wasn't saying much. There was no rival on the horizon. Libby recognized that with its existing weaponry and technology, the United States could remain the most powerful nation in the world for a decade or two, without even breaking a sweat. There would not even be much need to develop new weapons systems.

Libby wanted to shift the emphasis subtly. The main point shouldn't be to block rival powers, but rather for the United States to become so militarily strong, so overwhelming that no country would dream of ever becoming a rival. America should build up its military lead to such an extent that other countries would be dissuaded from even *starting* to compete with the United States. The costs would be too high; America's military technology would be so advanced, its defense budget so high that no one else could afford the huge sums necessary to embark on a long-term military buildup that, even if successful, would still not catch up to the United States for thirty years or more. Thus the United States would be the world's lone superpower not just today or ten years from now but permanently.

Libby set out to rewrite the leaked document. The aim was twofold: to smooth over some of Khalilzad's provocative language, the "keep-the-allies-down" theme that had made the White House uneasy, and at the same time to emphasize the broader idea of America's enduring military superiority.

Two months later Pentagon officials informed reporters that the document had been recast in such a way that it was dramatically different from the original. Officials suggested to reporters that the original draft had been toned down. The Pentagon had "abandoned" the idea that its strategy should be to block the emergence of a rival to American military supremacy, reported one Pentagon correspondent.[34]

However, the revised vision of American strategy contained most of the same ideas as the original. Libby's new draft came up with euphemisms in order to make the wording sound less confrontational. The final version didn't talk about stopping allies from emerging as rivals. But it said the United States should "preclude any hostile power from dominating a region critical to our interests." Presumably any nation that came to rival American power could be deemed potentially "hostile" if its policies weren't aligned with those of the United States.[35]

Libby's rewritten strategy didn't speak explicitly of a lone American superpower. Instead, it emphasized the need to preserve what was blandly termed America's strategic depth, its wide lead over other countries in military and technological capabilities. Libby's new document avoided saying that the United States would actively work to maintain its preeminence. Rather, it spoke vaguely about "shaping the future security environment." In other words, America would not sit back and wait for threats or rivals to emerge.[36] These ideas, preserving America's strategic depth and shaping the security environment, became key concepts that other Vulcans, such as Wolfowitz, would invoke over the coming years.

The new version of American strategy left as much latitude for unilateral American action as did Khalilzad's. Libby's revision (unlike the original) included numerous references to the importance of America's alliances and to the advisability of collective security. Yet it also repeatedly raised questions about whether collective action would work and left open the possibility the United States would act alone. "We will, therefore, not ignore the need to be prepared to protect our critical interests and honor our commitments with only limited additional help, or even alone, if necessary," the final version said. "A future President will need options allowing him to lead and, where the international reaction proves sluggish or inadequate, to act independently to protect our critical interests."[37]

Libby believed that overall, contrary to the press reports, his revised version had toughened rather than weakened the original draft. In its final form the Pentagon's Defense Planning Guidance had two parts: an overall statement of American strategy and a section on immediate implications, detailing the military capabilities the Pentagon needed to develop and the contingencies it needed to keep in mind in the coming years. The second part remains classified, but the statement of overall strategy—essentially Libby's rewrite of Khalilzad's draft—was declassified and published in January 1993, after the presidential election and shortly before the Bush administration left office.

This Pentagon's strategy for permanent American military superiority was issued under Cheney's name, and Cheney played the key role in making the document public. "He wanted to show that he stood for the idea," said Khalilzad. "He took ownership of it."[38]

Looking back many years later, Paul Wolfowitz insisted that he never understood why so much attention had been paid to the Defense Planning Guidance of 1992. "Why did it stir up so much fuss?" he asked in an interview. The document was designed, Wolfowitz said, to explain why America needed to maintain the core of its troop deployments overseas, even though it was making significant cutbacks. "What we were afraid of was people who would say . . . 'Let's bring all of the troops home, and let's abandon our position in Europe,'" he asserted. "It's hard to imagine just how uncertain the world looked after the end of the cold war."[39] In an article written at the end of the 1990s Wolfowitz argued that the ideas his office drafted in 1992 had turned into the consensus, mainstream view of America's post–cold war defense strategy.[40]

That claim may have been an exaggeration, but only a slight one. Over the following eight years of the Clinton administration, the Democrats did not specifically embrace the vision that America should operate as the world's sole superpower or that it should work to block other nations from emerging as rivals to the United States. Yet the Democrats' rhetoric and policies conformed in many respects to the ideas put forward by Wolfowitz's staff in 1992.

Clinton's secretary of state, Madeleine Albright, regularly referred to the United States as the "indispensable nation," embracing a vision of America's role in the world that was not substantially different from the idea of the United States as lone superpower. The Clinton administration distanced itself from the United Nations and the concept of collective security following the disastrous operation in Somalia in 1993. It conducted a large-scale massive military intervention in Kosovo without UN approval. (Indeed, when the George W. Bush administration was trying to decide in early 2003 whether to seek United Nations approval before launching its war against Iraq, Richard Holbrooke, Clinton's former UN ambassador, argued that the Kosovo precedent showed there was no need to go to the United Nations.) In short, while Democratic leaders often accused the Republicans of unilateralism, the truth was that the Clinton administration too gave far less weight to principles of collective security than had America's leaders from the 1940s through the 1980s.

After an initial review of defense issues when Clinton took office in 1993, his administration preserved the general outlines and structure of the post–cold war force structure that had been worked out under Cheney, Powell and Wolfowitz. The Pentagon strategy of 1992 had spoken vaguely of extending new security commitments to the new democracies of Eastern Europe; the Clinton administration did precisely that, expanding NATO to include Poland, Hungary and the Czech Republic.

The defense budget was never substantially reduced by either party; over the decade following the 1992 Defense Planning Guidance, the United States gave practical meaning to its vision of strategic depth by reaching the point where American defense spending was larger than that of the next fifteen nations combined.

Overall, the Democrats failed to come up with any clear alternative vision of American strategy that would forswear the 1992 vision of the United States as a sole superpower. When the Clinton administration sought to articulate its own view of America's role in the world, it stressed the importance of globalization, open markets and democracy. Those themes did not contradict the 1992 strategy, but rather described the economic and political basis of the new international system the United States intended to dominate. The Republicans didn't oppose Clinton's economic vision of globalization, and the Democrats did not challenge the Republican military vision of America as the sole superpower. It sometimes seemed as though America's two leading parties were playing the same recording. When Democrats held the White House, they turned up the economic treble. When the Republicans took over, they turned up the military bass.

CHAPTER FOURTEEN

Vulcans in Exile

IN THE LATE SPRING OF 1992 Dennis Ross, Secretary of State James Baker's leading adviser, began quietly suggesting that President Bush make a high-level change in his administration, a grand strategic gambit. The president, he argued, should alter the dynamics of the 1992 election by naming Colin Powell, the chairman of the Joint Chiefs of Staff, as his vice presidential running mate.[1]

Bush's reelection was increasingly in doubt. The American economy had just gone through two bouts of recession in 1990 and 1991. The unemployment rate stood at 7.8 percent. The polls showed that Bush's popularity was sinking. Many Americans believed that the president cared more about foreign policy than domestic issues. In Washington members of Bush's foreign policy team, which operated as a separate, favored elite within the administration, reflected the national unease. "Is the domestic team ever going to get its act together?" one foreign policy official asked a reporter.

The president, struggling to reverse his political decline, had his own notions for reshuffling his administration. Bush was thinking of moving Baker to the job of White House chief of staff, a job from which Baker could run the president's drive for reelection. Baker, who had already managed presidential campaigns first for Gerald Ford and then for Bush, didn't want to be dragged away from the State Department for yet another political campaign. "I was the guy who came up with the idea to dump [Vice President Dan] Quayle and have Powell become the vice president," recalled Ross. "Baker was saying, 'Hey, you've got to come up with something so that I don't have to go to the White House.' And this was the only thing I could come up with."

Meanwhile, within the Democratic party, after Bill Clinton had wrapped up the presidential nomination, the search was on for a vice presidential running mate who could boost Clinton's appeal. Some advisers began clandestinely exploring the possibility of a surprise choice: Colin Powell. In May, Vernon Jordan, Clinton's adviser and friend who was also close to Powell, approached the chairman of the Joint Chiefs. "Your polls are running off the chart," he said. "Are you interested in running as Clinton's VP?"[2] No American military leader since Eisenhower had been chosen to run as a major-party candidate for president or vice president. Now Powell, like Eisenhower, was being courted by both political parties.

Neither of these scenarios came to pass. On the Republican side Bush's intense sense of personal loyalty caused him to reject any suggestion of replacing Quayle. "He said, 'He's served me loyally, and I won't do it to him. If it means I lose the election, I lose the election,'" Ross recalled. Powell turned down the Democratic overtures. He still had more than a year to go in his second term as chairman, a job that he had transformed in such a way that it seemed to carry considerably more authority than did the vice presidency. Moreover, Powell admired Bush; the idea of running against the president who had appointed him chairman offended Powell's sense of fairness.

For Powell, that 1992 presidential campaign was merely the beginning. Throughout the 1990s, he was the perennial noncandidate. Virtually every time one of America's top civilian or foreign policy positions was open, Powell's name came up. During the transition of 1992–93, Vernon Jordan asked if Powell would be interested in becoming Clinton's secretary of state. He declined. After the 1994 congressional elections first Jordan and then Clinton sounded Powell out once again about becoming secretary of state, and Powell again said no.[3] In 1995, in the most public of these many flirtations, Powell examined the possibility of running for president, before deciding against the idea. Still, his name was mentioned again as a potential vice presidential nominee in 1996.

During this period two overarching realities became evident. The first was that Powell was never going to win the support of the conservative wing of the Republican party. His views on domestic social issues were outspokenly in favor of affirmative action and gun control; they were more in line with the Democrats than the Republicans. Nevertheless, and second, Powell was not going to join the Democratic party, for reasons that had almost entirely to do with foreign policy. He had served at senior levels in the national security apparatus under both Reagan and Bush. His identification with the Republicans was based not merely upon personal loyalties but also upon a vision of how to deal with the world that was closer to that of other Republicans than to the Democrats.

It is important to note that in this preference for Republican foreign policy, Powell was reflecting his own personal views and history, not necessarily that of the entire U.S. military leadership. William Crowe, Powell's immediate predecessor as chairman of the Joint Chiefs of Staff, endorsed Clinton in 1992 and later served as Clinton's ambassador to London. Powell saw things differently. He had some continuing differences with more conservative Republicans like Cheney and Wolfowitz, yet he shared with them a belief in American power, in the importance of a strong military and in the primacy of security issues over economic issues in U.S. foreign policy. He also believed that the Republicans simply were better managers of foreign policy than the Democrats, a view he had formed from his experiences in the Carter, Reagan and Bush administrations and his memory of the Democratic escalation of the Vietnam War.

In August, bowing to Bush's request, Baker resigned as secretary of state to become White House chief of staff. To close aides he confessed his unhappiness. "I'm being asked to go from resolving Arab-Israeli issues to determining whether we have ducks or balloons at a rally," he grumbled.[4] That fall Baker rarely traveled with the campaign; he stayed inside the White House, dispirited. Bush seemed to hope Baker might help him overcome his own lack of enthusiasm for domestic politics; instead, Baker merely amplified the sense of presidential ennui. The 1992 campaign left a residue of mistrust, not necessarily between Bush and Baker, who remained friends, but between Baker and others in the Bush family. Eight years later, when George W. Bush became president, the top foreign policy jobs went primarily to the protégés of Brent Scowcroft and Dick Cheney in the earlier Bush administration, while Baker's old team remained on the margins.

Cheney escaped Baker's fate. He was not formally drafted into the 1992 campaign. Nevertheless, the defense secretary participated. That summer Cheney asked what the Pentagon might do to help the president's reelection. In September, just as the general election campaign was beginning, the Bush administration announced two groundbreaking arms sales, first the approval of 150 F-16 jet fighters to Taiwan, a transaction estimated to be worth six billion dollars, and then a few days later 72 F-15 warplanes to Saudi Arabia, a sale valued at approximately nine billion dollars. The F-16s were manufactured in Texas and the F-15s in Missouri and California, all states important to Bush's hopes for reelection. A month later Kuwait agreed to purchase 236 M1 main battle tanks made in Michigan and Ohio, after Cheney wrote a personal letter to the Kuwaiti prime minister asking him to buy tanks from the United States rather than Britain. In an interview several years later Cheney maintained that these arms sales were legitimate and that he had kept the Pentagon divorced from presidential politics in 1992. He acknowledged, however, that the Bush campaign team might have "packaged" the public announcements of the Pentagon's arms sale for political reasons.[5]

Bush was headed for defeat, with or without the arms deals Cheney was arranging. In November, Clinton won 43 percent of the popular vote, Bush 38 percent and Ross Perot 19 percent. For the first time in twelve years the Republicans lost their hold over the White House and the executive branch of government.

Clinton's victory had not turned on foreign policy issues. He had proposed some modest reductions in the defense budget (laying out goals that in the end he did not keep). But he had also promised "an America with the world's strongest defense, ready and willing to use force when necessary."[6] He had criticized Bush for his reluctance to use force in Bosnia, thus suggesting that he might be more willing than the Republican president to send American troops on overseas missions. Clinton did not offer any alternative to the Vulcans' vision of America as the world's lone superpower.

Indeed, one of the main reasons for Clinton's victory was that with the cold war over, American voters felt secure enough to turn back to the Democrats, whose record on foreign policy had been a liability in presidential elections ever since the Vietnam War. In Clinton's acceptance speech at the Democratic National Convention he proclaimed, "Just as we have won the Cold War abroad, we are losing the battles for economic opportunity and social justice here at home."[7] The pithier, more famous version of the same theme came from Clinton's adviser James Carville: "It's the economy, stupid." To the Bush administration and especially to the Vulcans working in it, foreign policy was paramount. In 1992 they were out of tune with the mood of America.

Most of the Republican appointees at the Pentagon, including Cheney, Wolfowitz and Libby, left office with Bush. Colin Powell was among the few who stayed; his term as chairman of the Joint Chiefs ran until September 1993.

A few weeks before Clinton was sworn in, Lawrence Korb, a former Pentagon official who had become a proponent of deep cutbacks in the defense budget, talked over breakfast with Les Aspin, who had been appointed the new secretary of defense. Korb made a bold suggestion: Why shouldn't Clinton replace Colin Powell or at least announce immediately that he intended to do so?

Korb's logic was simple: As the new administration sought to carry out its policies, Powell would be placed in an impossible position. Clinton and Aspin had proposed to cut the defense budget back below the minimum or base force levels worked out by the Bush administration. Yet the budget Clinton had pledged to cut bore Powell's imprimatur; he had been its prime sponsor and had spent the previous three years of his life explaining to Congress why there could not be further reductions. Military leaders were supposed to carry out the directions of civilian leaders, yet one could not expect Powell to help cut the defense budget in ways he had long argued were unwise. He would be an impediment.[8]

Clinton and Aspin turned aside Korb's recommendation, as he must have known they would. Powell was by this time a prominent, popular national figure, and Clinton's own lack of military service had been a campaign issue. The new president was not willing to pose such a direct challenge to the military.

The next nine months were the most awkward in Powell's military career. He was out of step with the Clinton team, both stylistically and on the issues. With his passion for order and punctuality, Powell had believed that even the Bush administration's foreign policy meetings had been slightly too unstructured and windy; the Clinton administration's were much more so. Powell disagreed with the new administration's fumbling attempts to cut the defense budget. He opposed the administration's attempts to end the ban on discrimination against gays in the military. Above all, Powell found himself struggling yet again to defend his reluctance to send American troops into battle except under carefully delineated conditions and circumstances.

Since the summer of 1992 U.S. officials had been debating the possibility of air strikes in Bosnia to help protect the beleaguered Muslim population from Serbian atrocities. That fall Powell, again wielding his unprecedented power as chairman of the Joint Chiefs, had come out strongly against military intervention. In an op-ed article in the *New York Times*, writing as though he were in the midst of a political campaign, Powell boasted of the U.S. military's record of success under his leadership in Panama and the Persian Gulf. "There have been no Bay of Pigs, failed desert raids, Beirut bombings and no Vietnams," Powell said. The reason, he maintained, was that military force had been used only to accomplish narrow, carefully specified political objectives. ". . . You bet I get nervous when so-called experts suggest that all we need is a little surgical bombing or a limited attack. When the desired result isn't obtained, a new set of experts then comes forward with talk of a little escalation."[9]

Soon after the Clinton administration was sworn in, the Bosnia debate started up again. This time Powell was arguing against military intervention not merely with civilian leaders but with civilians from the Democratic party, the party that he remembered had sent hundreds of thousands of American troops to Vietnam. The bickering over Bosnia policy culminated in Powell's testy exchange with Madeleine Albright, then Clinton's ambassador to the United Nations. "What's the point of having this superb military that you're always talking about if we can't use it?" asked Albright. Recounting the incident in his memoirs, Powell said, "I thought I would have an aneurysm."[10]

It would be another two years before the Clinton administration finally decided upon the use of air strikes to help resolve the Bosnia conflict, and by that time Powell was in retirement. Even then Powell made plain to all who would listen his opposition to American intervention in the Balkans. In the earthiest rendition Powell ever gave of his views on the use of force, he told African-American scholar Henry Louis Gates, Jr., in a 1995 interview, "I believe in the bully's way of going to war. 'I'm on the street corner, I got my gun, I got my blade, *I'ma kick yo' ass.*'" Air strikes in Bosnia didn't meet Powell's standards.[11]

The initial, furious wrangling over Bosnia under Bush had one little-noticed consequence. It set the stage for the American decision to send forces on an entirely different mission to Somalia. In late 1992 the United States was asked to dispatch American troops to that African nation in order to help the United Nations deliver food shipments there. Bush, with Powell's acquiescence, approved the request.

The U.S. involvement in Somalia has often been explained as a reaction to televised pictures of starving African children. Yet the reasons were more complex. It is impossible to understand the surprising willingness to send troops to Somalia except in the context of the debates at the time over Bosnia and over cutting the U.S. defense budget. The Bush administration and Powell did not want to reject a second appeal for U.S. armed forces to carry out a humanitarian mission in Somalia after they had just also ruled out the use of force in Bosnia. A new Democratic administration was about to be sworn in, one with different priorities and different political constituencies; Powell would need to demonstrate to this new civilian leadership that the U.S. military was still a valuable tool of foreign policy. If the Pentagon had said no to military intervention in both Bosnia and Somalia, a Democratic administration and a Democratic Congress would certainly have asked what America was receiving for all the money it was spending on defense. Was the U.S. military merely sitting back and waiting for another major war against an enemy like the Soviet Union, even if such an enemy might never materialize?

Thus, whereas Powell determinedly resisted sending American forces to Bosnia, he went along in the case of Somalia. In Bush's final weeks in office he approved the initial decision to send American troops. Then, under the Clinton administration, Powell acquiesced, however reluctantly, when the mission of the American troops was expanded from protecting food shipments to supporting the United Nations' efforts at nation building and then to helping track down and apprehend the Somali clan leader Mohammed Farah Aidid. In the final weeks of his four years as chairman of the Joint Chiefs, Powell approved the dispatch of U.S. Rangers and the Delta Force to capture Aidid.

By the time this gradual Somalia escalation came to its disastrous end with the firefight that killed eighteen Americans, Powell had already retired. Clinton administration officials say that well before then, in early 1993, Powell had begun to distance himself from the Somalia operation, avoiding the high-level meetings and leaving details up to his deputy, Admiral David Jeremiah. "Powell was AWOL on Somalia," recalled a senior Clinton administration official.[12] Nevertheless, as chairman of the Joint Chiefs at the time the key decisions were made Powell bore some of the responsibility for the fiasco.

Somalia served as an ironic coda to Powell's military career. It managed to violate virtually all the lessons he had learned, the principles of the Powell doctrine. The military and political objectives were not narrowly defined. American public support was not assured. The mission was not vital to U.S. national interests. The United States did not go in with overwhelming force, and it did not get out quickly. Indeed, the American troops had been sent without any clear strategy for how and when the military operation would cease.

Powell's long military career may well have outlived the usefulness of his own doctrine. His rules on the use of force had been formulated in the aftermath of the Vietnam War. They proved to be of questionable application for the murky world of the 1990s, an era of cruise missiles and humanitarian missions, when America sometimes sent troops on overseas missions for different reasons and with different weaponry from the past and when in fact, it was sometimes hard to say what constituted a war or when it started or stopped. These were, however, problems for Powell's successors. On September 20, 1993, his term as chairman ended, and he retired from military service, joining the other Republican appointees in private life.

Besides Powell, only one other Vulcan, Richard Armitage, stayed on into the Clinton administration, and within barely a month he met a predictable fate.

In January 1992, soon after the conclusion of the Philippine base negotiations, Armitage had been appointed the Bush administration's aid coordinator for the former Soviet Union, organizing shipments of food, medical supplies and other relief to Russia and the other former Soviet republics. Once again Armitage was being placed in a post that did not require Senate approval and thus would not subject him to confirmation hearings or to attacks from Ross Perot. "He was put there because he could help get the Air Force involved in the job of delivering food," recalled Robert Fauver, a former State Department official. "There weren't that many people at the State Department who could work with the Department of Defense." Before long Armitage was at odds over the aid with Undersecretary of State Robert Zoellick, one of Baker's top aides. Zoellick kept wanting to attach conditions to the aid in order to reinforce market forces in the former Soviet republics; Armitage simply wanted to deliver the food.[13]

Yet Armitage's disagreements with Zoellick paled in comparison with his differences with the incoming Clinton team. The Russia aid job did not automatically change hands with a new administration, and Armitage continued his work in the first weeks after Clinton's inauguration. Inevitably his candor and his Republican ties led quickly to his departure. In mid-February 1993, speaking at Vanderbilt University, Armitage said he believed Russian President Boris Yeltsin lacked a "grand vision" and that his days were "somewhat numbered. . . . I think he's about at the end of his usefulness and someone else will step on the scene."[14]

Armitage explained afterward that he was merely voicing a personal opinion and not speaking for the U.S. government. For months higher-ranking American officials, including Cheney, the outgoing defense secretary, had been warning in public that Yeltsin might fall from power. Still, those explanations didn't satisfy Strobe Talbott, who had just taken office as President Clinton's new adviser on Russia policy. Bush administration officials, such as Condoleezza Rice, had thought poorly of Yeltsin, but Clinton and Talbott planned to deal with him and support him; in fact, they made Yeltsin the anchor of America's Russia policy for nearly eight years. Within a day after Armitage's remarks were reported, he was summarily replaced.

He soon set up his own private consulting business, Armitage Associates, bringing along as partners several former aides who had worked with him in the U.S. government. He also for a time employed Elizabeth Cheney, the daughter of the former defense secretary. The company attracted a number of clients, including defense firms and oil companies, involved in East Asia, the Middle East and the former Soviet Union, all regions where Armitage had worked while he was in government.

Armitage's firm had a policy that it would do no direct lobbying of Congress. However, it provided private companies with other sorts of help and advice on a range of foreign policy issues: water rights in the Middle East, defense contracts, oil pipelines and telecommunications. In December 1993, for example, Armitage was reported to have written to the U.S. ambassador in the former Soviet republic of Georgia on behalf of an American company seeking to restore its phone contract there. Later in the decade Armitage paid a visit to Heydar Aliyev, the president of Azerbaijan, on behalf of Texaco. Armitage Associates' client list included big American companies like Boeing, Goldman Sachs, Unocal and Brown & Root; firms that received Pentagon contracts, such as SAIC and MPRI; and foreign interests such as the Embassy of Japan, Toshiba, Mitsubishi and the Japan National Oil Corporation.[15]

At the firm's offices in Rosslyn, Virginia, Armitage received not only his formal clients but also a parade of other visitors. There were representatives of foreign governments seeking advice on how to deal with the Clinton administration or Congress and CIA station chiefs and journalists seeking to swap information or rumors. In private life, Armitage even quietly dispensed occasional advice to some of the Democrats: Kurt Campbell, the Pentagon official responsible for Asia during most of the Clinton administration, was a close friend. Above all, though, Armitage stayed active with the Republican network of former foreign policy officials eager to reminisce about the last administration and to plan the next one.

Condoleezza Rice left the Bush administration well before its final days. In early 1991, after two years at the National Security Council, she informed Scowcroft she wanted to depart. At first, there was talk of having her appointed to the California senate seat vacated by Pete Wilson after he was elected governor in 1990.[16] However, Wilson chose as his senate replacement a Republican state senator named John Seymour, who lost the 1992 election. Scowcroft believed that if Wilson had chosen Rice, she would have won.

Instead, Rice in 1991 returned to the Stanford University faculty. She made clear, however, that she was not returning to the routine academic life of an ordinary faculty member. She quickly befriended George Shultz, the former secretary of state, who was at Stanford's Hoover Institution. "I'd like to get more acquainted with American business and how it operates," Rice told Shultz. As Rice probably realized, the former secretary of state was serving on the board of Chevron at the time. "How would you feel about a big bad oil company?" Shultz asked Rice. Within months Rice was named to the Chevron board. The company later named one of its oil tankers the *Condoleezza Rice;* the ship, capable of holding one million barrels of crude oil in its tanks, was put to work bringing oil to the

United States from West Africa, Indonesia and the Middle East. At the end of the decade Rice reported holdings of more than $250,000 in Chevron stock, as well as annual directors' fees of $60,000. Chevron was not her sole company; over the following years, Rice also joined the boards of Transamerica, Hewlett-Packard and Charles Schwab and the advisory council of J. P. Morgan.[17]

In 1993, Stanford University President Gerhard Casper found himself searching for a new provost. He asked Shultz and other elders at Stanford for their advice. Shultz strongly recommended Rice, who had earlier served on the search committee that had chosen Casper for president, and she soon won the appointment. At the age of thirty-eight, she became Stanford's second-in-command; she was responsible for managing more than ten thousand employees and a budget of approximately one and one-half billion dollars.

Many of Stanford's provosts had remained on the job for only two or three years. Rice stayed for six, assuming a wide range of administrative tasks. She cut the budget by nearly seventeen million dollars in her first three years; her decisions engendered a wave of protests and a hunger strike by Chicano students dismayed by the layoff of a Chicano assistant dean. She supervised such new projects as graduate student housing and a science and engineering complex. She supported the principle of affirmative action but was also criticized for failing to bring more women to the Stanford faculty. "She learned a lot about how to run a complex organization," said her friend Stanford Professor Coit Blacker. "I think it gave her a profound sense of confidence in her abilities."[18]

Somehow, Rice managed to find time for other, less high-powered endeavors. While serving as provost, Rice taught an international relations course about the transformation of Europe at the end of the cold war. The class had approximately fifteen students, and Rice assigned a five-page paper each week. Kiron Skinner, an international relations scholar who served as her teaching assistant, was amazed to find that Rice personally read and graded each one of the papers. In her spare time, working with her father, Rice founded an organization called the Center for a New Generation, an after-school program to help students in the impoverished schools of East Palo Alto. Skinner, an African-American woman and Harvard graduate student who was a Rice protégée, completed a doctoral dissertation of more than six hundred pages. Rice, while Stanford provost, served on Skinner's thesis committee, read her dissertation, took part by telephone in her oral examinations and dispensed career help on the side.

Once, when someone had treated Skinner badly, Rice told her, "People may oppose you, but when they realize you can hurt them, they'll join your side." That was the advice of someone becoming familiar and comfortable with power.[19]

Less than three months after leaving the Pentagon at the end of the Bush administration, Paul Wolfowitz was appointed dean of the Johns Hopkins School of Advanced International Studies, one of Washington's most prestigious institutions, which runs graduate programs in foreign policy. The Hopkins position, which he held through the remainder of the decade, was virtually Wolfowitz's first job outside the U.S. government since he had joined the Nixon administration twenty years earlier. His only stints in private life since that time had been merely temporary bridges of a year or less between one job in the State or Defense Department and another.

Wolfowitz became immersed in fund-raising and academic pursuits at the school, yet he also never ventured far from the public issues to which he had devoted his career. He wrote a plethora of articles and op-ed pieces, and he testified before Congress regularly on subjects ranging from Bosnia to North Korea to Indonesia. He spoke regularly about America's preeminent role in the world, developing the themes that had first been put forward by his staff in the Pentagon's strategy document of 1992. Generally, instead of talking about a lone American superpower, he talked about preserving America's "strategic depth," the euphemism that conveyed the same idea. "American dominance gives us an opportunity to lead the world in building a peaceful relationship among the emerging great powers in the next century that will bring security to our children and our grandchildren," he told the House National Security Committee. "If we are unwilling to pay this price now, it will be like failing to buy insurance—there will be a much higher price to be paid later."[20]

Above all and with the greatest passion, Wolfowitz wrote and spoke about Iraq. In a lengthy essay in the *National Interest* published less than a year after he left the Pentagon, he argued that even though Iraq had been neutered militarily by the Gulf War, "Saddam Hussein's continuation in power is a problem." Wolfowitz predicted that it would be difficult to maintain the pressure on Saddam Hussein indefinitely because

some of America's partners from the Gulf War were "greedy for Iraqi contracts" and were eager to lift sanctions. "The United States and the entire
industrialized world have an enormous stake in the security of the Persian
Gulf, not primarily in order to save a few dollars per gallon of gasoline,
but rather because a hostile regime in control of those resources could
wreak untold damage on the world's economy, and could apply that
wealth to purposes that would endanger peace and security," Wolfowitz
concluded.[21]

Dick Cheney had been out of government scarcely more than had Wolfowitz. Since he first joined the Ford administration, there had only been
a single two-year hiatus in private life in 1977 and 1978, and Cheney had
spent most of that period running for Congress.

At the end of the Bush administration Cheney moved to the American Enterprise Institute, a leading Washington think tank with a corporate Republican tilt. He wasted no time in saying he might be interested
in the Republican presidential nomination in 1996. Precisely one week
after Clinton's inauguration, on January 27, 1993, Cheney appeared for
an interview on *Larry King Live* and was asked if he might run. "Obviously, it's something I'll take a look at," he said, his voice carrying its customary solemnity. ". . . Obviously, I've worked for three presidents and
watched two others up close, and so it is an idea that has occurred to
me."[22] Before long Cheney was speaking at Republican events around the
nation, meeting privately with party officials and fund-raisers and setting
up a political action committee. His message was that Clinton would
be vulnerable in 1996 to a challenge on foreign policy. "The American
people need leaders who are not afraid to engage the rest of the world and
do not tremble," he declared.[23]

The reception he received was respectful but not impassioned. On
January 3, 1995, just as local officials, political professionals and fund-
raisers were beginning to make commitments about whom they would
support for the Republican presidential nomination, Cheney announced
he had decided not to run. Like his mentor Donald Rumsfeld in the
1980s, Cheney found it difficult to attract enough support to win the
presidential nomination. The dynamics were much the same as for Rumsfeld: Cheney's service in Congress, as secretary of defense and as White
House chief of staff all added up to a wealth of experience in Washington.
However, they did not attract the money, the name recognition or the

core base of supporters that provide the ingredients of success in presidential politics.

That summer, Cheney accepted a new job as president and chief executive officer of the Halliburton Company, the oil field services and construction company. At a Dallas news conference to announce the appointment on August 10, 1995, Cheney spoke as though he were leaving public life forever. "When I made the decision earlier this year not to run for president, not to seek the White House, that really was a decision to wrap up my political career and move on to other things," he explained.[24]

For two years after his retirement, Colin Powell vanished into semiseclusion to write his autobiography. In September 1995, with his book ready for publication, he suddenly burst forth in public again with a series of television interviews and a nationwide book tour. The book was timed well to coincide with the early stages of the 1996 presidential campaign. Powell acted as though he were surprised by the outpouring of publicity concerning his book, which he had helped generate, and about the speculation about a presidential campaign, which he had done little to discourage.

The foreign policy hawks displayed considerable ambivalence about a Powell race. On the one hand, Powell was a symbol of American military power and a strong national defense; for the hawks, he was certainly preferable to Clinton. On the other hand, Powell had his undeniable moderate streak too. One day Frank Gaffney, a former Reagan administration official whose truculent anti-Soviet views had put him at the far right of the political spectrum, agreed to take part in a talk show debate about Powell's record in foreign policy and national security; Gaffney agreed to take the anti-Powell position. He forgot to ask in advance who would be on the pro-Powell side of the debate. When he arrived at the studio the next morning, Gaffney discovered his old mentor Richard Perle glowering at him. Perle, himself undeniably a hawk, had come to defend Powell's record.[25]

When Powell's book tour ended, and with public interest in his candidacy at its peak, he spent three weeks trying to decide whether he should run. His two closest friends, Richard Armitage and Kenneth Duberstein, worked closely with him to assess his chances. But the political dynamics hadn't changed. Powell had little prospect of winning either major-party nomination. The Democratic nomination was barely worth considering; Clinton obviously wasn't going to step aside for anyone, much less a loyal member of the last two Republican administrations. The Republican nomination was more open to competition; but to obtain it, Powell would have to go through primaries in which the support of the party's conservative supporters was crucial, and Powell was no more acceptable to the party's right wing than he had been in the past.

That left the possibility of running for president as an independent candidate. There were suggestions that Powell might be able to reach some bargain with Ross Perot, taking over the third-party machinery left over from Perot's candidacy in 1992. Those who proposed such a deal, however, didn't understand the legacy of bad blood stemming from Perot's old feuds with the Reagan and Bush administrations in general and with Powell's ally Richard Armitage in particular.

More fundamentally, Powell simply did not fit the personality or the profile of a third-party candidate. He was an insider's insider, someone who rose through the ranks of the existing order, not a challenger to it. He was a pragmatist, not a visionary. Even if Powell were to win election as an independent, he and his advisers wondered how he could run the country without the support of a political party. "Can you govern when you have no base in the Congress?" asked Duberstein. "You really have to run as part of a two-party system in order to govern effectively." That was a serious issue, and those who agonize about it aren't cut out to mount third-party candidacies.[26]

His wife was strongly opposed to a presidential race, and Powell concluded that he himself didn't have sufficient enthusiasm for it. "The calling was not there," he later wrote.[27] On November 8, 1995, Powell finally announced that he would not run for the presidency.

It was a decisive moment for Powell's role in American life. He would henceforth find himself in an uncomfortable position. He had risen to a position of stature and independence, with a popularity and public standing few political leaders achieve. Yet if he wanted any further career in government, he would have to work for someone else. There would be no Colin Powell administration.

In the end the 1996 Republican nomination went to Bob Dole, the former Senate majority leader, whom George H. W. Bush had defeated in the Republican primaries eight years earlier. Clinton easily won a second term. Dole's campaign was so lackluster that it was largely forgotten soon after the election.

Yet Dole's campaign was noteworthy, both for the views he espoused on foreign policy and for the people who served as his leading foreign policy advisers. At the outset Dole had relied on his own Senate aides, shunting aside better-known Republicans. By the summer of 1996, however, an old and familiar face had emerged at the top of the Dole organization: Donald Rumsfeld.

After his failed effort to win the 1988 Republican presidential nomination, Rumsfeld had decided to run another business. In 1990 he was named the chief executive officer of the General Instrument Corporation, a cable and communications firm. He moved the company's headquarters from New York City to Chicago, his hometown, and ran the firm for approximately three years. During that period the company went public. By taking shares from an initial public offering at fifteen dollars a share and later selling them at two or three times that value, Rumsfeld earned profits valued at twenty-four million dollars. There were stock options as well. According to a financial disclosure form he filed in 2001, Rumsfeld had managed by the end of the 1990s to accumulate assets of at least fifty million dollars and perhaps as much as two hundred million.[28]

Rumsfeld had served in Congress with Dole and once had the adjoining office on Capitol Hill. He agreed in the spring of 1996 to help the campaign as a two-day-a-week policy adviser. Within two months Rumsfeld was Dole's national campaign chairman, working six-day weeks and effectively running the organization. His principal deputy for foreign policy issues was Paul Wolfowitz. The two men had not worked closely together before; Wolfowitz had risen to prominence during the Reagan and Bush administrations, while Rumsfeld was out of Washington. The two men found themselves compatible in many ways; both had conservative views on foreign policy and supported a strong national defense. The Dole campaign thus served as the first tryout for the team of Rumsfeld and Wolfowitz, who together took over the civilian leadership of the Pentagon in 2001.

Throughout 1996 Dole staked out positions on foreign policy that were notably more conservative than those of the first Bush administration. Dole supported missile defense and was outspokenly hostile to the United

Nations. One of his principal applause lines throughout the campaign was a sardonic reference to "Boutros Boutros-Ghali," the UN secretary-general, whose Egyptian name Dole loved to invoke with ridicule. "I will never commit the American soldier to an ordeal without the prospect of victory," Dole said in his acceptance speech to the Republican National Convention. "And when I am president, every man and every woman in our armed forces will know the president is his commander-in-chief—not Boutros Boutros-Ghali or any other U.N. secretary general."

When Dole decided early in the campaign to give a speech about U.S. policy toward Asia, the submerged conflicts within the Republican party boiled to the surface. At first Dole's staff arranged for him to give this Asia speech during ceremonies at the Nixon library in Yorba Linda, California, in which Henry Kissinger was to be given an award as "America's statesman nonpareil." Dole's appearance there would have served to identify him closely with the notion of a close strategic relationship with China and, more broadly, with the Nixon-Kissinger school of realism in foreign policy. These plans did not sit well with congressional Republicans or with neoconservatives, such as Wolfowitz, who had opposed Kissinger since the 1970s; these groups favored stronger American support for Taiwan and for democracy in China. "A lot of people told him [Dole] that it was a mistake" to link his Asia policy symbolically to Kissinger," said former U.S. Ambassador to China James Lilley, one of Dole's advisers. Dole's appearance was moved from the Nixon library to a less sensitive Washington location.[29]

When Dole finally delivered his Asia speech, its tone was considerably more hawkish than anything Kissinger, Scowcroft or George H. W. Bush would have approved. He announced that the United States had an interest in "political pluralism" in China. "A 'one-China' policy does not mean a 'one party in China' policy," he asserted, thus implicitly criticizing the Chinese Communist party's monopoly on power. Dole's principal proposal was for ballistic missile defenses in Asia in cooperation with America's allies in Japan and South Korea, an idea he labeled the "Pacific Democracy Defense Program."[30]

In many ways Dole's Asia speech and his 1996 campaign amounted to a preview of the positions George W. Bush embraced after he arrived in the White House in 2001. Dole urged an unambiguous American commitment to the defense of Taiwan. The U.S. policy should be that "if force is used against Taiwan, America will respond," he said, thus presaging George W. Bush's pledge in 2001 that America would do "whatever it takes" to defend Taiwan. Dole also suggested more extensive American arms sales to Taiwan, specifically including submarines, which Bush authorized five years later. On North Korea, Dole argued that the United States should not have contact with the Pyongyang regime of Kim Jong Il until after he had opened the way for direct talks with South Korea. A half decade later, after the North Korean leader had held a summit meeting with South Korea's Kim Dae Jung (and after he had also clandestinely restarted the country's nuclear weapons program), President George W. Bush's position was an updated version of Dole's: no direct talks with North Korea until it agreed to multilateral talks about its nuclear program.

All of Dole's foreign policy positions, which Wolfowitz played a vital role in formulating, pointed to the broader underlying reality: By 1996 the center of gravity within the Republican party was shifting. The caution of the first Bush administration—its preoccupation with preserving a balance of power, its reverence for the status quo—was gradually giving way to policies that were more adventurous and more confrontational. For Republican political candidates the lesson of Bush's defeat in the 1992 election had been simple and clear: Bush had failed to court or to excite the party's conservative base.

Several years later the nation and the world were startled to discover that the administration of George W. Bush seemed different from that of his father. Yet when it came to foreign policy, the younger Bush was following closely along the lines of Dole's campaign, merely providing a more youthful face and stronger voice for roughly the same policies that advisers like Wolfowitz had tried out with Dole in 1996. The Republican party had already altered its tone well before the arrival of George W. Bush.

CHAPTER FIFTEEN

A Vulcan Agenda

THOSE WHO KNEW Paul Wolfowitz were amused when he was occasionally characterized as a reckless zealot. He was by nature perhaps the least daring member of the neoconservative movement from which he had arisen. His friends and allies on the right often called upon Wolfowitz to take stronger stands, to be more confrontational; they often found him unwilling to do so. While never abandoning his principles, Wolfowitz regularly worried about doing what was politically prudent.

Even on those issues with which he became publicly identified, Wolfowitz was sometimes a latecomer. For many years after the 1986 democratic revolution that ousted Ferdinand Marcos in the Philippines, Wolfowitz prided himself, fairly enough, on the role he had played in those events. Yet the record showed that at the time Wolfowitz was slow-moving and circumspect. He did not stand out as the leader of efforts within the Reagan administration to oust Marcos, and, in fact, for a time he defended the Marcos regime in the face of criticism from congressional Democrats.

He was deliberate in choosing his causes, careful with his rhetoric. During a press conference in the late 1990s in which Wolfowitz and other officials questioned the assumptions and conclusions of the CIA, a reporter asked Wolfowitz whether he was saying there had been a failure by the U.S. intelligence community. Wolfowitz's answer was immediately protective. "I don't think it's right to use that word *failure*," he said.[1]

His instinctive caution was what enabled Wolfowitz to maintain his credibility with those in positions of power and to keep on winning appointments in one administration after another. His friend Richard Perle had the freedom to be combative, provoking and belittling his adversaries, but Perle was usually an outsider to the policy-making circles of the executive branch that were Wolfowitz's home turf.

When Morton Abramowitz, one of America's leading Asia hands, led a series of studies in the late 1990s, he sometimes asked for Wolfowitz's signature. Wolfowitz hesitated until he knew what others were doing. "Paul would always ask me, 'Has Rich signed on?'" Abramowitz recalled.[2] "Rich" was Richard Armitage, Wolfowitz's partner and sometime rival on Asia policy within the Republican foreign policy elite.

On those occasions where Wolfowitz did elect to take a strong position, his views developed gradually, starting with vague pronouncements and then moving over time toward more detailed conclusions and policy proscriptions. So it was with his advocacy of an American military intervention against Saddam Hussein.

In the first half of the 1990s Wolfowitz did not call for a U.S. policy of regime change in Iraq. He argued that in hindsight, the United States had made a mistake when it missed the opportunity to get rid of Saddam Hussein after the Gulf War. However, he invariably went on to explain the many reasons for the first Bush administration's policies that left Hussein in power in 1991.

As the Clinton administration began to grapple with Saddam Hussein, Wolfowitz began to criticize the Democrats, both for failing to react more strongly to Iraq's defiance of United Nations weapons inspectors and for being ineffective in their attempts to contain the Iraqi leader. "The United States has virtually abandoned its commitment to protect a besieged people from a bloodthirsty dictator," he wrote during the 1996 presidential campaign.[3]

In 1997 Wolfowitz's ideas about Iraq began to harden. In a lengthy essay titled "The United States and Iraq," written for a book about Iraq's future, he sketched out America's three possible policy options: containment, engagement or replacement of Saddam Hussein with a new Iraqi regime. The existing policy of containment wasn't effective, he concluded. "Containment is not a static policy: the political dynamics of the Middle East will tend to weaken sanctions over time," he said.[4] The sanctions were harming the Iraqi people at least as much as the regime, he pointed out. Meanwhile, America's coalition against Iraq would steadily weaken, as France, Russia and China lined up to lift sanctions.

Engagement or normalization with Saddam Hussein wouldn't work either because it would enhance the Iraqi leader's power and destabilize the Middle East, Wolfowitz argued. Renewed access to significant oil resources would certainly lead to a strengthening of Iraq's armed forces and probably a resumption of nuclear, chemical and biological programs. Saddam Hussein would have more resources and opportunities to attempt to destabilize the weak regimes of the gulf through terrorism and other means. Finally, Saddam's revival would have a chilling effect on the Arab-Israeli peace process, already in deep difficulty.[5]

That left the third option, a new Iraqi regime. In the article Wolfowitz concluded that this was the best option, but still left vague what action the United States should take other than to "be prepared to seize opportunities."

By the end of 1997 Wolfowitz finally took these thoughts to their logical conclusion. He called directly and unequivocally for the use of military force to oust Saddam Hussein from power. "Overthrow Him," he urged in an article for the *Weekly Standard* he wrote with Zalmay Khalilzad, the longtime aide who in 1992 had drafted for Wolfowitz the strategic vision of America as the world's sole superpower. "Military force [against Iraq] is not enough," Khalilzad and Wolfowitz argued. "It must be part of an overall political strategy that sets as its goal not merely the containment of Saddam but the liberation of Iraq from his tyranny."[6]

From that point onward, "Overthrow Him" became Wolfowitz's regular refrain on Iraq, the theme he repeatedly emphasized in a deluge of magazine articles, congressional appearances and op-ed pieces (when Wolfowitz testified on Capitol Hill, he usually recycled his written testimony into an op-ed piece for the *Wall Street Journal* a few days later).

As part of this strategy, Wolfowitz urged American support for Iraqi opposition leaders, encouragement of a government-in-exile and the indictment of Saddam Hussein as a war criminal. He also proposed the creation of a liberated zone in southern Iraq comparable to the protected zone established in 1991 in northern Iraq. "There are a lot of political reasons why it's easier to operate in the south," Wolfowitz told a congressional hearing in 1998. "Kuwait is easier to work with than Turkey. Shia Arabs are a less disruptive force than the Kurds in the north."[7]

In the process of setting out his views on Iraq, Wolfowitz developed a striking set of arguments about America's relationship with its allies and friends in Europe and the Middle East. Wolfowitz was attempting to grapple with a dilemma. Many of these countries, ranging from France and Russia to Saudi Arabia, Egypt and Turkey, had helped the United States reverse Saddam Hussein's invasion of Kuwait; even in retrospect, Wolfowitz did not dispute the critical importance of that Gulf War coalition. Yet by the late 1990s, just as Wolfowitz was urging tougher action against Saddam Hussein, the coalition seemed to have weakened. On the surface, then, Wolfowitz was asking that America go further with Iraq than in 1991, but with fewer friends and allies.

To overcome this dilemma, he advanced two arguments. Both carried the implication that the opposition from America's friends and allies was spurious or transitory and that ultimately they would come to the side of the United States. The first argument was that other governments didn't support America on Iraq because they believed the Clinton administration was too weak and would therefore fail. "They do not wish to be associated with a U.S. military effort that is ineffective and that leaves them alone to face Iraq," he explained. Wolfowitz thus implied that with a stronger, more determined and hawkish American policy, the old coalition from 1991 would revive.[8]

His second, related argument was that America's friends and allies were by nature followers. Once the United States acted, the coalition would once again coalesce. "A willingness to act unilaterally can be the most effective way of securing effective collective action," Wolfowitz explained in 1997.[9] Before Congress, he testified: "France and Russia, I think, could be expected to follow their commercial noses when they saw—forgive the mixed metaphors—which way the oil wind was blowing."[10]

Both these Wolfowitz predictions about the behavior of America's friends and allies turned out to be untrue when, in 2002–03, the George W. Bush administration asked other countries to approve military action against Iraq. Stronger American policies produced stronger opposition. If, as Wolfowitz had argued in the late 1990s, other governments had been reluctant to join the United States only because they believed the Clinton administration might be too weak and timid to finish the job, then the George W. Bush administration left little room for doubt about its determination to be rid of Saddam Hussein. Yet when the United States took the lead, the 1991 coalition did not fall into line.

Wolfowitz's arguments in these late-1990s articles helped persuade other prominent Republicans to support the overthrow of Saddam Hussein without worrying too much about the allies and friends who had proved helpful during the Gulf War. In early 1998 the Project for a New American Century, the political arm of the neoconservative movement, released an open letter to Clinton signed by eighteen veterans of past Republican administrations. The letter called for a new American policy of "removing Saddam Hussein from power." The letter followed closely the arguments Wolfowitz had been making: The policy of containment wasn't working, and Saddam Hussein's continuation in power would be destabilizing to the Middle East. Those who signed the letter included Donald Rumsfeld, Richard Armitage, Wolfowitz, Khalilzad and several others who eventually joined the top ranks of the second Bush administration, including Elliott Abrams, John Bolton, Paula Dobriansky and Robert Zoellick.[11]

Martin Anderson was one of the Republican party's leading conservative intellectuals. He had worked for Richard Nixon as research director in the 1968 campaign, had served in the Nixon White House and had reemerged a decade later as an even more enthusiastic supporter of Ronald Reagan. From his office in the Hoover Institution at Stanford University, he pushed regularly for a variety of conservative causes he viewed as Reagan's legacy, especially tax cuts and missile defense. His forte was finding ways of translating ideas into policy, mostly by courting high-level politicians and persuading them to embrace those ideas.

Soon after Bob Dole's defeat in 1996, Anderson decided that with the Republicans shut out of the White House, the party needed a new institution through which leading experts and intellectuals could swap ideas with the Republican leadership in Congress. Anderson began meeting with Representative Chris Cox of California, the head of the House Republican Policy Committee. With the support of House Speaker Newt Gingrich, Anderson and Cox created a new organization called the Congressional Policy Advisory Board. The group brought together former cabinet members and other leading Republican officials from the Nixon, Reagan and first Bush administrations; the heads of the leading conservative think tanks, including Hoover, the American Enterprise Institute and the Heritage Foundation; and Republican members of Congress.

The organization began meeting in early 1998 and reconvened approximately every three months until 2001. The sessions, held in the Rayburn House Office Building, served several purposes. They helped Republicans in Congress think about possible legislation, topics for hearings and subjects for investigation. They enabled Republican leaders to develop their critiques of the Clinton administration, selecting issues and lines of attack, thus laying the groundwork for the next presidential campaign. The board also served as a meeting point for those who might occupy senior positions in the next Republican administration.

On foreign policy the leading members at the table included three men who later returned to office in the George W. Bush administration: Donald Rumsfeld, Dick Cheney and Paul Wolfowitz. Rumsfeld, independently wealthy, no longer running any private company that might consume his time and energy, proved to be the most active participant. In between the quarterly meetings he was on the phone regularly with congressional staff members. These three were joined by several other former cabinet members, including former Secretary of State George Shultz and former Defense Secretary Caspar Weinberger. Later a new member, Condoleezza Rice, was added to the group.[12]

It is revealing to note not only who attended these meetings from 1998 to 2000 but who was absent. Colin Powell was not at the table. No one had invited him to these top-level Republican strategy sessions, even though he had served as national security adviser in the Reagan administration, had been chairman of the Joint Chiefs under Bush and had been mentioned by the Dole team as a possible secretary of state if Dole was elected. Asked why Powell hadn't been brought into the group, Anderson replied, "Maybe he was too high up."[13] That was a curious perception, given Anderson's invitations to several former secretaries of state and defense; it accurately conveyed the undertone of respect, but also mistrust and alienation, with which conservative intellectuals viewed Powell. Richard Armitage was not asked to come to these Republican policy discussions either. Armitage was always on the list for meetings involving Asia policy, but he was not close to the conservative intellectuals and their think tanks.

Even if Powell had been invited, he would probably not have come. He avoided foreign policy study groups. In private life after retirement from the military, he devoted his energies to several youth organizations, including the Boys & Girls Clubs of America, Howard University and the United Negro College Fund. He prided himself that he liked to focus on kids, not think tanks. Given the choice of talking to the American Enterprise Institute or the Boys & Girls Clubs, he would have selected the latter.

Thus these meetings on Capitol Hill in the late 1990s provided an early glimpse of the political alignments of the next administration's foreign policy team. Cheney, Rumsfeld and Wolfowitz were working closely together, alongside conservative intellectuals and think tanks, with Rice as a late arrival in their ranks. Powell and Armitage were not part of this inner circle.

Among the issues discussed at these sessions, missile defense was first on the list. Anderson had been an especially fervent advocate of missile defense ever since he had accompanied Reagan on a tour of the North American Air Defense Command in Colorado in 1979.[14] North Korea was another frequent topic of discussion. Most of the Republicans didn't like the agreement the Clinton administration had signed with North Korea in 1994; in it, North Korean leader Kim Jong Il had agreed to freeze his nuclear weapons program in exchange for food and energy supplies, but he had not been willing to give up control of the fuel rods his country had already produced for future weapons. "A lot of my ideas about North Korea were formed in the cauldron of that advisory board," said Cox, who during the late 1990s introduced a series of legislative proposals aimed at challenging Clinton's Korea policy.

The group also talked about China, Russia and Iraq. In each instance the Republicans complained that the Clinton administration's policies were too conciliatory, too accommodating; they envisioned tougher policies in a new Republican administration.

In early 1998 Rumsfeld took charge of a more focused challenge to the Clinton administration's view of the world. The previous year Congress had created a new commission to examine all the available intelligence concerning the threat to the United States from ballistic missiles, and Rumsfeld was named chairman. Among the nine members of the commission was Wolfowitz. Once again, just as they had during the Dole campaign, Rumsfeld and Wolfowitz found themselves working together.

The missile commission had as its model the Team B study of Soviet military power in the 1970s. In that earlier work an outside group of experts had reviewed the available intelligence and concluded that the CIA might be offering too benign an interpretation of Soviet behavior. Wolfowitz had been one of the members of Team B. Rumsfeld too had been indirectly involved; as the secretary of defense in 1975 and 1976 he had been the leading opponent of détente within the Ford administration, and the findings of Team B had provided support for his views.

In 1995 the U.S. intelligence community had concluded in an official National Intelligence Estimate that no country other than the declared nuclear powers would be able to hit the continental United States with a ballistic missile for the next fifteen years. That intelligence study provided support for the Clinton administration's position that a national missile defense system was unnecessary anytime soon. Congressional Republican proponents of missile defense, including Gingrich, had appointed the Rumsfeld Commission because of their unhappiness with this intelligence estimate, which they suggested had been skewed to help the Clinton administration. During the first six months of 1998 the Rumsfeld Commission intensively examined the intelligence data on other nations' missile programs and conducted a series of interviews. The result was comparable to that of Team B: The Rumsfeld Commission warned that the danger to the United States from a missile attack was greater than the CIA and other U.S. intelligence agencies had been reporting. The commission report, issued in July 1998, concluded that "concerted efforts by a number of overtly or potentially hostile nations to acquire ballistic missiles with biological or nuclear payloads pose a growing threat to the United States, its deployed forces and its friends and allies." At least some countries would be able to "inflict major destruction" on the United States within five years of deciding to do so, the report said. [15]

The findings of the bipartisan commission were unanimous. Rumsfeld had succeeded in winning the endorsement of the three Democratic appointees of the commission—including a leading opponent of missile defense, Dr. Richard Garwin—by sticking to very specific factual findings about other nations' missile programs. The report did not come out in support of missile defense systems, which Garwin continued to oppose. (Garwin later wrote that he was favorably impressed with Rumsfeld, who he said was "eminently fair and energetic.") Nevertheless, within a day after the report was issued, House Republicans cited its findings as proving the need for missile defense; Gingrich called the Rumsfeld Commission report "the most important warning about our national security system since the end of the Cold War."[16]

Particularly noteworthy within the commission's report was its decision to list three specific countries as the most worrisome for the United States: North Korea, Iran and Iraq. The Rumsfeld Commission warned about the "newer, developing threats" from these three countries. The same triumvirate of nations was eventually singled out by President George W. Bush in his 2002 State of the Union address as the members of what he branded an "axis of evil."

Iraq, Iran and North Korea were the three countries whose missile and nuclear programs the United States was trying hardest to stop. This was by no means exclusively a Republican issue but rather an intrinsic part of America's overall policy for stopping the proliferation of nuclear weapons and missiles. During the mid-1990s Clinton administration officials also regularly grouped together Iraq, Iran and North Korea—not as an "axis of evil" but as the three toughest challenges the United States faced in curbing the spread of nuclear weaponry and missiles.[17] The Rumsfeld Commission's report, then, was one prominent manifestation of the way these three countries were being increasingly bracketed by Washington's foreign policy and intelligence communities, well before George W. Bush arrived in the White House.

As the Rumsfeld Commission was finishing its work, Cox and the House Republicans were starting a congressional investigation of the Clinton administration's China policy. In the spring of 1998, shortly before Clinton made the first presidential visit to China in nine years, the *New York Times* disclosed that two American firms, Hughes Electronics and Loral Space Communications, had given China expertise that helped improve the accuracy of its ballistic missiles.[18] In response, Congress appointed a special committee, headed by Cox, to investigate the transfers of American technology to China.

According to Cox, Rumsfeld played a significant behind-the-scenes role in the start-up of the committee. He offered a series of helpful suggestions about how to approach the investigation. Rumsfeld advised Cox, for example, to do whatever necessary to obtain bipartisan support for the committee's conclusions. In addition, Rumsfeld encouraged some of the departing staff members from the missile commission to go work for the Cox Committee.[19] Cox selected Wolfowitz's protégé and longtime assistant Scooter Libby as the committee's lawyer. The Cox Committee report, issued the following year, concluded unanimously that China had been seeking to acquire American military technology, that it had stolen information about some of the United States' most advanced nuclear weapons and that it had also illegally obtained American missile and space technology.[20]

The two firms accused of assisting China's missile program, Hughes and Loral, originally denied any wrongdoing. In late 1999 Hughes set up an independent task force to review its compliance with U.S. export control laws and appointed Wolfowitz its cochairman, along with former Senator Sam Nunn. (According to Wolfowitz's financial disclosure forms, he was paid a fee of three hundred thousand dollars for his work as cochair of this Hughes task force; the fee covered a period of about one year, during which Wolfowitz was spending most of his time working on the Bush presidential campaign and as a dean at Hopkins.[21]) Years later, midway through the George W. Bush administration, Hughes, Loral and two other aerospace firms agreed to pay a total of more than sixty million dollars in penalties to settle civil charges stemming from their help to China's rocket and satellite programs.[22]

Cox's committee was merely one part of the Republicans' multifaceted critique of the Clinton administration's China policy. Later that year the Heritage Foundation and the Project for a New American Century organized a joint statement that called for an end to America's policy of "strategic ambiguity" toward Taiwan. Under that policy, the roots of which dated back to the 1950s, the United States had always left unclear if it would respond with force to a military conflict between China and Taiwan. The conservatives' public statement of 1999 called upon the United States to "declare unambiguously that it will come to Taiwan's defense in the event of an attack or a blockade against Taiwan."

Among the twenty-three persons signing this Taiwan statement were Wolfowitz and Armitage, the Republicans' two leading Asia specialists. The two men checked with each other before they went along. "Paul called me, or I called him, and we told each other, 'It's a little too black-and-white,'" Armitage said several years later. "But we decided, we can't negotiate the language, we have to make a decision to get on or get off." Both signed.[23]

Shortly after Clinton was elected, Strobe Talbott, his friend and closest adviser on Russia policy, had suggested that Condoleezza Rice be appointed the ambassador to Moscow. As fellow specialists on the Soviet

Union, Talbott and Rice had known each other for years. Secretary of State Warren Christopher rejected the idea, arguing that the administration should send a professional diplomat to Russia.[24]

During Clinton's first term, as Rice devoted herself to her new job as Stanford provost, she said little about American policy toward Russia. The tempestuous Boris Yeltsin, with whom she had had the testy confrontation at the White House, was Russia's president. Like others from the first Bush administration, Rice in the early 1990s tended to focus less upon current events or the performance of Yeltsin's government than upon the period from 1989 to 1991, when the cold war came to a close. Together with Philip Zelikow, another former member of Brent Scowcroft's National Security Council, Rice wrote a book on the Western diplomacy with the Soviet Union that had led to the unification of Germany. Their conclusion was flattering to virtually everyone in power; they wrote that Bush, Margaret Thatcher, François Mitterrand and Helmut Kohl had acted "with skill, speed, and regard for the dignity of the Soviet Union" and that their performance had been "a testimony to statecraft."[25]

Rice's focus and her rhetoric began to change in the late 1990s, as the darker side of the new Russian state became more evident. She became ever more critical, both of Yeltsin's government and of the Clinton-Talbott policies toward it. The Russian economy had been opened up to privatization but in a crude way that had enriched a handful of crony capitalists and left most of the rest of the country impoverished and embittered. Corruption was endemic. Unemployment rates and mortality rates were climbing, while economic output was falling. At the grass roots the concept of a market economy remained even more a fiction than it had been in the early 1990s.[26]

In August 1998, the same month that Rice held an initial meeting with Texas Governor George W. Bush in Kennebunkport, Maine, to talk about a presidential race, the Russian economy virtually collapsed. The ruble dropped by more than 40 percent, foreign capital fled the country and Russia defaulted on some of its debt. The economic reformers in Yeltsin's government resigned. In both its economic and its foreign policies, Russia set itself upon a more conservative, more nationalistic course.

In the wake of these upheavals, a debate broke out in the United States over the question of "Who lost Russia?" The debate had strong political undertones. Vice President Al Gore, then preparing to run for the presidency in 2000, had been, along with Clinton and Talbott, one of the three principal architects of the administration's Russia policy.

At this point Rice emerged as the Republicans' leading critic of the Clinton administration's Russia policy. Her argument was that the Clinton team had concentrated too heavily on Yeltsin rather than the broader cause of economic reform; the administration had provided continuing support, including loans from the International Monetary Fund, without insisting on reforms or looking at how the money was being spent. "Support for democracy and economic reform became support for Yeltsin. His agenda became the American agenda," Rice wrote.[27] The Clinton policy "didn't recognize how mercurial Yeltsin is," Rice contended in another interview at the time. "It didn't react to the fact that an awful lot of money has been siphoned off. This gave a false sense of security to the Russians. They felt that no matter what reforms they didn't do, they would get the IMF money. No matter what behavior they showed, they would get friendship."[28]

Rice's prescription was that the United States should begin to detach itself from Russia, or at least from its top political leaders. "I think what's called for now is a major disengagement from Russia's domestic policies," she said.[29] She also urged much tougher action to stop Russia from carrying out its campaign against Chechnya. "I think the Russians have gone beyond the pale and I think that the international community can only speak out, and I also agree that international financial assistance needs to be at risk," she said in a television interview.[30] To some of Rice's fellow Russia scholars, she sounded as if she were proposing a new form of containment of Russia. "I was totally shocked," recalled Stanford University scholar Michael McFaul.[31]

In retrospect, it is hard to escape the conclusion that Rice's views on Russia during this period were influenced by political factors—that is, the desire to help the Republicans develop an issue for the 2000 presidential campaign. Rice's charge that the Clinton policy toward Russia had been too personalized and too dependent upon Yeltsin had a certain coherence at the time, yet within months after Rice returned to the White House in 2001, she helped guide the new President Bush toward a personalized relationship with Yeltsin's successor, Vladimir Putin. ("I looked the man in the eye. I was able to get a sense of his soul," Bush told reporters after his first meeting with Putin in 2001.[32]) Rice's call for tougher action against

Russia in Chechnya similarly softened after she and the Republicans returned to the White House.

Thus, during their years in exile under the Clinton administration, the Vulcans increasingly turned their attention above all to what they saw as new threats to American security. They issued regular warnings about missiles, about Iraq and North Korea, about the growing power of China and the growing instability of Russia. (Ironically, despite the Vulcans' preoccupation with these new dangers, they rarely dwelt upon the one threat that would eventually change their lives and those of the rest of America, terrorism.) The Vulcans were far less active in developing new institutions, diplomacy or other approaches that could deal with these threats. Rather, in most instances the Vulcans' preferred solution was the one it had been in the past: ever-greater American military power.

It would be unfair to say, as some Democrats and other critics did, that the Vulcans were exaggerating these perceived threats. In some instances, including Iraq and the North Korea, the Vulcans-in-exile were focusing upon serious, long-standing problems that the Clinton administration was addressing only through strategies of deferral. Moreover, even if the Vulcans had been overstating the nature of the threats, this would not have been unprecedented; the Democrats had come to power in 1961 after criticizing the Eisenhower administration for a missile gap with the Soviet Union that did not exist.

Rather, the more serious failing was that the Republicans' focus was backward-leaning. They were calling, in effect, for a restoration of the glory years from the first Bush administration. In their public speeches and private seminars they returned regularly to this recent past. "I was fortunate to be a part of the Bush administration during an extraordinary time, as the cold war ended," declared Rice in a speech to the Los Angeles World Affairs Council. She had almost turned down Scowcroft's offer of a job in Washington in 1989, she said. If she had, "I would have missed the unification of Germany, the liberation of Eastern Europe, the collapse of the Soviet Union. It was extraordinary!" Indeed, it was, but it was also no guidepost for the future, for a world in which, as Rice acknowledged in the same speech, there was "no longer the single unifying theme of the Soviet threat."[33]

Paradoxically, at the same time that the Vulcans were calling for a revival of the spirit of the first Bush administration, they were also beginning to embrace ideas and doctrines that would make sure there would be no such restoration. These changing ideas and doctrines meant that a new Republican administration would behave quite differently from its predecessor. The biggest of these changes was in America's view of the nature of its friends and allies. In the first Bush administration, these allies had been treated as partners. In the evolving view laid out by Wolfowitz on Iraq, the allies were treated as ducklings who would inevitably get in line behind their American mother. The Vulcans' eagerness for missile defense also presumed a different security relationship from that in the past between America and its allies. Yet during the 1990s the Vulcans continued to speak about the importance of America's alliances as though these would and could continue endlessly, without difficulty, in the face of their changing doctrines.

CHAPTER SIXTEEN

The Campaign

IN THE SPRING OF 1998 he was (so he said) merely running for reelection as governor of Texas. Nevertheless, George W. Bush and his political adviser, Karl Rove, had already taken care to register the Web site name www.Bush2000.org. At the time the polls showed (accurately, as it turned out) that Bush would run about dead even in a contest with Vice President Al Gore if the two men were to run against each other for the presidency. Bush was already making fund-raising expeditions around the country. One of those trips brought him to San Francisco, where he spoke at a Republican dinner in late April.

That night George Shultz, the crusty, imperturbable former labor negotiator who had served as Ronald Reagan's secretary of state, asked Bush if he might like to talk with some scholars at Stanford University's Hoover Institution the next day. Bush liked the idea. His schedule included a breakfast, lunch and late-afternoon reception in Silicon Valley near the Stanford campus, but he had several hours free between these events.

And so the following morning and afternoon, Bush, traveling with his California fund-raiser, Brad Freeman, sat down for several hours with a half dozen of the luminaries from Hoover. The sessions were held in the living room of Shultz's home on the Stanford campus. Besides Shultz, the scholars included Martin Anderson, the former adviser to both Richard Nixon and Ronald Reagan; Abraham Sofaer, a former Shultz aide; John Cogan and John Taylor, two economics professors; and the Stanford provost, Condoleezza Rice.[1]

Elsewhere that week, the UN Security Council was beset by new disagreements about the future of economic sanctions against Iraq, in the face of a new demand by Iraqi Deputy Prime Minister Tariq Aziz that they be lifted. In Washington a special interagency task force appointed by the Clinton administration had found widespread deficiencies in the government's ability to combat terrorism and an increase in activity by "small cells of terrorists" inside the United States.[2]

But in Palo Alto that cool, cloudy morning such events seemed relatively remote. The conversations in Shultz's living room meandered from one subject to another. This was not unlike other gatherings in which a politician and a group of experts are in turn eager to impress each other. Nothing in particular was decided, but the Hoover scholars concluded that they approved of the younger Bush. "He was very relaxed, with the sort of inner security some people have and some people don't," recalled Shultz.

Some of the participants realized that these talks had a precedent. As he listened to Bush, Martin Anderson recalled a similar session in 1979. Back then Anderson had been trying to line up support among intellectuals for Ronald Reagan's presidential campaign. Anderson had escorted Reagan to the Stanford campus, where the former California governor had talked with some Hoover scholars at Shultz's residence. Same house, Anderson thought, same living room, same chairs, some of the same scholars. Only the candidate was different.

That George W. Bush should be following in Reagan's footsteps was hardly predictable. His father, the forty-first president, had aroused the ire of loyal Reaganites by ousting them from key positions when he took over the White House in 1989, and conservatives had responded by giving his father no more than lukewarm support in his unsuccessful reelection campaign in 1992. Now the younger Bush was making a concerted bid for the support of the old Reagan crowd.

Bush invited the Hoover scholars, including Shultz, Rice and Anderson, to visit Austin for a follow-up meeting that July. They were joined there by former Defense Secretary Dick Cheney, now the head of the Halliburton Corporation, and by Cheney's former Pentagon aide Paul Wolfowitz, now the dean of the Johns Hopkins School of Advanced International Studies. This time Bush dropped the pretense that these talks were merely abstract explorations of interesting ideas. He told the visitors he was thinking of running for president, and he asked them for their help.

By the time of Bush's meetings with the Hoover scholars, Brent Scowcroft had already been working for more than a decade to advance Condoleezza Rice's career, mostly by bringing her to the attention of Bush's father. His endeavors on behalf of Rice continued even after she and the Bush administration had left Washington. When Scowcroft and Bush teamed up as coauthors to write *A World Transformed,* a memoir of the foreign policy of their administration, they called in former aides to help them review the events and themes they were planning to cover in the book. "I always made sure she [Rice] was in those groups," Scowcroft remembered. "And eventually he [Bush senior] was quite taken with her."[3]

In August 1998, the former president invited Rice to the Bush family compound in Kennebunkport, Maine. Rice had been there before, both to brief the president when she was on the National Security Council staff and to work on the Bush-Scowcroft memoir. This time, though, there was a different sort of business to address: George W. Bush was in Kennebunkport too, planning his presidential campaign.

Over a few days, the son of the former president and the protégée of the former national security adviser tested each other. They went fishing and worked out together on the treadmills, bikes and rowing machines at the Kennebunkport compound. They claimed later they had discussed America's relations with the world, and perhaps to an extent they had. There was much worth talking about; that summer, for example, Asia and Russia were in financial turmoil, Saddam Hussein ended Iraq's cooperation with UN weapons inspectors and Osama bin Laden's Al Qaeda organization bombed the American embassies in Kenya and Tanzania. But Bush and Rice also dwelt upon subjects of less cosmic significance, such as sports. The Texas Rangers, the baseball team Bush had once run as an owner and managing partner, were struggling to stay on top of their division. That summer America's baseball fans were watching Mark McGwire and Sammy Sosa compete to try to break the record of sixty-one home runs in a single season. In football the Cleveland Browns, the team Rice had rooted for as a child, were about to be taken over by Carmen Policy, the football executive Rice had befriended while she was at Stanford and he was running the San Francisco 49ers. Neither Bush nor Rice had to feign an interest in these events from the sports world, as politicians and scholars sometimes do.

"They bonded at Kennebunkport," said Coit Blacker. "She is a sports fanatic, and he's a sports fanatic too. . . . Condi has told me that one of the things she found most endearing about George W. is that he used sports metaphors, and Condi does too."[4]

Either at that 1998 meeting or shortly afterward Bush made the decision: Condoleezza Rice would be put in charge of foreign policy during his presidential campaign.

That fall Bush took on a second foreign policy adviser, Paul Wolfowitz. It was an obvious choice. Wolfowitz had served as a top aide to both Shultz and Cheney, the two guiding influences over foreign policy in these early stages of Bush's campaign. In a sense, Wolfowitz was merely picking up where he had left off, since he had also served as foreign policy adviser to Bob Dole in 1996.

Over the next two years, throughout the long presidential campaign, Rice and Wolfowitz served as Bush's two principal advisers on international affairs, coordinating daily events, preparing position papers and holding regular conference calls with the candidate. Rice was preeminent because she was closer to Bush. The more cerebral Wolfowitz seemed to find it harder to overcome the deep distrust of intellectuals Bush had nurtured since his undergraduate days at Yale. In one picture taken during the campaign at Bush's ranch in Crawford, Texas, the presidential candidate was photographed with his two advisers after an intelligence briefing. Bush and Rice were less than six inches from each other, relaxed and at ease, he in jeans and boots, she in chinos and running shoes. Wolfowitz, in contrast, stood noticeably more distant from Bush, wearing a dress shirt and work shoes, looking uncomfortable.[5]

In early 1999 Rice and Wolfowitz began to put together a formal team of foreign policy advisers for the Bush campaign. It was still remarkably early, with nearly two years remaining in the Clinton administration. Nevertheless, former Republican officials, unaccustomed to being out of office for nearly six years, were quietly jockeying to be named part of the Bush inner circle. For their part, Rice and Wolfowitz were maneuvering to lock up the best people before any other Republican candidate could get them. "The person who called me was Paul [Wolfowitz]," recalled Dov Zakheim, a specialist on the defense budget who had served in the Pentagon under Reagan. "He said, 'Do you want to do this? You've got to realize that once you're committed, you're committed.'" Zakheim gave his assent.[6]

The team had eight people, all of them alumni from the previous two Republican administrations. In addition to Rice and Wolfowitz, it included Richard Armitage, Richard Perle and Zakheim, all of whom had served in the Pentagon in the Reagan years; Stephen Hadley, a Pentagon aide to Wolfowitz in the Bush administration; Robert Blackwill, who had worked on the National Security Council with Rice; and Robert Zoellick, formerly a top aide to Secretary of State James Baker.

The advisers held their first session in Austin, with both Cheney and Shultz in attendance. They convened again over a weekend at Rice's home on the Stanford campus. Zakheim, an Orthodox Jew, doesn't drive on Saturdays, so while the other visitors stayed in a hotel, Rice, attentive to detail, made special arrangements for him to stay on campus within walking distance of her home. From then on, throughout Bush's presidential campaign, this team of eight spoke regularly, sometimes through telephone conference calls. It was this group that decided to call itself the Vulcans, after the mammoth statue overlooking Rice's hometown of Birmingham.[7] By coincidence, Armitage's wife had been raised in Birmingham, and so had the wife of Colin Powell, the most prominent alumnus of the Reagan and Bush administrations.

As the Bush presidential campaign progressed, several other illustrious figures worked alongside the Vulcans in advising Bush on foreign policy. They were not officially part of Rice's campaign group, but each was active on his own. By far the most influential of these was Dick Cheney. In the early stages of the campaign he was everywhere. He had been present in Austin when the Vulcans first convened. When Bush gave an initial speech on defense policy in September 1999, Rice and Armitage briefed the press on his ideas; Cheney flew to South Carolina to serve as master of ceremonies for their briefing.

In the late spring of 2000 Bush asked Cheney to take charge of choosing his running mate. After spending several weeks examining other possible candidates, including several Republican governors and senators, Cheney told Bush that he had changed his mind and would be willing to run for vice president himself. Bush needed no convincing; he had first suggested the idea months earlier. Reflecting on the weeklong review of possible running mates, Bush told reporters, "Gradually, I realized that the person who was best qualified to be my vice-presidential nominee was working by my side."[8]

The selection of Cheney was of surpassing importance for the future direction of foreign policy. It went further than any other single decision Bush made toward determining the nature and the policies of the administration he would head. Cheney combined an extensive knowledge of the inner workings of government with strong, conservative views about foreign policy and defense. He had already served in Congress, as White House chief of staff and as defense secretary. It was a breadth of experience in the executive and legislative branches that few others in America could match—virtually no one, that is, except for Cheney's former mentor, Donald Rumsfeld, who had once held precisely the same series of jobs as Cheney.

Rumsfeld had not occupied any permanent government position for two decades. But he too was playing an influential role behind the scenes to help the Bush campaign. During 1999 and 2000, while the Vulcans were meeting to decide what Bush's overall foreign policies should be, Rumsfeld was in charge of a separate, more clandestine campaign group. The idea for this group had been suggested by Martin Anderson from Hoover. It was dedicated to a single issue, one that Anderson in particular saw as Reagan's unfulfilled legacy: missile defense.

To a certain extent, the membership of Rumsfeld's missile-defense group overlapped with the Vulcans. Rice, Wolfowitz, Hadley and Perle, all of them Vulcans, took part in the Rumsfeld discussions. But this separate group also included Shultz, Anderson and some scientists long associated with proposals for missile defense, such as Lowell Wood of the Livermore lab. Having just finished serving as chairman of the 1998 commission on missile defense, Rumsfeld was a natural choice to head the group.

At one point the members of the missile defense team flew in from around the nation for a meeting in the living room of Rumsfeld's Chicago home. Such campaign sessions eventually enabled the Bush team to take office with a drive and determination to move forward as rapidly as possible on missile defense. These meetings also enabled Rumsfeld, while out of the public eye, to emerge once again as a driving force in Republican foreign policy.

There was one other foreign policy luminary hovering over the Bush campaign: Colin Powell. However, Powell's role in the campaign was different from that of Cheney or Rumsfeld. From the start Cheney played a central role both internally, in the campaign's discussions about what positions to take on foreign policy, and externally, as the vice presidential nominee. Rumsfeld was also active internally. Powell, by contrast, was important only externally, in helping to deal with the public and to help win political support for Bush. He was not active with the Vulcans or with Rumsfeld's missile defense group or any of the other campaign units through which the Bush team was formulating its foreign policies.

Powell had made clear early on and repeatedly that he was not interested in serving as Bush's running mate. Having decided in 1995 against running for president, he wanted no part of the vice presidential nomination, a job he had first rejected in the 1992 campaign. "I have no desire for political office," he said in a typical interview in March 2000.[9] But the key hidden qualifier in Powell's statement was the word *political.* Throughout 2000 Powell regularly left open the possibility that he would return to government as secretary of state.

Powell delivered one of the main speeches for Bush at the Republican National Convention in Philadelphia. Much of his address was devoted to the need for ending poverty and helping needy children; his speech thus served to buttress Bush's campaign theme of compassionate conservatism. On foreign policy Powell sounded a triumphal note, telling the Republican faithful: "The sick nations that still pursue the fool's gold of tyranny and weapons of mass destruction will soon find themselves left behind in the dustbin of history."[10]

In late October, at the peak of the fall campaign, Powell campaigned alongside Bush, thus helping Bush increase his appeal to minorities, moderates and veterans. By then Bush was making it clear he expected Powell to be one of the leading figures in his administration. "Tell us the names of people you would surround yourself with," a voter in Manchester, New Hampshire, asked Bush that month. He responded by listing, in order, Colin Powell, Condoleezza Rice and economics adviser Lawrence Lindsey. In an interview in Arkansas, Powell was asked if he would be Bush's secretary of state. "He's hinted at it, and I've hinted in return," Powell replied. On November 30, 2000, with the presidential election still in doubt and with the legal contests still continuing in Florida, Bush sought to demonstrate that the election was really over and that he was already acting as president-elect. His chosen method of doing so was to call Colin Powell down to his Texas ranch for a well-photographed meeting.[11]

Thus, while remaining at a distance from the Bush campaign's detailed foreign policy deliberations, Powell was central to its politics. Therein lay the seeds of problems for the future Bush administration.

Bush's team of advisers—Cheney, Powell, Rumsfeld, Rice, Wolfowitz, Armitage and all the other Vulcans—formed the core of his message to the nation on foreign policy during the 2000 campaign. Foreign policy would be in safe hands, he told voters, because he would rely on experienced people, all of them veterans of past administrations.

From the outset of his campaign Bush had struggled to assuage worries about his apparent lack of interest or experience in international affairs. In his youth and in private life he hadn't ventured to travel overseas for curiosity or pleasure in the fashion of many other affluent Americans of his generation. He had barely set foot in Europe, visiting London a couple of times and stopping once in Italy to see one of his daughters. He had traveled to Asia only once, on a visit to Beijing in 1975 while his father was head of the U.S. mission there. As governor of Texas Bush had of necessity spent his time on domestic issues, except for occasional dealings with Mexico.

The perceptions of Bush's inexperience in international affairs gained additional currency when at the start of his campaign he was ambushed in New Hampshire by a television reporter with a "pop quiz" in which Bush was asked to name the leaders of several foreign governments. He drew a blank when asked to come up with the name of the leader of Pakistan. "General . . ." Bush replied, struggling without success to come up with the name of Pervez Musharraf. Did he know the prime minister of India? "The new prime minister of India is—no," Bush replied. Similarly, the following spring Bush came up empty when a writer for *Glamour* magazine asked him to identify the Taliban. Finally the writer had to cue him. "Repression of women in Afghanistan?" he offered. "Oh, I thought you said some band," Bush replied. "The Taliban in Afghanistan. Absolutely. Repressive."[12]

And so throughout 1999 and 2000, seeking to counteract questions about his command of foreign policy, Bush had pressed the theme that he could be trusted as president because of his illustrious advisers and their long record of experience. "One of the things about a President Bush is that I'll be surrounded by good, strong, capable, smart people who understand the mission of the United States is to lead the world to peace," he said.[13]

The specific foreign policy issues Bush raised against Gore and the Clinton administration in the 2000 campaign were not particularly novel or surprising. They followed closely along the lines of attack traced earlier by congressional Republicans and by Bob Dole's campaign in 1996. Bush came out strongly in favor of national missile defense, saying he would be willing to abandon the 1972 Anti-Ballistic Missile (ABM) Treaty if necessary to pave the way. "Now is not the time to defend outdated treaties but to defend the American people," he thundered in his acceptance speech to the Republican convention. He also promised more money for the military. "America's armed forces need better equipment, better training and better pay," he said. Bush branded China a competitor, not a partner, of the United States. On Russia, Bush accused the Democrats of developing too personalized a relationship with President Boris Yeltsin and former Prime Minister Viktor Chernomyrdin.[14]

To the extent that Bush concentrated upon any foreign policy issue during his presidential campaign, it was a much broader, more general one. His message was that the Republicans were going to return to basics, to go back to the steady course the United States had followed from World War II through the end of the cold war. He pressed the theme that the Democrats of the 1990s had strayed too far from the traditional concerns of U.S. national security: strengthening America's alliances in Europe and Asia, building up a strong military and dealing with the challenges posed by major powers like Russia and China. He said he was opposed to using the military in small-scale humanitarian missions in places like Haiti, nor was he eager to concentrate on what some liberals were calling the new tasks of American foreign policy in the post–cold war world, such as combating AIDS and environmental degradation. As for the military, Bush said he would save it for major wars. "The vice president and I have a disagreement about the use of troops," he said during the presidential debate. "He believes in nation building. I would be very careful about using our troops as nation builders. I believe the role of the military is to fight and win war. . . . I don't want to try to put our troops in all places at all times. I don't want to be the world's policeman."[15]

The importance of alliances was one of Bush's regular refrains. In the main foreign policy speech of his campaign he declared that "all our goals in Eurasia will depend on America strengthening the alliances that sustain our influence." America's allies are "partners, not satellites," he said. These words grew out of Bush's criticism that President Clinton had bypassed Japan, America's ally, during a lengthy 1998 visit to China. But his message about alliances was phrased broadly to apply elsewhere too. "The

United States needs its European allies . . . to help us with security challenges as they arise," he said.

In the same vein, Bush charged that the Clinton administration had failed to preserve the Gulf War coalition his father had so skillfully put together to fight against Iraq. "Our coalition against Saddam is unraveling," he said during one of his televised debates with Gore.[16] The way to maintain its alliances and coalitions, Bush said, was for America to display humility. "If we're an arrogant nation, they'll resent us," he explained. "If we're a humble nation but strong, they'll welcome us."[17]

At one point during the second of their three campaign debates that fall, Gore declared that this was a "unique period in world history" in which the world was looking to America for leadership in such areas as the environment and the international economy. As he listened to Gore's words, Wolfowitz, who was serving as one of Bush's debate advisers, reflected that they sounded unexceptional. It's hard to respond to that without saying, "Me too," Wolfowitz thought.[18]

Instead, to Wolfowitz's surprise, Bush cut the vice president short. "I'm not so sure the role of the United States is to go around the world and say, 'This is the way it's gotta be,'" Bush retorted. "We can help. Maybe it's just our difference in the way we view government. . . . You know, I want to help people help themselves, not have government tell people what to do. I just don't think it's the role of the United States to walk into a country [and] say, 'We do it this way; so should you.'"[19] The answer was not one for which Rice and Wolfowitz had prepared the candidate; it was a spontaneous response from Bush. Wolfowitz rejoiced and considered it a revealing moment, underscoring Bush's belief in empowering people but not telling them what to do.[20]

A campaign debate, however, was not necessarily an accurate indication of future Bush foreign policy. Two years later, when Bush sought unsuccessfully to persuade the rest of the world to join the United States in a war against Iraq, his remarks about rebuilding alliances and about the importance of maintaining humility were recalled and replayed with no small sense of irony.

There were some issues that Bush and the Vulcans failed to address during the campaign and some underlying disagreements that they papered over or ignored.

Throughout the presidential race Bush and his foreign policy team said remarkably little about terrorism. Bush mentioned it only briefly during a speech about overhauling the nation's defenses. In the final month of the campaign, after Al Qaeda terrorists in Yemen had bombed the Navy destroyer USS *Cole* in the port of Aden, killing seventeen Americans, Bush, like Gore, called vaguely for retaliation against those responsible. Bush said the United States should send a "swift, sure and a clear signal to terrorists around the world that we are not going to tolerate terrorism." But there was virtually no discussion of any of the larger policy issues, such as how to improve homeland security or whether or how the U.S. government should mount a campaign against terrorism. Indeed, Bush never suggested that terrorism was one of the main problems for U.S. foreign policy, and he offered few criticisms of the Clinton administration's approach. Presidents have to set priorities, Bush said at the start of his campaign, "and let me just quickly run by the priorities: Russia and a strong NATO in Europe; China and our alliances in the Far East; our own hemisphere; as well as the Middle East."[21] A long article by Rice in *Foreign Affairs* magazine, written as an overview of the Bush campaign's view of the world, mentioned terrorism only once in passing, while concentrating instead upon the need to refocus American policy toward dealing with powerful states like Russia and China.[22]

Nor, for that matter, did the Bush campaign give any particular emphasis to the issue of Iraq. If George W. Bush thought that Saddam Hussein's brutal mistreatment of the Iraqi people, such as his use of gas against the Kurds in March 1988, was so outrageous as to require outside military intervention, he managed to get through an eighteen-month race for the presidency without saying so.

In this respect, Bush was merely following a well-worn path in the history of American electoral politics. Woodrow Wilson in 1916, Franklin Roosevelt in 1940 and Lyndon Johnson in 1964 all had run presidential campaigns without giving any indication that America might soon have to go to war. (Indeed, these predecessors had gone considerably further than Bush toward pledging to keep America *out* of war.) Still, by failing to give priority to Iraq during his 2000 campaign and by failing to focus at that time on Saddam Hussein's abuses, Bush weakened his argument two years later that this long history of cruelty provided justification for war. On March 16, 2003, as he was about to launch military action against Iraq, Bush declared, "On this very day fifteen years ago, Saddam

Hussein launched a chemical weapons attack on the Iraqi village of Halabja. With a single order, the Iraqi regime killed thousands of men and women and children without mercy and without shame."[23] That was true, but it left unexplained why America had waited to respond until fifteen years later.

To be sure, some members of Bush's Vulcans had signed the 1998 letter organized by the Project for a New American Century that had called for the overthrow of Saddam Hussein. But this neoconservative group did not itself represent the Bush team. In fact, although this fact was later forgotten, the neoconservatives generally did not support Bush during the Republican primaries. Instead, they were sympathetic to Senator John McCain, who had become a hero to the neoconservatives when he supported the Clinton administration's military intervention against Serbian dictator Slobodan Milosević in Kosovo, at a time when Republican congressional leaders were calling it Bill Clinton's War and were urging America to stay out. "I preferred McCain, and Kosovo was what did it for me, where he bucked a large chunk of the Republican party," recalled William Kristol, editor of the neoconservative *The Weekly Standard.* Although he remained on good terms with old friends in the Bush campaign, such as Wolfowitz, Kristol acknowledged that "it got a little bitter around January, February [2000]," as McCain easily defeated Bush in the New Hampshire primary and began to challenge him in South Carolina.[24]

Thus, although the neoconservatives were forthright in the support of military intervention to oust Saddam Hussein from power, it was by no means clear that the Bush campaign favored such action. Indeed, Rice, Bush's top adviser, suggested in 2000 that the Iraqi leader could be handled through the same policy of deterrence that had been carried out for decades against the Soviet Union. In her article in *Foreign Affairs*, Rice wrote that "rogue regimes," such as Iraq and North Korea, "are living on borrowed time, so there need be no sense of panic about them. Rather, the first line of defense should be a clear and classical statement of deterrence—if they do acquire weapons of mass destruction, that weapon will be unusable because any attempt to use them will bring national obliteration."[25] This deterrence argument could easily have been written by Rice's old boss Brent Scowcroft or by any other adherent of the realist school of foreign policy that had dominated American thinking during most of the cold war.

These submerged disagreements over Iraq were merely one example of the many tensions hidden within the Bush campaign in 2000. The neoconservatives favored tough policies toward China and greater support for Taiwan, but the business community, a core Republican constituency, was eager to maintain amicable relations with China. Bush criticized the Clinton administration's dispatch of troops to Haiti as a misguided exercise in "nation building," but the neoconservatives thought America's intervention in Haiti was a noble endeavor.[26]

Nor were the people lined up behind the Republican presidential candidate an entirely happy family. The Reaganites mistrusted the veterans of the first Bush administration, particularly those who had served on Scowcroft's staff, and both those groups were wary of the protégés of former Secretary of State Baker. There were unresolved frictions left over from the Gulf War between Powell, on the one hand, and Cheney and other conservatives, on the other. In his autobiography Powell had written, ostensibly jokingly, that Cheney and his civilian aides in the Pentagon (including, most prominently, Wolfowitz) were "right-wing nuts."[27] For their part, some of the conservatives, including Wolfowitz, had cooperated with some of the books and articles that attempted to puncture Powell's mystique and had criticized his cautious handling of the Gulf War.[28]

Nevertheless, these underlying tensions were set aside in the cause of a Republican return to power. On December 12, 2000, when the Supreme Court ruled, 5–4, that Florida's electoral votes should go to Bush, the experienced men and women who had run American foreign policy through several earlier Republican administrations prepared to return to government. The Vulcans were back.

CHAPTER SEVENTEEN

Who Runs the Pentagon?

THE COURSE OF George W. Bush's administration was set with surprising speed in late December 2000, in a momentous, though largely hidden, struggle over who would get the top foreign policy jobs in the new government, particularly the position of defense secretary. Rarely in American history has a new administration's foreign policy been so clearly determined by its initial round of appointments.

Bush was required to select his new team in unprecedented haste, making the clandestine maneuvering over jobs all the more frenetic. Ordinarily presidents-elect have about ten weeks to assemble a new administration. However, because the legal disputes over the Florida ballot lasted more than a month, the 2000 election was not settled until five and a half weeks before inauguration day. When it came to foreign policy, Bush had an impressive group of seasoned candidates from which to choose, since the Republicans had been in power for twenty of the previous thirty-two years. But all the Vulcans' collective experience didn't answer the tough questions: Who got which jobs?

The president-elect made his personnel choices in a series of meetings with three other people: Cheney; Andrew Card, whom Bush had already named the White House chief of staff; and Clay Johnson, Bush's Yale roommate, who had served as his chief of staff in the Texas governor's office and was soon to become the White House personnel director. Whenever Bush reached a final decision, this group would pass the name along to two others who served, in effect, as messengers to the outside world: Dave Gribben, the former Cheney aide and congressional relations specialist who was responsible for winning Senate confirmation for the nominees, and Ari Fleischer, the press spokesman, whose job was to tell the press.[1]

Some of the president-elect's foreign policy choices were easy. There was little question that Colin Powell would be secretary of state. Bush had all but promised the appointment during his campaign, and Powell had made clear he was interested. Similarly, there was no dispute over who would serve as the new national security adviser. Rice had worked so smoothly with Bush that it was plain she would get the job.

At the outset the choice for director of central intelligence seemed relatively clear too. Donald Rumsfeld seemed the likeliest candidate. His work two years earlier in chairing the commission on missile threats to the United States had given him direct, recent experience with the U.S. intelligence community and missile-related intelligence issues, and this was important to the new administration, which was eager above all to push forward on missile defense. Over the previous few years Rumsfeld's additional efforts as an adviser to the Dole campaign and to congressional Republicans had won him quite a few allies. When Bush began choosing his foreign policy team, "there was a cadre of people pushing Rumsfeld," recalled Republican Congressman Chris Cox. "Rumsfeld had his own chorus."[2]

Rumsfeld wasn't entirely sure he wanted the CIA job, according to friends. Nevertheless, he was already preparing for it. According to one former CIA director, Rumsfeld had begun to canvass various experts and insiders for their views about the problems and inner workings of the intelligence community. "They [the members of the Bush team] were talking about him and to him about being DCI [director of central intelligence]," Richard Allen, one of Rumsfeld's old friends, later recalled.[3]

The one job for which there was no obvious candidate was that of secretary of defense. Two of the Vulcans who had worked most actively in the presidential campaign, Paul Wolfowitz and Richard Armitage, were potential candidates; both had previously served in high-ranking jobs in the Pentagon. But neither of them was senior enough to wrap up such a prominent position, and each had some liabilities. Wolfowitz was admired, even by many of his adversaries, for his remarkable intelligence and diligence, but he was also criticized, even by some of his supporters, for his lack of skill or interest in administration. Memos passing through the bureaucracy tended to linger on his desk because Wolfowitz believed (usually rightly) that he could improve on the ideas or the writing. "Paul is a brilliant guy, but when you went down to his office at the State Department, you couldn't even find Paul, the papers were piled so high," remembered one high-ranking admirer.[4] His work habits were legendary. For a time during the first Bush administration, the Pentagon had two shifts of secretaries working with Wolfowitz—one that came in at 8:00 A.M. and left at 4:00 P.M., another that did the 4:00 to midnight shift. The Pentagon, a huge bureaucracy, was universally thought to need strong management at the top, and Wolfowitz didn't seem to fit that job description. By contrast, Armitage was regarded as a good manager, but he had little name recognition outside the foreign policy community or influence on Capitol Hill; indeed, amid Ross Perot's attacks Armitage had found it impossible to win Senate confirmation for secretary of the army in the first Bush administration. Wolfowitz and Armitage were clearly candidates for senior jobs in the new administration, but defense secretary seemed like a stretch for both.

Instead, as Bush began making his cabinet selections, a different scenario began to emerge for the Pentagon. It could be termed the politician plus Armitage package. Under this scenario Bush would name some prominent Republican political figure to take charge of the Pentagon; the leading candidates were Pennsylvania Governor Tom Ridge and former Indiana Senator Dan Coats, who had retired in 1998. Such a politician could help win congressional and public support for Bush's defense policies. A politician might not know much about the inner workings of the Department of Defense, so the thinking went, but that problem could be overcome if Bush appointed an experienced Pentagon veteran, such as Armitage, to be deputy secretary of defense. Armitage could run the building and deal with the details of policy and personnel, while Coats or Ridge was outside selling the programs and the message.

Ridge's prospects soon evaporated when conservatives raised alarms. He had been one of Bush's closest political allies and had won a Bronze Star for his service in Vietnam. However, during his days in Congress, Ridge's voting record on defense issues was surprisingly liberal; he had voted against Reagan's Strategic Defense Initiative and support for the contras. He was also a supporter of a woman's right to choose an abortion. The fact that Powell's allies were promoting Ridge for defense secretary made conservatives all the more suspicious.

Attention soon turned to Coats, and his candidacy for defense secretary developed strong momentum. Senate Majority Leader Trent Lott, an old ally from Capitol Hill, was pushing hard for him, and so were other Republican senators. Coats had ties to Cheney; Dave Gribben, Cheney's former Wyoming schoolmate and longtime Washington aide, had worked on Coats's staff. Coats also could claim familiarity with defense issues because he had served on the Senate Armed Services Committee.

Above all, Coats was a particular favorite of the religious right. "Mr. Coats is endorsed by social conservatives, who hope he will reverse what they view as eight years of 'social experimentation' at the Pentagon by Clinton appointees," reported the conservative *Washington Times* on its front page in one of several stories and editorials promoting Coats for defense secretary. "Mr. Coats opposes abortion and open homosexuality in the military and has reservations about mixing men and women during recruit training."[5]

Nevertheless, during a two-week period in late December, the politician plus Armitage scenario collapsed. The principal reason for this failure was a new factor, one that was to become the overriding dynamic of the Bush foreign policy team over the coming years—namely, the intense, continuing desire by others in the Bush administration and by conservatives outside it to limit the power and influence of Colin Powell.

On Saturday, December 16, 2000, within four days of the Supreme Court decision, Bush announced his first cabinet appointment, the selection of Powell as his secretary of state. The press conference at Bush's ranch in Crawford, Texas, was timed for the Sunday newspapers and talk shows. It was an event designed to show the country that the president-elect was beginning to form his new administration and that the disputed election was now ancient history.

"We must conduct our foreign policy in the spirit of national unity and bipartisanship," Bush declared, with Vice President–elect Cheney standing alongside. "Our next secretary of state believes, as I do, that we must work closely with our allies and friends in time of calm so that we will be able to work together in times of crises. He believes, as I do, that our nation is best when we project our strength and our purpose with humility."[6] No one recognized it at the time, but Colin Powell's standing inside the Bush administration may have peaked in the moments when the president-elect uttered those words. It began to decline soon afterward.

Taking the podium after Bush, Powell spoke for twice as long as the president-elect; the pair then took reporters' questions, almost all of which were directed to and were answered by Powell. The former general dominated the event. Physically he was taller and more imposing than Bush. Verbally he was vastly more confident. He spoke eloquently of the importance of his appointment to African-Americans. His remarks on foreign policy covered a breadth of subjects ranging from the Middle East to Russia to China to, unwisely for Powell, the defense budget, American troop deployments overseas and missile defense. He promised to help a new defense secretary "in getting what he needs for the military." He also suggested he might become involved in domestic policy, promising to help Bush show he was a president "for all of the people all of the time."[7]

On the surface, Powell's performance seemed unexceptional. This was his day, and indeed a historic one. He was trying, in the fashion of all newly appointed secretaries of state, to assure the rest of the world that American foreign policy would be in good hands. If Powell's remarks extended beyond the field of international diplomacy, he was in a sense responding to the political context in which the new Bush team had chosen to cast Powell's appointment: The underlying message of the press conference was one of postelectoral healing and national unity, themes that went well past the confines of foreign policy or the State Department.

Nevertheless, Powell's remarks, and the unrestrained confidence with which he expressed them, jeopardized his future role in the new administration. The more he spoke, the more he raised anxieties within key constituencies of the Republican party and the new administration. Neoconservatives were reminded of the Colin Powell who had opposed American military intervention in the Balkans and who favored affirmative action. Pentagon veterans from the first Bush administration, whose ranks included Vice President–elect Cheney, were reminded of the Colin Powell of 1990 and 1991, the politically skilled military leader who had quietly gone on his own to the president and the secretary of state to argue against war with Iraq. For alumni of the Reagan administration Powell's performance evoked memories of the time when Secretary of State Alexander Haig had sought to become the "vicar" of American foreign policy. It also seems possible that a president-elect, not yet secure in a job he had won only through a 5–4 Supreme Court decision, may have wondered about the implications of having a secretary of state with the potential to overshadow his boss.

Powell had been the most powerful chairman of the Joint Chiefs of Staff in American history. Would he also become the most powerful secretary of state? During the first Bush administration Cheney had felt obliged to warn Powell, "You're not the national security adviser . . . so stick to military matters."[8] Would this new Bush administration now have to warn Powell to stick to diplomacy and to stay away from military matters? "Powell spoke, and Powell spoke, and Powell spoke, and Powell spoke, and I thought, my God . . ." said Allen, an old hand on the Republican right. "It wasn't even clear to me until after Powell finished whether he was secretary of state or secretary of defense."[9]

If anxious conservatives tried to persuade themselves they had been merely imagining what had happened at the press conference, their fears were revived by the news coverage of the Bush-Powell event on the front page of the next day's *New York Times*. "The general's remarks were broader and more expansive than the incoming president's, and when the time came for questions, it was General Powell who answered them," wrote correspondent Alison Mitchell. ". . . At times, General Powell sounded as if he were speaking not just as the next secretary of state but as the next secretary of defense, too."[10]

The nation's newspapers generally reacted to the Powell appointment with effusive enthusiasm. In an editorial the *Washington Post* called him "impressive" and noted approvingly that "Mr. Powell suggested he wants to use his prestige to have an impact across the administration—on defense policy, on education, on the administration's outreach to the minority communities most embittered by the election results."[11] Such praise did nothing to ease the jitters on the right. The neoconservative *Weekly Standard* quickly published a piece that encapsulated the fears. Its headline was THE LONG ARM OF COLIN POWELL: WILL THE NEXT SECRETARY OF STATE ALSO RUN THE PENTAGON?"[12]

The result was that as the Bush team went about the job of choosing a defense secretary, it was quietly but increasingly preoccupied with the desire to circumscribe the influence of Colin Powell over the new administration's foreign policy.

The following day, to no one's surprise, Bush named Rice to become his national security adviser. On Monday, December 18, two days after the Powell news conference, Bush flew to Washington for a series of meetings, including an interview with Coats. The session, held at the Madison

Hotel, did not go well. At one point Coats specifically raised with the president-elect the issue of Powell's authority, asking whether he would have Bush's support if Powell tried to intrude on his turf as defense secretary. It was the wrong question to ask. The president-elect didn't want a defense secretary who needed to ask for White House support against Powell but rather a defense secretary who could deal with the secretary of state on his own.[13] Neither Coats nor any other Republican politician on the horizon seemed to have the experience on defense issues, the bureaucratic skills or the personal toughness that would be necessary if the defense secretary were to serve as a counterweight to Powell.

To the anti-Powell forces, the idea of Armitage's becoming deputy defense secretary seemed even more problematic. Armitage did not view himself merely as a sidekick to Powell. In the Reagan administration he had risen on his own inside the Pentagon to become one of the top aides to Secretary of Defense Caspar Weinberger. Armitage had his own interests in foreign policy toward Asia and the Middle East that had nothing to do with Powell and an extensive network of friends with little connection to Powell. Nevertheless, the fact remained that Armitage and Powell were best friends, that they talked regularly, if not daily, over the phone and that virtually everyone involved in foreign or defense policy was aware of their close bond. If Armitage was deputy defense secretary, effectively running the Pentagon while a boss such as Coats was out of the building, then Powell would have considerable indirect influence over the inner workings of defense policy. Yet if Armitage wasn't appointed Coats's deputy secretary, then who could be found to help Coats manage the Department of Defense?

Amid this maneuvering over the new defense secretary, there was one other consideration. It was introduced by former President George H. W. Bush, the president-elect's father. Bush senior did not like the idea of appointing Rumsfeld or anyone else the new director of central intelligence at the beginning of a new administration.

The issue was a seemingly abstract one, a question for political scientists: Should the job of the director of central intelligence be considered a political one that turned over each time the White House changed hands? Or should the job be kept separate from politics? Reasonable arguments could be advanced on either side of the debate. To the extent that the CIA director is supposed to give straight, unvarnished, objective information and analysis, the job would seem to call for someone in an independent position. On the other hand, to the extent that an intelligence chief runs extensive covert operations overseas, he is inextricably a part of the administration's foreign policy team and bears political responsibility along with the administration.

The former president possessed more than a little personal experience with this problem. In 1975 President Ford had brought him back from China to become CIA director, and he had been required by Congress to promise that if he took the job, he wouldn't be a Republican candidate for vice president. The senior Bush obliged and thus reluctantly postponed his political career in order to run the CIA. "I had to work hard to overcome the understandable concern about bringing politics into the agency," he later recalled.[14] When Ford lost, Bush hoped to continue as CIA director, and during a trip to Plains, Georgia, tried to persuade President-elect Carter to keep him on the job. To his considerable disappointment, Carter quickly replaced him.[15] From these events Bush had drawn the conclusion that a CIA director should carry over from one administration to the next, like the FBI director or the chairman of the Joint Chiefs of Staff. "Automatically replacing the director in each new administration would tend to politicize what essentially is a career service that is supposed to be beyond politics," he wrote in his memoir.[16] In 1989, when the elder Bush became president, he had chosen to leave DCI William Webster, whom Reagan had appointed, on the job for two years, even though Webster's performance had drawn mixed reviews.

In the face of the senior Bush's concerns about replacing the CIA director, there was some talk of having Rumsfeld appointed to head a presidential commission on intelligence, a position from which he might then replace DCI George Tenet after a decent interval.[17] But that seemed like a makeshift solution. It also didn't solve the problem of finding a secretary of defense.

Meanwhile, some of Rumsfeld's oldest and most illustrious friends were quietly lobbying hard for him—not for the job of director of central intelligence, but for secretary of defense. Among them was the former Secretary of State George Shultz, Rumsfeld's friend since the Nixon years. He talked both to Rice and to Clay Johnson. It seems extremely unlikely that Shultz would have done so without Rumsfeld's knowledge.

"I weighed in heavily," Shultz recalled in an interview. "I said he'd be a fine director of the CIA, but that they really [should] want him to be secretary of defense. What you need at Defense are three things: You need somebody who knows how to manage something big, somebody who knows the Congress and somebody who can fight a war, who's tough."[18]

Rumsfeld was no friend of the Bush family. Indeed, the senior Bush and Rumsfeld had been competitors within the Republican party for many years. Bush loyalists continued to blame Rumsfeld, then Ford's White House chief of staff, for the 1975 shake-up that had brought Bush to the CIA and taken him out of the running for the vice presidency. A decade later, when Rumsfeld tried to run for the 1988 Republican presidential nomination, the campaign undeniably reflected his judgment that Bush, even as a sitting vice president, wasn't a strong candidate.

Nevertheless, the bitterness between the senior Bush and Rumsfeld had evaporated by the end of the 1980s, according to Bush's former national security adviser, Brent Scowcroft.[19] It is something of a Republican tradition for presidents-elect to borrow the services of talented individuals from rival political camps: Henry Kissinger had been an adviser to Nelson Rockefeller's presidential campaign before working for Richard Nixon, and James Baker had run Bush's unsuccessful 1980 campaign before becoming Ronald Reagan's White House chief of staff. For the younger Bush to give a prominent job to Rumsfeld, his father's former adversary, was not as unusual as it may have seemed.

When the decision was made, it came with remarkable speed. About noon on Wednesday, December 27, Rumsfeld was still talking to old friends about heading the CIA. "I said, you're perfectly cut out for this job," Richard Allen told him that day in a phone call. "I don't know," Rumsfeld demurred. In a front-page story that same day the *Washington Times* reported that Rumsfeld had emerged as the leading candidate for the CIA post and quoted one official as saying the appointment was "a done deal"; other candidates, including Tenet, were said to have lost out.[20] That day the president-elect was in Boca Grande, Florida, fishing with his father and his brother Jeb.

The following morning the *New York Times* matched the *Washington Times* with its own account of how Rumsfeld was the top candidate for the CIA.[21] Bush meanwhile was on his way back to Washington. That afternoon, just after 2:00 P.M., the president-elect announced his nomination of Rumsfeld—not to be CIA director, as the newspapers had just reported, but to the Pentagon job Rumsfeld had held a quarter century earlier. "He's going to be a great secretary of defense, again," Bush told a press conference.

Bush touched briefly and delicately on the underlying issue, the relative clout of the individual members of the foreign policy team. ". . . General Powell's a strong figure, and Dick Cheney's no shrinking violet, but neither is Don Rumsfeld, nor Condi Rice," Bush said. "I view the four as being able to complement one another." The president-elect said one of Rumsfeld's first tasks would be "to challenge the status quo inside the Pentagon." Rumsfeld made clear he was not only willing but eager to do that. "It is clearly not a time at the Pentagon for presiding or calibrating modestly," he said.[22]

Bush kept Tenet on at the CIA, thus deferring to his father's belief that the job should not change hands each time a new president is elected. A couple of months later Bush quietly appointed Dan Coats his ambassador to Germany.

With the top foreign policy positions filled, the Bush team turned next to the number two positions and, at the same time, to the question of what to do with Paul Wolfowitz and Richard Armitage.

Wolfowitz hoped to be appointed Powell's deputy secretary of state. Although he had become closely identified with defense policy in the first Bush administration, he had also spent the Reagan years at the State Department; he had thoroughly enjoyed the issues and the work. Indeed, Wolfowitz seemed to believe he would be a more natural fit at State than inside the Pentagon, where his lack of military service, though rarely mentioned, was sometimes a subterranean issue. Conversely, over the years, Armitage, like other Pentagon officials, had often poked fun at the bureaucratic, stereotypically effete culture of the State Department. When Armitage served as Philippines base negotiator and was given a suite of offices on the State Department's ground floor, he had enlisted military officers to help run it and had behaved as if it were an outpost on alien soil, like Guantánamo Bay on Castro's Cuba. Wolfowitz didn't run down the State Department; he aspired to run it someday in the fashion of his old boss George Shultz.

There was, however, a problem: Wolfowitz's less than sterling relationship with Powell. It would have been awkward enough if the two men had never met, but even worse that they knew each other all too well. They had worked together in the Pentagon, where Wolfowitz had been among the most prominent of the group of civilians who mistrusted Powell's power and his instinctive caution and where Powell had thought of Wolfowitz and his whole staff as a group of "Reagan-era hardliners."[23]

Powell, after his appointment as secretary of state, enlisted the help of his friend Kenneth Duberstein to interview and help deal with candidates for the top jobs at the State Department. Duberstein, formerly Reagan's White House chief of staff, worked as a Washington lobbyist out of a suite of offices on Pennsylvania Avenue roughly a half mile from the State Department. Wolfowitz paid him a visit and said he was eager to be deputy secretary of state.

Powell wasn't interested. Instead, Duberstein, serving as Powell's go-between, offered Wolfowitz the position of ambassador to the United Nations, a job that, perhaps not coincidentally, would have sent Wolfowitz out of town. Wolfowitz wanted no part of a job in New York, a city that, despite its boundless self-importance, is merely a remote province when it comes to foreign policy decision making.

Richard Armitage's friends thought he seemed depressed after the Coats nomination fell through. Having spent much of the previous two years working for Bush's campaign, Armitage began talking about staying out of the new administration. He realized Rumsfeld wouldn't need or want him as deputy defense secretary. The two men had been on opposite sides of a Reagan-era divide: Armitage had been a close aide to Secretary of Defense Caspar Weinberger, and Rumsfeld had been a Shultz ally when Weinberger and Shultz were endlessly fighting about Lebanon and the Middle East. Ultimately, however, Armitage's difficulties stemmed not from ancient feuds but from modern-day friendships. However much Armitage saw himself as an independent actor, he was perceived in Washington first of all as Powell's ally. The Bush team simply didn't want an associate of Powell's to have one of the top jobs in the Pentagon. "For me, I think the question [of deputy secretary of defense] had to do with my relationship to General Powell," Armitage admitted in an interview the following year.[24]

Armitage went through the formalities of an interview with Rumsfeld for the job of deputy, but their conversation was icy. Associates insisted later on that Rumsfeld had originally intended to offer Armitage a position as a service secretary, perhaps secretary of the Navy, but if so, the conversation quickly took a different turn. After the pleasantries Rumsfeld bluntly informed Armitage the chances were "less than fifty-fifty" he would get the job of deputy secretary. Irritated, Armitage countered that he estimated there was "about zero" percent chance he would get or would take the job; you won't choose me, he told Rumsfeld, because I'm close to Powell.[25]

There were some other candidates on the list for deputy defense secretary, including William Schneider, once a senior administrator in Reagan's State Department, and Sean O'Keefe, the former Pentagon aide to Cheney. But the choice seemed, in retrospect, foreordained: Wolfowitz. Rumsfeld had worked with Wolfowitz both during the 1996 Dole campaign and on the 1998 missile defense commission. The vice president was Wolfowitz's strong supporter. Wolfowitz had served as idea man and policy expert in Cheney's Pentagon; he could play the same role once again for Rumsfeld, this time with the more senior title of deputy secretary. Rumsfeld himself could manage the Pentagon and could find other people, more interested in administration than Wolfowitz, to make sure the paperwork kept moving.

The final step seemed equally predictable: that Armitage should become Powell's number two, the deputy secretary of state. The two men were not merely friends but also viewed the world (and Washington) in a similar fashion. Both were Vietnam veterans, a rare credential in the Bush inner circle. Both were leery of military misadventures and civilian crusades. Both saw themselves as antielitists, men of modest upbringings who had achieved their successes without passing through the Ivy League schools as had many of the other men and women on the Bush team.

Yet curiously, it took a few days and some quiet persuasion before the deal was reached. Having hoped for a return to the Pentagon, Armitage wasn't sure he wanted to go to State. Working for Powell was to him like working for your brother. Meanwhile, having believed Armitage would be going to Defense, Powell had begun to consider other candidates to serve as his deputy.

Over the course of a week some of the veterans of past Republican administrations pleaded with Armitage to go work for Powell. "I told him he had an obligation," said Allen. "We had a little circuit going; [former

Undersecretary of Defense Fred] Iklé, a lot of people were banging on him."[26] The most powerful of the persuaders was Powell himself. Finally, after a long delay and after telling friends he wouldn't take the job, Armitage relented. He agreed to join the new administration as deputy secretary of state.

One day many months later, after the Bush administration was up and running and Wolfowitz and Armitage were trying to smooth over one of the many bitter disputes between the Pentagon and the State Department, Wolfowitz acknowledged the awkward, ironic truth that had never become public. You know, Rich, Wolfowitz said, you got the job that I wanted. And I got the job that you wanted.

This was not just a game of musical chairs. These personnel choices determined how much influence the individual members of the Bush team would have, the way in which foreign policy institutions would operate and the conceptual framework through which the administration would view the world.

The appointment of Rumsfeld as defense secretary served to limit the authority of Colin Powell over the administration's foreign policy. This was true not only because of Rumsfeld's aggressive personality, bureaucratic toughness and experience as a former defense secretary but also because of his three-decades-old personal ties to Vice President Cheney, whom Rumsfeld had once hired and groomed.

Nor was Cheney's influence limited to the Rumsfeld nomination. Wolfowitz, the new deputy secretary of defense, was close to Cheney. Several other people who had worked under Cheney and Wolfowitz in the Pentagon in the first Bush administration were placed in key positions on the new foreign policy team: Scooter Libby, Wolfowitz's protégé, became Cheney's chief of staff; Stephen Hadley, another Wolfowitz aide, became deputy national security adviser; Zalmay Khalilzad took charge of Afghanistan and Iraq policy at the National Security Council.

Thus, in what amounted to an unacknowledged struggle for influence over the Pentagon between Cheney and Powell—that is, between the former secretary of defense and the former chairman of the Joint Chiefs of Staff from the first Bush administration—Cheney emerged as the clear winner. Powell, despite his popularity and stature, couldn't match Cheney's network of friends among conservatives and within the Republican foreign policy elite. Powell would be left relatively free to run the

State Department in the new administration, but he would not be allowed, any more than Alexander Haig had, to become the "vicar" of American foreign policy. He would be merely one voice at the top, not the dominant one.

The series of appointments virtually guaranteed that the central preoccupation of the new foreign policy team would be American military power. Virtually everyone on the new team had spent some of his or her formative years in government in the Defense Department. Even Powell and Armitage, the State Department's two new leaders, had spent most of their careers in the Pentagon. (Whenever Powell and Armitage offended conservatives, the two men were accused of having been "captured" by the State Department bureaucracy.) The top ranks of the Bush foreign policy team included two former secretaries of defense and one former chairman of the Joint Chiefs.

There was no one among them whose career had been devoted primarily to diplomacy or to building international institutions. There was no one with the background of, say, Dean Acheson or Averell Harriman. The Vulcans were of comparable intelligence, drive and skill, but they had devoted their talents above all to helping America regain and build American military strength. Even some of the internal differences within the team—between Vietnam veterans Powell and Armitage, who were reluctant to commit troops to battle in inhospitable places, and the more hawkish Cheney, Rumsfeld and Wolfowitz—were ultimately debates about the application of military power.

The only member of the Vulcans' campaign team who had previously served in a senior job in the State Department was Robert Zoellick. He was named U.S. trade representative, an important position, but one that removed him from the table for discussions about the overall direction of American foreign policy. Some critics complained, fairly or not, about Zoellick's style and personality, but the underlying reality was that having never served in the Pentagon, Zoellick was one Vulcan who simply did not fit in with the new team or share its interests.

The appointments to the new administration, both at the top and at secondary levels, created a situation in which, over the following four years, the State Department and the Defense Department would be almost continually at odds with each other. Bush might have averted this problem either by appointing a defense secretary who would work closely with Powell or, on the other hand, by not appointing Powell secretary of state. That Bush failed to take either option grew directly out of the larger domestic politics surrounding Powell. The conservatives who constituted Bush's base of support never trusted Powell, yet they had not been able to win the election without Powell either. Powell had campaigned alongside Bush, had played a starring role at the Republican National Convention and had helped Bush put forward his theme of compassionate conservatism. Over the years there have been other instances in which a secretary of state and a secretary of defense were at odds with each other, but none of these other disagreements had such deep political roots as the one involving Powell.

The choices of Wolfowitz as deputy defense secretary and Armitage as deputy secretary of state further contributed to the acrimony between Defense and State. These appointments meant that Rumsfeld and Powell were seconded by powerful deputies who thought much as they did. If Wolfowitz had been named deputy secretary of state or Armitage deputy secretary of defense, some of the Bush administration's tensions might have been fought out *inside* each department, as personality disputes between a secretary and his deputy. Instead, there was relative harmony at the top within State and Defense and endless bickering between the two huge agencies.

During the Reagan and first Bush administrations many of the frictions at the top levels of the U.S. government had been quietly smoothed over by deputies or other lower-level officials. In the George W. Bush administration this rarely happened. Even the most casual visitor to the Pentagon quickly discovered that the State Department was the real enemy; at the State Department, by contrast, visitors were regularly offered unsolicited denunciations of the civilians in the Department of Defense.

This bureaucratic warfare meant that the White House was regularly called upon to resolve the disputes between the State and Defense departments. Thus the result was to leave Bush and Cheney with vastly greater power and leverage than they would have had if the State Department and the Pentagon had been working harmoniously together. Since the president-elect started out with virtually no experience in foreign policy, the dominant influence, particularly at the beginning of the administration, was Cheney.

To buttress his influence still further, Cheney took the step of appointing his own staff of foreign policy experts, who operated separately from the National Security Council, thus increasing the role of the vice president's office in international affairs well beyond what it had been in previous administrations. Foreign officials soon learned that when they visited Washington, it was no longer enough merely to talk to officials at the State Department, NSC and Pentagon; they had to make Cheney's office a regular stop on the itinerary.

One of Cheney's predecessors, John Nance Garner, had once memorably quipped that the vice presidency wasn't worth a bucket of warm spit. Cheney turned the same job into a flourishing vineyard.

Warnings and Signals

On January 20, 2001, George W. Bush was sworn in as America's forty-third president. Within weeks the hidden tensions over the role of Colin Powell burst into the open in a dispute over the incoming administration's policy toward North Korea. In the process the new Bush team revealed much about its underlying views and approach to the world.

Among foreign leaders there had been a quiet race to get in to see America's new leader. The winner—ironically, in retrospect—was French President Jacques Chirac, who deftly managed to arrange a meeting while on a trip to Washington in December 2000. "It looks like the French hit a home run . . . with President-elect Bush," reported the *Washington Post* at the time, suggesting that France was winning a battle for access to the new administration.[1]

In early March, South Korean President Kim Dae Jung flew to Washington to ascertain the future direction of the Bush White House. Kim was the first leader with serious diplomacy to transact. He was eager for the new Bush administration to give its imprimatur to his "sunshine" policy of conciliation toward North Korea. He also hoped the Bush team would promise to continue the drive that the Clinton administration launched in its final months for a new agreement with North Korea limiting its production and export of missiles.

On the day the South Korean president landed in Washington, it appeared he might get what he was seeking. "We do plan to engage with North Korea and to pick up where President Clinton and his administration left off," Powell told reporters at a State Department news conference.[2]

It was a surprise, then, when Kim visited Bush the next day and discovered that the new president was taking a different, considerably tougher line. Bush made clear he was in no rush for talks with North Korean leaders and was skeptical about the value of any agreements with them. "We're not certain as to whether they're keeping all terms of all agreements," the president asserted, thereby calling into question whether North Korea was honoring a 1994 deal in which the Clinton administration claimed it had won a suspension of North Korea's nuclear weapons program. "We look forward to, at some point in the future, having a dialogue with the North Koreans," said Bush, but he quickly added that any deal would require "complete verification" of North Korean promises.[3]

Months later Powell acknowledged he had erred by saying the new team would pick up where Clinton had left off because others in the administration hadn't agreed to do that. "Sometimes you get a little far forward on your skis," Powell said.[4] The new secretary of state was just learning the constraints of his new job. Over the coming years he often found the skiing to be difficult; the Bush White House repeatedly pushed him back on his heels.

Even the less hawkish members of the new Bush team took office with a considerably tougher line on North Korea than the Democrats had had. Powell's top advisers on Asia were Richard Armitage, the deputy secretary, and James Kelly, the newly appointed assistant secretary of state for East Asia. Both men had been critical of Clinton's North Korea policy. In the months before the Republicans took office, both men had made plain that they did not believe an American president should fly to Pyongyang for a summit meeting with North Korean President Kim Jong Il, as Clinton had been contemplating in his final months. Both also argued the Clinton administration had oversold its 1994 agreement with Pyongyang, in which North Korea had pledged to freeze its two known nuclear-weapons facilities in exchange for energy supplies; they suggested (rightly, as it turned out) that despite this deal, North Korea might be continuing its nuclear weapons program.[5]

Nevertheless, at the time Bush took office, neither they nor other Vulcans were proposing to undo the Clinton administration's agreement with North Korea. Asked at his confirmation if he favored abrogating the 1994 deal, Paul Wolfowitz had answered with a single word, "No." Armitage explained that the new team was not seeking a confrontation with North Korea. "We've got other fish to fry," he said, noting that the administration had other large ambitions, such as a tax cut, missile defense and peace in the Middle East.[6]

The problem was that the secretary of state's vague words had implied that Bush might, like Clinton, be in a hurry for a new deal with North Korea—or, even worse, that Bush might be willing to go off for a summit in Pyongyang, as Clinton had envisioned. In the hours before his meeting with Kim Dae Jung, Bush had huddled in the Oval Office with Vice President Cheney, National Security Adviser Condoleezza Rice, Chief of Staff Andrew Card and Bush's communications director, Karen Hughes; they decided to make it clear, in public, that Powell had gone too far. Bush's tough statement on North Korea soon followed. "It was an early signal that the President was not going to allow the secretary of state to say whatever he wanted," reflected one senior administration official many months later. "It was a useful signal to other cabinet members, too."[7]

At the time cynics minimized the significance of Bush's rhetoric, suggesting it represented short-term posturing by the new administration. The new administration was merely trying to show that it was different from Clinton, so this argument went; the Bush team would seek its own similar missile deal with North Korea after a decent interval, when Clinton could no longer be given any credit for it. By this theory, the Bush administration was merely being temporarily contrary, giving vent to campaign-style rhetoric in its early months before it confronted the realities of office.

In fact, Bush's rebuff to Kim Dae Jung represented something more broad and enduring than reflexive anti-Clintonism. It reflected the Vulcans' different view of the world. Leading members of the new Bush team, including Secretary of Defense Donald Rumsfeld, Cheney and Wolfowitz, had opposed Henry Kissinger's policies toward the Soviet Union in the 1970s. Rumsfeld had argued that an accommodation with the Soviets on arms control was unwise; Wolfowitz had further suggested that détente with the Moscow was immoral since it could serve to perpetuate a repressive, antidemocratic regime. But if a relatively weaker America had decided against any accommodation with the Soviet Union in the 1970s, then why should the United States at the peak of its power in 2001 need to compromise with North Korea, a regime vastly smaller, more impoverished and more repressive than the one in Moscow? If the United States had successfully challenged totalitarianism in the Soviet

Union and eventually witnessed the collapse of the regime, why couldn't it do likewise in North Korea?

On the day after Kim Dae Jung visited the White House, a senior official pointedly told a reporter that North Korea was not a democracy and that the new administration had doubts about the extent to which it should do business with its leaders. During the early months of the new administration one of America's leading military commanders came home from overseas for a visit to the Pentagon and was startled to be told, "We don't *do* 'engagement.'"[8]

The abrupt turnaround on North Korea policy perfectly illustrated the new administration's style and underlying assumptions about foreign policy. The Vulcans were not eager to enter into agreements—certainly not for their own sake. No deal was better than one that didn't work or one that helped keep a brutal regime in power. Far more than their predecessors, the Vulcans were willing to base American foreign policy on moral judgments, such as whether a regime (or an individual leader, such as Kim Jong Il) was undemocratic or repressive.

Wolfowitz was particularly pleased with the direction of the new administration. During those early months Bush had interrupted a discussion of foreign policy by commenting about one country's leadership, "We're talking about them as though they were members of the Chevy Chase Country Club. What are they really like? . . . How brutal are these people?" Wolfowitz felt that these questions offered an important perspective, one that had been too rare in Washington. (In an interview Wolfowitz would not say which country had flunked the Chevy Chase test, but it was almost certainly North Korea or Iraq.)[9]

Yet there were some difficulties with the administration's uncompromising approach. If the underlying strategy was to wait for a regime like North Korea either to yield to American demands or to collapse entirely, then that strategy left little for the U.S. government to do in the meantime. It ran the risk that a tottering regime with which America was refusing to make a deal might survive and do serious harm before it collapsed. Thus over the following years North Korea would become an intractable problem for the Bush administration. Starting in late 2002, after the administration had confronted North Korea with evidence it had been continuing to develop nuclear weapons, the Pyongyang regime restarted its nuclear reactor, removed seals from its nuclear facilities, ordered international inspectors to leave the country, withdrew from the nuclear nonproliferation treaty, test-fired missiles and claimed it was reprocessing plutonium. Meanwhile, as it moved toward becoming a full-fledged nuclear state, North Korea sought to goad the Bush administration into talks. The Vulcans didn't want direct negotiations. The administration's response instead was to be patient, hoping for an eventual capitulation or a collapse. In August 2003, the United States entered into six-party talks with North Korea in which China, Russia, Japan and South Korea also took part—but even after the talks started, the administration was still in no rush for an agreement.

Condoleezza Rice was not a China expert. Yet during the very first weeks of the new administration the new national security adviser had clearly already been contemplating how to deal with the world's most populous nation, which Bush had labeled a "strategic competitor." Sitting in her White House office, Rice explained to a visitor that the administration anticipated some conflicts with China but was seeking to have them early, during the first year, in order to get them out of the way. China's Communist party chooses new leaders at a party congress every five years, Rice noted, and the next one was scheduled for the fall of 2002. She hoped that in the months leading up to that party congress, the United States could avoid controversy with China and keep a low profile. The aim was to avoid doing anything then that might set off an outpouring of Chinese anti-Americanism of the sort that had followed the accidental U.S. bombing of the Chinese Embassy in Belgrade in 1999. Thus one element in the new administration's strategy was to try to ensure that any confrontations with Beijing took place in 2001, not 2002. Rice, ever disciplined, had come up with a novel approach to China policy; it was a question of setting the calendar and keeping to it.[10]

She could not have known what was about to unfold. When Rice spoke of possible conflicts between Washington and Beijing, she was thinking primarily about Taiwan. The new Bush team was on record in favor of stronger American support for the island and its democratic government. In its final years the Clinton administration had postponed action on a series of requests by Taiwan for new weapons systems, leaving the decisions up to the next administration. Bush had to act on Taiwan's requests by late April 2001.

Suddenly, as that deadline approached, the new Bush team found itself in an unanticipated, more serious confrontation with China and its

People's Liberation Army. On Sunday, April 1, 2001, an American EP-3 reconnaissance plane on an intelligence mission near China's coastline collided with a Chinese fighter jet. The Chinese plane fell into the ocean, and its pilot was never found. The American plane landed on Hainan Island, where the twenty-four crew members were detained. China refused to release the Americans until it received a formal apology from the United States.

Chinese jets had been challenging American reconnaissance missions for months. They came primarily from a navy squadron based on Hainan, where Chinese pilots appeared to compete with one another to see how close they could come to the American spy planes. Indeed, in December 2000 the United States had lodged a formal protest with China's Ministry of Defense over the dangerous airmanship.[11] Nothing had changed.

The collision of the two planes and China's detention of the crew constituted the most serious military confrontation between the United States and China in more than three decades. For more than a week the halls of Congress and talk shows across the United States filled up with speculation of war or economic retaliation. China had shown the United States that it was "a hostile power," declared Representative Dana Rohrabacher of California. Another congressman, Duncan Hunter, introduced legislation to revoke China's trade benefits with the United States. "While we trade with China, they prepare for war," Hunter said.[12]

For a time the new administration had trouble even getting through to the Chinese leadership. Chinese President Jiang Zemin was on a trip to Latin America, along with Qian Qichen, his leading foreign policy adviser. Rice tried to put through a phone call to Qian, but he wouldn't come to the phone. Jiang boasted to one of his Latin American hosts that after the bombing of the embassy in Belgrade, Clinton had tried to phone him six times before Jiang finally took a call.[13]

In Beijing U.S. Ambassador Joseph Prueher at first found himself unable to see anyone other than lower-level officials in the Foreign Ministry. Members of the Bush team were irked that the Chinese were behaving in such a brusque manner. Beijing seemed to react primarily to public pressure from Bush himself. Only after the president made statements calling for U.S. access to the detained crew members and for higher-level talks between the two governments did China begin to respond.

Finally, serious talks got under way between Prueher and Chinese Foreign Ministry officials in Beijing and between Chinese Ambassador Yang Jiechi and Armitage in Washington. Quickly the talks centered on how to resolve China's demand for an apology. The two sides worked out a deal in which Prueher handed Chinese officials a letter stating that the United States was "very sorry" for the loss of the Chinese pilot and for the fact that the American plane had landed on Hainan without official clearance. The English-language text of Prueher's letter did not use the word *apology*, but in Beijing, authorities translated the letter into Chinese with wording that suggests a "deep expression of apology or regret." With that linguistic subterfuge the eleven-day crisis eased, and China released the American crew.[14]

The new administration's approach for dealing with China contrasted sharply with its policy toward North Korea. With China the administration set carefully limited goals that could be achieved without either a collapse or a capitulation by the Chinese regime. The administration was willing to negotiate directly with Beijing to try to achieve these goals. The Bush team did not refrain from dealing with China because of judgments about the unsavory nature of the Chinese regime or its leaders; Jiang, for example, had been primarily responsible for China's brutal repression of the Falun Gong spiritual movement and for China's eradication of a tiny democracy movement. The Chinese leadership, however, was apparently not subjected to Bush's Chevy Chase Country Club test (or if it was, it passed on grounds of affluence).

This differential handling of China was of course attributable in part to the fact that it was far bigger and militarily more powerful than North Korea. There was another factor as well, a desire to avoid disturbing the American business relationship with China. The Vulcans, since the earliest days of the Bush campaign, had developed a framework of ideas for China in which they would be more assertive than the Democrats on security issues and on Taiwan but would not jeopardize U.S. investment in China or trade between the two countries.

In one speech during the campaign, Wolfowitz, the Vulcans' leading theoretician, had said he thought China was "probably the single most serious foreign policy challenge of the coming decades." Yet while China's power was increasing, Wolfowitz continued, "I think it would be a mistake to treat China like the old Soviet Union during the Cold War." Unlike the Soviet Union, Wolfowitz explained, China has "a substantial private sector whose scope and sphere is [*sic*] growing." Rice had praised the emergence in China of what she called "an entrepreneurial class that does not owe its livelihood to the state."[15]

Such assertions tended to exaggerate the extent to which Chinese businesses operated independently of the Chinese state. Nevertheless, these ideas and analyses served an important political purpose: They provided the underpinnings for a policy of continued American trade with China. The Republican party enjoyed strong backing from the American business community, and none of the Vulcans was eager to jeopardize that support. During the campaign, while often challenging the Democrats' China policy in other ways, Bush had not allowed any daylight to emerge between himself and the Clinton administration on the central issue of trade.

During the cold war the Vulcans had elected to challenge the Soviet Union rather than accommodate it. But the Soviet Union had not been tied to the global economic system, and China increasingly was. As a result, the Vulcans were willing to do business with China's Communist party leadership in a manner that they never would have countenanced with Moscow.

When Bush authorized the letter of regret over the spy plane, some of the neoconservatives were outraged. Writing in the *Weekly Standard,* Robert Kagan and William Kristol said Bush had brought a "profound national humiliation" upon the United States; they branded the Bush policy one of appeasement and called for the revocation of China's trade benefits. For a time relations between the neoconservatives and the Bush White House were strained.[16]

Bush quickly moved to win back support from the political right. Less than two weeks after China's release of the Americans, he announced that his administration was authorizing the largest package of new weapons systems for Taiwan in many years, including submarines, which Taiwan had been trying to obtain since the 1970s. China was taken by surprise. During the early months of 2001 Chinese officials had spent considerable energy in a campaign to dissuade the Bush administration from letting Taiwan buy a different weapons system, new, advanced destroyers equipped with Aegis advanced radar systems. Beijing had won the battle over the Aegis but hadn't realized that submarines were in the offing. The Chinese were "bait-and-switched," reflected Armitage many months later.[17]

The Bush administration quickly followed with another surprise. During a television interview about his first hundred days in office the new president was asked if the United States had an obligation to defend Taiwan. "Yes, we do, and the Chinese must understand that," he replied. With the full force of the American military? "Whatever it took to help Taiwan defend itself."[18] The president's words, at least on the surface, represented a change in the long-standing American policy of "strategic ambiguity" concerning Taiwan. Ever since the 1950s, when John Foster Dulles was trying to persuade Chiang Kai-shek not to invade the Chinese mainland, the United States had refused to specify if, or under exactly what circumstances, America would come to Taiwan's aid in a military conflict with China. Ending this policy of ambiguity had been one of the top items on the neoconservatives' agenda; their Project for a New American Century had organized the 1999 letter, signed by Wolfowitz and Armitage, that called for revising America's Taiwan policy. Such a change was seen as a step toward moral clarity, toward putting America clearly on the side of democratic Taiwan.

In fact, the practical significance of Bush's "whatever it takes" declaration was open to question. Bush had indicated that the United States would come to Taiwan's defense if it were attacked; he had left unclear what the United States would do if war broke out under other circumstances, such as if Taiwan were provoked into starting hostilities. Yet it was these blurry situations that the policy of ambiguity had been intended to cover. In an interview three days later Cheney, while saying ambiguity "may be" wrong, also said Bush's statement had served to "reinforce" and "reiterate" the existing U.S. policy, thus leaving unclear exactly how much the policy had changed.[19] Bush's declaration was not followed by any specific orders to the U.S. military to alter its planning or resources for possible conflicts in the Taiwan Straits. China's own military planners had appeared to take it for granted since the mid-1990s that if the People's Liberation Army attacked Taiwan, the United States would intervene with force to help defend the island; that had been clear ever since the Clinton administration dispatched two aircraft carriers to help defend Taiwan in the crises of 1995 and 1996. Thus Bush's statement may have meant more in the United States, as a symbolically important gesture to American conservatives and their goal of moral clarity, than it meant for China and Taiwan.

The same week the Bush administration quietly pushed through one final policy change, one with long-term consequences for Taiwan, this time subtly undercutting Taiwan's position. The president announced that he was abolishing the process of yearly reviews of Taiwan's requests for American weaponry.[20] Those annual reviews had made it easier for Taiwan to win support in the United States for its arms requests because each spring, in the weeks before the deadline, Congress and the news media focused intensively on the question of what arms Taiwan should get. Bush's change cleared the way for the White House to make decisions on arms for Taiwan in a more quiet and leisurely manner, less driven by deadlines and congressional pressure. Indeed, in 2002 and 2003, for the first time in several years, there were no public disputes over weaponry for Taiwan.

In a general sense, the Vulcans carried out the calendar-based China strategy Rice had sketched out in early 2001; the administration posed most of its challenges to Beijing during Bush's first months in office. Thereafter the Bush team avoided public confrontations in dealing with China, especially throughout 2002 before and during the Communist party congress. After initially making clear that the new administration should not be considered a friend of China, the Bush team then proceeded to do business quietly and regularly with China's leaders. The Vulcans were selective; they knew how to choose their adversaries.

By the time of Bush's first trip to Europe in June 2001, a perception had already taken hold, one that would endure. His administration, it was said, was "unilateralist" in its approach. The first question the new president was asked on his first trip overseas was if the United States was willing to "go it alone" in the world. Bush quickly found himself both denying accusations of unilateralism and attempting to redefine the word in a narrow fashion that wouldn't apply to the administration: "I hope the notion of a unilateralist approach died in some people's minds here today. . . . Unilateralists don't ask opinions of world leaders."[21]

These European perceptions had been prompted above all by the administration's decision earlier that spring to abandon the Kyoto Protocol on global warming, the international agreement reached in 1997 to reduce emissions of carbon dioxide, methane and other pollutants. The Clinton administration had signed this agreement but then decided not to submit it to the Senate for ratification; over the protests of European governments, the new Bush team took the more drastic step of withdrawing entirely from the proposed treaty.

The rejection of the Kyoto agreement was not an isolated occurrence. During its first nine months in office the new administration took several other steps the impact of which was to undercut existing treaties or agreements. Bush announced in May that the administration, in its drive for a national missile defense system, was hoping to move "beyond the constraints" of the 1972 Anti-Ballistic Missile Treaty. In July the administration turned down a draft protocol to set up enforcement mechanisms for an international ban on biological weapons. With each new example in which the Bush team rejected or even voiced doubts about an international agreement, the word *unilateralist* further attached itself to the administration.

The accusation was at once accurate and unfair, insofar as it seemed to imply that the phenomenon had started in 2001. There had indeed been a tendency toward unilateralism—that is, a tendency by the United States to act on its own, rather than in concert with other countries or with international organizations. That drift, however, had begun in the 1990s, not with the George W. Bush administration. It was above all an outgrowth of the end of the cold war and America's new status as the world's only superpower. On the one hand, the United States felt freer to advance its own national interests rather than the larger interests of the West or of its allies. On the other hand, other governments became more acutely sensitive than in the past to demonstrations of American power.

The Clinton administration too had been subject to accusations of unilateralism, although this fact seemed to have been quickly forgotten after Bush took office. During the late 1990s the Clinton administration refused to sign the international treaty banning the use of land mines (1997), declined to join the International Criminal Court (1998) and declined to submit the Kyoto treaty to Congress.[22] In 1999 the Senate rejected ratification of the Comprehensive Test Ban Treaty. During this period State Department officials spoke regularly of America's "hegemony problem" overseas. Countries such as China, Russia and France began to consult with one another about how they could counterbalance American power. When the Clinton administration mounted military action against Iraq in 1998, only Britain was willing to join with it.[23]

To be sure, some of these actions perceived as unilateralist in the

1990s had been more the responsibility of the Republican Congress than the Clinton White House. But in other instances, including the rejections of the land mine treaty and the International Criminal Court, the Clinton administration had acted on its own, on the basis of strong objections from the Pentagon. Some analysts in the 1990s had attributed America's drift toward unilateralism to the personal failings of Clinton, just as many later blamed the inadequacies of Bush. "We've got a president who's not interested in foreign policy, so domestic lobbies are decisive when foreign policy issues arrive," former national security adviser Zbigniew Brzezinski had said of the Democratic president during his final year in the White House.[24] In sum, the new Bush administration was continuing and accelerating a drift toward unilateralism in American foreign policy that was already under way well before it took office.

In Europe, on the final stop of his trip, Bush met for the first time with Russian President Vladimir Putin. It was after this session that Bush uttered his famously quick judgment of the Russian leader. He told reporters he had looked Putin in the eye and "found him to be very straightforward and trustworthy. . . . I was able to get a sense of his soul." Hearing those words, some scholars were reminded of Rice's past critique of the Democrats; she had argued that the Clinton administration overly personalized American policy toward Russia by relying too heavily on Clinton's ties to Boris Yeltsin. "Knowing Condi, I'm sure her stomach turned" when Bush spoke of his deep new bond with Putin, said Stanford University Russia specialist Michael McFaul.[25]

Rice insisted her earlier criticisms of Clinton's Russia policy had been misunderstood. "No one has ever said that it's not a good thing for the President of Russia and the President of the United States to have a good, warm relationship. . . . The issue was whether or not the United States started to equate reform with Boris Yeltsin," Rice explained to reporters. But by that same logic, the question for the future was whether Bush and Rice were starting to equate Russian foreign policy with Vladimir Putin (whom the president eventually began referring to as Pootie-Poot).[26]

In returning to the Pentagon after twenty-four years, Donald Rumsfeld seemed like a modern-day Rip Van Winkle. When President Ford first appointed him in 1975, he had been, at the age of forty-three, the youngest defense secretary in history. This time, at sixty-eight, he was the second oldest, ranking just behind George C. Marshall. When Rumsfeld first ran the Pentagon, he had been locked in bureaucratic combat with Henry Kissinger over détente and the nature of the Soviet threat. By the time he returned, the Soviet Union had already been dead for nine years. "We lived in a different world," Rumsfeld said at his confirmation hearing, reflecting upon the Defense Department he had left behind. During his first weeks back on the job Rumsfeld felt obliged to remind people that although he had been out of the public eye since the 1970s, he had kept up-to-date on foreign policy and defense issues. "Well, you know, I've not been living in a cellophane package these last twenty-five years," he bristled during one television interview, pointing to his work on the missile commission in the 1990s and his brief stint as Mideast peace coordinator in the 1980s.[27]

Rumsfeld's principal task in those early months was to try to bring radical change to the American armed forces and their weapons systems. During his presidential campaign Bush had vaguely pledged a "transformation" of the military, one that would bring it into line with the revolutionary improvements in military technology and the changing nature of the world. "Our military is still organized more for cold war threats than for the challenges of a new century," he had declared. American forces, Bush continued, needed to be "agile, lethal, readily deployable and require a minimum of logistical support."[28] In saying this, Bush was identifying himself with the cause of reform of the Pentagon, but in a safe way that avoided too many specifics.

Over the years the Vulcans had championed the cause of building up American military power. Yet the issue of defense transformation presented questions and trade-offs for which the Vulcans, for all their commitment to military might, had few ready answers. Just *how* should America build up military power? Should the United States spend its defense dollars on more of the existing tanks, planes and other hardware, or should it phase out these older systems and try to develop new generations of advanced weaponry? Would an administration's civilian leaders promote a stronger national defense by giving strong support to the generals and admirals or by challenging them and trying to shake things up?

Defense transformation hadn't been the top priority for the last few Republican administrations. Under Reagan, Defense Secretary Caspar Weinberger had concentrated on buying as many ships and planes as possible as quickly as possible, in order to build up America's arsenal against the Soviet Union. In the first Bush administration, amid the pressure for budget cutbacks that followed the end of the cold war, Cheney and Powell had been preoccupied with the need to preserve a base force, a minimum level of troop deployments that would enable the United States to maintain its position overseas.

In the early months of 2001 Bush and Cheney gave top priority not to defense but to the administration's $1.3 trillion tax cut. They repeatedly turned aside Rumsfeld's requests for additional money for the Pentagon. Within weeks after the inauguration the White House spurned an initial plea for additional funds for defense beyond what Clinton had requested for that fiscal year. A few months later the White House cut back by more than half Rumsfeld's request for budget increases in the following year. Consequently, if the Pentagon were going to spend more money for new generations of weaponry, it would have to find the money to do so by cutting back on some of the older systems still under development.

Tensions erupted between those Bush supporters who favored tax cuts and those who espoused an assertive foreign policy. Neoconservatives rushed to the support of Rumsfeld, Wolfowitz and the Pentagon; they excoriated Bush and Cheney for their supposed stinginess on defense. "So much for Vice President Cheney's campaign promise to the military: 'Help is on the way,'" wrote columnist Robert Kagan. ". . . After years of berating Clinton, Republicans are suddenly mute—what [defense] budget crisis?—while Rumsfeld and Wolfowitz are hung out to dry." The *Weekly Standard* suggested in an editorial that Rumsfeld and Wolfowitz should resign.[29]

Rumsfeld began to retreat from promises of reform. With a trace of bitterness he told one news conference, "The reality is that no one is going to be making any dramatic changes in anything, because that's just not how Washington works." He began to emphasize that defense transformation had originally been Bush's idea, not his: "We had a situation where you have a new president who asked the secretary of defense to undertake some studies with respect to some issues that he campaigned on and cares about and believes should be looked at. The new defense secretary is doing exactly that."[30]

Yet even while scaling back expectations, Rumsfeld pursued defense transformation in the confrontational style that had been the hallmark of his career inside and outside of government. Before long he had begun to alienate senior military leaders and members of Congress, and some of them began to air their grievances against Rumsfeld in the press.[31]

By the late summer of 2001 Rumsfeld was clearly in trouble. Critics claimed that he had been away from the Pentagon too long, that he was from a different era, that he was an outsider who no longer knew the players or understood the issues. There was speculation that he might be on the way out. "The sweepstakes have already begun on who might succeed Secretary of Defense Donald Rumsfeld if and when he steps down," reported the *Washington Post*'s Al Kamen in his "In the Loop" column. At a Pentagon briefing in early September a reporter trying to show sympathy for Rumsfeld asked him gently, "Do you feel a little beat up, kind of like a punching bag?"

Rumsfeld all but conceded he did. "The new group comes in, everyone's kind of nice for five minutes, and then they start throwing them in the barrel and beating them up a little bit. And life goes on, we'll all survive." That exchange took place at the Pentagon on September 6, 2001. No one had any idea what was about to hit.[32]

In early June, seven months after the Bush administration took office, Paul Wolfowitz delivered what was, in hindsight, a remarkable commencement address at West Point. He noted that 2001 would mark the sixtieth anniversary of the American disaster at Pearl Harbor. "Interestingly, that 'surprise attack' was preceded by an astonishing number of unheeded warnings and missed signals," Wolfowitz told the graduating cadets. He was reflecting the classic analysis of intelligence failure contained in the book *Pearl Harbor: Warning and Decision* by Roberta Wohlstetter, the wife of Wolfowitz's former dissertation adviser, Albert Wohlstetter.[33] ". . . Surprise happens so often that it's surprising that we're still surprised by it," Wolfowitz continued. He said America needed to overcome a sense of complacency and to "replace a poverty of expectations with an anticipation of the unfamiliar and the unlikely."[34]

He was more prescient than he could have imagined. America was about to be attacked. Once again the United States was unable to deal with the unfamiliar and the unlikely. Once again there were unheeded warnings and missed signals.

Soon after Wolfowitz's speech an FBI agent named Kenneth Williams in the Phoenix field office noticed that eight men of Middle Eastern descent, all under investigation for possible terrorist ties, were enrolled in pilot-training courses at the Embry-Riddle Aeronautical University in Prescott, Arizona. On July 10, 2001, this agent wrote FBI headquarters in Washington and the New York field office, suggesting that the FBI should talk to other civil aviation schools and alert the intelligence community. The FBI decided it didn't have enough manpower to pursue Williams's lead. No one informed the CIA or the National Security Council of what Williams had noticed.[35] On August 16 the FBI's field office in Minneapolis detained Zacarias Moussaoui, a French citizen of Moroccan descent who had gone to a flight school seeking lessons on a simulator, but only to learn how to steer planes, not to land them. FBI headquarters turned down a request for a warrant to examine his computer. No one at the FBI connected Moussaoui with the earlier Phoenix memo.

Throughout the spring and summer of 2001, meanwhile, the U.S. intelligence community was picking up signals that Osama bin Laden's Al Qaeda organization was planning a big new strike against the United States. Cofer Black, the head of the CIA's counterterrorism center, reported in May that a major attack was in the offing. Over the summer, by Director of Central Intelligence George Tenet's account, there were thirty-four communications intercepts by bin Laden adherents referring to "zero hour" or "something spectacular." But the CIA believed that bin Laden's organization would strike against Americans overseas, as it had in the earlier attacks on U.S. embassies in Africa and the USS *Cole* in Yemen.[36] On August 6 intelligence officials gave Rice and the president a written report on Al Qaeda's plans. The report discussed the possibility of airplane hijackings, but only in the context of similar events in the past; the suggestion was that terrorists might try to land a plane, take the passengers hostage and seek to trade them for something, such as a prisoner release.

During this same period the new administration's efforts to come up with broader policies for homeland security were moving at a leisurely pace. On May 8, 2001, Cheney had been appointed the head of a new Bush administration task force on domestic terrorism, aimed at examining the possibility of a terrorist attack upon the United States and how the U.S. government should respond. But by early September Cheney's task force had still not gotten off the ground.[37]

A separate interagency review of how to combat Al Qaeda was scheduled for early August, then postponed to the middle of the month, then finally held in early September, with top administration officials, including Rice, Powell and Wolfowitz, in attendance. The participants agreed to devote more money and effort to help the Northern Alliance and Uzbek opponents of the Taliban regime that was harboring bin Laden in Afghanistan. Most of the debate centered on the question of whether to use a new weapon, the armed, unmanned Predator drone, to attack Al Qaeda. The CIA didn't want responsibility for employing the armed Predator, and neither did the Joint Chiefs of Staff. The meeting ended without a decision.[38]

The Vulcans had prided themselves on their experience. In their earlier years in office they had helped America recover from Vietnam, presided over the Soviet collapse and won the Gulf War of 1991. They had returned to office under George W. Bush brimming with confidence. They were fully prepared to deal with security threats of the sorts they had confronted in the past—major powers, rogue states, dictators and land armies, all entities that operated inside fixed territories and identifiable borders—but they were not as ready to combat a stateless, amorphous terrorist organization like Al Qaeda.

As Wolfowitz made clear in his West Point speech, the Vulcans had been prepared to be surprised. Still, they were caught looking in the wrong direction. On Tuesday, September 11, 2001, as the three hijacked airplanes crashed into the World Trade Center and the Pentagon, the Vulcans were every bit as stunned as a previous generation of Americans had been on that sleepy Sunday sixty years earlier, when Japanese planes appeared over Honolulu.

CHAPTER NINETEEN

History Starts Today

In times of adversity many of the Vulcans instinctively sought inspiration from Winston Churchill. He was their patron saint. Churchill had combated tyranny; he had been willing to stand up against the prevailing mood; he had grasped that compromise and negotiation with a dictator were futile; he had led a nation through its darkest hour. The admiration for Churchill was based largely on his extraordinary personal qualities, factors that rose above partisan politics or petty domestic issues. But it also didn't hurt that Churchill had also been a Tory, a conservative. The American president who had worked hand in hand with Churchill during World War II (a man with not inconsiderable leadership ability, vision and eloquence of his own) had been a Democrat and a liberal; among the Vulcans he did not enjoy the same iconic status.

It was not surprising, then, that as Scooter Libby, the chief of staff to Vice President Dick Cheney, watched his boss inside the White House throughout the cataclysmic hours of September 11, 2001, some of Winston Churchill's words came to Libby's mind. In the final paragraph of *The Gathering Storm*, Churchill's memoir of the years leading up to the war, he had written about the moment when he finally became British prime minister: "I felt as if I were walking with destiny, and that all my past life had been but a preparation for this hour and for this trial." That sentence, Libby believed, could easily have applied to Cheney on September 11.[1]

The comparison was grandiose, particularly for someone like Cheney who shunned rhetorical flourishes as much as Churchill relished them.

Yet the underlying meaning made sense. If anyone in America had the government experience to respond to a terrorist attack upon Washington, it was Cheney. As President Ford's deputy chief of staff and then chief of staff, Cheney had mastered the inner workings of White House operations right down to the salt shakers and plumbing. In Congress he had worked on the House Intelligence Committee, learning how the CIA and America's several other intelligence agencies operate. As defense secretary he had been in charge of the U.S. armed forces. Above all, although almost nobody knew it, during the 1980s Cheney had been one of the leading participants in the highly classified planning to maintain continuity of government and set up a new presidential chain of command if America was under nuclear attack (see chapter nine).

On September 11 Cheney had just returned to the White House from a trip to Kentucky the previous day. He was in a morning meeting with his speechwriter when his secretary interrupted to say that a plane had struck the World Trade Center. Having turned on the television, the vice president watched the second plane hit the tower. He hurriedly convened a meeting in his West Wing office with Condoleezza Rice, Libby and other officials; they put in a call to Bush, who was traveling in Florida, to discuss what statement he might make. Suddenly Secret Service agents burst in shouting, "Sir, we have to leave immediately." They feared that American Airlines Flight 77, which had left Dulles Airport, might be headed for the White House. The agents lifted Cheney off his feet and moved him down flights of stairs into the Presidential Emergency Operations Center. That hardened underground shelter, called PEOC, had been set up during the cold war to enable White House leaders to survive a nuclear attack.[2]

The American Airlines plane slammed into the Pentagon. Inside the White House bunker the vice president picked up the phone, called Bush and told him to postpone his return to the nation's capital. Since Cheney was already in Washington, the president should remain outside so that both men could not be hit in the same attack, the vice president reasoned. Cheney was going through the drills he had learned concerning the continuity of government; he was playing defense, trying above all to prevent what the nuclear war experts had called decapitation—that is, the elimination of all of a country's top decision makers, leaving the nation leaderless and unable to respond. (Nineteen months later, when the Bush administration decided to go to war against Saddam Hussein's Iraq, decapitation of the enemy became a core element in the American offensive military strategy.)

Cheney was the dominant figure on September 11. It was he who urged the president to fly to Offutt Air Force Base in Nebraska, which had secure communications facilities. It was he who ordered that House Speaker Dennis Hastert and other congressional leaders be taken out of town to one of the Eisenhower-era bunkers built for use if America was under nuclear attack. In subsequent interviews explaining his actions on September 11, the vice president spoke blandly about the importance of ensuring presidential succession in a crisis. He never mentioned the clandestine exercises in which he and Donald Rumsfeld, accompanied by scores of civil servants, had occasionally sneaked out of Washington in the middle of the night to practice, for several days at a time, how to run America during a nuclear war.

Soon after Bush returned to Washington on the night of September 11, Cheney began spending time at Camp David, so that he was outside the capital while the president was at home. As the autumn progressed and as American forces went to war in Afghanistan, the vice president was often reported to be working in an "undisclosed location" out of Washington. Eventually, the "undisclosed location" turned into a national joke, a routine for the comedy shows. It became part of Cheney's identity. The blend of solemnity and mystery was fitting for a man who, throughout his career, had embodied the twin propositions that (a) running government was weighty, unglamorous business and that (b) he always had some secrets he could not discuss.

On September 11 there was one thing Cheney did not do: He did not address the nation. While running the Presidential Emergency Operations Center, he sent out no words of reassurance, delivered no "fight-them-on-the-beaches" oratory. That was the president's job, and for Cheney, the Silent Man, it was certainly just as well; if he was playing the role of Churchill, then it was Churchill without vocal cords. The president stumbled as he spoke to the country that night, but he recovered his public standing in a speech the following week.[3]

While Cheney was by nature uncommunicative, there were also political forces at work to keep him mute. Inside the White House, a number of powerful people—staff members like Karl Rove, Bush's political adviser, and Karen Hughes, the communications director—spent their days ensuring that the president got full public attention and credit for being in charge of the battle against terrorism. After Cheney appeared on television on the Sunday after September 11 and gave an extraordinarily detailed, coherent account both of the events of that day and of the administration's emerging response, the vice president virtually disappeared from the airwaves for months. There were delicate suggestions that in the early days of the crisis he might have overshadowed the president.[4]

Still, out of public view, Cheney was omnipresent, even when he was off in an undisclosed location and was participating in the administration's meetings only with his image and voice piped in on Secvid, the secure video teleconferencing system. It was Cheney's specter that hovered over the administration's policy deliberations, its internal wrangling, its decision making. Other administration officials could handle the TV interviews, the show business. But over virtually every foreign policy action the Bush administration took, whether on terrorism or Afghanistan, the Middle East or Iraq, there always loomed the ghost of this balding, white-haired, slightly pudgy, bespectacled man of deeply conservative views who took government seriously and worked as the consummate inside operator.

In the days immediately after September 11, the Vulcans were determined to do things differently from in the past. Now they were no longer willing to listen to old excuses, old rationalizations, old ways of thinking of the sort that they had had to tolerate when they had dealt with the world in previous administrations. This blend of resolve and righteous indignation cut across the Bush administration, from hawks to moderates and from central issues of terrorism to peripheral ones. Richard Armitage was a perfect example of the new mood.

That month a delegation of fourteen journalists from local Chinese television stations happened to be touring the United States as guests of the Institute of International Education. On September 11, the delegation was in Washington. Inside a meeting room, as a large-screen television set aired the pictures of the planes hitting the World Trade Center, American onlookers saw to their amazement that a few of the Chinese journalists were laughing or cheering.

The incident touched off a brief, intense debate inside the State Department. The department's East Asia bureau wanted to send the journalists home. But the separate State Department unit responsible for educational and cultural affairs resisted. Its officials argued that what looked like laughter might have been merely a sign of tension or embarrassment; perhaps the behavior was just a reflection of cultural differences between Americans and Chinese. Moreover, these doves argued, the journalists were potentially important people who could prove to be influential in China in the future. No matter, responded the hawks; the laughter was simply unacceptable behavior, and the delegation should be expelled. The American Embassy in Beijing began to weigh in on the side of the doves. The internal wrangling made its way up the State Department bureaucracy to Armitage, who was asked at a Saturday morning meeting to resolve the deadlock.

The deputy secretary was in no mood for a Solomonic splitting of differences or for cultural relativism. "Send them home," Armitage ordered. "Those people ought to be on the next plane out of here." Afterward the State Department covered up the reasons for its action. U.S. officials refused to acknowledge that the delegation had been expelled, explaining only that "the visit was curtailed" and implying that the U.S. government had been acting out of concern for the journalists' safety. But accounts of the dispute and of Armitage's handling of it made the rounds of the State Department. It was taken as a sign of a new era, one in which Americans would reject long-winded explanations of the inexplicable.[5]

Earlier that summer, Director of Central Intelligence George Tenet had made a secret trip to Pakistan to swap information about Osama bin Laden. When the World Trade Center was bombed, Pakistan's spymaster, General Mahmoud Ahmad, the head of Inter-Services Intelligence (ISI), happened to be in Washington on a return visit to the CIA. Armitage asked to see him.

As Ahmad sat in Armitage's office with Pakistani Ambassador Maleeha Lodhi at his side, the deputy secretary of state kept returning to a single theme. "Are you with us or against us?" he asked. Pakistan had been the prime supporter of the Taliban, the Afghan regime that had harbored and protected Osama bin Laden and his Al Qaeda supporters. Now, Armitage said, Pakistan faced a choice. Pakistan was either on America's side or not. You can report that back to General Pervez Musharraf, the Pakistani president, Armitage said. When Ahmad tried to explain the background to Pakistan's relationship with the Taliban, Armitage cut him short. "History starts today," he said.

At a second meeting the following day Armitage presented Ahmad with a list of seven specific demands. Above all, the Bush administration wanted the right to fly over Pakistani territory and to land on it for military and intelligence operations; the United States needed to be able to move its warplanes from aircraft carriers over and onto Pakistani territory in order to bomb Taliban forces in Afghanistan. The United States sought other help too, including logistical support for the American military and access to all available intelligence information about the Taliban and Al Qaeda.[6] There would be no bargaining over these demands, Armitage told the Pakistani intelligence chief. The United States didn't intend to play the game of entering the souk to start haggling over price. In Islamabad, Musharraf got the message; in Washington, Ahmad told Armitage that Pakistan would agree to all the American requests.[7]

Armitage's warning was one that the Vulcans and their president, George W. Bush, delivered again and again over the following years: "You're either with us or against us." To the Vulcans these words were meant to demonstrate that it was a new era and that America had changed after September 11. "History starts today." There would be no more long-winded explanations, no more shades of gray.

However, not all foreign officials took these words the way they were intended. Lodhi, the Pakistani ambassador, was an admirer of the new Bush administration. She told friends she liked the Bush people better than their predecessors; the Bush foreign policy team seemed to think in strategic terms and didn't seem so obsessed with issues such as human rights and nonproliferation as the Clinton crowd. Nevertheless, Lodhi confessed, when she heard that refrain, "You're with us or against us," she didn't think of the message as representative of a new era. On the contrary, Lodhi thought America was retreating to the modes of thought of the past. "You're with us or against us" was the message the Americans had delivered during the cold war when it told other governments they would have to choose between the United States and the Soviet Union. With such a message the United States was refusing to recognize the complexities of other countries.

Over the following months Musharraf gave considerable (though not unqualified) support to the Bush administration in its military campaign

against the Taliban. The following year the United States quietly acquiesced as Musharraf amended Pakistan's constitution in a way that extended his presidency for another five years and gave him the power to
dissolve Parliament. The Bush administration's admirable belief in the
importance of democracy did not seem to extend to Pakistan.

"I think everyone understands that we have, unfortunately, entered a new
era," Paul Wolfowitz told reporters inside the badly damaged Pentagon
two days after the terrorist attacks, picking up the same theme as Armitage.

On September 11 Rumsfeld, a key figure, along with Cheney, in the
clandestine continuity of government exercises of the 1980s, had ordered
Wolfowitz to get out of town to the safety of one of the old nuclear
bunkers, so that both the defense secretary and his deputy would not be
in the nation's capital at the same time. But Wolfowitz had stayed only
briefly and hurried back to Washington. Like Libby, he had taken to
quoting Churchill for solace and inspiration. "As Winston Churchill
commented on the day after Pearl Harbor, dictators underestimate America's strength," said Wolfowitz in an interview that week.[8]

But what, exactly, should America do? How should it answer the terrorist attacks? It was assumed from the start that there would be some
form of military retaliation. None of the Vulcans was unfamiliar with the
use of force; all had spent some of their formative years in the Pentagon.
Even the Clinton administration had come up with a limited military response (that is, cruise missiles) to bin Laden's 1998 attacks on the American embassies in Africa. That had proved ineffective, and now America
had been hit at home in a manner vastly more serious than in the past.
Against whom should America retaliate, though? Against bin Laden?
Against the Taliban regime that served as his protector and host in
Afghanistan? Would that stop terrorism by itself, or should the United
States go further?

In those early days Wolfowitz pushed for the broadest possible response.
"It's not going to stop if a few criminals are taken care of," he said. The
United States should mount a broad campaign to cut off all the terrorists'
support systems. In words that created a brief furor, Wolfowitz called for
a strategy of "ending states who sponsor terrorism." Although a day later
he corrected himself, asserting that he had meant "ending state support

for terrorism," the earlier version had already caught everyone's eye. Wolfowitz, it seemed, was proposing to move to overthrow some existing governments. And what regimes could Wolfowitz have in mind? Speculation turned immediately to Iraq and Saddam Hussein. Wolfowitz, who had been warning for more than two decades about the dangers of a powerful Iraq, did little to dispel that idea. "He [Hussein] is one of the most active supporters of state terrorism," he asserted during that first week.[9]

The previous February, just after taking office, the new administration had delivered to Iraq a brief warning of its willingness to resort to military power. While Bush was on a visit to Mexico, American and British forces carried out a wave of air strikes against Iraqi radar and air defense command centers, including targets near Baghdad, in response to Iraqi artillery and missile attacks on the allies' airplanes. However, that was only a temporary measure. During its early months the Bush administration focused its attention on other issues, such as China. Iraq policy was left primarily in the hands of Secretary of State Colin Powell. He proposed an initiative to make the economic sanctions against Iraq more effective by easing restrictions on trade in civilian goods and, at the same time, further tightening Iraq's ability to buy anything that could be used for military purposes. The hope was that by refining the sanctions, the Bush administration could begin to win back the support of allies and rebuild the international coalition that had fought the Gulf War of 1991.

Among hawks in the new administration Powell's policy (known as smart sanctions) was unpopular. Opponents feared that by allowing wider civilian trade, the policy could bolster the Iraqi regime. The policy wouldn't bring about the overthrow of Saddam Hussein, the goal that several Vulcans had publicly endorsed in the late 1990s. At his confirmation hearing to be deputy secretary of defense, Wolfowitz had pointedly asserted that sanctions could be only one component of an effective Iraq policy.[10]

Powell's effort soon bogged down at the United Nations. The French, Chinese and Russians all disliked the American proposal; they were hoping for a much broader easing of sanctions that would permit, for example, French investment in Iraq's oil industry. The Russians didn't like the tighter restrictions on military-related sales to Iraq. Over the summer the sanctions issue was shelved.

If history had really started on September 11, then no one would have contemplated military action against Iraq immediately afterward. The United States had plenty of other grounds for complaint against Saddam Hussein's regime: its threat to American geopolitical interests; its brutality toward the Iraqi people; its past history of trying to develop weapons of mass destruction. But there was no evidence Iraq was behind the terrorist attacks (and none would be found in the months afterward either).[11]

Nevertheless, as the administration weighed what to do in the week after September 11, Wolfowitz, joined by Cheney's chief of staff, Scooter Libby, laid out the case for military action against Iraq. The forces behind terrorism in the Middle East were all interconnected, they argued. Saddam Hussein was the most powerful opponent America faced. If the United States could defeat him, it would weaken terrorist groups throughout the Middle East. The issue was broader than merely Al Qaeda, they maintained. "What we were really arguing about was, do you keep [America's response] to one particular, obnoxious terrorist network, or did September 11 mean your whole attitude towards terrorism has to change?" asserted Wolfowitz in a later interview.[12] He urged that the administration should not limit its military response to Afghanistan.

Powell countered that the United States would not be able to obtain the support of other governments for military action against Iraq. Let's stick to Afghanistan for now, he urged. In public, the secretary of state delivered a blunt rebuke to Wolfowitz's call for action against other states. "We're after ending terrorism," Powell said. "And if there are states and regimes, nations, that support terrorism, we hope to persuade them that it is in their interest to stop doing that. But I think 'ending terrorism' is where I would leave it and let Mr. Wolfowitz speak for himself."[13]

Thus the old tensions between Powell and Wolfowitz, which had first emerged inside the Pentagon in the first Bush administration, surfaced once again, exacerbated by the larger institutional frictions between the State Department and the Pentagon. In the following weeks there were occasional attempts to smooth things over. At one point Armitage, who had worked closely with Wolfowitz throughout the 1980s, invited him to lunch at the State Department. He reminded Wolfowitz of his own intense loyalty to Powell and said he took the Pentagon's sniping at Powell as a personal affront. The tensions eased, but only temporarily.

On Iraq, Bush seemed at first to side with Powell. He chose to focus on Afghanistan as the place where America would first take military action in response to the terrorism of September 11. At the time this was taken as a defeat for Wolfowitz, the strongest proponent of action against Iraq. Powell had "won the argument," newspapers reported.[14] But that was a misinterpretation. The administration hadn't decided *against* going to war in Iraq; it had decided merely to postpone any decision about Iraq while concentrating first on Afghanistan. More generally, the administration hadn't limited the war on terrorism to Al Qaeda but had left open the possibility of a wider campaign.

As was often the case, it was Cheney who pointed the way to the Vulcans' actual policy. The administration had concluded, he said, that it would bring down "the full wrath of the United States" upon nations that provide sanctuary or support for terrorists. Those words were not too different from Wolfowitz's formulation of ending state support for terrorism. Asked about action against Iraq, the vice president said that Osama bin Laden was the American target "at the moment . . . at this stage."[15] Iraq's time would come.

In the weeks immediately after September 11, a new myth took hold about the Bush administration. The conventional wisdom, passed around in newspaper stories and television talk shows, held that Bush and his team had decided to forsake the unilateralism of their first nine months.

"The world changed at 9 a.m. Tuesday," wrote one of the many proponents of this theory. "Out went the old Bush, the unilateralist. In came the new Bush, a multilateralist. . . . Until now, Bush had given allies the impression that he needed them less than they needed him. But now, he's dialing 911 around the world." The Bush administration "will have to temper its unilateral instincts on many issues," asserted C. Fred Bergsten of the Institute for International Economics.[16]

This misconception that the administration had suddenly discovered the need for its allies took hold during a period when the president was seeking to win as much international approval as possible for American action against terrorism. In Europe there had been an outpouring of support for the United States. In France, *Le Monde* had published what became a famous editorial of support. "We are all Americans," wrote editor Jean-Marie Colombani. "We are all New Yorkers, as surely as John F. Kennedy, in 1963 in Berlin, was a Berliner." In Brussels, after Powell had requested a demonstration of support, NATO's nineteen governments for the first time in history invoked Article 5 of the treaty, the collective defense provision that obliges all members to respond with armed force if necessary to protect the territory of any member of the alliance.[17]

Nevertheless, these portrayals of a chastened administration's discovering that it could no longer go it alone in the world were inaccurate, much as the early caricatures of the Bush team had been. Before September 11 the administration's tendencies toward unilateralism had not been so new or unique as critics had claimed; after September 11 these same unilateral tendencies were never abandoned.

During the 1990s European and American leaders had developed widely disparate points of view about international affairs and about military power. Europeans increasingly tended to rely upon negotiations, diplomacy and international law in resolving disputes; by contrast, Americans tended to emphasize the continuing importance and necessity of a strong military.[18] These differences in outlook were not altered by the terrorist attacks. Despite their proclamations of support after September 11, European leaders soon made plain that their backing for American foreign policy was not unqualified. "I stress, we are prepared for risks and also military risks, but not for any adventures," Chancellor Gerhard Schroeder told the German Parliament. French President Jacques Chirac rushed to become the first foreign leader to visit the White House after September 11, just as he had been the first to meet with Bush after the end of the 2000 election. But when the two presidents appeared together at a joint press conference, Bush repeatedly spoke of the new campaign against terrorism as a "war," while Chirac said he was reluctant to call it a war.[19] These two European leaders were clearly reluctant to endorse any American military campaign against Iraq. They feared the United States might do something that would destabilize the existing order in the Middle East, which their countries had strong interests in preserving.

The Americans too balked at transatlantic cooperation, but in a different way. That fall, when French officials went to the U.S. Central Command in Tampa, Florida, volunteering to provide French forces for the American-led military campaign in Afghanistan, they found to their dismay that U.S. military commanders weren't interested in their help. Thanks for the offer, the French were told, but we don't want to wage war by committee.[20]

French Ambassador to Washington François Bujon de L'Estang called this the Kosovo syndrome. During the 1990s American military leaders had been exasperated by the process of seeking consensus within NATO for military action in the Balkans. Now, faced with the arduous task of hurriedly mounting a military campaign in a remote part of the world, American military leaders viewed the prospect of working with European forces not as a help but as a nuisance.

It is worth underscoring here that the driving force in spurning these European offers was the uniformed military, not the Bush White House or Rumsfeld's civilian leadership in the Pentagon. French officials discovered that at the top levels the Bush administration seemed willing and indeed eager to have an international coalition carry out the campaign in Afghanistan. Yet in Tampa U.S. military officials were slow to respond to their offers or to define what they needed.[21] This particular strand of American unilateralism, then, did not originate with the Bush administration. It grew directly out of the military realities of the 1990s: the operational difficulties between U.S. and allied forces in the Balkans and the overall disparity in military power between America and Europe.

Still, even at the peak of apparent transatlantic harmony in the weeks after September 11, the Europeans were rarely accorded the deference by the Bush White House to which they had become accustomed in earlier administrations. French officials found it hard to obtain appointments or sufficient time with Rice or Cheney or Rumsfeld. When Chirac visited Washington, he of course got top-level meetings, but he told aides afterward he was unsure whether anyone was paying much attention to what he said. The French began grasping at slender hopes. A conservative member of the French National Assembly, Pierre Lellouche, had been a long-standing friend of Wolfowitz's. Perhaps that connection would help, one French official mused. But it proved of little consequence; the gulf between America and France was broader than any personal relationships could overcome.

Bujon finally concluded that the Bush administration was the first in modern American history that did not place Europe at the center of its strategic thinking. For the new administration Europe simply wasn't as great a problem as it had been throughout the cold war and during the wars in the Balkans. The concerns and the strategic thinking of the new Bush team were now focused on an area that started with the Middle East and stretched east across to northeastern Asia.

The Bush administration's views of the relative importance of various countries inside Europe also seemed to be different from those of its predecessors. France and Germany no longer enjoyed center stage. On Bush's

initial visit to Europe in the spring of 2001 he made the obligatory appearances at NATO and European Union meetings and then visited three
countries: Spain, Poland and Slovenia. He did not stop in Paris or Berlin.
"The subtle reminder has been delivered to the French and the Germans
that American diplomacy in Europe has other options," one commenta-
tor, Martin Walker, wrote at the time.[22] Bush's itinerary on that initial
foray offered an important clue to what was to come: Two years later,
when the Bush administration waged war against Iraq, its European supporters included Spain and Poland, not France and Germany.

On the morning of September 11, over breakfast in a private dining room
at the Pentagon, Rumsfeld was discussing with a group of Republican
representatives how to win greater Capitol Hill support for his programs,
particularly ballistic missile defense. As usual, the defense secretary
warned about the threats to the United States posed by terrorist groups
and rogue states. America should be prepared for surprises, he said. Just
before the breakfast ended, the first hijacked airplane crashed into the
World Trade Center. Within an hour another slammed into the Pentagon
itself. The entire building shook. Rumsfeld dashed outside to lead rescue
efforts amid the rubble for fifteen minutes, then went back inside the
smoky Pentagon to the National Military Command Center, where he
remained throughout the day.[23]
    The terrorist attacks and their aftermath proved to be decisive events
for Rumsfeld's fortunes in the Bush administration and indeed for his entire career. He had served as secretary of defense before, but not at the
time of military action. His battles in the past had been over abstract issues of policy, intelligence and budgets; his adversaries had been rival
American officials, such as Henry Kissinger. Now the exigencies of fighting a genuine war made Rumsfeld and his Pentagon the leading agency in
the internal deliberations inside the U.S. government. Even more important, Rumsfeld took on a new role with the public too. Over the following months, as the Pentagon carried out military action against Al Qaeda
and Taliban forces in Afghanistan, Rumsfeld began to conduct televised
press briefings several times a week, sometimes even daily. In the process,
he became a media star.
    Suddenly the American public was able to see in Rumsfeld what
Richard Nixon had detected more than three decades earlier: his talent and

quickness on his feet; his nimbleness in answering or evading questions; his overflowing self-confidence; his knack for cutting through jargon; his relentless counterattacks on those who challenged him. "He's young, he's thirty-nine years old, he's a hell of a spokesman," Nixon had said of the White House operative with seemingly limitless potential, ego and ambitions. By 2001 the youth had gone and the presidential ambitions seemingly subsided, but Rumsfeld's skill as a spokesman was as sharp as ever.

The media coverage of Rumsfeld focused largely on his style, personality and mastery of the news media. Articles chronicled his speech patterns, the old-fashioned expressions like "golly" and "you bet" with which he had punctuated his thoughts throughout his career. *People* magazine decided to put him on a list of the world's sexiest men; the president gave him the nickname Rumstud.[24] A famous *Saturday Night Live* skit showed Rumsfeld intimidating reporters to the point where they were scared to ask further questions.

These lionizing portraits often overlooked the larger context of Rumsfeld's performances. The defense secretary was asserting his dominance not merely over the press corps (a relatively easy target) but, far more important, over American military leaders. As Rumsfeld stood at the Pentagon podium day after day, Air Force General Richard Myers usually stood behind him, saying little, looking on as though he had been reduced to serving as a minor spear-carrier. It was a startling reversal of the roles that Cheney and Colin Powell had played at press conferences at the time of the Panama invasion and the Gulf War. Back then Powell, the chairman of the Joint Chiefs of Staff, had done most of the talking and dominated the podium, while Cheney, the defense secretary, stood mute in the background. A decade later Rumsfeld was taking care to ensure that no uniformed military leader would attract as much power, attention or independent authority as Powell had once commanded.

Rumsfeld made clear in other ways too that he was in charge of the military—not just in a broad supervisory role but with respect to the everyday details. During the war in Afghanistan he talked daily with General Tommy Franks, the CENTCOM commander in charge of the campaign. That too was a change in role for a defense secretary. (By contrast, throughout the war in Kosovo the American military commander, General Wesley Clark, had no direct contact with William Cohen, Rumsfeld's predecessor.[25])

The American and British forces began carrying out air strikes against the Taliban forces in Afghanistan on October 7, 2001. For three weeks there appeared to be little progress in what was called Operation Enduring Freedom. By the end of October commentators were warning that the military campaign was turning into a quagmire. Reporters and columnists began rehashing anecdotes and quotes from the 1980s, when Soviet forces, despite their vastly superior power, had bogged down in a war in Afghanistan. The more ambitious among them reread Rudyard Kipling and dredged up stories of the British frustrations in Afghanistan during the nineteenth century. In order to have any chance of winning the war, it was said, the U.S. forces would have to endure a long, punishing winter. In his public appearances Rumsfeld began trying to plead for patience. "We said it would be long, we said it would be difficult," he asserted in one Sunday talk show.[26]

In fact, military successes were not far off. On November 9, under intense bombardment from American warplanes, Taliban forces abandoned the city of Mazar-e-Sharif and quickly lost control of virtually all of northern Afghanistan. Four days later the Northern Alliance, the anti-Taliban forces backed by the United States, marched into Kabul, the Afghan capital. The Taliban retreated to the southern city of Kandahar, the home base of their movement. On December 7, under heavy air attacks, they were forced to pull out of that city too. With that defeat, the Taliban rule in Afghanistan came to an end.

Yet the Americans and their allies failed to accomplish the goal Bush had originally envisioned: to capture Osama bin Laden "dead or alive." In late November and early December as many as fifteen hundred Arab and Chechen fighters from the Al Qaeda network took shelter in cave complexes at Tora Bora, high in the mountains of eastern Afghanistan, not far from the border with Pakistan. American warplanes pounded the facility from the air, Afghan units attacked on the ground, and on December 16, the Al Qaeda holdouts abandoned Tora Bora. But by then bin Laden had already slipped away into the nearby mountains.[27]

On that day Rumsfeld happened to be inside Afghanistan, making a triumphal visit to American forces at Bagram Airfield outside Kabul. He made clear that the war would not come to an end with the close of the Afghan campaign. "Your job is certainly not over," he told the troops.

"There are a number of countries that are known as being on the terrorist list."[28]

What came next? The Bush team had determined at the outset that Afghanistan represented the initial focus of a global campaign. "Our war on terrorism begins with Al Qaeda, but it does not end there," the president had told the nation. Powell had regularly employed the formula that Afghanistan represented "phase one" of a larger war.[29] In the late fall, with Al Qaeda fleeing from Afghanistan, the administration entered a weeks-long period of uncertainty over its next goals and targets.

It appeared at first that the administration would seek to follow up Operation Enduring Freedom with a similar military campaign against one or more countries that, like Afghanistan, had served as home bases for Al Qaeda forces. For a time in November U.S. defense and intelligence officials had Somalia under intense surveillance in what was seen as a prelude to a military strike. There was talk of American forces going into the Sudan, Yemen, the Philippines.[30]

From overseas American military commanders sent home long, detailed proposals for military action in these and other countries. Inside the Washington bureaucracies, defense and intelligence officials were set to work drawing up targeting packages and contingency plans for virtually every country in which Al Qaeda leaders had ever been based.[31]

Yet in the end none of these proposed new ventures seemed important enough to merit designation as the prime target for "phase two" of the war on terrorism. None of them had a regime as recognizably malevolent as the Taliban; Somalia had virtually no government at all, and the leaders of Yemen and the Philippines were in different ways friendly to the United States. None of the regimes had the same close ties with Al Qaeda as the Taliban either. Osama bin Laden hadn't lived in the Sudan since 1996, when he was expelled from the country.

There were other problems too. It would be hard for the administration to sustain public attention and support for "phase two" of the war on terrorism if it were waged against some other marginal country. After the Afghan campaign an American military strike in Somalia or the Sudan would seem at best duplicative and at worst anticlimactic. It might be different if American forces could capture Osama bin Laden, but he had just slipped away once, and there was no sign he had taken refuge in any of these other countries. "Finding handfuls of people is indeed like finding needles in a haystack," Rumsfeld had warned.[32] Once Operation Enduring Freedom was over, the American effort against Al Qaeda seemed to be best suited for a quiet, covert intelligence war, not a new public or military campaign.

Still hanging was of course the question of Iraq. Wolfowitz and others in the administration were still pushing for a change in regime there. Yet Wolfowitz himself was talking during this period about making countries like Somalia the next targets for the antiterrorist campaign.[33] At this stage, in late 2001 and January 2002, participants on both sides of the continuing Iraq debate were preoccupied with the question of whether Saddam Hussein's regime could be linked to Al Qaeda. Hawks kept searching for possible connections that would justify making Iraq a target of the war on terrorism, but the evidence couldn't be found. "A lot of folks out of the administration have spent a lot of time and energy trying to tie Iraq and Al Qaeda together, but thus far it hasn't been able to be done," said Armitage in late November. "My view is, we've got enough problems with Iraq with its weapons of mass destruction. They've got to pay a price for that, but that'll be at our time and our pace."[34]

America's campaign against terrorism seemed to be stalled after Afghanistan, awaiting new direction. The administration was searching for some conceptual breakthrough, a broader statement of vision, goals and ambitions. These were soon forthcoming. The Vulcans were in the process of redefining America's entire strategy and approach for dealing with the world.

CHAPTER TWENTY

A New Strategy

DURING THE EARLY STAGES of the war on terrorism the Vulcans had concentrated primarily on the specific tasks they had set out for themselves: defeating the Taliban and ousting Al Qaeda from Afghanistan. By early 2002, after roughly one year in office, they were ready to move on to something larger—not merely another country or another terrorist group but a whole new way of thinking about America's relations with the world. They were preparing to wage a new campaign in the realm of ideas. "Phase two," it turned out, would be conducted not with troops and warplanes but through speeches and strategy papers. Although the Vulcans had for decades operated within the framework of the ideas developed during the cold war, by 2002, more than a decade after the collapse of the Soviet Union, many of them seemed to be eager to cut loose from these intellectual moorings.

The underlying ethos of the cold war had been a sense of caution and limits. There were some things the United States had been unwilling to do because of the risks of a full-scale war with the Soviet Union (or, for a time, China). President Truman had fought a limited war in Korea, firing General Douglas MacArthur after he sought to carry the war onto Chinese soil. The Eisenhower administration had held back from supporting freedom fighters in Hungary; the Kennedy, Johnson and Nixon administrations had waged another limited war in Vietnam. The principal strategies of the cold war had been essentially defensive in nature: containment and deterrence.

After the fall of the Berlin Wall it had taken some time for the United States to absorb the implications of the change. In 1991 President George

H. W. Bush had vaguely spoken of a new world order, an idea that rested on the unprecedented, temporary cooperation between America and the Soviet Union against Iraq. Yet there had been little time to rethink the underlying principles governing American foreign policy; the members of the first Bush administration had been obliged to spend most of their time simply coping with the massive changes around the world, including the Soviet collapse and the reunification of Germany. The first signs of a new intellectual framework had emerged from the Pentagon in 1992, when Paul Wolfowitz and his aides had sketched out their vision for a world in which America was the world's only superpower. These novel ideas, however, were never officially embraced because they were too controversial to win approval at the White House and because in any event, the Bush administration was forced to leave office less than a year later.

Over the following decade the United States had continued to augment its military power to the point where by 2002 it had surpassed not merely that of any other country, but that of any imaginable combination of nations. At the same time, the nature of potential threats to American security was also changing. The dangers seemed to arise not from a rival power like Nazi Germany or the Soviet Union but from what was called asymmetric warfare. A "rogue" nation or a terrorist group could not defeat the U.S. Army on the battlefield, but it might launch missiles or crash airplanes in ways that could kill thousands of Americans.

In the 1970s and 1980s many of the Vulcans had proposed a greater American effort to confront the Soviet Union. Rumsfeld had challenged détente. Dick Cheney had led the way in accepting the "Morality in Foreign Policy" plank at the 1976 Republican National Convention. Wolfowitz had questioned Kissinger's belief in realpolitik, his preoccupation with balance of power diplomacy. Armitage had helped implement the Reagan doctrine, the efforts to challenge the Soviet Union in the third world. At the time, however, none of these men had questioned the underlying doctrine of containment that lay at the heart of American strategy. All had accepted the cold war framework and the limits it imposed.

But by early 2002 the Vulcans were in a hurry for new ideas. After the shock of September 11 their inclination was to reach for broad, enduring changes in the underlying principles guiding American foreign policy. They were convinced America had entered a new era and needed new concepts to guide it. While Winston Churchill provided inspiration for the

Vulcans in the midst of the September 11 crisis, in its aftermath they began turning to other historical models: to Harry Truman, George Kennan and Dean Acheson, the group of men who had crafted a new foreign policy and a new set of ideas to help America cope with the Soviet Union after World War II.

The Vulcans' eagerness to jettison the past did not begin with the terrorist attacks of September 11. In one policy area, at least, the Bush administration had come into office with the specific intent of burying the legacy of the cold war. In its determination to push forward with missile defense, the new administration regularly and explicitly questioned the underlying assumptions that had governed national security for decades.

Touring Europe in the first months after he took office, Wolfowitz repeatedly argued that the Anti-Ballistic Missile Treaty negotiated by the Nixon administration no longer made sense. "The world of 2001 is fundamentally different from that of 1972," he said. America faced new challenges from the proliferation of missiles and weapons of mass destruction. In Berlin, Wolfowitz questioned why twelve years after the Berlin Wall came down, "we are still in some ways . . . wedded to old Cold War notions of deterrence." From the White House, Condoleezza Rice poked a bit of self-mocking fun at the old cold war mind-set. "For much of my career, I was a Soviet specialist. . . . I was one of the High Priestesses of Arms Control—a true believer."[1]

Then September 11 greatly accelerated the administration's willingness to rethink cold war ideas about national security. Far from forcing the administration to revert to the time-honored multilateral approaches of the past, as many analysts predicted immediately afterward, the attacks instead created a new climate in which the administration was prepared to reconsider the fundamental tenets that had guided American security since World War II.

A half year after September 11 a veteran intelligence official said he thought the operating style of the George W. Bush administration was different from its predecessors. The foreign policy team, he said, seemed to have a sense of impatience that was unlike anything he had observed in either the first Bush administration or the Reagan administration. "I'm surprised every day, because I've been schooled for thirty years that things go back to normal within six weeks or two months or so after a crisis. But these people aren't changing. There's a clear commitment on their part to make a difference. They refuse to go back to business-as-usual."[2]

In December 2001 the administration took its first big step toward abandoning the rules and restrictions of the cold war when President Bush announced that the United States would withdraw from the ABM Treaty. That agreement, he said, "was written in a different era, for a different enemy."

The abandonment of the ABM Treaty represented the culmination of efforts that had begun in the Reagan administration and picked up momentum in the late 1990s. Rumsfeld had played a central role. He had not only headed the formal commission that warned in 1998 of missile attacks on American soil but had also been in charge of the more secretive campaign group that had planned for missile defense while Bush was running for president.

Powell had supported missile defense since the days when he served as Reagan's national security adviser. In 2001, however, he had sought to work out a compromise with Moscow that would enable the United States to move ahead on missile defense without withdrawing from the ABM Treaty. In the end the secretary of state's attempts to preserve the treaty fell through. Bush and Rice sided with Rumsfeld, opting for a complete break with the past.[3]

There were soon signs that the drive for missile defense, while extraordinarily important on its own, represented only one facet of a broader change in strategy. In early 2002 the Pentagon delivered to Congress a classified document called the Nuclear Posture Review. In it, the administration proposed the development of new, smaller nuclear weapons that could be used not just against the major nuclear powers, Russia and China, but also against Iraq, North Korea, Iran, Syria and Libya. The Clinton administration had laid the groundwork to some extent. It had drawn up a presidential directive that included some contingency plans for targeting "rogue nations" with nuclear weapons.[4] The Bush team made this policy explicit. The thrust of the new Bush strategy was to shift the underlying purpose of America's nuclear weapons away from the notions of defense and deterrence and toward the goal of war fighting. Bunkerbusting nuclear weapons, the report envisaged, could be employed against enemy supplies of chemical or biological weapons. America's nuclear weapons might also conceivably be used in response to "an Iraqi attack on Israel or its neighbors, or a North Korean attack on the South, or a military confrontation over the status of Taiwan," the document said. Washington was no longer worrying about all-out nuclear exchanges with Moscow that could lead to Armageddon. It was, instead, thinking about the role that America's nuclear weapons might play in future conflicts in the third world.[5]

"The terrorists who struck us on Sept. 11 were clearly not deterred from doing so by the massive U.S. nuclear arsenal," explained Rumsfeld in a speech in January 2002. Deterrence, the central element of American military strategy for decades, was a concept coming into disfavor. Increasingly the Vulcans were gravitating toward strategies that focused on offensive military action. "Defending against terrorism and other emerging 21st Century threats requires that we take the war to the enemy," said Rumsfeld. "The best and in some cases the only defense is a good offense."[6]

The central figure in these larger conceptual changes was Condoleezza Rice. Bush's national security adviser was outweighed in the administration's inner circles by the older, more experienced figures of Cheney, Powell and Rumsfeld. Yet she was of critical importance in several ways. Of all the top-level officials, she was by far the closest to Bush. When the Defense and State departments were divided, or when Rumsfeld and Cheney advised one course of action and Powell a different one, it was Rice who helped the president reach a decision. She operated at the interface between the president and his political advisers, on the one hand, and his foreign policy team, on the other.

Of all the Vulcans, it was Rice who best personified the profound intellectual shift from the first Bush administration to the second one. Rice had not merely been a "high priestess of arms control." She had risen to prominence as the heir to the foreign policy traditions of Henry Kissinger and Brent Scowcroft. At Stanford and during the first Bush administration she had been an avowed proponent of the doctrine of realism, the belief in a tough-minded foreign policy based on national interests and balance of power diplomacy. During the 2000 presidential campaign and during Bush's initial months in office, Rice appeared to be advocating an updated, modified version of those same realist traditions. American foreign policy, she argued, should focus on the biggest, most powerful countries, particularly China and Russia, and should avoid becoming bogged down in nation-building enterprises. America should not use its military as "the world's 911," she wrote. ". . . This overly broad definition of America's national interest is bound to backfire as others arrogate the same authority to themselves."[7]

Still, Rice had taken care to avoid alienating the conservatives, who bitterly opposed Kissinger-style realism. Like George W. Bush himself, Rice sought to avoid being swept up in the factional disputes among Republicans that had badly damaged Bush's father and, long before him, Gerald Ford. She made sure that the younger Bush, during his presidential campaign, called for "realism in the service of ideals," a slogan that sought to straddle the old Republican divide.[8]

In mid-2001, not long after the editors of the *Weekly Standard* had excoriated the new president for his handling of the spy plane dispute with China, Rice quietly reached out to the neoconservative movement that the magazine represented. Come by my office some time, she told William Kristol, the neoconservative leader; let's talk, instead of merely reading each other's quotes in the newspapers. When Kristol went into the White House for a chat, Rice told him that during a visit to Poland she had been personally moved by the importance and power of democracy there. She had become, she suggested to Kristol, a bit less of a believer in realpolitik.[9]

It was Rice, more than anyone else, who viewed the mission of the Vulcans after September 11 as a historic one comparable to that of the post–World War II generation. America was not merely combating terrorism but constructing a whole new order. "The international system has been in flux since the collapse of Soviet power," she told one audience. "Now, it is possible—indeed probable—that that transition is coming to an end. . . . This is, then, a period akin to 1945 to 1947, when American leadership expanded the number of free and democratic states—Japan and Germany among the great powers—to create a new balance of power that favored freedom."[10]

When Richard Haass, a senior Powell aide and the director of policy planning at the State Department, drafted for the administration an overview of America's national security strategy, Rice ordered that the document be completely rewritten. She thought the Bush administration needed something bolder, something that would represent a more dramatic break with the ideas of the past. Rice turned the writing over to her old colleague, University of Virginia Professor Philip Zelikow, who had worked alongside Rice in the first Bush administration and had been her coauthor for a book about the unification of Germany.[11]

In November 2001, during the last stages of the war in Afghanistan, there was a curious, subtle shift in the public rhetoric of the Bush administration. Top officials increasingly emphasized the danger that Al Qaeda might obtain weapons of mass destruction. Rumsfeld said in one television interview that it was "reasonable to assume" Osama bin Laden had some access to chemical and biological weapons. Speaking to the UN General Assembly, Bush warned that terrorists were "searching for weapons of mass destruction, the tools to turn their hatred into holocaust."[12]

On the surface the administration was offering merely one more rationale for the war on terrorism—and seemingly an unnecessary one. Al Qaeda had just killed three thousand Americans with its attacks on the World Trade Center and Pentagon. What more justification was needed? In fact, although this was little recognized at the time, the administration's new stress on weapons of mass destruction was the earliest sign of a far broader campaign, one that would dominate the Bush administration's policy long after Afghanistan, Operation Enduring Freedom and even Al Qaeda were out of the headlines.

At the time the government of Pakistan had just arrested three scientists working on the country's nuclear weapons program for questioning about their visits to Afghanistan and their ties to the Taliban.[13] Inside the United States, five people had died and more than twenty others were infected when letters containing anthrax spores were put into the mail. In the end neither of these incidents was tied to Al Qaeda. But the terrorist attacks had prompted the administration to examine the "what if" scenarios: What if on September 11 the terrorists had used a nuclear weapon, or a chemical or biological one? What if, instead of three thousand deaths, there had been three hundred thousand?

Initially the focus was on the terrorists who might obtain weapons of mass destruction. But of course the weapons had to be obtained somewhere. Before long the administration began to switch its attention to the potential suppliers.

On January 29, 2002, Bush took the next, momentous step in the redirection of the war on terrorism. In his State of the Union address he surprised the nation and the world by proclaiming that the administration was seeking to combat an "axis of evil," a group of nations that were seeking to develop weapons of mass destruction and could potentially provide these weapons to terrorists. He specifically named North Korea, Iran and Iraq as members of the "axis."

Thus over a period of less than five months the administration had progressively shifted the focus of the war on terrorism from (a) retaliating against the perpetrators of the September 11 attacks to (b) stopping terrorists from acquiring weapons of mass destruction to (c) preventing states from supplying terrorists with these weapons. Indeed, there were suggestions in Bush's speech that a link between the states and terrorism wasn't absolutely necessary; what mattered above all were (d) the axis-of-evil states and their weapons programs. "By seeking weapons of mass destruction, these regimes pose a grave and growing danger," the president said.[14]

David Frum, then one of Bush's speechwriters, later claimed that the original aim of the axis-of-evil speech was specifically to target Iraq. Mark Gerson, Bush's chief speechwriter, had asked Frum first to find a justification for war against Iraq, he wrote; later Iran was added, and finally North Korea as a seemingly casual afterthought.[15] Frum's perspective reflected both his experience as a speechwriter and also the thinking of neoconservatives within the administration, who were eager for a regime change in Iraq.[16]

Yet Frum was not himself part of the Vulcans' foreign policy deliberations, and his analysis overlooked the other, broader dimensions of the axis-of-evil speech. Iraq, Iran and North Korea weren't joined together entirely randomly or just for Bush's State of the Union. Rumsfeld's 1998 commission on missile threats had cited precisely these three countries as ones of special worry. The Clinton administration too had singled out Iraq, Iran and North Korea[17]—not as "evil" or an "axis" but as the three nations that had rapidly advancing nuclear and missile programs in seeming violation of the nuclear nonproliferation treaty and that were also considered hostile to American interests.[18]

Thus, for the Bush administration, the axis-of-evil speech served several purposes. It underscored the Vulcans' mounting concern about terrorist groups' acquiring nuclear, chemical or biological weapons. It enabled the Bush White House to shift attention away from the murky, often frustrating task of catching terrorists with no fixed address (where was

Osama bin Laden?) to the more familiar ground of dealing with conventional states, such as Iraq, North Korea and Iran. It linked up the new war on terrorism, which had been in need of new direction after Afghanistan, to long-standing U.S. policies aimed at stopping the spread of weapons of mass destruction.

Finally, for those within the Bush administration, such as Wolfowitz, who had argued long before September 11 for the overthrow of Saddam Hussein, Bush's axis-of-evil speech also provided a new, broader conceptual framework within which to pursue the goal of regime change in Iraq. Yet in this respect the axis-of-evil speech had profound implications for the eventual campaign against Iraq. Over the next fourteen months, as the Bush administration moved toward military action against Iraq, officials repeatedly emphasized the theme that Saddam Hussein was developing weapons of mass destruction; this, more than the Iraqi leader's brutality or danger to the region, became the primary justification for war. In the months after the war ended, Iraq's weapons of mass destruction could not be found, and the administration faced a torrent of questions about its previous claims.

The State of the Union address set the Bush administration on a new course. Hunting terrorists was deemphasized, at least in public; instead, stopping rogue states from developing weapons of mass destruction became the administration's top priority. Bush's speech led to abrupt changes in American foreign policy. The State Department's intermittent attempts at diplomacy with North Korea and with Iran were temporarily frozen. The American people were unlikely to support any broad accommodation with regimes branded as evil, and conversely, North Korean and Iranian leaders labeled as evil were less likely to negotiate with the United States. Thus the Vulcans were once again reverting to the approach they had taken when they opposed détente in the 1970s and when they labeled the Soviet Union an evil empire in the early 1980s: Avoid compromise or accommodation with morally objectionable regimes, and rely instead on American military power.

After Bush's State of the Union, a myth developed that the phrase *axis of evil* represented only empty rhetoric or the last-minute wording of the speechwriters. "Some senior State Department officials, for example, didn't find out that Mr. Bush would refer to the three nations as an 'axis of evil' until the rest of America did," reported the *New York Times*.[19]

That may indeed have been true of some State Department officials, yet in fact, Powell and Armitage, the two top State Department officials, had carefully reviewed and signed off on Bush's speech, including the *axis-of-evil* phraseology. "It [the speech] was cleared completely here," acknowledged Armitage in an interview later that year. "The secretary [Powell] and I had read it time and again, had made a lot of changes to it. It didn't go through the whole bureaucracy, but it went through us, in several iterations. Never did we look at [changing the phrase] 'axis of evil.' That just didn't strike us as out of the ordinary." Powell and Armitage had heard comparable words before; both were serving in government when Ronald Reagan branded the Soviet Union "the evil empire."[20]

The Bush speech took many governments overseas by surprise. They included America's allies in Europe, many of which had ongoing relationships with Iran, and in Asia, where Japan and South Korea were trying to figure out how to deal with North Korea. The administration had not warned the allies in advance of what was, by any measure, a significant change in direction for the war on terrorism.

Wolfowitz insisted that the Bush administration was not downgrading the importance of its allies. Asked if the administration had consulted with them about the State of the Union speech, he replied that the speech itself represented the beginning of a process of consultation. "They could read it," he said. ". . . The State of the Union speech, I consider, was an invitation to a whole bunch of people to consult, to discuss, to debate, to get on board hopefully [*sic*]." He argued that America was simply demonstrating leadership and telling its allies what the United States wanted to undertake, then asking the allies for their views. By way of comparison, Wolfowitz pointed out that after Iraq invaded Kuwait in 1990, the first Bush administration had gone to Saudi Arabia not to ask what the United States should do but to state clearly that America planned and intended to drive Saddam Hussein's forces back to Iraq.[21]

However, Wolfowitz's explanation papered over a significant change. During the cold war, "consultation" with allies hadn't usually meant giving a landmark public speech and then asking afterward what other governments thought about it; rather, it had meant talking and soliciting ideas in private before such a speech was given.[22] The comparison to the 1990 diplomacy with Saudi Arabia underscored this crucial difference;

Cheney and Wolfowitz had consulted with Saudi officials in private, not in public. The axis-of-evil speech represented a different form of "consultation" with America's allies—on television in prime time. It seemed like an unnecessary slight.

The reaction among America's allies was compounded by the further problem that other than Pakistan, the only countries singled out for praise in the State of the Union were Russia, China and India; this was a reflection of Rice's belief in the importance of great powers. Bush's speech never referred to South Korea or Japan. Nor did the president thank (or mention) NATO, which after September 11 had passed an unprecedented resolution in support of the United States; or Germany, which ventured to send troops on an overseas combat mission for the first time since World War II; or even Britain, whose troops and warplanes fought alongside the Americans in Afghanistan. Crediting these overseas partners in Bush's speech would have cost the administration nothing more than a few words.

As it turned out, the axis-of-evil speech represented a watershed for American relations with Europe. The transatlantic tensions that had been slowly heating up throughout the late 1990s and simmering during the first year of the Bush administration now came to a boil. French Foreign Minister Hubert Védrine called the State of the Union speech "simplistic." German Foreign Minister Joschka Fischer warned that "alliance partners are not satellites." Christopher Patten, the British Conservative party leader working for the European Union, reminded Washington of the words of Winston Churchill: "In working with allies, it sometimes happens that they develop opinions of their own." That was, as Patten undoubtedly realized, a gibe at the Churchill admirers in the Bush administration.

Americans inside and outside the administration were equally caustic about the Europeans, arguing that they were blind to the dangers from weapons of mass destruction and in any event had been marginalized by their own prolonged unwillingness to spend money on defense. Neoconservative columnist Charles Krauthammer called Europe an "axis of petulance. . . . The ostensible complaint is American primitivism. The real problem is their irrelevance." Taking the lead for the Bush administration, Powell dismissed the French criticisms by saying that Védrine was "getting the vapors." The stage was being set for the drama that was to unfold one year later at the United Nations.[23]

On January 3, 2002, about three hundred miles off Israel's coast, commandos from the Israeli Navy boarded a ship called the *Karine A*. On it, they seized fifty tons of weaponry, including Katyusha rockets, mortars, explosives and ammunition. Israeli officials claimed that Yasser Arafat's Palestinian Authority had purchased the ship, that the arms had been obtained in Iran and that they were in the process of being smuggled into the Gaza Strip for possible use in the Palestinian uprisings against Israel. U.S. officials later said their intelligence confirmed these Israeli accounts. "Leaders in the Palestinian Authority had to know about this, and there were Palestinian Authority personnel on the ship," said Powell. ". . . It's a pretty big smoking gun." The Palestinian leadership, which had repeatedly promised the United States to take steps to curb violence, had been caught red-handed, just at the time when the Bush administration was contemplating its future policies.[24]

Over the following six months the Bush administration made a concerted attempt to ease the conflict between the Israeli government of Ariel Sharon and Arafat's Palestinian Authority. Vice President Cheney and Powell, the leading spokesmen for two opposing viewpoints within the administration on the Middle East, each made extensive trips through the region. In the end it was Cheney's vision that won out.

All the Vulcans started with the same broad underlying premise: that the dispute between Israel and the Palestinians could not be separated from the larger politics of the Middle East and the Persian Gulf. But the two factions in the administration disagreed about the nature of this linkage and what should be done about it.

To the hawks, including Cheney, Rumsfeld and Wolfowitz, the most important factor was the underlying confluence of interests between Arafat's Palestinian leadership and Saddam Hussein in Iraq. Each one reinforced the other, they believed: The Palestinian uprisings against Israel distracted America from trying to deal with Iraq; correspondingly, Saddam Hussein's continuing presence in Iraq provided sustenance to the Palestinian uprisings against Israel. Remember, argued the hawks, Arafat was most willing to make concessions when he was most isolated, such as after Saddam Hussein's military defeat in 1991.[25] For the hawks, the short-term priority was to end the Palestinian uprisings, and the way to achieving long-term progress was to find a way to make the Palestinian leadership more accommodating.

The opposing group, including Powell, Armitage and others at the State Department, saw the relationship between Israel-Palestine policy and larger Middle East strategy differently. From their viewpoint it would be impossible for the Bush administration to move against Saddam Hussein until after there was progress toward a settlement of the Israeli-Palestinian conflict. Under this logic, the American support of Sharon had aroused anger throughout the Middle East; therefore, in order for the United States to win support from Arab governments for action against Iraq, the Bush administration would first have to address the Israeli-Palestinian dispute. For this group of officials, the short-term priority was to get Sharon's government to relax its crackdown on the Palestinians, and the key to a longer-term solution was to induce Israel to make concessions in its conditions for a peace settlement.

In early March, Cheney embarked upon a ten-day tour through the Middle East. The trip was reminiscent of Cheney's groundbreaking 1990 visit to Saudi Arabia and other Arab capitals following Saddam Hussein's invasion of Kuwait. Twelve years later Cheney was once again seeking to build up support in the Middle East for another U.S. military campaign against Iraq.

On virtually every stop, however, Iraq was treated as a secondary issue. Arab leaders told the vice president that the United States needed to do more to promote a settlement between Israel and the Palestinians. In particular, Cheney was urged to persuade Israel that it should let Arafat leave the West Bank so that he could participate in an Arab summit in Beirut.

Neither Bush nor Cheney had met with Arafat since taking office; they believed that in the late 1990s President Clinton had become too personally involved in dealing with the Palestinian leader and that he had proved unreliable. Cheney made no plans to see Arafat in the Middle East. But in Israel near the end of his trip Cheney suddenly announced he would be willing to meet with Arafat within a week if the Palestinian leader would take action to stop Palestinian violence and to work out a cease-fire with Israel. After Cheney met with Sharon, the Israeli leader said he would allow Arafat to leave the West Bank for the Beirut summit. It appeared as though the Bush administration were on the verge of concerted diplomacy to goad Sharon and Arafat toward peace.[26]

As usual in the Middle East, events intervened. That month there had already been several other suicide bombings in Israel. On March 27 came the deadliest of all: Twenty-nine Israelis died in a suicide bombing at a hotel in Netanya as they were sitting down for a Passover seder. In response, Israel launched what it called Operation Defensive Shield, a military offensive in the West Bank. Backed by tanks and helicopters, Israeli forces occupied Ramallah, putting Arafat's headquarters under siege and confining him and his aides to a few rooms.

Even beforehand there had been clear signs Cheney's initiative was in trouble. Sharon had held up on allowing Arafat go to the Beirut conference because he had not taken enough steps against terrorism, and the Palestinian leader had balked at leaving the West Bank because he was afraid Israel might not let him return. After the Netanya bombing and the subsequent Israeli offensive, everything was once again put on hold. Cheney went back to Washington and stayed there; his meeting with Arafat never took place. A year later one of Cheney's aides reflected that the vice president's trip of March 2002 had represented Arafat's last opportunity and that the Palestinian leader had failed to seize it.[27]

In early April Bush responded to the continuing violence by sending Powell to the Middle East in a renewed push for peace. The president asked Arafat to take steps to stop terrorism; he called upon Israel to stop building settlements, to pull its forces back from the occupied territories and open up border checkpoints to let Palestinians go back to work. It was the usual approach, seeking concessions from both sides.

Powell hadn't traveled to Israel for nearly a year. Like other senior officials in the Bush administration, he had avoided becoming entangled in time-consuming Middle East peacemaking at a time when Israeli and Palestinian leaders didn't seem ready. The secretary of state's April trip merely deepened the pessimism. Arab governments called for Israel to end its siege of Arafat's headquarters and to pull back the forces it had sent into the West Bank. Bush himself had in fact called for Israel to act "without delay." Yet Sharon was unwilling to comply, and Powell, after talking to him, failed to get any timetable for a pullback. In Washington, Rumsfeld, Wolfowitz and other Pentagon leaders resisted the idea that the administration should come down hard on Sharon; they argued that the Israeli military operations were part of a legitimate campaign against terrorism. Powell also met with Arafat, still confined and surrounded by Israeli troops in Ramallah, but said afterward he was disappointed the Palestinian leader had not done more to stop the violence against Israelis.

"The world is looking for him to make a strategic choice and lead his people down the path of peace," Powell said.[28]

By this point the Middle East turmoil was beginning to arouse the sort of passions inside the United States that can have lasting political repercussions. Supporters of Israel started to organize a demonstration in Washington. The Bush administration had to decide whom to dispatch to the rally as its representative. It couldn't send someone as high-ranking as a cabinet member. The issue was a sensitive one; Karl Rove, Bush's political adviser, played a key role in the discussions.

The choice boiled down to three of the Vulcans: Rice, Armitage or Wolfowitz. But sending Armitage, a State Department official, might have conveyed a degree of official sponsorship of the pro-Israeli demonstration, at the very time of Powell's diplomacy in the Middle East. That left Rice and Wolfowitz. The decision was predictable: Wolfowitz, the one official at the top ranks of the Bush foreign policy team who was Jewish. Rove called Wolfowitz to give him the news.

Wolfowitz didn't relish the assignment. He argued back that it would be more appropriate to send Rice. Why not send Condi? No luck; in fact, he was told, Rice had been in the room when the decision was made to send him. It was a telling reminder of the differing roles of the two Vulcan intellectuals: Rice was more of an insider than Wolfowitz was; she was always nearer the locus of political power.[29]

At the rally Wolfowitz delivered a speech that was strongly supportive of Israel but also included a few words of sympathy for Palestinians. "Innocent Palestinians are suffering and dying in great numbers as well," he told the crowd. "It is critical that we recognize and acknowledge that fact." Those words brought forth boos, catcalls and chants of "Down with Arafat."[30]

Wolfowitz was stunned. He hadn't expected his words about the Palestinians to be popular with the crowd, but he had figured they might be greeted with something like a stony silence. He was not prepared for the outpouring of hostility.[31] It was an awkward moment. The administration's leading theoretician confronted the fury of the street.

After Powell returned to Washington, both the suicide bombings and Israel's military offensive continued. In May the secretary of state put forward the idea of an American-sponsored international peace conference on the Middle East, in which Sharon's government and Arafat's Palestinian Authority would participate. Administration officials began drafting a speech in which the president would unveil the American proposal for the conference.

By this time, however, the climate of opinion within the top ranks of the administration was beginning to shift. Arafat, after previously frustrating Clinton's efforts at peacemaking, had done nothing since then to give the Bush team hope about the prospects for negotiations with him. At the Pentagon, Rumsfeld, Wolfowitz and others argued against any return to the kinds of diplomacy that had failed in the past. Meanwhile, Sharon was urging the administration to stop dealing with Arafat. In Israel there were four suicide bombings in May and two more in early June.

Bush's Middle East speech went through at least twenty-eight drafts. Near the end of the process, on June 19, 2002, yet another bombing killed seven Israelis; a group called the Al Aksa Martyrs Brigade claimed responsibility for the attack. The following day an Israeli military attaché brought to the National Security Council intelligence that Arafat had authorized a payment of twenty thousand dollars to the Al Aksa Martyrs Brigade. That was all the information administration officials needed to take their Middle East policy where it was already heading.[32]

On June 24, in the Rose Garden of the White House, Bush finally delivered his long-awaited speech on the Middle East. He did not call for an international peace conference, as Powell had proposed. Instead, the president urged the Palestinian people to elect new leaders, ones who were "not compromised by terror." After a new, democratic Palestinian leadership was in place, Bush promised, the United States would support the creation of a Palestinian state.

In many respects this speech was a milestone. For the first time the United States had explicitly abandoned Arafat, declaring that America would support a Palestinian state only if it was not under his leadership. Over the previous months Powell had said repeatedly that the United States intended to work with Arafat; now Powell's diplomacy was being cast aside. The administration was also discarding the past approach of seeking concessions from both Israelis and Palestinians at the same time. Under Bush's new policy, it would be up to the Palestinians to change their leadership first, before Israel was required to take new steps of its own toward peace.

Bush's speech had significance for other countries in the Middle East too. The president explicitly called upon the Palestinians to build "a prac-

ticing democracy." The existing Palestinian legislature had no power,
Bush complained. Any Palestinian state should have "a new constitution," a legislature with genuine power and "a truly independent judici-
ary."[33] Bush was for the first time applying to the Middle East the
principles and democratic ideals that officials such as Wolfowitz had begun to embrace in East Asia during the late 1980s. Most of the other governments in the region, including America's longtime partners in Saudi
Arabia and Egypt, could not meet the democratic standard Bush was setting for the Palestinians.

Once again the Vulcans had opted for the far-reaching approach. What
had started as a proposal for yet another Middle East peace conference resulted instead in another dramatic break with the long-standing policies
of the past. In the months since September 11 the administration had
abandoned the ABM Treaty, moved away from cold war strategies of deterrence, recast America's doctrines on nuclear weapons and turned the
war on terror into a campaign against weapons of mass destruction. Now
it was reshaping American policy toward Israel and the Palestinians in
fundamental ways. And there was still more to come.

The administration had been dropping hints of a fundamental change in
military strategy since the beginning of 2002. In one section of the State
of the Union, Bush had asserted, "I will not stand by while peril draws
closer and closer." America, he said, would not permit "the world's most
dangerous regimes to threaten us with the world's most destructive
weapons." In the spring Rice had begun to mention vaguely in public the
document Zelikow was drafting for the administration that would lay out
an entirely new national security strategy for the United States.[34]

   In June, Bush unveiled the heart of this new strategy. The president
delivered the commencement address at West Point, the same venue at
which, exactly one year earlier, Wolfowitz had mused about the prospects
of a surprise attack. There for the first time Bush warned that Americans
should be ready for "preemptive action" to protect national security. "We
must take the battle to the enemy, disrupt his plans and confront the
worst threats before they emerge," the president said.[35]

   This was a considerable step beyond the previous talk about the need
for offense instead of defense. "Preemptive action" meant that the United
States would be willing to start a war if it thought it was going to be at-

tacked or, in Bush's formulation, if it felt threatened. America would no longer rely on strategies of containment and deterrence to prevent war from breaking out. The United States was discarding, or at least redefining, the principle it had helped enshrine in the United Nations Charter: that a nation should go to war only in self-defense.

To be sure, without ever saying so, the United States had always implicitly reserved for itself the right of preemptive action. American officials had not ruled out the possibility of a first strike against the Soviet Union if the Soviet Union had been found to be preparing to launch a war with the United States. The Kennedy administration had imposed its naval quarantine during the Cuban missile crisis in what was arguably a preemptive move. But that action had fallen short of war, and over the years American officials had repeatedly condemned the general principle of preemption. The United States had condemned Israel for its 1981 preemptive attack on Iraq's budding nuclear facilities at Osirak. Who was to say what sort of threat would justify an American decision to strike first? If the United States claimed the right to launch a preemptive attack, what would stop other countries from doing so? What would U.S. officials say if, for example, India decided to launch a preemptive strike against Pakistan?[36]

The answer to these questions appeared to be that the United States was establishing itself, the world's preeminent power, as the chief judge and enforcer of international stability. In another section of Bush's West Point speech that was no less significant than the passage on preemptive action, the president embraced the vision put forward by Wolfowitz's Pentagon staff ten years earlier: the notion of a world dominated by an American superpower so militarily strong that no one else could possibly match it and that attempts to do so would be not worth starting. "Competition between great nations is inevitable, but armed conflict in our world is not," Bush said. ". . . America has, and intends to keep, military strengths beyond challenge, thereby making the destabilizing arms races of other eras pointless."[37]

The West Point speech was merely a preview. Three months later the Bush administration issued its entire new National Security Strategy, a comprehensive thirty-one-page document in which it laid out, in written form, its vision for America's relations with the world.

The Goldwater-Nichols Act of 1986 required every administration to file approximately once a year an overview of its national security strategy. In previous administrations these documents had been relatively anodyne. But the strategy made public in September 2002 was the first one from George W. Bush's administration and also the first since the terrorist attacks.[38]

The document blended together the three crucial elements of the Vulcans' new vision. First was the advocacy of preemptive action. "We will not hesitate to act alone, if necessary, to exercise our right of self-defense by acting preemptively" against terrorists, the document said. Second, the document adopted the notion of an unchallengeable American superpower: "Our forces will be strong enough to dissuade potential adversaries from pursuing a military build-up in hopes of surpassing, or equaling, the power of the United States." Third, in dealing with the world, the American superpower would seek to promote overseas the country's democratic values. The ideals of Woodrow Wilson were to be revived, this time linked hand in hand with America's unprecedented military power. There is only "a single sustainable model for national success: freedom, democracy and free enterprise," asserted the National Security Strategy. America "must stand firmly for" the rule of law, limits on the power of the state, free speech, freedom of worship, equal justice, respect for women, religious and ethnic tolerance and respect for private property.[39]

The document made a few nods in the direction of continuity with the past. It spoke of the importance of cooperation with other major powers, including Russia, India and China. It incorporated Rice's favorite phrase, that America would seek a "balance of power that favors human freedom," a slogan that represented another effort to combine the realism ("balance of power") Rice had learned from mentors like Scowcroft and the ideals ("human freedom") of the neoconservatives. But these references to cooperation and a balance of power seemed to be potentially in conflict with the vision of an unchallengeable American superpower promoting democracy throughout the world.

Overall, the scope of the National Security Strategy was breathtaking. To be sure, even some of the Bush administration's critics had conceded that the rise of Al Qaeda had made necessary some readjustment in old cold war doctrines, which had assumed that the threats to American security would come from existing states occupying well-defined territory.

"To respond to the threat of mega-terrorism does require some stretching of international law to accommodate the reasonable security needs of sovereign states," admitted one such critic.[40] Yet the Bush administration had once again opted to go beyond mere tinkering with the past and to put forth something bolder, a more fundamental change.

In short, over the course of less than nine months, from January to September 2002, the Vulcans managed to set down an entire new set of ideas and principles. They were deliberately choosing to create a new conception of American foreign policy, just as the Truman administration had constructed a new framework of ideas and institutions at the beginning of the cold war.

By the end of this period the Vulcans were beginning to talk about the cold war, in which all of them had participated, as though they no longer remembered it. In one curiously ironic section of the new National Security Strategy, the administration spoke almost longingly of the Soviet Union, suggesting the Soviets had been less threatening and more predictable than Al Qaeda. "In the Cold War, especially following the Cuban missile crisis, we faced a generally status quo, risk-averse adversary," the document said.[41] This was of course a strikingly different view of the Soviet Union from the one the Vulcans had held in the 1970s, when Rumsfeld was opposing détente and when Wolfowitz was taking part in the Team B review of intelligence about Soviet intentions. In that earlier period neither had believed that Moscow was risk-averse or an upholder of the status quo.

Thus, a decade after the Soviet collapse, both sides of the American political spectrum seemed to have developed amnesia about the nature of the cold war. Among liberals one of the shibboleths of the 1990s was that during the cold war Americans had shared a unity of purpose, but that ever since, U.S. foreign policy had been cast adrift. "For fifty years after the end of World War II and until the fall of the Berlin Wall in 1989, we were sure about one thing: We knew where we stood on foreign policy," declared Bill Bradley at the start of his 2000 presidential campaign.[42] Such clichés forgot the furious foreign policy debates of the cold war; the supposed unity in dealing with the Soviet Union and with communism could be detected only in hindsight. Conversely, the Vulcans and their allies on the political right were creating in retrospect a Soviet Union more benign than the one they had inveighed against for many decades.

The new National Security Strategy had been largely an initiative of Rice's National Security Council. Oddly, the hawks in the Pentagon and in Vice President Cheney's office hadn't been closely involved, even though the document incorporated many of their key ideas. They had left the details and the drafting in the hands of Rice and Zelikow, along with Rice's deputy, Stephen Hadley.

The hawks were preoccupied with something far more concrete; they believed in the overriding importance of regime change in Iraq. And to move against Iraq, they believed, the United States did not require a new national security strategy. It did not even need a new doctrine of preemptive war. The United States simply needed to enforce the existing United Nations resolutions on Iraq, with which Saddam Hussein had failed to comply.[43]

Nevertheless, now that the new strategy was in place, the Vulcans were in position to put it into practice. They were ready for a demonstration of how the administration's new doctrine of preemption would work. The obvious candidate was a regime with a history of developing weapons of mass destruction, a proven hostility to American power and interests and a long record of brutal repression that offended democratic ideals. It was time to deal with Iraq.

Toward War with Iraq

THE AXIS-OF-EVIL SPEECH brought Iraq to center stage and kept it there. From January 2002 through the war of 2003 the question of what the Bush administration should do about Saddam Hussein's regime became the dominant issue in U.S. foreign policy and, indeed, in all of American political life. Occasionally, other countries and other problems would float into consciousness, only to fade away after a few days, largely because the Bush administration did not want to divert attention or resources away from Iraq. When North Korea confirmed it had an ongoing nuclear weapons program, for example, the Bush administration insisted there was no sense of crisis or urgency. Soon after Bush's State of the Union, Secretary of State Colin Powell noted that "with respect to Iran and with respect to North Korea, there is no plan to start a war with those nations." Powell pointedly omitted Iraq from his no-war list.[1]

In the late winter and spring of 2002 the Bush administration launched a running internal review of America's policy options on Iraq. The participants were the second- and third-ranking officials in each of the main foreign policy agencies. For the Pentagon, the representatives were Wolfowitz and Undersecretary for Policy Douglas Feith. From State came Armitage and Undersecretary Marc Grossman. The National Security Council's representatives included Rice's deputy, Stephen Hadley; Zalmay Khalilzad, the regional specialist for Iraq; and for a time General Wayne Downing, the NSC's counterterrorism specialist. John McLaughlin, the deputy director of the CIA, and Peter Pace, the vice chairman of the Joint Chiefs of Staff, also took part.[2]

The group agreed that containment was no longer a viable strategy for dealing with Saddam Hussein. Even the Clinton administration, in its final years, had gone on record in favor of regime change in Iraq, at least in the abstract. Now, in the wake of the overthrow of the Taliban in Afghanistan, the members of the Bush team were determined to oust Saddam Hussein. They wanted to make regime change in Iraq not merely a goal but a reality.

But how? There were three different possibilities. The first option was called the enclave strategy. It was an idea that had been proposed in the late 1990s by exile leaders of the Iraqi National Congress and by some of its American supporters, including Wolfowitz and Khalilzad. Under this approach, Iraqi opposition groups, with the help of the United States, would establish an enclave in southern Iraq, in northern Iraq or in both. The United States would recognize the leadership of such an enclave as the legitimate government of Iraq and provide military support. From inside the enclave the opponents of Saddam Hussein might then challenge his regime and mount a military campaign against it until it collapsed.

The second option was a coup d'état to overthrow Saddam Hussein. The CIA had tried that during the 1990s, without success. The third option was a full-scale American invasion of Iraq, with ground forces; this was of course precisely the option that the first Bush administration had rejected at the time of the 1991 Gulf War.

Administration officials dismissed the enclave strategy. That approach was too slow and too unlikely to work. It raised fears of a disaster like the Kennedy administration's Bay of Pigs invasion in Cuba. The Iraqi opposition groups couldn't defeat Saddam Hussein on their own militarily, and in the end the United States might well have to intervene with force of its own to bail them out.[3] Even if things went well, the enclave strategy would be too messy. The participants wanted something quicker and more decisive.

So the remaining choices were a coup or an invasion. The participants didn't rule out the possibility of a coup, and indeed, the CIA was encouraged to keep on trying. But the Bush officials also realized that the chances of a successful coup remained slim, and that the administration simply couldn't count on this strategy to oust Saddam Hussein. Moreover, administration officials thought that even a successful coup would probably not by itself be sufficient to accomplish all their goals; after a coup there might still need to be some form of American military intervention in Iraq to make sure some new Iraqi leader did not gain control of and resume the programs for weapons of mass destruction that Saddam Hussein had launched many years earlier.

All these factors pointed to option three, a full-scale American invasion. That seemed the option most likely to succeed in bringing about a change in regime in Iraq. As early as the fall of 2001 the Pentagon had started to draw up plans for a possible military campaign against Iraq that would, for once and for all, dislodge Saddam Hussein from power. In early 2002 this military planning became far more serious and detailed. Rumsfeld began working closely with General Tommy Franks, the head of the U.S. Central Command, to develop plans for an invasion. In the most general sense, the course for military intervention in Iraq was charted in the spring of 2002, roughly a year before the start of the war.

Not surprisingly, the administration's intensifying focus on Iraq began to trickle into the newspapers. So did the military planning. The Pentagon "is concentrating on a major air campaign and ground invasion," said one report. The phrase *shock and awe*—first coined by strategist Harlan Ullman to signify a massive, humbling display of American military power, crept into the public lexicon during this period.[4]

Outside the administration, throughout the spring and early summer, several former officials, led by Richard Perle and James Woolsey, pressed the argument for war with Iraq. "The *casus belli* is that we know Saddam Hussein possesses chemical and biological weapons," explained Perle at a Washington forum. "We know that he hates the United States. We know that he is working on nuclear weapons." Perle, who was close to the Iraqi exile leader Ahmed Chalabi, specifically warned against a policy of overthrowing Saddam Hussein through a coup d'état, a strategy that would almost certainly result in some senior military officer from inside Hussein's regime's becoming the next leader, rather than an exile, such as Chalabi. "It would be a tragedy if Saddam is removed only to be replaced by another tyrant," he said.[5]

Perle also began to press the theme that America needed to act soon on Iraq. The threat, he argued, was becoming ever more serious. "We have no time to lose," he said in a television interview."[6] This was a modified version of the warnings once issued about the Soviet Union by Perle and his mentors Albert Wohlstetter and Paul Nitze.

Inside Colin Powell's State Department, Perle was sarcastically dubbed the "Unpaid Adviser." That sobriquet referred to the fact that while Perle was often treated as though he were a member of the Bush foreign policy team, he had no real responsibilities; his sole official title was chairman of the Defense Policy Board, a group of former officials who convened every two or three months to offer their views to Rumsfeld.[7] At times it seemed as though both Perle's adversaries on the political left and Perle himself, for different reasons, tended to exaggerate his influence over the Bush administration's decision making.

Nevertheless, although Perle and Woolsey were outsiders, the network of personal ties connecting them to some of the Vulcans (particularly Wolfowitz, but also Rumsfeld and Cheney) was intricate and long-standing. As a result, when they called for military action against Iraq, they were seen as reflecting views inside the administration. Wolfowitz and Perle had been allies since their arrival in Washington as students in 1969, and Woolsey had befriended both men during the late 1970s. The three were not just intellectual soul mates but neighbors. "We all live within a stone's throw of each other in Chevy Chase," said Woolsey, a conservative Democrat who served a brief, unhappy tenure as President Clinton's first director of central intelligence.[8] Woolsey had also become acquainted with Cheney and Rumsfeld when all three men served as team leaders and would-be White House chiefs of staff in the clandestine doomsday exercises of the Reagan administration. In the 1990s Woolsey served on Rumsfeld's missile commission; after 2001 he served with Perle on the Defense Policy Board.

Woolsey dismissed suggestions that in his television interviews and newspaper articles about Iraq he was serving as a conduit for the views of Wolfowitz and Rumsfeld. "There are no secret meetings, or secret handshakes or conclaves or anything," he explained in an interview in the spring of 2002. Since the beginning of the new administration, he had seen Wolfowitz only rarely, usually at meetings of the Defense Policy Board. Their proposals for military intervention in Iraq—Perle and Woolsey outside the administration, Wolfowitz inside—were similar simply because their views were so alike, not because they were coordinated with one another, Woolsey explained.[9]

The administration's internal discussions and military planning led to continuing speculation in the press about war with Iraq. The public calls for action by the Vulcans' friends helped intensify the press coverage. Conversely, the steady stream of stories about possible war spurred on the internal planning since if there was to be a war, no one wanted to be caught unprepared. By the midsummer of 2002 so much momentum was building toward action against Saddam Hussein's regime that the question seemed to be not if the administration would go to war but when. Yet there had been, until that point, only a limited public debate about Iraq. That was soon to change.

Brent Scowcroft had watched the movement toward war with growing dismay. The national security adviser of the first Bush administration couldn't believe where the second Bush administration was heading. Scowcroft possessed at least as many personal connections to the administration as Perle or Woolsey. In 1989 he had brought Rice to the National Security Council and personally picked out Cheney to be defense secretary. Throughout the first Bush administration he had worked closely with Powell, chairman of the Joint Chiefs.

Scowcroft remained, at age seventy-seven, a strong proponent of realism in foreign policy. He prided himself that his views had not changed much for a quarter century; in the 1970s he had been categorized as a leading hawk, and by 2002, to his bemusement, he was portrayed as a dove.[10] At all times his preoccupation was in furthering American interests through stable relations with other major powers, no matter what form of government those powers had; he was leery of efforts to turn American foreign policy into a crusade for democratic reform throughout the world. One of Scowcroft's greatest sources of pride was the extensive international coalition the first Bush administration had put together before the Gulf War of 1991. He operated his own private consulting firm with offices a few blocks from the White House; he maintained close ties with Saudi Arabia and the other Arab governments in the Middle East that had joined with America in the Gulf War.

During the first months after George W. Bush took office, Scowcroft had been uneasy with what he thought was the unilateralist drift of the new administration. However, in the immediate aftermath of September 11 he believed that the new Bush team had become more pragmatic and was beginning to recognize the importance of working in concert with other countries. He was taken aback, then, when the administration seemed in the spring and summer of 2002 to be focusing on war with

Iraq. He was convinced that moving against Saddam Hussein would divert attention from the campaign against terrorism and would damage America's standing with other governments in the Middle East. Scowcroft did not hide these views; for months he offered them to anyone who asked, both privately and, from time to time, in public. At first, however, what he said attracted little notice.

In early August Scowcroft laid out his views on a Sunday television show. He argued that the administration should not go to war with Iraq until after making progress toward peace between Israel and the Palestinians. He also maintained that the administration should first go to the United Nations and get it to insist on the return of weapons inspectors to Iraq. "If he [Hussein] doesn't agree to it, that gives you the *casus belli* that we really don't have right now," Scowcroft said.[11]

There was little immediate reaction. The following week Scowcroft's aide Arnold Kanter suggested that he put his views about Iraq into an op-ed piece.[12] Scowcroft did, and the article was published in the *Wall Street Journal* on August 16. This time, he sharpened his argument with a series of ominous predictions of what might happen if America went to war with Iraq. Saddam Hussein, concluding he had nothing to lose, might use his weapons of mass destruction. Iraq might attack Israel, which could respond with nuclear weapons, "unleashing an Armageddon in the Middle East." Elsewhere in the region there would be an "explosion of outrage" against the United States, and the result might be to destabilize other Arab governments.[13]

This time Scowcroft's views attracted attention, not only in the press but inside the White House. Newspapers gave prominent coverage to his op-ed piece, using it as a starting part for broader articles about opposition to the war.[14] Rice called Scowcroft and chided him for taking the administration by surprise. "Why didn't you tell me?" she asked her former boss. Scowcroft pointed out that he was merely repeating what he'd said a few days earlier on *Face the Nation*. He reminded her he'd sent her an advance copy of the op-ed piece. It hadn't reached Rice's desk, however, until the morning the article was published.

Over the following days James Baker and Lawrence Eagleburger, the two secretaries of state of the first Bush administration, issued their own warnings against any immediate war with Iraq. Both called upon the administration to slow down the pace of events and to go to the United Nations to seek international support against Hussein's regime. "We should try our best not to have to go it alone, and the president should reject the advice of those who counsel doing so," said Baker, who had played a key role in helping George W. Bush win the presidency by representing him during the disputed vote counting in Florida.[15]

What accounted for the intense differences in outlook between Scowcroft and Rice, the teacher and his carefully groomed protégée? How could one explain why the stalwarts of the foreign policy team of Bush the Elder were becoming the loyal opposition in the tenure of George W. Bush?

Scowcroft tended to attribute the differences to domestic politics. The younger Bush and his political adviser, Karl Rove, he thought, were couching the administration's foreign policy in a way that would appeal to the Republican party's conservative wing, the bedrock of its support. They were trying to learn from the political mistakes of Bush's father, who had lost the 1992 election. Scowcroft cared far more about foreign policy than politics, but a decade after that election even he acknowledged that in failing to pay enough attention to the Republican party's conservative base, the first Bush administration had made a serious mistake.[16]

Still, domestic politics could provide only part of the explanation for the metamorphosis from the first Bush administration to the second. The Vulcans were serious about foreign policy and had spent most of their careers on it. They were in the process of rewriting some of the fundamental doctrines that had guided America's relations with the world for a half century. They were doing far more than was necessary for domestic politics, and they clearly believed in what they were doing.

Some of Rice's colleagues advanced another explanation: that the changes from Bush I to Bush II reflected age and generational differences. By this theory, Scowcroft, Baker and Eagleburger represented an older generation that was still guided by the caution and restraint of the cold war in which they had spent most of their lives. By contrast, Rice and some of her associates, such as Deputy National Security Adviser Stephen Hadley, had had their formative experiences in foreign policy during the first Bush administration, when they were able to witness the possibilities for positive change throughout the world.[17]

But this age-based analysis too seemed to fall short. The prime movers in the second Bush administration included Cheney, Rumsfeld and Wolfowitz. All three of these men had first risen to prominence not during the first Bush administration but far earlier, during the Nixon-Ford years, during almost exactly the same period as Scowcroft and Baker.

In fact, the changes from Bush I to Bush II reflected not so much questions of age as the underlying disagreements on foreign policy among the Republicans since the 1970s. Although everyone had accepted the restraints imposed by the cold war, Cheney, Rumsfeld and Wolfowitz had at the time been more eager to test those limits than Scowcroft and other realists. They had been less accepting of détente with the Soviet Union; they had been more eager to confront it with American ideals and sheer military power.

Added to these long-standing philosophical cleavages was the powerful impact of September 11. Indeed, some of what set the members of George W. Bush's foreign policy team apart from that of his father was not their experiences in the cold war but their experience more than a decade after its demise. Scowcroft, Baker and Eagleburger were not responsible for American security when New York City and Washington were attacked by terrorism. The Vulcans were. Scowcroft, Baker and Eagleburger had worked in government almost entirely before the end of the cold war; by contrast, the defining characteristic of the Vulcans was that their careers stretched out on both sides of that momentous change. For the Vulcans, the end of the cold war had been only the middle of the story, and terrorism was the dominant theme of the later years. This made for a considerable difference in outlook. For example, on the basis of the events of 1990 and 1991, Scowcroft and Baker could plausibly view Saudi Arabia as America's friend and partner. From the equally valid perspective of officials in the second Bush administration, the role of Saudi Arabia was, at best, problematic; over the decade since 1991 there had been a series of intermittent terrorist attacks in which Osama bin Laden and other Saudis had played significant roles.

After their testy exchange about the op-ed, Rice and Scowcroft remained on amicable terms. From then on, whenever Scowcroft planned to write an article, he let Rice know in advance; sometimes she asked to talk to him first. Scowcroft didn't change his views. Many months later, when George W. Bush and British Prime Minister Tony Blair began planning for a U.S.-British interim authority to govern Iraq after the end of Saddam Hussein's regime, Scowcroft declared that bypassing the United Nations could provoke the "wrath and enmity" of the Muslim world. "I'm a skeptic about the ability to transform Iraq into a democracy in any realistic period of time," he said.[18]

Scowcroft became, in a way, America's most unlikely high-level dissident, the friend and coauthor of George H. W. Bush, voicing clear public challenges to the policies put forward by George W. Bush and the foreign policy officials Scowcroft had worked alongside or groomed. After he began to speak out, others within Washington's foreign policy elite noticed that he was treated cordially but with a certain distance. When officials like Rumsfeld held quiet, confidential briefings for former secretaries of state and national security advisers, sometimes Scowcroft wasn't there.

Within the administration, Colin Powell was putting forward many of the same arguments that Brent Scowcroft made. Indeed, Powell-and-Scowcroft served as the counterpoint to Wolfowitz-and-Perle. In each instance, two men who thought alike and had worked closely together in the past were working along parallel paths, one of them in public and the other on the inside.

To the president and others in the administration, Powell emphasized that he was not opposed in principle to military intervention in Iraq. The important questions, he argued, were how and when to intervene, with whom and how to clean up Iraq afterward. The United States should move against Saddam Hussein not alone but in a coalition with like-minded friends and allies, Powell said. There was no rush, he said; the administration should act at a time of the administration's own choosing.

Powell recommended a more deliberate course of action, starting with an attempt at the United Nations to win support for the return of weapons inspectors to Iraq. But in the administration's internal discussions, Cheney argued that the administration should not seek any new authorization from the United Nations; the United States should merely inform the UN it was time to move against Iraq for failing to comply with past Security Council resolutions.[19]

On August 26, in a speech to the Veterans of Foreign Wars in Nashville, Cheney took direct aim in public at some of the arguments Powell had been making. Above all, the vice president rejected the argument that the Bush administration should seek to have UN weapons inspectors sent back to Iraq. "Saddam has perfected the art of cheat and retreat, and is very skilled in the art of denial and deception," Cheney said. "A return of inspectors would provide no assurance whatsoever of his compliance with U.N. resolutions." He said, without qualification, that Saddam Hussein had resumed his attempts to acquire nuclear weapons and also to enhance Iraq's capabilities in chemical and biological weapons.

The vice president also gave a concise statement of how Iraqi oil fitted into the administration's calculations. Iraq had 10 percent of the world's oil reserves, Cheney noted, and if Saddam Hussein had weapons of mass destruction, he "could then be expected to seek domination of the entire Middle East, taking control of a great portion of the world's energy supplies." Cheney dismissed the argument by Scowcroft that moving against Iraq would inflame tensions throughout the Middle East and undercut the war on terror. On the contrary, he said, "extremists in the region would have to rethink their strategy of jihad. Moderates throughout the region would take heart."[20]

Delivering that VFW speech represented something of a new role for Cheney, one that surprised some who had worked for him in the past. Cheney—the quintessential insider, the former congressman who had almost never given floor speeches, the former defense secretary who had allowed Colin Powell to dominate their joint Pentagon press conferences—was electing to take the lead in an open public debate. That was a job he had in the past usually left to others. It was a sign of how intensely Cheney felt about Iraq and how strongly he was arguing the case for war inside the administration in the closed-door meetings that were, in effect, Cheney's natural habitat.

By the late summer of 2002 the dispute over Iraq within the Republican foreign policy elite was beginning to turn rancorous. The old antagonisms between those who fought in Vietnam and those who hadn't burst into the open once again. Nebraska Senator Chuck Hagel, a veteran, questioned whether Perle, who had not served in the military, would be willing "to be in the first wave of those who go into Baghdad." On Web sites and in Internet chat rooms, the epithet "chicken hawk," meaning a person who advocates war without having had experience in combat, was applied to Cheney, Wolfowitz and others in the Bush administration who were not veterans.[21] Some of the proponents of war unleashed attacks on opponents that were equally personalized and nasty. There were suggestions that Scowcroft's and Baker's views on Iraq were merely the result of friendships with the Saudis or the need for consulting contracts and that

Powell had somehow been brainwashed by the bureaucracy of the State Department.

In short order, Bush moved to end the bickering within his own party and administration. The president decided to take the Iraq issue to the United Nations. In a speech to the UN General Assembly on September 12, Bush announced that the United States would go to the Security Council for passage of a new resolution on Iraq. Saddam Hussein's regime was "a grave and growing danger," he said. If Iraq wanted peace, it should "disclose and remove or destroy" all weapons of mass destruction.[22]

Bush's decision appeared to be, on the surface, a victory for the secretary of state over the vice president. In the short run it was. The administration was taking the more deliberate course that Powell and Scowcroft had recommended, seeking a return of UN weapons inspectors before going to war with Iraq, rather than bypassing this step, as Cheney had proposed. Just as Bush had gone along with Powell after the September 11 attacks by deciding to focus on Afghanistan rather than Iraq, so now again the president was deferring any immediate action against Saddam Hussein while he sought international support.

Yet in a larger sense the result of the summer-long Iraq debate inside and outside the administration was a compromise that benefited the hawks. In order to win the argument for going to the United Nations, Powell and Scowcroft had felt compelled to make arguments that ultimately worked in favor of war. Both men had stressed that they were not opposed to the idea of regime change or to eventual American military intervention in Iraq. Scowcroft had said that if Iraq did not cooperate with UN weapons inspectors, that might give America a cause for war. Powell had argued that the issue wasn't whether to go to war with Iraq but how.

In fact, Bush was giving up very little by deciding to take the Iraq issue to the United Nations. At that time, in September 2002, the United States wasn't ready for war with Iraq anyway.[23] The Pentagon hadn't yet put enough troops into position for an invasion. Inside the administration the assumption was that Saddam Hussein wouldn't comply with the United Nations; he wouldn't come clean about the status of his programs for weapons of mass destruction. Moreover, if the United States wanted to walk away from the United Nations later on, when troops were in the region, it could still do so.

Meanwhile, going to the UN could help the administration to gain support for war not just overseas but at home as well. At the time polls consistently showed that the American people would support a war with Iraq only if it had the support of the international community. "Our most recent poll found that 64 per cent generally favor military action against Iraq, but that withers to 33 per cent if our allies do not join us," Andrew Kohut of the Pew Research Center for the People and the Press wrote in September. Such poll results help explain why the administration, when it eventually invaded Iraq, went to such extraordinary lengths to claim it was acting with the support of a broad international coalition, even though that flimsy coalition included many tiny nations and excluded some of America's oldest allies.

No one realized it then, but in retrospect, the wrangling among the Republicans in the summer of 2002 was America's only serious public debate about war with Iraq. The Democrats were badly divided and also hesitant to challenge Bush on Iraq; their arguments about whether to go to war never reached the intensity of the intra-Republican bickering. That fall, following a desultory debate, both houses of Congress voted by large margins to authorize Bush to "use the armed forces of the United States as he determines to be necessary and appropriate . . . against the continuing threat posed by Iraq."[24] After Bush and the Republicans gained seats in the November congressional elections, the Democrats became even less willing to question the administration's Iraq policy. The dissenting Republicans grew quieter too. Once the president agreed to go to the United Nations, Scowcroft, Baker and the other veterans of the first Bush administration became more guarded in their critiques of the administration. They never again mounted a direct public challenge on Iraq. Powell eventually closed ranks with the rest of the administration and supported military action to overthrow Saddam Hussein.

Overall, Bush's decision to seek United Nations authorization in September 2002 turned out to be a shrewd political move. Whether by design or not, it served the purpose of transforming the politics of the Iraq issue at a crucial moment. Over the following months, everyone waited to see what the United Nations would do about Iraq, and during this interval the passions in America subsided. By the time the Iraq debate picked up again, the parties to it had changed; the leading protagonists were not individuals or factions in Washington (Cheney versus Powell, Perle versus

Scowcroft, realists versus neoconservatives) but rather entire countries (America and Britain versus France, Germany and Russia). The Bush administration succeeded in internationalizing the debate and, in the process, defused opposition inside America.

In mid-September James Kelly, the assistant secretary of state for East Asia and the Pacific, followed with growing excitement in Washington a visit by Japanese Prime Minister Junichiro Koizumi to North Korea. Koizumi had been accorded a warm welcome, and North Korean leader Kim Jong Il had confessed, after years of denial, that his regime had years earlier kidnapped Japanese citizens. "I think he [Koizumi] will get a big bounce in the polls," Kelly said.[25]

Kelly had good reason to be following these events closely. He was himself quietly preparing to make the first visit to Pyongyang by anyone in the Bush administration. Powell and Armitage had persuaded the administration it was time to try to talk to North Korea and see whether it would be willing to abandon its nuclear weapons program. Officials in the Pentagon and in Vice President Cheney's office had voiced skepticism about the value of such a trip, arguing that it was too soon to achieve results and that there was no reason to talk with North Korea just for the sake of talking. The underlying disagreements within the administration were far deeper than Kelly's itinerary. Some of the Vulcans did not believe the United States should enter into an accommodation that might help perpetuate one of the world's most repressive regimes.

North Korea had been a continuing headache for the Bush administration, on matters big and small. There had been minor crises that never made it into the press. A team of American nuclear experts from a private company had been visiting North Korea for several years under a Department of Energy contract to help put the country's spent nuclear fuel into containers. In the fall of 2001 members of this team were suddenly barred from leaving North Korea; some were also relieved of sizable amounts of cash. After high-level intervention by the administration the visitors were freed.[26]

Of vastly greater consequence, U.S. intelligence agencies had reported that North Korea was continuing its nuclear weapons program. The Clinton administration believed it had obtained a freeze in this program under a 1994 agreement in which North Korea agreed to stop amassing plutonium, a crucial ingredient for manufacturing a nuclear weapon. However, U.S. intelligence reports, starting in 2000, concluded that North Korea was clandestinely seeking to enrich uranium, an alternative method for making a bomb.[27]

The Bush administration decided Kelly should inform North Korea that the United States knew of this secret uranium enrichment program and insist that it stop. Most officials expected North Korea would simply deny that the uranium program existed. In a way, such a denial would have suited all sides in the Bush administration's internal debates. The hawks would have been satisfied because a North Korean denial would have resulted in a protracted delay while the two sides argued the question of what North Korea was doing. The doves would have treated such a denial as merely the first step in a long process of bringing North Korea into the international community.

North Korea surprised everyone. When the talks opened in Pyongyang on October 3 and Kelly brought up the uranium program, North Korean officials issued no denial. Instead, the following day they informed Kelly that North Korea was "entitled to have nuclear weapons."[28]

After Kelly returned home with this news, the Bush administration at first kept it secret. Some officials hoped that the United States might quickly get China and Russia to persuade North Korea to abandon the program. But there was no immediate help, and within less than two weeks the story of North Korea's admission leaked out.[29]

The disclosure created a series of difficulties for the Bush administration. It threatened to distract attention away from Iraq just when the Bush team was trying to win domestic and international support for military action against Saddam Hussein. Even worse, North Korea's admission seemed to call into question the administration's rationale for moving against Iraq. The North Korea nuclear program was more advanced and more dangerous than Iraq's, and so, critics wondered, what was the justification for going to war in one case and not in another? To be sure, the existence of one advanced nuclear weapons program in North Korea didn't oblige the United States to accept the possibility of a second on in Iraq. But still: If America was going to tolerate North Korea's nuclear program, treating it with patience, then what was the sense of urgency about Iraq?

The underlying problem was that the new doctrines the Vulcans had been developing didn't work for North Korea in the way that they did for Iraq. North Korea wasn't a likely candidate for preemptive war because it had the capacity to attack South Korea and devastate the capital city of Seoul as soon as hostilities broke out. North Korea couldn't be turned into a demonstration project for the spread of democracy either. Some of the Vulcans hoped that in overthrowing Saddam Hussein, the United States could turn Iraq into a model for democracy that would transform Arab political culture and the politics of the entire Middle East, but in East Asia some governments were already democratic, and the rest wouldn't follow North Korea's example. Iraq lay in the middle of a troubled region and was intricately connected to it; North Korea sat in the middle of a thriving region from which it was isolated.

And so when it came to North Korea, the Vulcans temporized. While tending elsewhere in the world to push for bold approaches and quick, permanent solutions, when it came to North Korea, they elected to wait, even at the risk of allowing a dangerous nuclear weapons program to move forward. They still hoped that China and Russia might eventually help bring pressure to bear on Kim Jong Il, the North Korean leader; they yearned for the day when North Korea's desperate economic problems might force it to be more accommodating. Some of the Vulcans hoped, further, for a collapse and a change of regime in Pyongyang.

The Bush administration played for time, insisting there was no emergency. "It is not a crisis," said Colin Powell, giving voice to what became the administration's regular refrain on North Korea.[30] It was not a crisis, officials said, when North Korea restarted its nuclear reactors. It was not a crisis when North Korea forced international inspectors to leave the country. It was not a crisis when North Korea started to produce plutonium for nuclear weapons once again.

As a group the Vulcans had been preoccupied throughout their careers with military power. Yet North Korea was one case in which there seemed to be no good military solution, as they felt there was in Iraq. The Bush administration seemed to be searching for one but unable to find it. "North Korea is a threat, to be sure, but it's a different kind of threat, one that, for now at least, can be handled through diplomacy, and differently," said Rumsfeld.[31]

Throughout late 2002 and early 2003, as the Bush administration prepared to move against Iraq and as Pyongyang moved ahead with its nuclear program, the essence of America's uncertain, temporizing policy toward North Korea was encapsulated by that careful qualification from Rumsfeld; "for now, at least," the administration was leaving it up to the diplomats.

During the fall of 2002 Powell directed an American campaign of diplomacy at the United Nations to win approval for a tough new resolution on Iraq. Saddam Hussein suddenly announced he would allow UN weapons inspectors to return to Iraq for the first time in four years, but his last-minute concession did not deter the Security Council from further action. The United States sought wording that would authorize UN members to use "all necessary means," a euphemism for force, to make sure Saddam Hussein's regime gave up weapons of mass destruction. Other governments, led by France and Russia, balked, saying they wanted the UN first to carry out new, tougher weapons inspections and then afterward to hold a second round of discussions about the use of force.

The result, brokered by Powell and French Foreign Minister Dominique de Villepin, was a compromise. The United States abandoned the "all necessary means" wording that would have authorized war after this one single UN resolution. In return, France went along with language saying that if Iraq didn't yield its weapons of mass destruction, it could be declared in "material breach" of UN resolutions, including the one in which Iraq had promised to disarm at the end of the 1991 war. Those words gave the United States leeway to claim that it was using force against Iraq because the eleven-year-old cease-fire had broken down. On November 8, the UN Security Council approved this compromise by a vote of 15–0.[32]

At the time this UN resolution was widely portrayed as a triumph for Powell over the hawks within the administration. He had succeeded, it was said, in winning unanimous backing at the United Nations for the administration's Iraq policy, and at the same time he was credited with winning support in Washington for a multilateral approach in dealing with Iraq. Powell was said to have emerged once again as the dominant figure within the Bush foreign policy team. "Colin Powell has carried the day on what may be the most important national security debate of the Bush presidency," wrote Michael O'Hanlon of the Brookings Institution, in a column titled "How the Hard-Liners Lost." He concluded: "There is now a real possibility that the president, together with his secretary of state, will achieve a peaceful outcome in Iraq that rewrites the books on coercive diplomacy—as well as the early histories about who really calls the shots in this administration."[33]

This was a misjudgment of the Bush administration, of the secretary of state's role within it and arguably of Powell himself. The president and all the Vulcans, including Powell, were still pursuing the goal of a change in regime in Iraq. To be sure, the administration had decided to obtain as much support from the United Nations as possible, but there was never any abandonment of the broader goal of dislodging Saddam Hussein from power. Administration officials viewed the two goals of disarmament and regime change as inseparable because they assumed Saddam Hussein would never give up the programs for weapons of mass destruction they were convinced he possessed.

At one point in the midst of the UN debate Bush had declared, "Saddam Hussein must disarm himself—or, for the sake of peace, we will lead a coalition to disarm him."[34] Those vague words seemed to leave some room for the Iraqi leader to avoid war and still hold on to power. Yet in the Bush administration's internal deliberations there was never any delineation of exactly what actions by the Iraqi regime would qualify as disarmament and thus avert a military attack. Some, including Powell, believed that at least in theory, Saddam Hussein could remain in power by transforming his regime; he would have to comply with the international demands, disclose fully what weapons programs Iraq had developed and then dismantle them. But others in the administration thought that even if Saddam Hussein had walked outside his palace and handed over large amounts of chemical and biological weapons stocks, this would still not have been sufficient. "The belief was that as long as you had Saddam [in power], he could change his mind [about weapons of mass destruction]," Zalmay Khalilzad, who was handling Iraq policy for Rice's National Security Council, explained many months later. Asked what the administration's bottom-line condition was for refraining from military action, Khalilzad replied, "It was literally that Saddam Hussein would have to leave the country."[35]

Throughout the autumn of 2002 the Bush administration had been slowly and quietly moving troops and equipment to the areas around Iraq and making other military preparations. By late fall there were nearly sixty thousand American troops in the region.[36] Countries opposed to

war with Iraq, such as France, did not object; they believed that in sending these troops, the Bush administration was merely engaging in coercive diplomacy, putting some military muscle behind the new Security
Council resolution.[37]

As the New Year approached, there were clear signs that the Iraq resolution worked out by Powell and de Villepin had failed to bridge the
differences within the UN Security Council. Iraq submitted a twelve-
thousand-page report on its weapons programs that everyone believed
was full of omissions and based on old materials. The response of opponents of war such as France, Russia, China and Germany was to call for
additional inspections. In Washington, however, officials grew increasingly worried that inspections could be dragged out endlessly.

In late December the Pentagon began dispatching air, land and sea
forces to the Persian Gulf in large numbers. One deployment order was
signed on December 24, followed by several others. The military buildup
continued throughout the next ten weeks, until there were approximately
250,000 American troops—joined by 45,000 British personnel and
about 2,000 Australians—in the vicinity of Iraq.

By early January French officials had recognized that the American ar-
mada in the Gulf was becoming far bigger than was needed for coercive
diplomacy. The United States was openly preparing for war. Indeed, the
huge buildup seemed to close off other possibilities; if Bush were to reverse course and bring the forces home without a war, he would look silly
to the American public, and the United States would lose face overseas.
French President Jacques Chirac dispatched a top aide to Washington for
a private meeting with Rice. The aide, Maurice Gourdault-Montagne,
warned that a war could be dangerous, that it could destabilize other
Middle Eastern countries, trigger a wave of demonstrations and increase
recruitment for Al Qaeda. Point by point, Rice rejected his arguments.
War might carry these risks, but the status quo, with Saddam Hussein
still in power and in position to threaten his neighbors someday, wasn't
tolerable either, she replied.[38]

In mid-January de Villepin, the French foreign minister, requested a new
UN session, ostensibly to talk about terrorism. During the formal meetings de Villepin stuck to that subject. But at a press conference he delivered an impassioned warning against war with Iraq. "We believe today
that nothing justifies military intervention," he said. The diplomatic

battle lines were being drawn; the French were serving notice that they would oppose war and might veto any attempt to get UN authorization for it.

This French move later became known as the ambush. Powell's aides indicated the secretary of state, expecting a UN session on terrorism, had been taken by surprise by de Villepin's sudden, public break with the Bush administration on Iraq. Over the following days Powell's rhetoric on Iraq grew noticeably tougher. Instead of speaking about the importance of weapons inspections, he began to argue that the inspections wouldn't work. He warned of possible American military action and made clear he would support it.

News stories now began to suggest that Powell had been transformed into a hawk. This theme reverberated around the country and the world. In a typical exchange at a press conference in Beijing, a Chinese reporter asked the American secretary of state: "You now become a hawk in Iraqi issues and speak words just like Rumsfeld, so why [did] you change?" In a reply that could have summarized his entire career, Powell countered that "it's very unwise to stereotype people with one-word labels." For their part, French officials concluded that Powell had used the de Villepin incident as a pretext for taking a harder line. "Colin Powell knew that the decision [for war] was taken, and it was a golden opportunity to justify to the world that the dove was becoming a hawk," said one diplomat.[39]

In fact, Powell had never been the dove that he was assumed to be. Those who thought of him as a liberal on questions of foreign policy did not know his history: his work for Defense Secretary Caspar Weinberger and President Reagan, his key role in the decision to invade Panama. Throughout Powell's career, he had believed, at least as much as any other of the Vulcans, in the importance of American military power. His one caution, the one giving rise to his image as a dove, was that the United States should avoid military interventions that could be long, bloody or costly. But Powell's underlying rationale was ultimately pragmatic, not pacifistic; he was seeking to maintain and build the strength of the U.S. armed forces by avoiding another draining venture like the Vietnam War. To be sure, Powell had questioned the wisdom of America's 1991 war with Iraq and had actively campaigned against intervention in Bosnia. Yet the prospect of a second conflict with Iraq in 2003 was nothing like these earlier ventures. There was no danger of a stalemate; Powell had the military expertise to know that any new Iraq war fought along conventional lines would result in a quick American victory.

Other than his famous reservations about military intervention, Powell was not given to grand principles. He saw himself as primarily a problem solver, a pragmatist. He did not possess any sweeping vision for America's role in the world that would have served as an alternative to the Wolfowitz team's notion of America as an unchallengeable superpower. Nor did he put forward any substitute for Rice's National Security Strategy, with its doctrine of preemption. Throughout his career he regularly fell into the role of the good soldier; he might fight a few side battles inside the bureaucracy, but in the end he fell into line behind the presidents he served. This particular president wanted to oust Saddam Hussein from power, and in military terms the best time for an invasion was in the first three months of the year, before the weather in the Middle East grew swelteringly hot.

Powell had already said that he was not opposed in principle to military intervention in Iraq. He had favored the UN diplomacy as a part of the administration's attempt to win international support for a war to replace Saddam Hussein. The compromise he had negotiated at the United Nations had been a vague one; Powell viewed the UN resolution passed in November as a way of rounding up international support for regime change in Iraq, while the French and their allies viewed the same resolution as a substitute for war and regime change. By mid-January the compromise was falling apart. Countries like France and Germany made clear they were not going to support military action in Iraq. And so Powell began shifting focus. He made it clear that the United States was going to move against Saddam Hussein with as many allies as it could get, but that it was going to move, one way or another.

In February, as war approached, the Vulcans laid another cornerstone in the construction of a new American foreign policy. The administration embraced the cause of democracy in the Middle East. A post-Saddam Iraq was to serve as a model for political liberalization throughout the whole region.

In a speech to the American Enterprise Institute, Bush voiced the hope that the liberation of Iraq could help transform the Middle East: "A new regime in Iraq would serve as a dramatic and inspiring example of freedom for other nations in the region. It is presumptuous and insulting to suggest that a whole region of the world or the one-fifth of humanity that is Muslim is somehow untouched by the most basic aspirations of life."[40] Bush had first touched on this theme the previous year, when he proposed democracy specifically for the Palestinians. Now he was explicitly broadening the idea to apply to other undemocratic governments in the region—among them Saudi Arabia and Egypt—that had for decades supported American policy while, at the same time, repressing dissent inside their borders.

Bush's speech was a triumph for neoconservatives in the administration, such as Wolfowitz. They had been espousing the cause of spreading democracy overseas with increasing conviction ever since the 1986 "people's power" revolution in the Philippines. Whereas realists such as Scowcroft maintained that supporting authoritarian governments was a necessary component of American foreign policy, the neoconservatives countered that such a policy was harmful in the long run; democratic governments were more stable. At first the neoconservatives had focused on democracy in East Asia, as the Philippines, South Korea and Taiwan all opened up their political systems. Now the neoconservatives were transporting these same democratic ideals to the Middle East. Intellectually the neoconservatives had been influenced by the ideas of Bernard Lewis, the scholar who had written of the failings of political institutions in the Islamic world. Politically, they were responding to the September 11 attacks, which had demonstrated the negative aspects of America's support for undemocratic regimes like Saudi Arabia's.

In calling for democratic change in the Middle East, the neoconservatives had come full circle. In the late 1970s leading neoconservatives such as Jeane Kirkpatrick had passionately criticized the Carter administration for pushing the shah of Iran to make his regime more open and democratic. In that era, greater tolerance for autocratic regimes had not been some obscure or marginal issue for the neoconservatives; it had been an important theme for the movement, and one with far-reaching political implications. When the neoconservatives gravitated to the Republicans for the first time in the Reagan administration, Kirkpatrick had been in the vanguard of that change, and Reagan's praise for Kirkpatrick's views on the shah of Iran had been one of the main factors in her willingness to switch parties.

Now, two decades later, the neoconservatives were proposing for the entire Middle East the same sort of democratic reforms they had once found objectionable when applied to the shah's Iran. What had changed? First, the cold war had ended; that had removed the argument that America should support authoritarian allies for the larger cause of combating the Soviet Union. Second, America had become so militarily powerful that it was no longer dependent on the support of authoritarian regimes to the extent that it had been in the 1970s.

The underlying interest for the neoconservatives, which remained constant over the quarter century period, was the advancement of American military power and ideals in such a way as to defeat the principal adversaries of the United States: the Soviet Union in the cold war and terrorism and so-called rogue nations in the George W. Bush administration. In the 1970s that cause, overcoming America's biggest enemy, entailed supporting the shah of Iran as a partner against communism. In the 1980s it meant withdrawing support from Ferdinand Marcos in the Philippines because his repressive regime had raised the specter of a Communist takeover in a country that housed two large American military installations. In 2003 it meant supporting democracy in the Middle East as a wedge against terrorism.

Director of Central Intelligence George Tenet had planned to go to the Middle East in early February 2003, but Powell wouldn't let him go.

The secretary of state was in the midst of a last concerted drive to win the support of America's European allies and the UN Security Council for military action against Iraq. On February 5 he was scheduled to give the Security Council an overview of U.S. intelligence concerning Iraq's weapons of mass destruction. Powell was unwilling simply to go to New York City and read what the U.S. intelligence community had written for him. Powell requested that Tenet postpone his overseas trip, come to the United Nations and sit directly behind him, in such a way that Tenet's head could be seen on television nodding in agreement with Powell's presentation. As director of central intelligence Tenet supervised not only the CIA but all the agencies in the U.S. intelligence community. The secretary of state was insisting that Tenet give his personal imprimatur to all the intelligence information Powell gave to the United Nations about Iraq.[41]

When the day came, Powell outlined the American intelligence in detail, complete with reconnaissance photographs of Iraqi facilities and transcripts of intercepted conversations in which Iraqi officials talked about hiding things from the UN weapons inspectors. The presentation had little impact overseas. Those who were opposed to the use of force were skeptical about the American claims, and they argued that in any event the U.S. intelligence pointed to the need not for war but for more aggressive UN inspections. Nine days later, in an impassioned speech to a cheering UN Security Council chamber, de Villepin grandiosely proclaimed that France "has never ceased to stand upright in the face of history and before mankind." France was hardly alone in opposing American military intervention in Iraq; while it took the lead, France was working in close cooperation with Germany and Russia.[42]

The American diplomacy was made more complicated by the secretary of defense. During this period Rumsfeld displayed his career-long penchant for confronting opponents head-on, challenging their core values and assumptions. He seemed incapable of the sort of polite obfuscations, evasions and repetitions on which diplomacy is usually based.

In a press conference for foreign correspondents in Washington, Rumsfeld belittled France and Germany and their aspirations to be the leading countries in a united Europe. Although the French and Germans opposed America's policy on Iraq, Rumsfeld said, they did not represent Europe but merely "old Europe." Europe's center of gravity, he noted, was shifting eastward with the addition of new members from what was once the Soviet bloc. "[If] you look at vast numbers of other countries in Europe, they're not with France and Germany on this, they're with the United States," he concluded.[43] Those words contained a germ of truth (several European governments supported the United States, at least to a degree) and a dollop of exaggeration ("vast numbers"). Most important, Rumsfeld's remarks represented a considerable departure from America's longstanding support for the unity of Europe. They were all the more remarkable because what seemed like a new American policy toward Europe—that is, an attempt to foster divisions within it—was put forward not by the president or secretary of state but by the secretary of defense.

At a press briefing a few weeks later Rumsfeld suggested that the United States could go to war against Iraq without British troops if necessary. "To the extent they [British forces] are able to participate, . . . that would obviously be welcomed," the secretary of defense said. "To the extent they're not, there are workarounds and they would not be involved, at least in that phase of it."[44] Those words were devastating for British Prime Minister Tony Blair, who was at that time trying to persuade his

Parliament that Britain should join in the military action because the United States desperately needed the help of its old ally. A British journalist who was accompanying the British prime minister that month recorded the impact of Rumsfeld's words on Blair: "To be stabbed by Britain's traditional French rival is one thing. To be kicked by his transatlantic ally, to be told that all his effort to win . . . a parliamentary majority at home is a waste of time; that is something else."[45] After Blair made two late-night phone calls to Bush expressing his dismay, Rumsfeld issued a written clarification, saying he hadn't meant what his words had clearly implied.

Bush and the Vulcans had pledged during the presidential campaign to restore the strength of U.S. alliances. But as the Iraq debate reached its climax at the United Nations, America's relationships with some of its leading European allies reached a nadir. On February 17, a holiday in Washington, Vice President Cheney met French Ambassador Jean-David Levitte in his residence and confronted him. "Is France an ally or a foe?" he asked. Levitte insisted France was still an ally. Cheney demurred. "We have many reasons to conclude that you are not really a friend or an ally," the vice president said.[46]

The final weeks of maneuvering at the United Nations were an admixture of paradox, intrigue and histrionics. Throughout the fall the Bush administration had argued that there was no need for a second Security Council resolution authorizing the use of force; the American position had consistently been that existing UN resolutions gave all the authorization that was necessary. But in February the United States decided to reverse course and seek approval for a second UN resolution specifically authorizing military action. The Bush administration did so largely at the behest of Britain. Seeking to defuse opposition at home, Blair had promised that he would go back to the United Nations to seek new approval before going to war.

Meanwhile, France, which had all along insisted on the necessity of a second UN resolution before military action against Iraq, did an about-face in the opposite direction. The French ambassador, on instructions from Chirac, secretly went to the White House; he argued that the United States should abandon its attempt to win approval of a second UN resolution and, if America was determined to do so, go to war without it.[47] French officials explained that they wanted to avoid a bitter, damaging fight in the United Nations. What the French left unsaid was that in clandestinely seeking to persuade the United States to go to war without the second UN resolution, they were moving to undercut Blair, who needed to go back to the UN. In effect, then, the last weeks of diplomacy before the Iraq War brought forth a new diplomatic "Battle for Britain" between Washington and Paris. The United States was seeking to retain Britain's support, while France was attempting to bolster Blair's domestic opposition and thus perhaps to separate Britain from the United States.

On the night of March 6, 2003, in a private meeting at the Waldorf-Astoria Hotel in New York, Powell and de Villepin waged what amounted to the climactic prewar showdown between the United States and France. De Villepin couched what he was about to say as a matter of diplomatic courtesy. I don't want there to be any surprises, the French foreign minister told the American secretary of state. France, he said, was determined to veto a second UN resolution on Iraq. Don't think that this is just a negotiating ploy, he told Powell. France wasn't bluffing; it would cast its veto.

Thank you, Dominique, replied Powell. And you need to understand that even if you do veto the second resolution, we're going to use 1441 (the first UN resolution) and if Saddam Hussein doesn't change course at the last minute, we're going to go ahead against him.[48]

The French had signaled their unalterable opposition; the Americans had made clear their determination to go to war against Iraq.

The Bush administration pressed ahead in its pursuit of a new UN resolution. Powell repeatedly expressed optimism that the United States could win the support of undecided Security Council members. On March 9 he was still insisting there was a "strong chance" that at least a majority of the fifteen Security Council members would support the United States.[49]

The following day, however, with six of the fifteen members of the UN Security Council still undecided, Chirac announced in public that France would oppose the new U.S.-British proposal "whatever the circumstances." After Chirac's declaration America and Britain found it impossible to win over the undecided countries. A week later U.S. and British officials gave in, conceding that they were unable to win approval for a new UN resolution.

Both Bush and Blair blamed Chirac. They argued that when the French president came out clearly in opposition to the second UN resolution, he effectively ended any chance the Americans and British had had for winning over those countries on the Security Council that hadn't yet taken sides—because these governments then concluded there was no point in trying to decide whether they should support a resolution the French could veto. For their part, French officials later claimed that Chirac had been quietly urged on by leaders such as Mexico's Vincente Fox, who didn't want to be forced to cast a vote for or against the United States in a showdown at the United Nations.[50]

For American diplomacy, the six-month venture at the United Nations was a remarkable failure. The Bush administration had come into office promising to give new emphasis to ties with Mexico and, more generally, Latin America, but had failed to win the backing of either Mexico or Chile, the two Latin American countries on the Security Council. Similarly, Rice had sought to forge a new American relationship with Russian President Vladimir Putin, but at the United Nations, Russia stood with France and Germany in opposition to the United States. Powell and Armitage had labored to develop strong relations with Pakistan's President Pervez Musharraf, but Pakistan wouldn't come out in support the American position either.

Some of the Vulcans' most fundamental assumptions had been erroneous. Since the late 1990s, Wolfowitz had argued that if the United States showed greater resolve in dealing with Iraq, America's friends and allies would support it. When governments in Europe and the Middle East had voiced opposition to America's Iraq policies, Wolfowitz had contended that what they said in public shouldn't be taken at face value; the allies and friends were simply unsure America had the stamina for a successful campaign against Saddam Hussein. But in reality, as the Bush administration took an ever-stronger stand on Iraq, friends and allies overseas didn't rush to America's side; instead, contrary to Wolfowitz's prediction, tougher policies produced ever-greater opposition.

"All our goals in Eurasia will depend on America strengthening the alliances that sustain our influence," Bush had declared during his run for the presidency, in a speech drafted for him by the Vulcans.[51] The Bush administration's campaign at the United Nations so seriously eroded America's main European alliance and so badly damaged its influence overseas as to raise questions about whether the whole UN venture had been worth the extraordinary costs.

For the Vulcans, there would be no accommodation, no deal on Iraq, any more than there had been any compromise with the Soviet Union in the 1970s when they were in the early stages of their careers. Diplomacy was not their strongest suit. They would rely ultimately on American military power.

On March 17, within an hour after the United States conceded the defeat of its diplomacy at the United Nations, President Bush met at the White House with Rumsfeld and Wolfowitz to review military preparations for an invasion. Two days later, on the evening of March 19, he announced the start of Operation Iraqi Freedom. "Now that the conflict has come, the only way to limit its duration is to apply decisive force," the president declared.[52]

The Bush administration unleashed against Iraq the awesome military power that all the Vulcans had helped to develop in the decades since America's defeat in Vietnam. They put this military strength to work on behalf of their vision: the goal of an America whose values and ideals would prevail throughout the world because the United States was so powerful no other country could afford the costs of competing with it and no one would even begin to try.

Conclusion

As it turned out, both sides in the acrimonious debate over war with Iraq were wrong, and in serious ways. Opponents had warned that an invasion of Iraq would lead to a cataclysm in the surrounding countries in the Middle East. They argued that an American-led war would trigger an explosion of demonstrations throughout the region, threatening the stability of other Arab governments. Iraq might attack Israel, and Israel might counter with nuclear weapons, some opponents had said.

These were among the most prominent arguments advanced by the opponents. Yet few, if any, of the dire consequences they had predicted came to pass. Once the invasion started, the American and British forces (together with a few tiny contingents from other countries to provide the fig leaf of a broad "coalition") managed to seize Baghdad and oust Saddam Hussein from power in a campaign that lasted three weeks; it took another three weeks to complete major military operations elsewhere in Iraq. None of the other governments in the regime fell; none, it seemed, were significantly destabilized by the war. Iraq didn't lash out at Israel or bring it into the conflict. There was no nuclear Armageddon. Iraqi forces didn't use biological or chemical weapons against the allied troops. For the invading forces, casualties were remarkably light. By the time President Bush proclaimed victory on May 1, only 138 Americans had been killed, fewer than in the four-day Desert Storm operation of 1991.

Afterward some of the opponents of war attempted to explain away the fact that the parade of horribles they had forecast was mostly imaginary. French officials, after warning repeatedly that an invasion of Iraq would set off a paroxysm of rage in other Arab countries that could destabilize the entire Middle East, later said these consequences might eventually have transpired if the war had not ended so quickly. They hadn't anticipated that the American and British forces would achieve such an easy victory in Iraq, French officials explained.[1] If this was indeed the reasoning, then French officials seriously misjudged the military situation. While denouncing American power, they had also managed to underestimate its capabilities, as applied to modern conventional warfare.

But while the opponents of war had erred, so certainly had the most fervent American proponents of the invasion of Iraq. After the war ended, many of the forecasts of the hawks proved inaccurate. They had envisioned that once Saddam Hussein and a handful of his top aides were removed from power, the rest of the country would rise up in joy at Iraq's liberation. Just as decapitation of the Iraqi leadership had been a central element in U.S. military planning, so too had it been a key part of the strategy for postwar reconstruction. The aim was not to rebuild Iraq from the bottom up but to let Iraqis take over, once they were freed of the onus of Saddam Hussein and his top aides. The proponents of war had believed that Iraq possessed a civil service and a civil society that would keep the country running and transfer loyalties over to a new, more representative Iraqi leadership.

But Iraq failed to conform to the hawks' prewar conceptions. "Some important assumptions turned out to underestimate the problem," Paul Wolfowitz gingerly acknowledged three months after the end of the war.[2] The hold of Saddam Hussein's Baath party over Iraqi society was far deeper and more entrenched than the Bush administration had anticipated. Iraqi army and police forces were unwilling to work for or with the Americans. As a result, American occupation forces found themselves dealing with a fearful and suspicious Iraqi population, one quite unlike the cheering nation the hawks had suggested would turn out to greet the invaders.

When President Bush declared an end to major combat operations in his May 1 speech aboard the USS *Abraham Lincoln,* he asserted that "the battle of Iraq is one victory in a war on terrorism that began on September 11, 2001."[3] Yet the victory was incomplete. In the following months, American forces confronted a campaign of armed resistance in Iraq that produced more casualties than the war itself. Secretary of Defense Donald Rumsfeld, who as White House chief of staff in the final moments of the Vietnam War had mourned that the conflict had been "marked by so many lies and evasions," responded to America's postwar situation in Iraq with evasions of his own. For more than two weeks he tried to maintain that American troops were not confronting a guerrilla war; finally the U.S. military commander in Iraq, General John P. Abizaid, acknowledged that his troops were dealing with a "classic guerrilla-type" conflict.[4]

Still more at variance with the hawks' prewar predictions, the allied forces that took control of Iraq were unable to find the weapons of mass destruction that the Bush administration had repeatedly said Saddam Hussein's forces possessed. The risk of Iraqi weapons of mass destruction had constituted the principal justification put forward for war as the Bush administration sought support for the invasion both overseas and at home. Yet months of intensive searching uncovered no stocks of chemical or biological weapons. Nor did the administration find evidence that Iraq had a large-scale, active nuclear weapons program in the years before the invasion, much less that it was moving rapidly (in the fashion of North Korea) toward acquisition of a nuclear bomb. David Kay, the former UN weapons inspector appointed to run the CIA's postwar search for weapons of mass destruction in Iraq, told Congress in October 2003 that Iraq's nuclear program had been in only "the very most rudimentary" state.[5]

Overall, the Bush administration faced a far more troubled occupation of Iraq than the one for which it had planned. It found itself devoting more American forces to postwar Iraq than it had expected and for longer periods of time. In November 2003, six months after Bush's triumphal May 1 declaration that major combat had ended, approximately 130,000 American troops were in Iraq, confronting regular armed attacks. By that time, the number of American deaths in the postwar occupation was nearing 300, more than twice as many as during the war itself. The costs of the occupation to the Pentagon were running four billion dollars a month, and Congress was obliged to authorize approximately seventy billion dollars in additional spending for military operations and reconstruction in Iraq.

Those who had forecast that the overthrow of Saddam Hussein would produce a burst of exhilaration across Iraq later argued that this did not take place because many Iraqis were intimidated; they were fearful of the continuing power of the underground Baath organization or even haunted by the specter that Saddam Hussein might someday return to power. That argument was plausible enough. But it pointed to another error: a misunderstanding of Saddam Hussein's brutal regime, the breadth of its hold over the Iraqi people and the effort required to replace it with a new Iraqi leadership. Just as the opponents of an invasion of Iraq had overstated the consequences of war upon the rest of the Middle East, so the proponents of an invasion had overestimated the impact inside Iraq itself of an allied military victory.

The decision to invade Iraq had encapsulated virtually all the key elements in the Vulcans' views of the world. It reflected the foreign policy ideas and themes that the Vulcans had gradually developed over the previous three decades.

The first, of course, was their belief in the centrality and the efficacy of American military power, which they had worked to restore and build up ever since the defeat in Vietnam. In 2003 the Bush administration managed to mount a full-scale invasion, with relatively limited outside help, in the Persian Gulf, a region where in the 1970s the United States had had barely a token military presence and where it had once been forced to rely on a partnership with Iran (or, for a time, Iraq). No other military operation could have better demonstrated the thirty-year rise in American military capabilities or the extent to which the United States had come to rely on those capabilities as America's principal tool in dealing with the world.

Second, the war against Iraq reflected the Vulcans' belief in America as a force for good around the globe. Others might worry that war and invasion would cause as many harmful effects as beneficial ones or that the liberal ideals of freedom and democracy might not easily take root in a place like Iraq. On the whole, the Vulcans didn't worry about such things; indeed, they portrayed Iraq as merely the first step in an effort to spread democracy throughout the Middle East. They viewed this larger campaign against the backdrop of their own experiences in dealing with Eastern Europe and East Asia. Skeptics had said South Korea and Taiwan weren't ready for democracy either, the Vulcans pointed out—until it turned out that they were. (One difference, however, was that democracy didn't arrive in these Asian countries as the result of a military invasion.)

The third theme was the Vulcans' extraordinarily optimistic assessment of American capabilities. This was a factor separate from the belief in liberal values or in American benevolence. It was possible to agree in principle upon the need for democracy in Iraq or in the rest of the Middle East yet also to conclude that achieving that objective might be beyond America's resources. The United States might not have the money, the troops, the commitment or the staying power to accomplish its aims; its goals might be too ambitious for its budgets or its military deployments. Once again the Vulcans weren't dissuaded by such obstacles. They had been arguing for thirty years that America was not in decline and that it had vastly more power in reserve for international affairs than others believed.

Fourth, the decision to invade epitomized the Vulcans' reluctance to enter into agreements or accommodations with other countries. Despite the campaign speeches about the importance of alliances, it was, in their view, far better to have few or no allies than to make a deal that would constrain America's freedom of action overseas. Indeed, Rumsfeld had momentarily suggested that the United States would be willing, if not eager, to go to war without the backing of Britain, its closest ally and partner in international affairs. Even Colin Powell, the most accommodation-minded of the Vulcans, had no hesitation in endorsing a military invasion that several of America's most important allies (as well as other leading members of the UN Security Council) had opposed.

Finally, the war in Iraq served as a demonstration of the Vulcans' commitment to the strategy Paul Wolfowitz's Pentagon staff had drafted at the end of the cold war: America would build up its military power to such an extent that it would be fruitless and financially crippling for any other country to hope to compete with it. The first draft of that 1992 Pentagon report spoke of the need for the United States to block the emergence of any rival power. The later version, rewritten by Wolfowitz's aide Scooter Libby and released in early 1993 under Dick Cheney's name, had spoken more vaguely of the need to "shape the future security environment." In going to war against Iraq and in attempting to democratize the Middle East, the George W. Bush administration was providing a classic example of what that concept meant. The internal logic was simple. Terrorism had emerged as America's principal security threat; terrorism arose primarily in the Middle East; therefore, "shaping the future security environment" meant transforming the entire politics and social fabric of the Middle East.

Sometimes the Vulcans claimed that the only history of consequence for understanding their decision to invade Iraq was the terrorism of September 11. "For me, September 11 was a transforming event, in the sense of seeing that terrorism had the potential to kill not just three thousand people, but three hundred thousand or three million," said Wolfowitz.[6]

There is no doubt that the attacks of September 11 had a profound impact upon the Vulcans, as they did on the rest of the nation. The question was, What shaped the Vulcans' distinctive response to that trauma? Not all American leaders would have reacted in the same way as the Vulcans; not all foreign policy teams would have carried out a war on terrorism that led, with ever-greater determination, to the invasion of Iraq. What were the instincts, the attitudes, the experiences that lay beneath the Vulcans' decisions and choices after September 11? The answers to such questions could be found in the careers and ideas of the Vulcans over the previous thirty years. Much as they sometimes denied it, the Vulcans were influenced by their own history.

The invasion of Iraq, by any reckoning the most significant foreign policy decision of the Bush administration, affected the individual members of the Vulcans in different ways.

The war turned Donald Rumsfeld once again into America's dominant public figure, even more so than during the military operations in Afghanistan of 2001. Seizing the Pentagon podium for his near-daily news conferences, Rumsfeld held forth with his usual confidence. "Was there ever a better Washington briefer than Donald Rumsfeld?" asked a *Washington Post* correspondent.[7] Uniformed military leaders remained in Rumsfeld's shadow; none of them was allowed to occupy center stage in the way that Colin Powell had as chairman of the Joint Chiefs of Staff or in the fashion that Norman Schwarzkopf had during Operation Desert Storm.

For a brief period, a few days into the war, Rumsfeld appeared to be in serious trouble. When American forces slowed down in their drive to Baghdad and it appeared the United States might be heading into a tough, protracted campaign, critics accused Rumsfeld of developing a faulty war plan. Some, including retired military leaders, complained that the secretary of defense had allowed an invasion that was undermanned. "I know a lot more about fighting than he [Rumsfeld] does," said General Barry McCaffrey. ". . . The problem is that they chose to attack 250 miles into Iraq with one armored division and no rear-area security and no second front."[8] But within only a few more days, American forces drove on to Baghdad, Iraqi resistance vanished and the attacks on Rumsfeld's war plan quickly ceased.

Rumsfeld's breezy combativeness got him into further difficulty at the end of the war. When looting broke out and Baghdad deteriorated into chaos, the secretary of defense reacted casually to the news, treating it as the expectable by-product of war and the end of a repressive regime. "Stuff happens!" Rumsfeld quipped. "It's untidy, and freedom's untidy."[9] Thirty-two years earlier, as a young domestic policy official in the Nixon administration, Rumsfeld had first sought to become involved in foreign policy by volunteering to take charge of postwar reconstruction in Southeast Asia. Now, as secretary of defense, he displayed considerably less interest in what happened after the war than in the war itself and in the task of developing American military power for future wars.

Serving as defense secretary in the Bush administration was, for Rumsfeld, the role of a lifetime. In the 1970s Rumsfeld had run the Pentagon in an era when the United States was struggling to recover from military defeat, when there were no new wars and when American foreign policy was set largely by the State Department. This time he was in charge of a Pentagon that was vigorously engaged in military operations overseas and had become the driving force in American foreign policy. The Pentagon gave Rumsfeld a chance to demonstrate both his skills in dealing with the press and his considerable experience in shaking up and cowing large organizations. The job of defense secretary also offered him endless bureaucratic battles to wage and a phalanx of powerful personal and institutional interests to challenge.

He had never achieved his early ambition of becoming president of the United States. Rumsfeld's destiny was to become America's consummate war minister, a cabinet secretary who sometimes appeared more powerful than a president. His performance in the second Bush administration would have warmed the heart of his old boss Richard Nixon.

The American invasion of Iraq represented something less than a personal triumph for Colin Powell. The American military strategy demonstrated that the Pentagon was beginning to turn away from Powell's approach to warfare; the emphasis of the Iraqi operation was not upon the application of overwhelming force but upon speed and mobility. So too the occupation of Iraq that followed the war seemed to contradict the cautious principles that Powell and his boss Defense Secretary Caspar Weinberger had set down in the 1980s: a long-term commitment of American troops without any clear plan for when or how the operation might end.

Powell was the member of the Vulcans who, during his long career, served in more top foreign policy jobs in the U.S. government than anyone else. Yet he had the misfortune to take on the job of secretary of state within an administration where the task of diplomacy was often greeted with profound mistrust. Powell's considerable skills were those of a problem solver and a manager. He never pretended to be a visionary. Yet in the wake of the September 11 attacks it sometimes seemed as if the job of secretary of state required a visionary. America was in the process of redefining its relations with the rest of the world. Others in the administration were putting forth their own well-articulated visions of a world in which the United States relied above all on its military strength. Powell offered no clear alternative.

Powell's role was a curious one, shared by a handful of others at other times and places. He was the loyal henchman/suspected opponent, the top-level official who, while carrying out the policies of a leader, also seeks to reshape and moderate those policies in such a way that they are more acceptable to the public. Powell was the American version of Zhou Enlai, the Chinese premier and second-in-command to Mao Zedong. Like Zhou, Powell was most admired by the opponents of the government for which he worked, and most intensely disliked by the regime's most zealous supporters. Both factions tended to assume that he was secretly opposing the very policies that in public he could be seen to be carrying out. Yet Powell never opposed the policies strongly enough to resign, and he continued to enjoy the support of the leader for whom he toiled.

As the war in Iraq drew to a close, former House Speaker Newt Gingrich launched a public campaign against Powell's State Department, accusing it of undermining the president's policies and of failing to win support for the United States overseas. "America cannot lead the world with a broken instrument of diplomacy," declared Gingrich, who enjoyed long-standing ties to both Cheney and Rumsfeld. Deputy Secretary of State Richard Armitage offered a memorably savage response: Gingrich, he said, was "off his meds and out of therapy."[10]

The White House kept its distance from this acrimony, but it demonstrated how in the wake of the Iraq War, the hawks, who since the earliest days of the administration had campaigned against Powell mostly in private, became increasingly willing to challenge him in public.

Powell had played a vital role in the Vulcans' history. He had been one of the leading figures in the decades-long process of restoring American military power after Vietnam. Yet as he neared the end of his public career, it remained unclear the extent to which his legacy, his message of caution and overpowering force, would endure.

As always, Condoleezza Rice managed skillfully to stay out of the crossfire. During the first Bush administration Rice had usually been able to persuade both factions in the running disputes over Soviet policy that she was on their side. In the second Bush administration once again she avoided too close an identification with any particular faction or ideology.

Those who opposed the invasion of Iraq directed their ire primarily at others in the administration, toward Cheney, Rumsfeld, Wolfowitz and the president himself. They rarely paid as much attention to Rice, despite the fact that as national security adviser, she had quietly played at least as significant a role as any of the others. She had been the prime mover behind the drafting of a new National Security Strategy that laid the framework for a preventive war. She had served as the White House coordinator and as the president's closest adviser, throughout the entire Iraq operation. And she emerged after the war as the principal spokesman for the administration's expansive vision of its mission in the Middle East. Rice began to speak of the need for a "generational commitment" by America and its allies to bring about the political transformation of the entire region.[11]

Months after the end of the war Rice's performance as national security adviser was called into question when it turned out she had allowed the president to give the American people faulty intelligence information about Iraq's weapons of mass destruction.[12] But the criticisms did not seem to take hold. Rice, the youngest of the Vulcans, seemed to be in a position to carry their legacy into some future administration.

In contrast with Condoleezza Rice, Paul Wolfowitz could never manage to operate primarily behind the scenes. He had been too willing for too long to stake out strong positions in public. Instead, Wolfowitz became the administration official most closely identified with the invasion of Iraq. In the midst of the invasion Americans working in the war zone came up with the nickname Wolfowitz of Arabia for the deputy secretary of defense;[13] the phrase captured the degree of intensity, passion and even, it sometimes seemed, romantic fervor with which he pursued the goals of overthrowing Saddam Hussein and bringing democracy to the Middle East.

Yet despite such stereotypes, his underlying motivations remained an enigma. Did Wolfowitz support U.S. military power as a tool in the larger goal of furthering American ideals? Or was it the reverse? Was his invocation of the cause of democracy the method by which he advanced the larger goal of advancing American power? Wolfowitz portrayed his vision of U.S. foreign policy as the outgrowth of idealism, in contrast with the strategic thinking of Henry Kissinger and others. The idealism was heartfelt, yet an examination of Wolfowitz's long career also showed that his idealism usually followed along behind hard-nosed judgments about American interests. Wolfowitz had been among the first to warn about the dangers of Iraq, yet it is worth remembering that his late-1970s interest in the country arose from the fear that some regime hostile to U.S. interests might come to dominate the oil reserves of the Persian Gulf. These same strategic concerns continued to affect Wolfowitz's thinking over the following quarter century; only later did the ideals of freedom and democracy enter into the calculations.

Reflecting on his long career, Wolfowitz had remarked that in the early 1980s, when he switched his focus for a time from the Middle East to East Asia, "it was like walking out of some oppressive stuffy room into sunlight and fresh air." In the Middle East, he said, people knew only how to create problems; in East Asia, people knew how to solve them.[14] But for Wolfowitz, there was no permanent escape from that stuffy room. After the American decision to invade Iraq, Wolfowitz's future, more than any other of the Vulcans, seemed to be tied to the outcome of events in the Middle East.

Richard Armitage did not play any central role in the invasion of Iraq. As the war progressed, he went about his work at the State Department, helping run the organization for Powell, managing its budgets and personnel and other administrative matters. He took part in the interagency meetings. But the man who had once hoped to run the Pentagon for the Bush administration watched the new military operations from a distance.

It was a paradox. Armitage was the one Vulcan who best exemplified, in his own life and upbringing, the spirit of an American warrior. He had once been in fact precisely the sort of soldier that the Bush administration hoped to send to Iraq. Armitage knew about special forces and about covert operations, not through Washington meetings but from slogging through the villages of Vietnam. He had volunteered for combat duty again and again, growing to love the country in which he fought. He had opposed a negotiated settlement and bitterly resented the American military withdrawal from Vietnam. Now, three decades later, Armitage was relegated to the sidelines in a new military venture for which, it seemed, his experience would make him useful.

On the surface Armitage's relegation to a minor role stemmed from his friendship with and loyalty to Powell. That was what had cost him a job at the Pentagon when the Bush administration was being formed; that was the underlying cause of the frosty relationship between Rumsfeld and Armitage. Yet the problem also went deeper: Armitage didn't quite fit in with the top levels of the administration. He wasn't as coolly detached as Cheney, as ruthless as Rumsfeld, as cerebral as Wolfowitz or as politically adept as Rice. He was a Republican centrist surrounded by conservatives.

Throughout the summer and fall of 2003 the United States struggled to suppress an increasingly tough guerrilla campaign against its occupation in Iraq. Within the top ranks of the Bush administration, Armitage was the single official with hands-on experience in guerrilla warfare; he had in fact served within the military as a counterinsurgency instructor. Yet once again his experience was not put to use.

Armitage was no more a visionary than Powell was; like Powell, he wasn't prepared to offer grand conceptions of the role America should play in the world. In fact, Armitage said in the summer of 2003 that by the end of a single four-year term as deputy secretary of state he would probably have run out of new ideas altogether. He was making plans to leave the Bush administration after the end of a single four-year term.[15]

The invasion of Iraq was in many ways Dick Cheney's war, just as the George W. Bush administration had been in some respects Cheney's administration. Within the top ranks the vice president had been the leading proponent of a war to oust Saddam Hussein from power. Inside the administration Cheney had also been the most forceful in arguing that Iraq possessed weapons of mass destruction. In the year before the start of the war Cheney had made numerous visits to the CIA to talk with its analysts about the evidence of Iraq's involvement in weapons programs. It was a remarkable, hands-on role for a vice president of the United States.[16]

Serving in the George W. Bush administration permitted Cheney to give much freer vent to his own determinedly conservative views than he ever had in the Ford administration or the first Bush administration. His unique talent, as he recognized early in his career, was to convey a sense of soothing solemnity; Cheney could make whatever he said sound so obvious, reasonable and self-evident that listeners often didn't stop to question it. His cool demeanor and his aura of chamber of commerce prudence were the traits that had once caused congressional reporters to describe Cheney inaccurately (to his own irritation) as a "moderate," while labeling others whose views and voting records were similar as conservatives. In fact, the higher Cheney rose, the more conservative he became.

Cheney had discovered in the mid-1990s that he was unable to run a successful campaign for president himself. He didn't have enough funds, name recognition or popular appeal. But Cheney had managed to link up with George W. Bush, who proved to be the most proficient fund-raiser in the history of American politics. The result of that partnership was to give Cheney a large part of what he had sought from the job of president (a dominant role in running the federal government) while sparing him from the parts of the job he liked the least (the ceremonial and symbolic aspects of the presidency).

When it came to military and intelligence issues, Cheney, as a former defense secretary and member of the House Intelligence Committee, wielded extraordinary influence in the administration's back room decision making. He had his own staff and an extensive network of former aides throughout the foreign policy apparatus; they recognized that he took defense and foreign policy issues seriously. This network of aides and former aides had joined with Cheney in pushing for military intervention to overthrow Saddam Hussein. A picture taken in the midst of the Iraq War, the day before American troops captured Baghdad, shows Cheney pointing happily at Wolfowitz, with Scooter Libby, Cheney's chief of staff, sitting behind the vice president and Douglas Feith, the undersecretary of defense, alongside Wolfowitz: hawks at the peak of triumph.[17]

Cheney had come a long way from the era when he had served as Donald Rumsfeld's doorkeeper, supervising Christmas card lists and the repairs of the White House plumbing. He had become perhaps the most powerful vice president in American history.

During the thirty-five-years from 1968 through 2003, the Vulcans reflected the moods and the beliefs of America as a whole. One reason that these six Republican foreign policy hands had been able to build up more experience in the executive branch of government than their counterparts in the Democratic party was simply that by and large the country kept on electing Republican presidents.

During this period the Republicans won six of the nine presidential elections, establishing a dominance over the White House comparable to that of the Democrats from 1932 to 1968. To be sure, foreign policy hadn't been the sole reason for the Republican victories, but it had certainly been an important factor. Vietnam had led to Richard Nixon's victory; the revolution in Iran and the second oil crisis had enabled Ronald Reagan to defeat Jimmy Carter; the image of Michael Dukakis raised questions about his experience in national security and helped George H. W. Bush win the 1988 election.

The Vulcans themselves tended to have closer ties and greater personal familiarity with electoral politics than the foreign policy leaders in the Democratic party. Two of the Vulcans (Rumsfeld and Cheney) had served in Congress, winning election and reelection; Cheney had also faced the electorate as a candidate for vice president in 2000. Indeed, at one time or another, three of the Vulcans (Rumsfeld, Cheney and Powell) had flirted with running for president themselves. The Democrats could find few counterparts. Generally, those who ran foreign policy in Democratic administrations weren't politicians.[18] Conversely, the elected Democratic politicians who were seriously interested in foreign policy, such as former Vice President Al Gore, never managed to acquire the hands-on, cabinet-level experience in running the bureaucracy that Cheney, Rumsfeld and Powell all had previously acquired as secretaries of defense or chairman of the Joint Chiefs of Staff. For the Democrats, foreign policy and electoral politics tended to be separate occupations; for the Vulcans, they were closely intertwined.

Beyond these ties to electoral politics the Vulcans from 1968 to 2003 also tended more often than not to reflect more closely than the Democrats the views of the military. They usually favored bigger defense budgets and more ambitious strategies, positions that were good for the Pentagon. Even when the Vulcans were out of office, they still tended to retain their close ties to the national security apparatus. It was revealing that during the clandestine planning of the 1980s, when the U.S. government selected individuals who might run America during a nuclear war, two of the three leaders chosen were Rumsfeld and Cheney.

In short, over a thirty-five-year period, the Vulcans can be said to have represented their generation, one that pursued unchallengeable military strength for the United States. Many Americans disagreed with them, but not enough to dislodge them from power for long.[19] When the Vulcans dealt with the world, they were a stand-in for America: its government, its national security establishment, its political beliefs and choices.

The question remained whether the venture into Iraq in 2003 marked the point where history turned once again. Did it represent the outer limits of the expansion of American power and ideals? From the perspective of the Vulcans themselves, it clearly did not; they portrayed Iraq as merely a way station on the road toward democratizing the entire Middle East.

It was unclear, however, how difficult and costly the occupation of Iraq would prove to be. More significantly, it remained uncertain the extent to which the American people would support the goal of trying to transform an entire region and culture. Was this one instance in which the Vulcans, despite their close ties to electoral politics, had taken a few steps beyond the will, the mood and the resources of the American people? Or conversely, would the American public once again support their expansive, optimistic view of the nation's capabilities?

There was no question that the Vulcans' venture into Iraq grew out of their previous thirty-five years of thinking about America's role in the world. It represented a final step in the transfer of ideas that the Vulcans had formed during the cold war into a post–cold war world—the ideas that the United States should emphasize military strength, should spread its ideals and should not accommodate other centers of power.

Over the past few years modern historians have drawn a picture of world events in which one era, the cold war, ended in 1989 and a new era, the post–cold war, started then. But hidden within this picture, there lay another, entirely different historical narrative, one that began in the two decades before 1989 and continued for at least fifteen years afterward. It was the story of the pursuit of unrivaled American power, the story of the rise of the Vulcans.

Acknowledgments

I WAS LUCKY. In the early fall of 2001 I was offered an opportunity to write my next book at a think tank called the Center for Strategic & International Studies, one of Washington's premier institutions in the field of foreign policy. For the next two years CSIS served as my home base as I went about the research and writing of *Rise of the Vulcans*. Remarkably, the people at CSIS were willing to have me in their midst, contributing a writer's idiosyncratic perspectives, even though no one knew the subject of the book until I had chosen it and no one saw anything I had written until the manuscript was finished and delivered. Their forbearance is, I think a testament to CSIS's commitment to the world of ideas and the spirit of free inquiry. It goes without saying that CSIS bears no responsibility for the contents of this book; the ideas and the views in it are strictly my own.

At CSIS, I am especially grateful to two people, director John Hamre and Kurt Campbell, the director of the International Security Program, for the extraordinary support they provided. I am also thankful to Stephanie Kaplan, Julianne Smith and Jessica Cox, who helped manage the ISP program in which I worked. And I am profoundly indebted to three talented assistants who, each for several months in turn, helped with research on the book: Andrew Peterson, who set up the files and got me started; Valerie Lincy, who furthered the research and contributed valuable insights; and Brian Kennedy, who finished the research, collected photographs and then displayed remarkable skills in helping with copyediting the manuscript.

I am also thankful to the Gerald R. Ford Library, which provided a travel grant that enabled me to examine its presidential archives in Ann Arbor for several days in the summer of 2002. David A. Horrocks, the supervisory archivist, and his team at the Ford Library were most helpful in helping me examine information from the Ford administration about Dick Cheney and Donald Rumsfeld.

Lastly, I am grateful to one other wonderful institution, the *Los Angeles Times,* the newspaper where I worked for more than twenty years, where I covered several of the Vulcans and where I developed a deep interest in American foreign policy. When I decided it was time to make the jump from daily reporting to full-time book writing, editors John Carroll and Dean Baquet and Washington bureau chief Doyle McManus were understanding, gracious and supportive.

I conducted well over a hundred interviews for this book, in some instances returning to the same person several times. I am grateful to the following people, all of whom contributed ideas, insights or information that helped my research: Morton Abramowitz, Elliott Abrams, Harry Aderholt, Richard Allen, Martin Anderson, Michael Armacost, Richard Armitage, Scott Armstrong, Jeffrey Bergner, Coit Blacker, Dennis Blair, Tom Blanton, Robert Borosage, Frederick Brown, Zbigniew Brzezinski, François Bujon, John Carbaugh, Frank Carlucci, Richard Childress, Chris Cox, Susan Crowder, Matt Daley, François Delattre, Kenneth Duberstein, Robert Ellsworth, Fritz Ermath, Robert Fauver, Jeffrey Fiedler, Daren Flitcroft, Carl Ford, Francis Fukuyama, Frank Gaffney, Len Garment, Dave Gribben, David Hatcher, Kent Harrington, Charles Horner, Fred Iklé, Karl Jackson, Chalmers Johnson, James Kelly, Geoffrey Kemp, Zalmay Khalilzad, Jeane Kirkpatrick, Lawrence Korb, William Kristol, Jean-David Levitte, I. Lewis (Scooter) Libby, James Lilley, Maleela Lodhi, Edward Luttwak, Robert McFarlane, Michael McFaul, Michael Malbin, Mike Matrinko, William Odom, Douglas Paal, Torkel Patterson, Michael Pillsbury, Jonathan Pollack, Colin Powell, James Reichley, Condoleeza Rice, Larry Ropka, Dennis Ross, Stanley Roth, Henry Rowan, Robin Sakoda, Jean-André Sauvageot, James Schlesinger, Gary Schmitt, Bill Schneider, Randall Schriver, Brent Scowcroft, Richard Secord, George Shultz, Kiron Skinner, Stephen Solarz, Ed Timberlake, Bill Triplett, Chase Untermeyer, Erich von Marbod, Susan Wallace, Paul Wilkinson, Peter Wilson, Paul Wolfowitz, James Woolsey, Dov Zakheim and Philip Zelikow. There are a handful of other sources who cannot be named, but to whom I am at least equally thankful.

Two great historians and friends, Warren I. Cohen and Nancy Bernkopf Tucker, were kind enough to read the manuscript and to offer reactions and corrections. Two other talented friends, Henry Allen and Ellen Bork, each gave valuable suggestions on portions of the manuscript. They all helped the book considerably yet should not be held accountable for its opinions and interpretations.

Finally, I was remarkably thankful to have a thoughtful, encouraging editor at Viking Penguin, Adrian Zackheim, who spotted an interesting book idea and was willing to support it, even at an early stage when the Bush administration's foreign policy team seemed like a fairly obscure subject. At Viking, Mark Ippoliti also provided invaluable help on the book. And throughout the process, I was fortunate to have Rafe Sagalyn as my agent; it was Rafe who encouraged me to pursue the idea of a collective biography.

It's true that I couldn't have done the previous two books without my wife, Caroline, but I *really* couldn't have done this one. And my two grown kids, Elizabeth and Ted, helped immeasurably by contributing to happiness.

Notes

INTRODUCTION

1. CNBC News Transcript, "George W. Bush Stumped When Asked to Name the Leaders," November 4, 1999.

2. Frank Bruni, "Bush Questions Gore's Fitness for Commander in Chief," *New York Times,* May 31, 2000, p. 20.

3. See Maureen Dowd, "Hail Anhedonia," *New York Times,* November 12, 2000; Thomas L. Friedman, "The Way We Win," *New York Times,* November 14, 2000; Dowd, "When the Boy King Ruled," *New York Times,* December 31, 2000.

4. Author interview with Yang Jiemian, January 19, 2000.

5. Walter Isaacson and Evan Thomas, *The Wise Men* (New York: Simon & Schuster, 1986); David Halberstam, *The Best and the Brightest* (New York: Random House, 1969).

**CHAPTER ONE: A RISING POLITICIAN AMID WAR
AND DIRTY TRICKS**

1. Richard Nixon conversation with H. R. Haldeman and Henry Kissinger, April 7, 1971, conversation 246-7, Nixon tape collection, National Archives.

2. Nixon telephone call with Kissinger, April 6, 1971, conversation 1-4, National Archives.

3. Terri Shaw, "GI Deaths in Vietnam Pass Korea," *Washington Post,* April 9, 1971, p. 1; Chalmers M. Roberts, "President Prodded on War: Nine in GOP Urge 'Finality,'" *Washington Post,* April 7, 1971, p. 1.

4. Memorandum for the President from Donald Rumsfeld, February 27, 1971, in National Security Files, Name Files, Donald Rumsfeld, in Nixon papers, National Archives.

5. Memorandum for Jon Huntsman from General Haig, May 4, 1971, ibid.

6. Nixon conversation with Donald Rumsfeld, March 8, 1971, conversation 463-6, Nixon tape collection, National Archives.

7. Conversation 246-7, ibid.

8. Gerald Ford, *A Time to Heal* (New York: Harper & Row), 1979, p. 130.

9. Nixon conversation with Kissinger and Haldeman, July 23, 1971, conversation 544-4, Nixon tape collection, National Archives.

10. Ibid.

11. For these and other details of Rumsfeld's early career, see Steve Neal, "Donald Rumsfeld Gets Down to the Business of Running for President," *Chicago Tribune Magazine,* January 26, 1986, p. 6. Princeton wrestling: Interview with Frank Carlucci, June 28, 2002.

12. Neal, op. cit.

13. Interview with Robert Ellsworth, January 13, 2002.

14. Neal, op. cit.

15. Vernon Loeb, "Rumsfeld Apologizes for Remarks on Draftees," *Washington Post,* January 22, 2003, p. A1.

16. Interview with Richard Allen, December 21, 2001.

17. Ellsworth interview.

18. John Osborne, "The President and the Poor," *New Republic* (May 24, 1969).

19. Ellsworth interview. The Nixon outpost at the Hilton also included Patrick Buchanan and William Safire. See William Safire, *Before the Fall: An Inside View of the Pre-Watergate White House* (New York: Doubleday & Co., 1975), pp. 60–61.

20. Memorandum of William H. Rehnquist, April 14, 1969, in White House Central Files, Subject Files, EX-FG, Office of Economic Opportunity, Nixon papers, National Archives.

21. Interview with David Gribben, July 18, 2002; Michael Medved, *The Shadow Presidents* (New York: Times Books, 1979), p. 334.

22. Medved, op. cit.; Melissa Healy, "Cheney Courts Support as Nomination Hearings Begin," *Los Angeles Times,* March 15, 1989, p. A1; George C. Wilson, "Cheney Believes Gorbachev Sincere," *Washington Post,* April 5, 1989, p. A12.

23. Richard Cheney, "Government Must Help Business Flourish," *American Business and the Quest for Freedom* (Washington, D.C.: Ethics and Public Policy Center, 1986), p. 13.

24. Interview with David Gribben, December 17, 2001.

25. Carlucci interview.

26. Lyndon B. Johnson, special message to Congress, March 16, 1964.

27. Interview with Leonard Garment, June 28, 2002.

28. "Statement by the President on the Office of Economic Opportunity," August 11, 1969, and "Redirection of the Office of Economic Opportunity," in White House Central Files, Subject Files, EX FG 6-7, Office of Economic Opportunity, Nixon papers, National Archives.

29. Carlucci interview.

30. Donald Rumsfeld, National Press Club address, December 16, 1969, in White House Central Files, Subject Files, EX FG 6-7, Office of Economic Opportunity, Nixon papers, National Archives.

31. Donald Rumsfeld, address to San Francisco Chamber of Commerce, September 23, 1970, in White House Central Files, Subject Files EX FG 6-7, Office of Economic Opportunity, Nixon papers, National Archives.

32. Rumsfeld, memorandum for the President, October 16, 1970, in White House Central Files, Subject Files EX FG 6-7, Office of Economic Opportunity, Nixon papers, National Archives.

33. Richard Allen interview.

34. H. R. Haldeman, *The Haldeman Diaries* (New York: G. P. Putman, 1994), p. 208.

35. Nixon conversation with Rumsfeld, March 8, 1971, conversation 463-6, Nixon tape collection, National Archives.

36. Conversation of July 23, 1971.

37. Conversation of March 8, 1971.

38. Ibid.

39. Ibid. for March conversation; Nixon conversation with Donald Rumsfeld, July 22, 1971, conversation 542-5, Nixon tape collection, National Archives.

40. Nixon phone call to Colson, July 23, 1971, conversation 6-197, Nixon tape collection, National Archives.

41. Nixon conversation with Rumsfeld, October 19, 1971, conversation 11-135, Nixon tape collection, National Archives.

42. Nixon conversation with Rumsfeld and Finch, Oval Office, May 19, 1971, conversation 501-29, Nixon tape collection, National Archives.

43. Conversation with Donald Rumsfeld, March 8, 1971.

44. John Ehrlichman, *Witness to Power* (New York: Simon & Schuster, 1982), p. 103.

45. Nixon conversation with Haldeman, July 2, 1971, conversation 537-2, Nixon tape collection, National Archives.

46. Nixon conversation with Rumsfeld, July 22, 1971, Nixon tape collection, National Archives.

47. Nixon conversation with Haldeman, July 28, 1971, conversation 550-1, Nixon tape collection, National Archives.

48. Haldeman, op. cit., p. 540.

CHAPTER TWO: THE INTELLECTUAL AS PROTÉGÉ

1. See "Bibliographical Note on Jacob Wolfowitz," Jack Kiefer, ed., *Selected Papers of Jacob Wolfowitz* (New York: Springer-Verlag, 1980), and *Dictionary of Scientific Biography* (New York: Scribner, 1970), vol. 18, supplement 2, pp. 996–97.

2. Interview with Paul Wolfowitz, June 19, 2003.

3. Interview with Francis Fukuyama, July 19, 2002.

4. Saul Bellow, *Ravelstein* (New York: Penguin Books, 2000), pp. 15, 19–20.

5. Ibid., p. 58.

6. D. T. Max, "With Friends Like Saul Bellow," *New York Times Magazine,* April 16, 2000, p. 70.

7. Wolfowitz interview.

8. Walter Nicgorski, "Allen Bloom: Strauss, Socrates and Liberal Education," in *Leo Strauss, the Straussians and the American Regime,* ed. Kenneth L. Deutsch and John A. Murley (Lanham, Md.: Rowman & Littlefield, 1999), pp. 206, 208.

9. Wolfowitz interview.

10. See William Galston, "A Student of Leo Strauss in the Clinton Administration," in *Leo Strauss*, loc. cit., pp. 429–37.

11. Thomas Pangle, *The Rebirth of Classical Political Rationalism: Essays and Lectures by Leo Strauss* (Chicago: University of Chicago Press, 1989), p. 17.

12. Ibid., p. xxv. This quotation is from Pangle, not from Strauss.

13. Jacob Weisberg, "The Cult of Leo Strauss," *Newsweek* (August 3, 1987), p. 61. Over the years, Wolfowitz attended some of the Straussian reunions in Washington, including one in 2003.

14. Quoted in Harry V. Jaffa, "Strauss at One Hundred," in *Leo Strauss*, loc. cit., pp. 43–44.

15. Allan Bloom, *The Closing of the American Mind* (New York: Simon & Schuster, 1987), pp. 141–42.

16. Mark Blitz, "Government Practice and the School of Strauss," in *Leo Strauss*, loc. cit., pp. 429–30.

17. Gary J. Schmitt and Abram N. Shulsky, "Leo Strauss and the World of Intelligence (by Which We Do Not Mean *Nous*)," in *Leo Strauss*, pp. 407–12.

18. Interview with Peter Wilson, August 1, 2002.

19. Interview with Jeane Kirkpatrick, April 24, 2002.

20. Wolfowitz interview.

21. For a lucid account of Wohlstetter's work, see Fred Kaplan, *The Wizards of Armageddon* (New York: Simon & Schuster, 1983), pp. 89–110 and 117–24.

22. Wolfowitz interview.

23. Paul D. Wolfowitz, "Nuclear Proliferation in the Middle East: The Politics and Economics of Proposals for Nuclear Desalting," doctoral dissertation, University of Chicago, June 1972, pp. 32–33.

24. This account is based upon interviews with two sources with firsthand knowledge of the committee, who did not wish to be named. The details of the office and ABM debate are also covered in Paul H. Nitze, *From Hiroshima to Glasnost* (New York: Grove Weidenfeld, 1989), pp. 294–95; in Kaplan, op. cit., pp. 342–55; and in Jay Winik, *On the Brink* (New York: Simon & Schuster, 1996), pp. 52–53.

25. Kaplan, op. cit., p. 349–50.

26. Robert G. Kaufman, *Henry M. Jackson: A Life in Politics* (Seattle: University of Washington Press, 2000), p. 211.

27. Nitze, op. cit., p. 295.

28. Max Frankel, "The Missile Vote: Both Sides Can Claim a Victory," *New York Times*, August 4, 1969, p. 22.

29. Kaplan, op. cit., pp. 354–55.

30. I am referring here to Nitze's views in 1969. Later Nitze himself served as an arms control negotiator for the United States.

31. Henry Kissinger, *Years of Renewal* (New York: Simon & Schuster, 1999), p. 114.

32. For accounts of the firings at the ACDA, see Raymond L. Garthoff, *A Journey Through the Cold War* (Washington, D.C.: Brookings Institution Press, 2001), pp. 273–74; Kaufman, op. cit., p. 258; Seymour Hersh, *The Price of Power* (New York: Summit Books, 1983), pp. 559–60.

33. Interview with Fred Iklé.

34. In the George W. Bush administration Perle served for a time as head of the Defense Policy Board, an advisory group, but did not hold any job inside the administration itself.

CHAPTER THREE: A SOLDIER AND A SAILOR

1. This account is based upon an interview with Richard Armitage, August 21, 2002.

2. *Lucky Bag* 1967 yearbook note, supplied by U.S. Naval Academy Archives. Nickname and weight room supplied in an interview with a classmate at the academy.

3. Armitage interview.

4. Colin Powell, *My American Journey* (New York: Ballantine Books, 1995), pp. 27, 34.

5. Ibid., p. 59.

6. Ibid., p. 66.

7. Cheney obtained deferments first as a student and then as a parent. Wolfowitz had deferments as a student.

8. Robert Timberg, *The Nightingale's Song* (New York: Touchstone Books, 1995), p. 91.

9. Michael Hirsh, "Hawks, Doves and Dubya," *Newsweek* (September 2, 2002), p. 24.

10. Peter Beinart, "First Serve," *New Republic* (September 2, 2002), p. 6.

11. Powell, op. cit., pp. 77–101.

12. Ibid., pp. 78, 86, 100–101, 127.

13. Ibid., pp. 126–45.

14. Ibid., pp. 138–39.

15. Glen's letter is quoted in Charles Lane, "Anatomy of an Establishment Career," *New Republic* (April 17, 1995), p. 20, and was first made public by a British journalist named Michael Bilton.

16. Ibid.

17. Powell, op. cit., p. 120.

18. Ibid., pp. 143–45.

19. Ibid.

20. Interview with James Kelly, September 17, 2002.

21. Interview with Richard Allen, December 21, 2001; interviews with Fred Iklé, December 10, 2001, and July 23, 2002.

22. Interview with Larry Ropka, October 22, 2002.

23. Stanley Karnow, *Vietnam: A History* (New York: Penguin Books, 1984), pp. 601–2; Elaine Sciolino, "Cloak and Dagger Retired, Ex-Chief of CIA Remains Hard to Predict," *New York Times,* March 30, 1992, p. 10.

24. Shackley responded to questions that were relayed from the author to him through James Lilley, another former CIA official, November 8, 2002.

25. Interview with Richard Armitage, June 23, 2003.

26. Kelly interview.

27. J. Edward Lee and Toby Haynsworth, *White Christmas in April* (New York: Peter Lang Publishing, 1995), p. 85.

28. Ibid., p. 84.

29. Ibid.; interview with Richard Childress, October 16, 2002.

30. Kelly interview.

31. Armitage interview.

32. Kelly interview.

33. Interview with a source who served as a senior official in the Defense Department in the 1970s.

34. Kelly interview.

35. Ropka interview.

36. Armitage interview.

37. Interview with Erich von Marbod, March 4, 2003.

38. Armitage interview.

39. Interviews with Armitage and Kelly.

40. Written statement by Erich von Marbod; Armitage interview; Lee and Haynsworth, op. cit.

41. Armitage interview.

42. Frank Snepp, *Decent Interval* (New York: Random House, 1977), p. 459; von Marbod statement.

43. Von Marbod statement to Undersecretary of Defense Walter Slocombe, April 26, 2000.

44. See Walter Isaacson and Evan Thomas, *The Wise Men* (New York: Simon & Schuster, 1986).

45. Interview with Paul Wolfowitz, March 12, 2002.

46. Interview with Peter Wilson, August 1, 2002.

47. Powell, op. cit., p. 393.

48. Interview with a former senior official of the Nixon and Ford administrations, who was interviewed on the condition he would not be named.

49. Armitage interview.

CHAPTER 4: COMBATING THE SOVIETS, DÉTENTE AND HENRY KISSINGER

1. Richard Nixon, *RN* (New York: Grosset & Dunlap, 1978), p. 1042.

2. Interview with Richard Cheney, December 6, 1996.

3. Memo to the president from Henry A. Kissinger re NSC Meeting, Saturday August 10, 1974, in National Security Adviser: NSC Meeting File, box 1, folder "NSC Meeting, August 10, 1974," Gerald R. Ford Library.

4. Anatoly Dobrynin, *In Confidence* (New York: Times Books, 1995), pp. 325–26.

5. Robert T. Hartmann, *Palace Politics* (New York: McGraw-Hill, 1980), p. 283.

6. Interview with Robert Ellsworth, December 13, 2001.

7. "Gerald R. Ford's Remarks on Taking the Oath of Office as President," Gerald R. Ford Library.

8. Ron Nessen, *It Sure Looks Different from the Inside* (Chicago: Playboy Paperbacks, 1978), p. 150.

9. Michael Medved, *The Shadow Presidents* (New York: Times Books, 1979), p. 36.

10. Files of Jerry H. Jones, 1974–77, box 10, Richard Cheney, Gerald R. Ford Library.

11. Ibid.

12. Cheney interview with Stephen Wayne, Hyde and Wayne collection, Gerald R. Ford Library.

13. Handwritten notes from Richard Cheney, May 29, 1975, in Richard Cheney Files, box 6, folder "Intelligence—New York Times Articles by Seymour Hersh (1)," Gerald R. Ford Library.

14. John Hersey, *The President* (New York: Alfred A. Knopf, 1975), pp. 120–21.

15. Nessen, op. cit., p. 132.

16. John Osborne, *White House Watch: The Ford Years* (New York: New Republic Books, 1977), pp. 142–43.

17. Hartmann, op. cit. pp. 321–23; Nessen, op. cit., 108–9; Kissinger, *Years of Renewal* (New York: Simon & Schuster, 1999), pp. 534–35.

18. Nessen, op. cit., pp. 112–13.

19. Kissinger, op. cit., pp. 98–99.

20. Ibid. p. 105.

21. Ibid. p. 175.

22. Hartmann, op. cit., p. 283.

23. Memorandum for Don Rumsfeld from Dick Cheney, July 8, 1975, in Richard Cheney files, box 10, folder "Solzhenitsyn, Alexander," Gerald R. Ford Library.

24. Callaway memo to Cheney, November 3, 1975, in Callaway papers, box 5, Gerald R. Ford Library.

25. Interview with Winston Lord, December 11, 1996; Walter Isaacson, *Kissinger* (New York: Simon & Schuster, 1992), p. 671.

26. Osborne, op. cit., p. xxiv.

27. Ford, *A Time to Heal* (New York: Harper & Row, 1979), pp. 320–27.

28. Medved, op. cit., p. 337.

29. Osborne, op. cit., p. 11.

30. Ibid., pp. xxiv–xxv.

31. Interview with Morton Abramowitz, December 12, 2001.

32. Interview with Brent Scowcroft, June 6, 2002.

33. Interview with Fred Iklé, December 10, 2001.

34. Kissinger, op. cit., p. 850.

35. Ford, op. cit., 357–58; Raymond Garthoff, *Détente and Confrontation* (Washington, D.C.: Brookings Institution Press, 1985), pp. 540–43.

36. "Implications of Recent Trends in the United States and Soviet Military Balance," by Donald Rumsfeld, James E. Connor files, box 1, folder "Defense, Donald Rumsfeld (3)," Gerald R. Ford Library.

37. Memorandum of Conversation: President Ford, Dr. Henry A. Kissinger, Don-

ald Rumsfeld and Brent Scowcroft, Oval Office, March 29, 1976, in National Security Advisor Memoranda of Conversations collection, box 18, Gerald R. Ford Library.

38. Teeter memo to Cheney, "Analysis of Early Research," November 12, 1975, in Robert M. Teeter papers, box 63, Gerald R. Ford Library. Cheney comments to Hartmann in Hartmann Papers, box 120, Ford Library.

39. *Weekly Compilation of Presidential Documents,* vol. 12, pp. 22, 350, quoted in Garthoff, op. cit., pp. 547–48.

40. Ford, op. cit., p. 374.

41. Medved, op. cit., pp. 337, 339.

42. Cheney interview, December 6, 1995.

43. Republican platform, "Morality in Foreign Policy," proceedings of the 1976 Republican National Convention.

44. Nessen, op. cit., pp. 229–31; Ford, op. cit., 398; memo from Mike Duval to Dick Cheney, August 17, 1976, in Gerald R. Ford Library.

45. See Don Oberdorfer, "Report Saw Soviet Buildup for War," CIA Declassifies Controversial 1976 "Team B" Analysis, *Washington Post,* October 12, 1992, p. A11.

46. Jack Davis, "The Challenge of Managing Uncertainty: Paul Wolfowitz on Intelligence Policy-Relations," *Studies in Intelligence,* vol. 39, no. 5 (1996).

47. See Robert Dreyfuss, "The Pentagon Muzzles the CIA," *American Prospect,* vol. 13, issue 22 (December 16, 2002), and Seymour M. Hersh, "Selective Intelligence," *New Yorker* (May 12, 2003), p. 44.

48. Interview with Francis Fukuyama, July 19, 2002.

49. Henry Kissinger, *A World Restored* (Boston: Houghton Mifflin, 1973), p. 316.

50. Kissinger, *Years of Renewal,* p. 97.

51. Iklé interview; interview with Zbigniew Brzezinski, November 26, 2001.

52. A. James Reichley interviews with Winston Lord and Brent Scowcroft, Gerald R. Ford Library.

53. Kissinger, *Years of Renewal,* p. 652.

CHAPTER FIVE: ENTER THE PERSIAN GULF

1. Interview with Paul Wolfowitz, June 19, 2003.

2. The overall account of the Limited Contingency Study is based upon interviews with Geoffrey Kemp (February 21, 2002), Dennis Ross (April 18, 2002) and Paul Wolfowitz (March 12, 2002 and June 19, 1993).

3. Pentagon study, "Capabilities for Limited Contingencies in the Persian Gulf," June 15, 1979, executive summary, p. 1. The full study was declassified on April 23, 2003, and released to author. An earlier, unclassified version of this study had been provided to authors Michael R. Gordon and General Bernard E. Trainor for their book *The Generals' War* (Boston: Little, Brown, 1995), pp. 6–9, 480, fn. 2.

4. Ibid., pp. 6–7.

5. Ross interview.

6. Ross interview; conversation with Harold Brown, February 28, 2002.

7. William Odom, "The Cold War Origins of the U.S. Central Command," unpublished paper, pp. 25–26.

8. Gary Sick, *All Fall Down* (New York: Random House, 1985), p. 13.

9. See William Branigan, "Iran Cancels Arms Orders with U.S.," *Washington Post,* April 9, 1979, p. A1.

10. Walter Isaacson, *Kissinger* (New York: Simon & Schuster, 1992), pp. 562–65.

11. Sick, op. cit., p. 15. Kissinger maintains that this language, whose wording he does not quote, was meant to apply to only one specific decision: whether the shah should be permitted to buy F-14 or F-15 warplanes. See also Henry Kissinger, *Years of Upheaval* (New York: Little, Brown, 1982), p. 670.

12. Memorandum of conversation, Ford, Kissinger, Scowcroft and shah of Iran, May 15, 1975, box 11, National Security Adviser files, Gerald R. Ford Library.

13. Sick, op. cit., p. 17.

14. Interview with Larry Ropka, October 22, 2002; interview with an eyewitness at the Helms-Secord ceremonies.

15. Interview with Richard Armitage, June 23, 2003.

16. Colin Powell, *My American Journey* (New York: Ballantine Books, 1995), pp. 232–33.

17. Interview with William Odom, March 28, 2002; Zbigniew Brzezinski, *Power and Principle* (New York: Farrar, Straus & Giroux, 1985), p. 456.

18. President Jimmy Carter, State of the Union address, January 21, 1980.

19. Odom, op. cit., pp. 25–32.

20. Powell, op. cit., p. 234.

21. Ibid., p. 241.

22. Irving Kristol, "American Conservatism 1945–1995," *Public Interest,* no. 121 (September 1995), p. 84.

23. Jeane Kirkpatrick, "Dictatorships and Double Standards," *Commentary,* vol. 68 (November 1979), p. 41.

24. Ibid., p. 37.

25. Interview with Jeane Kirkpatrick, April 24, 2002.

26. The best example of recent neoconservative views about democracy is Lawrence F. Kaplan and William Kristol, *The War over Iraq* (San Francisco: Encounter Books, 2003), pp. 96–111. It includes an explicit rejection of Kirkpatrick's "Dictatorships and Double Standards," pp. 102–3.

27. Lou Cannon and David S. Broder, "Anticipating Carter, Reagan Adds Key Advisers," *Washington Post,* March 23, 1980, p. A1.

CHAPTER SIX: TRANSITIONS

1. Lou Cannon, "From the White House to the Hustings: Richard Cheney Wants to Work on Capitol Hill," *Washington Post,* October 16, 1978, p. B1.

2. Interviews with Dave Gribben, December 17, 2001, and July 18, 2002.

3. See Matthew Vita and Dan Morgan, "A Hard-Liner with a Soft Touch," *Washington Post,* August 5, 2000, p. A1.

4. Gribben interview.

5. Interview with Fred Iklé, December 10, 2001.

6. Interview with Jeane Kirkpatrick, April 24, 2002.

7. Interview with one of Jackson's Senate aides, who eventually joined the Reagan administration.

8. Interview with Paul Wolfowitz, June 19, 2003.

9. See Colin Powell, *My American Journey* (New York: Ballantine Books, 1995), pp. 136–37.

10. Ibid., pp. 156–57.

11. Interview with Frank Carlucci, January 11, 2002.

12. Interview with William Odom, March 28, 2002.

13. Powell, op. cit., p. 226.

14. Lynn Langway, "Unsnuffing Searle," *Newsweek* (June 6, 1977), p. 36.

15. "Action at Searle Will Strengthen Position," *Chemical Week* (January 18, 1989), p. 9; Hugh D. Menzies, "Ten Toughest Bosses," *Fortune* (April 21, 1980), p. 62; Thomas M. Chesser, "It Was Tough Medicine, but G. D. Searle Breathes Easier Now," *New York Times,* January 31, 1982, section 3, p. 6.

16. Chesser, op. cit., and Roy Rowan, "A Politician Turned Executive," *Fortune* (September 10, 1979), p. 94.

17. Jim Adams, untitled article, Associated Press, November 26, 1979.

18. Rowan, op. cit.

19. A. James Reichley interview with Richard Allen, Gerald R. Ford Library.

20. For the most detailed version of these negotiations, see Richard Allen, "George Herbert Walker Bush: The Accidental Vice President," *New York Times Magazine,* July 30, 2000, p. 36.

21. Ronald Reagan, *An American Life* (New York: Simon & Schuster, 1990), p. 215.

22. Ibid., p. 216; Allen, op. cit.

23. Interview with Richard Allen, July 16, 2002.

24. Interview with James Kelly, September 17, 2002.

25. These operations, and Aderholt's life, are described in detail in Warren A. Trest, *Air Commando One* (Washington, D.C.: Smithsonian Institution Press, 2000).

26. Interview with James Lilley, April 25, 2002.

27. Interview with Richard Armitage, August 21, 2002; Trest, op. cit., pp. 251–52.

28. Interview with Heinie Aderholt, October 11, 2002.

29. Armitage interview.

30. Aderholt interview.

31. Armitage interview.

32. Kelly interview.

33. Kelly interview; Richard Armitage, "Hanoi's Crumbling Policy," *Christian Science Monitor,* August 21, 1980.

34. Lilley interview.

35. Interview with Lawrence Korb, February 12, 2003.

36. Interview with John Carbaugh, December 21, 2001.

37. Powell, op. cit., pp. 242–43.

CHAPTER SEVEN: CAMELOT OF THE CONSERVATIVES

1. Interview with I. Lewis Libby, May 7, 2002.

2. Chris Madison, "Haig's Planning Chief Finds Rewards, Risks in Helping Keep State Straight," *National Journal* (April 10, 1982), p. 621.

3. Interview with Paul Wolfowitz, October 31, 1996; James Mann, *About Face* (New York: Alfred A. Knopf, 1998), pp. 128–29.

4. Libby interview.

5. Francis X. Clines and Warren Weaver, "Briefing," *New York Times,* March 30, 1982, p. 12.

6. Alexander M. Haig, *Caveat* (New York: Macmillan, 1984), p. 314.

7. Interview with George Shultz, February 12, 2002.

8. Interview with Paul Wolfowitz, June 19, 2003.

9. George P. Shultz, *Turmoil and Triumph* (New York: Scribner, 1993), pp. 381–83.

10. Daniel F. Gilmore, "Vietnam Veteran Awarded Medal of Honor," United Press International, February 25, 1981; Caspar Weinberger, *Fighting for Peace* (New York: Warner Books, 1990), pp. 52–56.

11. Colin Powell, *My American Journey* (New York: Ballantine Books, 1995), pp. 242, 248.

12. Weinberger, op. cit., p. 47.

13. Powell, op. cit., pp. 269–70.

14. Interview with Lawrence Korb, February 12, 2003.

15. Powell, op. cit., pp. 280–81.

16. Weinberger, op. cit., pp. 433–45; Powell, op. cit., p. 292.

17. Powell, op. cit., p. 293.

18. Interview with Dov Zakheim, June 28, 2002; Weinberger, op. cit., pp. 167, 175–201.

19. Interview with Robert Ellsworth, December 13, 2001.

20. Interview with Jeane Kirkpatrick, April 24, 2002.

21. Doyle McManus, "U.S. Shaping Assertive Policy for Third World," *Los Angeles Times,* June 16, 1985, p. 7.

22. Interview with Richard Armitage, November 30, 2001.

23. McManus, op. cit.

24. Interviews with Fred Iklé, December 10, 2001, and Edward Luttwak, April 4, 2002.

25. Iklé interview.

26. Shultz interview; "Rumsfeld Said to Take Job as Mideast Envoy," *New York Times,* November 3, 1983, p. A13.

27. Department of State cable, December 21, 1983, "Rumsfeld mission: Dec. 20 meeting with Iraqi President Saddam Hussein," National Security Archive.

28. Hearing of Senate Armed Services Committee on U.S. Policy on Iraq, September 19, 2002.

29. Department of State cable, Dec. 21, 1983, "Rumsfeld One-on-One Meeting

with Iraqi Deputy Prime Minister and Foreign Minister Tariq Aziz," National Security Archive.

30. Department of State cable, December 21, 1983, of Rumsfeld meeting with Saddam Hussein, National Security Archive.

31. Shultz, op. cit., p. 235.

32. Ibid., p. 238; David B. Ottaway, "U.S. Says Iraq Used Gas Again in War with Iran," *Washington Post,* March 27, 1985, p. A25.

33. Interview with Secretary of Defense Donald M. Rumsfeld, *Newshour with Jim Lehrer,* September 18, 2002.

34. Shultz interview.

CHAPTER EIGHT: OF DICTATORSHIPS AND DEMOCRACY

1. Interview with Karl Jackson, November 19, 2001.

2. Interview with James Lilley, November 8, 2002.

3. Interview with Richard Armitage, November 20, 2001.

4. Interview with Elliott Abrams, February 1, 2002.

5. Interview with William Kristol, December 7, 2001.

6. Abrams interview.

7. Ronald Reagan address to Members of the British Parliament, June 8, 1982; Barton Reppert, "Political Parties Urge Democracy Group," Associated Press, April 18, 1983.

8. George P. Shultz, *Turmoil and Triumph* (New York: Scribner's, 1993), p. 970.

9. Raymond Bonner, *Waltzing with a Dictator* (New York: Times Books, 1987), pp. 362–63.

10. State Department Cable, "Assistant Secretary Wolfowitz Meetings with Opposition Figures," National Security Archive.

11. Interview with Stanley O. Roth, November 26, 2002.

12. Lena H. Sun, "Philippine Crisis Grows, Top U.S. Officials Warn," *Washington Post,* March 13, 1985, p. A19.

13. Shultz, op. cit., p. 603.

14. Ibid., pp. 627–42.

15. Henry A. Kissinger, "What Next When U.S. Intervenes," *Los Angeles Times,* March 9, 1986.

16. Interview with Paul Wolfowitz, March 12, 2002.

17. Henry Kissinger, *Years of Renewal* (New York: Simon & Schuster, 1999), p. 108.

18. Paul Wolfowitz, "Asian Democracy and American Interests," B. C. Lee Lecture, Heritage Foundation, September 23, 2000.

19. Wolfowitz interview.

20. Paul Wolfowitz, "U.S. Encourages Constructive Change in the Philippines," *Wall Street Journal,* April 15, 1985, p. 29.

CHAPTER NINE: IN THE MIDST OF ARMAGEDDON

1. This account of the Reagan program and of Cheney and Rumsfeld's central roles within it was provided by three separate individuals who were participants in the secret exercises. The interviews were conducted in 2002.

2. Robert Scheer, *With Enough Shovels* (New York: Random House, 1982), pp. 232–34, 250–51; Richard Halloran, "Pentagon Draws Up First Strategy for Fighting a Long Nuclear War," *New York Times,* May 30, 1982, p. A1.

3. Halloran, op. cit.

4. Ted Gup, "The Ultimate Congressional Hideaway," *Washington Post Magazine,* May 31, 1992, p. W11.

5. Interview with Robert McFarlane, December 17, 2002.

6. See transcripts, CNN Special Reports, November 17 and December 19, 1991.

7. Tim Weiner, "Pentagon Book for Doomsday to Be Closed," *New York Times,* April 18, 1994, p. A1.

8. President Reagan speech to National Association of Evangelicals, March 8, 1983.

9. Condoleezza Rice, "The Soviet Alliance System," in Alexander Dallin and Condoleezza Rice, eds., *The Gorbachev Era* (Stanford, CA: Stanford Alumni Association, 1986), p. 158.

10. Interview with Brent Scowcroft, January 3, 2002.

11. Dale Russakoff, "Lessons of Might and Right: While Others Marched for Civil Rights," *Washington Post Magazine,* September 9, 2001, p. W23.

12. "From Not College Material to Stanford's No. 2 Job," *New York Times,* June 23, 1993, p. B7.

13. Jay Nordlinger, "Star-in-Waiting: Meet George W.'s Foreign-Policy Czarina," *National Review,* vol. 50, no. 16 (August 30, 1999), p. 35.

14. Interview with Michael McFaul, February 14, 2002.

15. Interview with Coit Blacker, February 13, 2002; Russakoff, op. cit.

16. Condoleezza Rice, "Small Steps, Giant Leaps," in *A Voice of Our Own,* ed. Nancy M. Newman (San Francisco: Jossey-Bass, 1996), p. 226.

17. McFaul interview; interview with Kiron Skinner, February 11, 2002.

18. Interview with Francis Fukuyama, July 19, 2002.

CHAPTER TEN: A SCANDAL AND ITS AFTERMATH

1. Interviews with James Lilley, November 20, 2001, and Torkel Patterson, August 1, 2002.

2. Interview with Larry Ropka, October 22, 2002.

3. For the impact of Vietnam on these Iran-contra principals, see Robert Timberg, *The Nightingale's Song* (New York: Touchstone, 1995).

4. Karen Tumulty and Sara Fritz, "President, Panel Agree on Covert Action Rules," *Los Angeles Times,* August 8, 1987, p. 1.

5. Theodore Draper, *A Very Thin Line* (New York: Hill and Wang, 1991), pp. 148–50.

6. Interview with William Odom, March 28, 2002; Lawrence Walsh, *Final Report of the Independent Counsel for Iran/Contra Matters,* August 4, 1993, vol. I, part VIII, Officers of the Department of Defense (*U.S. vs. Caspar Weinberger and Related Investigations*), p. 432, fn. 223.

7. Colin Powell, *My American Journey* (New York: Ballantine Books, 1995), pp. 299–301.

8. Walsh, op. cit., p. 432.

9. Powell, op. cit., p. 318.

10. David Corn, *Blond Ghosts* (New York: Simon & Schuster, 1994), pp. 376–80.

11. Ibid., pp. 382–98.

12. Ropka interview.

13. Interview with Fritz Ermath, March 14, 2002.

14. Powell, op. cit., p. 332.

15. Interview with Kenneth Duberstein, July 11, 2002.

16. Powell, op. cit., pp. 328–29.

17. Duberstein interview.

18. Anatoly Dobrynin, *In Confidence* (New York: Times Books, 1995), p. 612.

19. David S. Broder and Thomas Edsall, "Arms Agreement Improves GOP's Chances in 1988," *Washington Post,* September 20, 1987, p. A20; Richard Morin, "Post-Summit Poll Shows Reagan Gains," *Washington Post,* December 15, 1987, p. A1; Steven V. Roberts, "Reagan's Final Rating Is Best of Any President Since 40's," *New York Times,* January 18, 1989, p. 1.

20. See, for example, Bill Keller, "The Radical Presidency of George W. Bush," *New York Times Magazine,* January 26, 2003, p. 26.

21. Powell, op. cit., pp. 350–51, 382–83; George Shultz, *Turmoil and Triumph* (New York: Scribner, 1993), p. 1011.

22. Paul Kennedy, *The Rise and Fall of the Great Powers* (New York: Random House, 1987), p. 515.

23. William H. Honan, "The Lessons of War Sell in Peacetime," *New York Times,* December 19, 1988, p. D12.

24. Jim Mann, "Officials Upset by Book Saying U.S. Is Courting Decline," *Los Angeles Times,* May 31, 1988, part I, p. 15.

25. Kennedy, op. cit., pp. 533–34.

26. Samuel Huntington, "The U.S.: Decline or Renewal?," *Foreign Affairs* (Winter 1988–1989), p. 76.

27. Glenn Kessler, "Diplomatic Gap Between U.S., Its Allies Widens," *Washington Post,* September 1, 2002, p. A1.

CHAPTER ELEVEN: A NEW REPUBLICAN PRESIDENT, A NEW FOREIGN POLICY TEAM

1. Interviews with William Kristol, November 12 and December 7, 2001.

2. Rumsfeld speech to annual meeting of shareholders, G. D. Searle & Co., Business Wire, May 23, 1985.

3. See Jack W. Germond and Jules Witcover, "Doubts About Bush Prompt Search for New Faces," *National Journal,* vol. 18, no. 7 (February 15, 1986), p. 402.

4. Interview with George Shultz, February 12, 2002.

5. Steve Neal, "Rumsfeld Almost Off and Running," *Chicago Tribune,* April 4, 1985, p. 19; "Rumsfeld Frowns on Spy Swap," United Press International, September 23, 1986.

6. Stephen Chapman, "Can Rumsfeld Add Another Line to a Strong Résumé?" *Chicago Tribune,* February 15, 1987, perspective section, p. 3.

7. Shultz interview.

8. Interview with Frank Carlucci, January 11, 2002.

9. Raymond Coffey, "Rumsfeld Decides He's Not Running; Rules on Campaign Finances Cited," *Chicago Tribune,* April 3, 1987, p. 7.

10. George Bush and Brent Scowcroft, *A World Transformed* (New York: Alfred A. Knopf, 1998), p. 26.

11. Dick Cheney, "Covert Operations: Who's in Charge?" *Wall Street Journal,* May 3, 1988, p. A30.

12. Interview with Brent Scowcroft, January 3, 2002.

13. Interview with Brent Scowcroft, June 6, 2002.

14. Interview with Fred Iklé, December 1, 2001.

15. Robert M. Gates, *From the Shadows* (New York: Simon & Schuster, 1996), pp. 472–73; Bush and Scowcroft, op. cit., p. 36.

16. Scowcroft interviews; interview with Dennis Ross, April 18, 2002.

17. Interview with Fritz Ermath, March 14, 2002.

18. Interview with Coit Blacker, February 13, 2002.

19. Philip Zelikow and Condoleezza Rice, *Germany United and Europe Transformed* (Cambridge, Mass.: Harvard University Press, 1995), p. 379, fn. 57.

20. Interview with Michael McFaul, February 14, 2002.

21. Interviews with I. Lewis (Scooter) Libby, May 7, 2002, and with Ermath.

22. This account of Perot's activities on Vietnam POWs is taken from Gerald Posner, *Citizen Perot* (New York: Random House, 1996), pp. 190–217.

23. Carlucci interview.

24. Interview with James Kelly, September 17, 2002.

25. Posner, op. cit., p. 197.

26. John Mintz, "Va. Police Raid Vietnamese Businesses, Homes," *Washington Post,* October 30, 1984, p. B2; Posner, op. cit., pp. 202–3.

27. As a reporter for the *Los Angeles Times* the author personally witnessed one of Perot's attacks on Armitage, which included unsubstantiated suggestions of corruption and hushed references to secret police files. Perot continued to offer these allegations to various reporters from 1987 through the 1992 presidential campaign. See, for example, Morton M. Kondracke, "Perot vs. Armitage," *Roll Call,* June 29, 1992, p. 6, and Sidney Blumenthal, "Perotmania," *New Republic,* vol. 206, no. 24 (June 15, 1992), p. 23.

28. Interview with a former Pentagon official who requested not to be identified.

29. Interview with Richard Armitage, August 21, 2002.

30. Armitage interview.

31. Interview with a longtime friend of Armitage's.

32. See Powell, *My American Journey* (New York: Ballantine Books, 1995), pp. 316–17, 355, 393.

33. Bush and Scowcroft, op. cit., p. 23.

34. Interview with David Gribben, December 17, 2001.

CHAPTER TWELVE: USE OF FORCE

1. James A. Baker III, *The Politics of Diplomacy* (New York: G. P. Putnam's, 1995), p. 194.

2. George Shultz, *Turmoil and Triumph* (New York: Scribner, 1993), pp. 1051–79.

3. Colin Powell, *My American Journey* (New York: Ballantine Books, 1995), p. 412.

4. Transcript of Department of Defense briefing on Panama, December 20, 1989.

5. Susanne M. Schafer, "Powell Steps into New Leadership Role," Associated Press, December 23, 1989; Saul Friedman, "Four Star Warrior," *Newsday Magazine,* February 11, 1990, p. 10.

6. R. W. Apple, "Washington Talk: Instincts to Be Cautious With Panama Prevail," *New York Times,* October 10, 1989, p. 22.

7. Yossi Melman and Dan Raviv, *Friends in Deed: Inside the U.S.-Israeli Alliance* (New York: Hyperion, 1994).

8. Baker, op. cit., p. 263.

9. This account of the events on the eve of the Iraqi invasion is based on Michael Gordon and General Bernard E. Trainor, *The Generals' War* (Boston: Little, Brown, 1995), pp. 4–30.

10. Powell, op. cit., pp. 448–49.

11. General H. Norman Schwarzkopf, *It Doesn't Take a Hero* (New York: Bantam Books, 1992), p. 297.

12. Powell, op. cit., pp. 451–52.

13. George Bush and Brent Scowcroft, *A World Transformed* (New York: Alfred A. Knopf, 1998), pp. 316–17.

14. Interview with Dennis Ross, April 18, 2002.

15. Powell, op. cit., p. 451.

16. Ross interview.

17. Interview with Brent Scowcroft, January 3, 2001.

18. Interview with Henry Rowen, February 11, 2002.

19. Rowen interview. See also Gordon and Trainor, op. cit., pp. 142–58, a detailed account of this alternative war plan.

20. Interviews with Rowen and with I. Lewis Libby, September 16, 2002.

21. Schwarzkopf, op. cit., p. 368.

22. Rowen interview.

23. Powell, op. cit., p. 474.

24. Paul Wolfowitz testimony to House National Security Committee, September 16, 1998.

25. Ross interview.

26. Paul Wolfowitz, "The United States and Iraq," in *The Future of Iraq,* ed. John Calabrese (Middle East Institute, 1997), pp. 107–13.

27. Paul Wolfowitz, "Victory Came Too Easily," *National Interest,* no. 35 (Spring 1994), p. 87.

28. Powell, op. cit., p. 505.

29. Baker, op. cit., p. 410.

30. Libby interview.

31. Rowan interview.

32. Gordon and Trainor, op. cit., p. 429.

33. Wolfowitz, in *The Future of Iraq,* loc. cit., pp. 108–9; see also Wolfowitz, "Victory Came Too Easily," loc. cit., p. 87.

34. Ross interview; Bush and Scowcroft, op. cit., p. 490.

35. Powell, op. cit., p. 516.

36. Ross interview.

37. Bush and Scowcroft, op. cit., pp. 370, 400.

38. "Quotes from Defense Secretary Richard Cheney and Gen. Colin Powell," Associated Press, account of military briefing, January 23, 1991; John Broder, "Presidential Timber? Cheney Lets Chips Fall as He Gains Stature," *Los Angeles Times,* October 30, 1990, p. H3.

39. Robert D. McFadden, "In a Ticker-Tape Blizzard, New York Honors the Troops," *New York Times,* June 11, 1991, p. A1.

CHAPTER THIRTEEN: DEATH OF AN EMPIRE, BIRTH OF A VISION

1. Transcript, remarks by Undersecretary of Defense Paul Wolfowitz to the American Bar Association, November 21, 1991, Federal News Service.

2. Ibid.

3. Patrick E. Tyler, "U.S. Strategy Plan Calls for Insuring No Rivals Develop," *New York Times,* March 8, 1992, p. I1.

4. Ibid.

5. Interview with a former aide to Cheney.

6. Dick Cheney address to the American Enterprise Institute Forum, February 21, 1991.

7. George Bush and Brent Scowcroft, *A World Transformed* (New York: Alfred A. Knopf, 1998), p. 44.

8. Colin Powell, *An American Journey* (New York: Ballantine Books, 1995), p. 423.

9. David Rosenbaum, "From Guns to Butter," *New York Times,* December 14, 1989, p. A1.

10. John M. Broder and Melissa Healy, "Cheney Labels as 'Hogwash' Complaints About His Defense Budget Cuts Strategy," *Los Angeles Times,* December 16, 1989, A29.

11. George Bush remarks at the Aspen Institute Symposium, August 2, 1990.

12. Dick Cheney address to the tenth anniversary celebration of the World Affairs Council of Washington, D.C., June 8, 1990.

13. Ibid.

14. Testimony of Dick Cheney, Hearing of the House Armed Services Committee, Subject: Fiscal Year 1992–93 Defense Authorization, February 7, 1991.

15. Powell, op. cit., p. 438.

16. Jim Wolffe, "Powell: I'm Running Out of Demons," *Army Times,* April 5, 1991.

17. Don Oberdorfer, "Strategy for Solo Superpower; Pentagon Looks to 'Regional Contingencies,'" *Washington Post,* May 19, 1991, p. A1.

18. Hearing of the Senate Armed Services Committee, February 21, 1991.

19. Interview with Brent Scowcroft, June 6, 2002; Public Papers of the Presidents, Presidential Document 1230, August 10, 1990.

20. This account is based on Bush and Scowcroft, op. cit., pp. 131–33, and on Robert M. Gates, *From the Shadows* (New York: Simon & Schuster, 1996), pp. 478–79.

21. Paul Hendrickson, "Yeltsin's Smashing Day," *Washington Post,* September 13, 1989, p. D1.

22. Interviews with Fritz Ermath, March 14, 2002, and with Dennis Ross, April 18, 2002; Gates, op. cit., pp. 495, 499, 501, 528.

23. Seth Mydans, "U.S. 'Father Image' Is Blamed for Low Filipino Self-Esteem," *New York Times,* December 28, 1987, p. A6.

24. The Philippines found its way back into Washington's strategic calculations after September 11, 2001, when it was viewed as an important battleground of the American war on terrorism.

25. Michael Putzel, "Battle Joined on 'Peace Dividend,'" *Boston Globe,* January 12, 1992, p. 1.

26. Remarks by Paul Wolfowitz to the Defense Writers Group, March 5, 1992, Federal News Service.

27. Interview with Zalmay Khalilzad, May 28, 2003.

28. Tyler, op. cit.

29. Barton Gellman, "Keeping the U.S. First: Pentagon Would Preclude a Rival Superpower," *Washington Post,* March 11, 1992, p. A1; Patrick E. Tyler, "Pentagon Drops Goal of Blocking New Superpowers," *New York Times,* May 24, 1992, p. A1.

30. Doyle McManus, "U.S. Role Abroad Splits Presidential Candidates," *Los Angeles Times,* March 13, 1992, p. A4; Jim Mann and Doyle McManus, "Longtime Allies—the U.S., Germany and Japan—Are Drifting Apart," *Los Angeles Times,* June 7, 1992, p. A1; Doyle McManus and Jim Mann, "Big 3 Tested: Will Economic Rivalry Break Up the Allies," *Los Angeles Times,* June 9, 1992, p. A1; Lester Thurow, *Head to Head* (New York: William Morrow, 1992).

31. McManus and Mann, op. cit., Patrick E. Tyler, "Lone Superpower Plan: Ammunition for Critics," *New York Times,* March 10, 1992, p. A12; Charles Krauthammer, "What's Wrong with the Pentagon Paper?" *Washington Post,* March 13, 1992, p. A25.

32. Khalilzad interview.

33. This section is based upon interviews with I. Lewis Libby, April 24 and June 16, 2003.

34. Barton Gellman, "Pentagon Abandons Goal of Thwarting U.S. Rivals," *Washington Post,* May 24, 1992, p. A1.

35. Secretary of Defense Richard Cheney, "Defense Strategy for the 1990s: The Regional Defense Strategy," Pentagon document, January 1993, p. 3.

36. Ibid., pp. 6–7.

37. Ibid., p. 9.

38. Khalilzad interview.

39. Wolfowitz interview, March 12, 2002.

40. Paul Wolfowitz, "Remembering the Future," *National Interest,* no. 59 (Spring 2000), pp. 35–37.

CHAPTER FOURTEEN: VULCANS IN EXILE

1. The quotes in this and the following paragraphs are based on an interview with Dennis Ross, April 18, 2002.

2. Colin Powell, *My American Journey* (New York: Ballantine Books, 1995), p. 539.

3. See ibid., pp. 547, 586–87.

4. Ross interview.

5. James Mann, *About Face* (New York: Alfred A. Knopf, 1999), p. 268; interview with Richard Cheney, December 6, 1996; Eric Schmitt, "Kuwaitis Will Buy Tanks Made in U.S.," *New York Times,* October 13, 1992, p. A1.

6. Clinton acceptance speech to Democratic National Convention, July 16, 1992.

7. Ibid.

8. Interview with Lawrence Korb, February 12, 2003.

9. Colin L. Powell, "Why Generals Get Nervous," *New York Times,* October 8, 1992, p. A35.

10. Powell, *My American Journey,* loc. cit., p. 562.

11. Henry Louis Gates, Jr., "Powell and the Black Elite," *New Yorker* (September 25, 1995), p. 73.

12. Interview with a senior Clinton administration official who asked not to be identified by name.

13. Interview with Robert Fauver, December 18, 2001.

14. Art Pine, "Clinton Replacing Aid Official Armitage," *Los Angeles Times,* February 23, 1993, p. A13.

15. Barry Meier and Raymond Bonner, "A Deal Done in U.S. Style Dazes an Ex-Soviet State," *New York Times,* December 7, 1993, p. A1; Peter H. Stone, "Caspian Wells Come In for K Street," *National Journal* (March 13, 1999); Richard L. Armitage public financial disclosure report, February 2, 2001.

16. Interview with Brent Scowcroft, June 6, 2002.

17. Interview with George Shultz, February 12, 2002; Chevron Corp., "Chevron Christens New Tanker, the *Condoleezza Rice,* in Brazil," PR Newswire, August 23, 1993; Condoleezza Rice public financial disclosure report, January 20, 2001.

18. Interview with Coit Blacker, February 13, 2002; Ed Guzman and Adam Kemezis, "Budget Cuts, Student Relations Highlight Six Outstanding Years as Provost," *Stanford Daily,* January 4, 1999.

19. Interview with Kiron Skinner, February 11, 2002.

20. Paul Wolfowitz, "National Security Interests in the Post Cold War World," testimony to House National Security Committee, June 6, 1996.

21. Paul Wolfowitz, "Victory Came Too Easily," *National Interest,* no. 35 (Spring 1993–1994), p. 87.

22. CNN Transcript No. 750, "Dick Cheney Comments on the Military Scene," *Larry King Live,* January 27, 1993.

23. Richard L. Berke, "Presidential Hopefuls at a Republican Forum Jab at Clinton's Foreign Policy," *New York Times,* July 28, 1994, p. A10.

24. Allen R. Meyerson, "Halliburton Picks Cheney to Be Chief," *New York Times,* August 11, 1995, p. D3.

25. Interview with Frank Gaffney, February 28, 2002.

26. Interview with Kenneth Duberstein, July 11, 2002.

27. Powell, *My American Journey,* loc. cit., p. 600.

28. Frederick H. Lowe, "Rumsfeld Resigns at General Instrument," *Chicago Sun-Times,* August 12, 1993, p. 58; William Gruber, "Rumsfeld Reflects on Politics, Business," *Chicago Tribune,* October 20,1993, business section p. 3; Donald Rumsfeld public financial disclosure report, January 18, 2003.

29. Jim Mann, "Dole Struggling to Shape His Stand on China," *Los Angeles Times,* April 12, 1996, p. A18; Elaine Sciolino, "Facing Split over China, Dole Delays Asia Policy Speech," *New York Times,* April 13, 1996, p. A9.

30. Bob Dole, "America and Asia: Restoring U.S. Leadership in the Pacific," speech to Center for Strategic and International Studies Statesmen Forum, May 9, 1996.

CHAPTER FIFTEEN: A VULCAN AGENDA

1. Federal News Service transcript, press conference of the Commission to Assess the Ballistic Missile Threat, July 15, 1998.

2. Interview with Morton Abramowitz, December 12, 2001.

3. Paul Wolfowitz, "Clinton's Bay of Pigs," *Wall Street Journal,* September 27, 1996, p. A18.

4. Paul Wolfowitz, "The United States and Iraq," in *The Future of Iraq,* ed. John Calabrese (Washington, D.C.: Middle East Institute, 1997), p. 111.

5. Ibid., p. 112.

6. Zalmay Khalilzad and Paul Wolfowitz, "Overthrow Him," *Weekly Standard* (December 1, 1997), p. 14.

7. Paul Wolfowitz testimony before House National Security Committee hearing on U.S. policy on Iraq, September 16, 1998.

8. Paul Wolfowitz, "Rebuilding the Anti-Saddam Coalition," *Wall Street Journal,* November 18, 1997, p. A22.

9. Ibid.

10. Paul Wolfowitz, testimony before the House National Security Committee hearing on U.S. policy on Iraq, September 16, 1998.

11. Project for a New American Century, open letter to President Clinton, January 26, 1998.

12. Interview with Chris Cox, March 3, 2003.

13. Interviews with Martin Anderson, February 12, 2002, and March 3, 2003.

14. For a detailed account of Reagan's visit and Anderson's role, see Frances FitzGerald, *Way Out There in the Blue* (New York: Touchstone, 2000), pp. 19–28.

15. "Executive Summary of the Report of the Commission to Assess the Ballistic Missile Threat to the United States," July 15, 1998.

16. Richard L. Garwin, "What We Did," *Bulletin of the Atomic Scientists* vol. 54, no. 6 (November–December 1998), pp. 40–45; Michael Killian, "Panel Disputes CIA Assessment, Fears Attacks by Rogue States," *Chicago Tribune,* July 16, 1998, p. 8.

17. Interview with Robert Einhorn, March 6, 2003. For examples of Clinton administration's lumping together North Korea, Iran and Iraq, see William Perry, remarks to Commonwealth Club of California, February 23, 1996; Madeleine Albright, testimony to Senate Appropriations Committee, June 16, 1998; Sandy Berger, briefing on President Clinton's State of the Union address, January 27, 2000, and William Cohen, press conference in Beijing, July 13, 2000, Federal News Service.

18. Jeff Gerth with Raymond Bonner, "Companies Are Investigated for Aid to China on Rockets," *New York Times,* April 4, 1998, p. A1.

19. Cox interview.

20. In the wake of the congressional investigation the Justice Department attempted to prosecute Wen Ho Lee, a Taiwan-born nuclear scientist, on charges of mishandling classified information stemming from the theft of American nuclear weapons designs. Eventually prosecutors agreed to a plea bargain in which they permitted Lee to be set free and dropped fifty-eight felony charges against him, in exchange for his plea of guilty to a single felony count and his agreement to submit to debriefings by the FBI.

21. "Nunn, Wolfowitz to Head Special Hughes Task Force," Hughes Electronics Corporation press release, December 3, 1999; Paul Wolfowitz public financial disclosure report, February 15, 2001.

22. Renae Merle, "Hughes, Boeing Settle with U.S.," *Washington Post,* March 6, 2003, p. E1; Jeff Gerth, "Two Companies Pay Penalties for Improving China's Rockets," *New York Times,* March 6, 2003, p. A9.

23. Project for a New American Century, statement on the defense of Taiwan, August 20, 1999; interview with Richard Armitage, November 30, 2001.

24. Strobe Talbott, *The Russia Hand* (New York: Random House, 2002), pp. 39–40.

25. Philip Zelikow and Condoleezza Rice, *Germany Unified and Europe Transformed* (Cambridge, Mass.: Harvard University Press, 1995), p. 370.

26. Clifford G. Gaddy and Barry W. Ickes, "Russia's Virtual Economy," *Foreign Affairs* vol. 77, no. 5 (September–October 1998), pp. 53–63.

27. Condoleezza Rice, "Promoting the National Interest," *Foreign Affairs,* vol. 79, no. 1 (January–February 2000), p. 58.

28. John Lloyd, "The Russian Devolution," *New York Times Magazine,* August 15, 1999, p. 34.

29. Ibid.

30. Transcript of interview with Condoleezza Rice on ABC's *This Week,* November 28, 1999.

31. Interview with Michael McFaul, February 14, 2002. In his book, Talbott, who was the architect of the democratic Russia policy that Rice was criticizing, accused her of advocating a quarantine of Russia during the late 1990s. Talbott, op. cit., pp. 292, 403.

32. Frank Bruni, "Putin Urges Bush Not to Act Alone on Missile Shield," *New York Times,* June 17, 2001, p. A1.

33. Condoleezza Rice, speech to Los Angeles World Affairs Council, January 15, 1999.

CHAPTER SIXTEEN: THE CAMPAIGN

1. This account is based upon interviews with George Shultz and Martin Anderson, February 12, 2002, and corroborating information subsequently supplied by Shultz. For overall Bush campaign in 1998, see Sam Howe Verhovek, "Riding High, Bush Eases into 2000 Election," *New York Times,* May 25, 1998, p. A1.

2. Roberto Suro, "U.S. Lacking in Terrorism Defenses," *Washington Post,* April 24, 1998. p. A1.

3. Interview with Brent Scowcroft, January 3, 2002.

4. Interview with Coit Blacker, February 13, 2002.

5. Walter M. Mears, "Bush Gets CIA Briefing," Associated Press, September 2, 2000, and accompanying Associated Press picture.

6. Interview with Dov Zakheim, June 28, 2002.

7. Interview with Richard Armitage, November 30, 2001.

8. Transcript of George W. Bush remarks at press conference with Richard Cheney, July 25, 2000, Federal News Service.

9. Unsigned article, "Colin Powell Rules Out Vice Presidential Bid," Associated Press, March 21, 2000.

10. Transcript of Colin Powell speech to Republican National Convention, Federal Documents Clearing House, July 31, 2000.

11. Sandy Davis, "Colin Powell Throws Full Weight Behind Bush Presidential Quest," *Arkansas Democrat-Gazette,* October 25, 2000, p. A1; Dave Boyer, "Bush Speculates About His Cabinet," *Washington Times,* October 21, 2000, p. A4; Tom Raum, "Bush Meets Powell at His Ranch," Associated Press, November 30, 2000.

12. CNBC News Transcript, "George W. Bush Stumped When Asked to Name the Leaders," November 4, 1999; Elaine Sciolino, "Bush's Foreign Policy Tutor," *New York Times,* June 16, 2000, p. A1.

13. Transcript of NBC's *Meet the Press,* November 21, 1999.

14. Governor George W. Bush, speech to Republican National Convention, August 3, 2000; *Meet the Press* interview, November 21, 1999.

15. Transcript of second Gore-Bush debate, October 11, 2000.

16. Governor George W. Bush, "A Distinctly American Internationalism," speech at Ronald Reagan Presidential Library, November 19, 1999. Transcript of third Gore-Bush Debate, October 17, 2000.

17. Transcript of second Gore-Bush debate, October 11, 2000.

18. Interview with Paul Wolfowitz, March 12, 2002.

19. Transcript of second Gore-Bush debate, October 11, 2000.

20. Wolfowitz interview.

21. *Meet the Press* interview.

22. Condoleezza Rice, "Promoting the National Interest," *Foreign Affairs,* vol. 79, no. 1 (January–February 2000), pp. 45–62.

23. Excerpts from joint news conference in Lajes, Azores, *New York Times,* March 17, 2003, p. A13.

24. Interview with William Kristol, December 7, 2001; see also Robert Kagan, "The Biggest Issue of Them All," *Washington Post,* February 15, 2000, p. A23.

25. Rice, op. cit.

26. Robert Kagan, "A World of Problems," *Washington Post,* April 10, 2000, p. A21.

27. See Colin Powell, *My American Journey* (New York: Ballantine Books, 1995), p. 526.

28. See Michael Gordon and Bernard E. Trainor, *The Generals' War* (Boston: Little, Brown, 1995), pp. 150–52, 468–69.

CHAPTER SEVENTEEN: WHO RUNS THE PENTAGON?

1. Interview with Dave Gribben, December 17, 2001.

2. Interview with Chris Cox, March 3, 2003.

3. Interviews with Richard Allen, December 21, 2001, Brent Scowcroft, January 3, 2002, Morton Abramowitz, December 12, 2001, and a former director of central intelligence.

4. Interview with a former State Department official.

5. Rowan Scarborough, "GOP Right Clamoring for Coats as Defense Chief," *Washington Times,* December 22, 2000, p. A1.

6. Transcript of Bush-Powell news conference, December 16, 2000, Federal News Service.

7. Ibid.

8. See chapter twelve.

9. Allen interview.

10. Alison Mitchell, "Powell to Head State Dept. as Bush's First Cabinet Pick," *New York Times,* December 17, 2000, p. A1.

11. Editorial, "Colin Powell's Message," *Washington Post,* December 18, 2000, p. A26.

12. Matthew Rees, "The Long Arm of Colin Powell," *Weekly Standard,* December 25, 2000, p. 17.

13. This account is based on interviews with David Gribben, December 17, 2000, Allen and two other sources who asked not to be identified.

14. George Bush and Brent Scowcroft, *A World Transformed* (New York: Alfred A. Knopf, 1998), p. 21.

15. The author was among the reporters covering Bush's visit to Plains in late 1976. Bush found it impossible to conceal his eagerness to keep the job before he saw Carter and his deep disappointment after his effort failed.

16. Ibid.

17. On Rumsfeld and the commission, see Walter Pincus, "Intelligence Shakeup Would Boost CIA," *Washington Post,* November 8, 2001, p. A1.

18. Interview with George Shultz, February 12, 2002.

19. Interview with Brent Scowcroft, June 6, 2002.

20. Ralph Z. Hallow and Bill Gertz, "Rumsfeld Atop List to Take Over as CIA Director," *Washington Times,* December 27, 2002, p. A1.

21. Eric Schmitt, "Ex-Defense Chief Seens to Be Bush Choice for CIA," *New York Times,* December 28, 2000, p. A18.

22. Transcript, CNN Live Event, Bush Nominates Donald Rumsfeld as Secretary of Defense, December 28, 2000.

23. Colin Powell, *My American Journey* (New York: Ballantine Books, 1995), p. 525.

24. Interview with Richard Armitage, November 30, 2001.

25. This account is based on interviews with two associates of Armitage's and one associate of Rumsfeld's.

26. Allen interview.

CHAPTER EIGHTEEN: WARNINGS AND SIGNALS

1. Nora Boustany, "Bush Drops by the French Ambassador's House and Gets to Know Chirac," *Washington Post,* December 20, 2000, p. A30.

2. State Department transcript of Colin Powell media availability with Swedish Foreign Minister Anna Lindh and EU representatives, March 6, 2001.

3. White House transcript of remarks by President Bush and President Kim Dae Jung, March 7, 2001.

4. William Douglas, "Powell Acknowledges Some Miscues," *Newsday,* May 5, 2001, p. A7.

5. Author conversations with James Kelly and with Richard Armitage, December 2000 to February 2001.

6. Ibid.; Senate Armed Services Committee confirmation hearing of Paul Wolfowitz, February 27, 2001.

7. Interview with two senior Bush administration officials who took part in the administration's deliberations.

8. Interviews with a senior Bush administration official, March 9, 2001, and with a senior American military officer.

9. Interview with Paul Wolfowitz, March 12, 2002.

10. Interview with Condoleezza Rice, March 30, 2001.

11. Interview with Admiral Dennis Blair, former commander of U.S. forces in the Pacific, April 3, 2003.

12. Transcript of Rohrabacher interview, *CBS Morning News,* April 5, 2001; Jim Puzzanghera, "California Lawmakers at Center of Capitol Hill's Debate on China," Knight Ridder News Service, April 6, 2001.

13. Interview with a Bush administration official directly involved in the handling of the EP-3 incident, August 1, 2002.

14. On the talks, interview with Richard Armitage, November 30, 2001; on differing translations, John Pomfret, "Resolving Crisis Was a Matter of Interpretation," *Washington Post,* April 12, 2001, p. A1.

15. Paul Wolfowitz, "Asian Democracy and Asian Values," B. C. Lee Lecture, the Heritage Foundation, March 2, 2000; Condoleezza Rice, "Promoting the National Interest," *Foreign Affairs,* vol. 79, no. 1 (January–February 2000), p. 45.

16. Robert Kagan and William Kristol, "A National Humiliation," *Weekly Standard* (April 16, 2001), p. 11; interview with William Kristol, December 7, 2001.

17. Interview with Richard Armitage, November 30, 2001. See Jim Mann, "U.S. Promised Subs to Taiwan It Doesn't Have," *Los Angeles Times,* July 15, 2001, p. A1.

18. "President Bush Discusses His First 100 Days In Office," ABC News transcript, April 25, 2001.

19. CNN transcript, "Vice President Cheney on Larry King Live," April 27, 2001.

20. "A Huge Honor to Be in This Office," transcript of George W. Bush interview, *Washington Post,* April 25, 2001, p. A22.

21. White House transcripts, joint press Conference with President George W. Bush and President José María Aznar, June 12, 2001; press availability with President Bush and NATO Secretary General Lord Robertson, June 13, 2001.

22. The Clinton administration later reversed itself and signed the treaty establishing the International Criminal Court, but only on December 31, 2000, when Clinton was a lame-duck president preparing to leave office. Even in doing so, Clinton said he would not submit the treaty to the Senate because he had concerns about the court's powers. He also said he would not recommend that the incoming Bush administration submit the treaty for ratification. See Thomas Ricks, "U.S. Signs Treaty on War Crimes Tribunal," *Washington Post,* January 1, 2003, p. A1.

23. For American unilateralism under Clinton, see Martin Woollacott, "It's Time America Woke Up to the Rest of the Planet," *Guardian,* October 20, 2000, p. 24; Tyler Marshall and Jim Mann, "Goodwill Towards U.S. Is Dwindling Globally," *Los Angeles Times,* March 26, 2000, p. A1.

24. Marshall and Mann, op. cit.

25. White House transcript, "Press Conference by President Bush and Russian Federation President Putin," June 16, 2001; interview with Michael McFaul, February 14, 2002.

26. "Press Briefing by Secretary of State Colin Powell and National Security Adviser Condoleezza Rice," June 16, 2001; James Carney, "Our New Best Friend," *Time* (May 27, 2002), p. 42.

27. Transcript, Senate Armed Services Committee hearing on the nomination of Donald Rumsfeld, January 11, 2001; transcript, Secretary of Defense Donald Rumsfeld interview on *Newshour with Jim Lehrer,* February 14, 2001.

28. "A Period of Consequences," George W. Bush speech, The Citadel, September 23, 1999.

29. Robert Kagan, "Indefensible Defense Budget," *Washington Post,* July 20, 2001, p. A31; "No Defense," *Weekly Standard* (July 23, 2001), p. 11.

30. Pamela Hess, "Rumsfeld Plays Down Pentagon Reform," United Press International, May 24, 2001.

31. Thomas Ricks, "For Rumsfeld, Many Roadblocks," *Washington Post,* August 7, 2001, p. A1.

32. Transcript of Donald Rumsfeld press conference, September 6, 2001; Al Kamen, "Donny, We Hardly Knew Ye," *Washington Post,* September 7, 2001, p. A27.

33. See Roberta Wohlstetter, *Pearl Harbor: Warning and Decision* (Stanford, Calif.: Stanford University Press, 1989).

34. Paul Wolfowitz, commencement address at the U.S. Military Academy, West Point, June 2, 2001.

35. Factual Finding 5(e), Final Report of the Congressional Joint Inquiry into 9/11, December 10, 2002; Dan Eggen, "FBI Pigeonholed Agent's Request," *Washington Post,* May 22, 2002, p. A1.

36. For an extensive account of the intelligence and counterterrorism deliberations in Washington in the months preceding September 11, see Daniel Benjamin and Steven Simon, *The Age of Sacred Terror* (New York: Random House, 2002), pp. 326–49. On Tenet's perspective, see Bob Woodward, *Bush at War* (New York: Simon & Schuster, 2002), pp. 3–7.

37. White House statement on domestic preparedness against weapons of mass destruction, May 8, 2001; Barton Gellman, "Before September 11, the Bush Anti-Terror Effort Was Mostly Ambition," *Washington Post,* January 20, 2002, p. A1.

38. Benjamin and Simon, op. cit., pp. 345–46.

CHAPTER NINETEEN: HISTORY STARTS TODAY

1. Interview with I. Lewis Libby, December 11, 2001; Winston Churchill, *The Gathering Storm* (Boston: Houghton Mifflin/Mariner Books, 1948), p. 601.

2. The most detailed version of Cheney's account of this day is in his interview with Tim Russert on NBC's *Meet the Press,* September 16. 2001.

3. For a critical analysis of Bush's September 11 speech and of his subsequent recovery, see David Frum, *The Right Man* (New York: Random House, 2002), pp. 124–51.

4. Eric Schmitt, "Out Front or Low Profile, Cheney Keeps Powerful Role," *New York Times,* October 7, 2001, section 1B, p. 4.

5. This story was based on an interview with two State Department officials and was confirmed by Richard Armitage in an interview, November 30, 2001. See also transcript of State Department daily briefing, September 19, 2001.

6. Armitage's list also included the demands that Pakistan close its borders to all Al Qaeda operatives and all arms shipments to Al Qaeda, that Pakistan curb all domestic expressions of support for terrorism, that it cut off fuel shipments to the Taliban and that it break diplomatic relations with the Taliban once the evidence implicated Al Qaeda in the September 11 attacks.
The list of demands was provided by Armitage's office.

7. The account of these meetings is based upon interviews with Armitage, November 30, 2001, and with Ambassador Maleela Lodhi, March 18, 2002.

8. Transcript of Defense Department briefing by Paul Wolfowitz, September 13, 2001; interview with Paul Wolfowitz on *Newshour with Jim Lehrer,* September 14, 2001.

9. Wolfowitz Defense Department briefing, September 13, 2001; Wolfowitz interview on National Public Radio, September 14, 2001; Wolfowitz interview on *Fox News with Brit Hume,* September 13, 2001.

10. Jane Perlez, "Capital Hawks Seek Tougher Line on Iraq," *New York Times,* March 7, 2001, p. A10.

11. Soon after September 11 there were allegations that Mohammed Atta, the ringleader of the hijackings, had met with an Iraqi official in Prague in April 2001. The reports had been based upon the Czech Republic's intelligence. However, the CIA and the Czechs further investigated this report and concluded there was no evidence to support it. See Walter Pincus, "No Link Between Hijackers, Iraq Found, U.S. Says," *Washington Post,* May 1, 2002, p. A9; Dana Priest, "U.S. Not Claiming Iraqi Link to Terror," *Washington Post,* September 10, 2002, p. A1.

12. Interview with Paul Wolfowitz, June 18, 2003.

13. Interview with senior administration official; see also Patrick Tyler and Elaine Sciolino, "Bush's Advisers Split on Scope of Retaliation," *New York Times,* September 20, 2001, p. A5; Bob Woodward and Dan Balz, "At Camp David, Advise and Dissent," *Washington Post,* January 31, 2002, p. A1; transcript of Colin Powell briefing at the State Department, September 17, 2001.

14. See, for example, Mark Mathews, "The Resurrection of Colin Powell," *Baltimore Sun,* October 8, 2001, p. 2A; Richard A. Ryan, "Powell Resists Rumsfeld's Vision to Broaden Battles," *Detroit News,* October 7, 2001, p. 15A.

15. Cheney, *Meet the Press,* September 16, 2001.

16. Dick Polman, "Amid Crisis, Bush Has Abandoned His Unilateral Ways," *Philadelphia Inquirer,* September 14, 2001, p. A3; Joseph Kahn, "Awakening to Terror, and Asking the World for Help," *New York Times,* September 16, 2001, section 4, p. 12.

17. "Old Friends, Best Friends," *Economist,* Special Report (September 15, 2001); Jean Marie Colombani, "Nous sommes tous Americains," *Le Monde,* September 13, 2001; William Drozdiak, "Attack On U.S. Is Attack on All, NATO Agrees," *Washington Post,* September 13, 2001, p. A25.

18. See Robert Kagan, *Of Paradise and Power* (New York: Alfred A. Knopf, 2003).

19. "German Parliament Approves Possible U.S. Military Aid," *Deutsche Presse-Agentur,* September 19, 2001; Norman Kempster, "Chirac Visits White House," *Los Angeles Times,* September 19, 2001, p. A18.

20. Interview with French Ambassador to Washington François Bujon de L'Estang, April 17, 2002.

21. Bujon interview. The French eventually provided about two thousand troops during the early months of the Afghanistan campaign for auxiliary missions such as intelligence, reconnaissance and refueling.

22. Martin Walker, "Bush Avoiding France and Germany?," United Press International, June 20, 2001.

23. Interview with Chris Cox, March 3, 2003; Don Van Atta and Lizette Alvarez,

"A Hijacked Boeing 757 Slams into the Pentagon, Halting the Government," *New York Times,* September 12, 2001, p. A5.

24. "Donald Rumsfeld, Sexiest Cabinet Member," *People* (December 2, 2002), p. 92.

25. See Susan Baer, "Playing by His Own Rules," *Baltimore Sun,* December 9, 2001, p. 6E.

26. *CNN Late Edition,* October 28, 2001.

27. For a detailed construction of bin Laden's escape, see Philip Smucker, "How bin Laden Got Away," *Christian Science Monitor,* March 4, 2002, p. 1.

28. "Secretary Rumsfeld with U.S. Troops at Bagram," Department of Defense transcript, December 16, 2001.

29. President Bush address to a joint session of Congress, September 20, 2001; transcript of Colin Powell interview on *Meet the Press,* September 23, 2001.

30. Interviews with two senior State Department officials, November 2001.

31. Interview with a senior U.S. intelligence official March 2002; Thomas Ricks, "Pacific Plan Seeks Clues to Al Qaeda Contacts," *Washington Post,* November 4, 2001, p. A23.

32. Defense Department transcript, "Rumsfeld Media Availability with New York City Mayor Giuliani," November 14, 2001.

33. James Dao and Eric Schmitt, "U.S. Sees Battles in Lawless Areas After Afghan War," *New York Times,* January 8, 2002, p. A1.

34. Interview with Richard Armitage, November 30, 2001.

CHAPTER TWENTY: A NEW STRATEGY

1. Defense Department transcript, "Press Availability with Deputy Secretary Wolfowitz in Berlin," May 10, 2001; remarks by Condoleezza Rice at the National Press Club newsmaker luncheon, July 13, 2001.

2. Interview with a senior intelligence official.

3. David E. Sanger and Elisabeth Bumiller, "U.S. to Pull Out of ABM Treaty, Clearing Path for Antimissile Tests," *New York Times,* December 12, 2001, p. A1.

4. Walter Pincus, "'Rogue' Nations Policy Builds on Clinton's Lead," *Washington Post,* March 12, 2002, p. A4.

5. William H. Arkin, "Secret Plan Outlines the Unthinkable," *Los Angeles Times,* March 10, 2002, p. M1; Michael R. Gordon, "U.S. Nuclear Plan Sees New Targets and New Weapons," *New York Times,* March 10, 2002, p. A1; Michael A. Gordon, "Nuclear Arms: For Deterrence or Fighting?" *New York Times,* March 11, 2002, p. A1.

6. Defense Department transcript, "Secretary Rumsfeld Speaks on 21st Century Transformation of the U.S. Armed Forces," address to National Defense University, January 31, 2002.

7. Condoleezza Rice, "Promoting the National Interest," *Foreign Affairs,* vol. 79, no. 1 (January–February 2000), pp. 45–62.

8. Governor George W. Bush, "A Distinctly American Internationalism," speech at Ronald Reagan Presidential Library, November 19, 1999.

9. Interview with William Kristol, December 7, 2001.

10. White House transcript, "Remarks by National Security Adviser Condoleezza Rice on Terrorism and Foreign Policy," speech to Paul H. Nitze School of Advanced International Studies, Johns Hopkins University, April 29, 2002.

11. Interview with Philip Zelikow, May 29, 2003.

12. President George W. Bush, address to UN General Assembly, November 10, 2001; CBS news transcript, "Secretary of Defense Donald Rumsfeld Discusses the War on Terrorism," *Face the Nation*, November 11, 2001.

13. John Burns, "Pakistan Releases 3 Scientists Questioned on Ties to Taliban," *New York Times*, November 3, 2001, p. B-5.

14. George W. Bush, State of the Union address, January 29, 2002.

15. The term *axis* was first popularized by Benito Mussolini, who used it in a 1936 speech to describe the new agreement Italy had just signed with Germany. Kenneth Janda and Stafano Mula, "Dubya, Meet Il Duce," *Chicago Tribune*, April 21, 2002, perspective section, p. 1. Bush did not claim that Iraq, Iran and North Korea were collaborating closely with one another in the manner of the World War II axis of Germany, Japan and Italy.

16. David Frum, *The Right Man* (New York: Random House, 2003), pp. 225–45.

17. On the Clinton administration, see chapter fifteen, note seventeen.

18. Other than the five members of the UN Security Council, only six other countries had advanced programs for nuclear weapons and missiles: Iran, Iraq, North Korea, Israel, India and Pakistan. The first three had signed the nuclear nonproliferation treaty and thus were in potential violation of it; the latter three did not join the treaty.

19. See, for example, Elisabeth Bumiller, "Axis of Debate: Hawkish Words," *New York Times*, February 3, 2002, section 4, p. 5.

20. Interview with Richard Armitage, August 21, 2002.

21. Interview with Paul Wolfowitz, March 12, 2002.

22. There were a few notable exceptions in the cold war. The Nixon administration arranged Henry Kissinger's landmark visit to China without informing Japan in advance.

23. Steven Erlanger, "German Joins Europe's Cry That the U.S. Won't Consult," *New York Times*, February 13, 2002, p. A18; Gerald Baker and Richard Wolffe, "Powell Shrugs Off European Dismay over 'Axis of Evil'"; *Financial Times*, February 14, 2002; p. 1; Charles Krauthammer, "The Axis of Petulance," *Washington Post*, March 1, 2002, p. A25.

24. James Bennet with Joel Greenberg, "Israel Seizes Ship It Says Was Arming Palestinians," *New York Times*, January 5, 2002, p. A1; Hanna Rosin, "Israel Says Ship with Weapons Was Loaded in Iran," *Washington Post*, January 6, 2002, p. A19; State Department transcript, Colin Powell interview with Jim Lehrer on the *Newshour*, January 25, 2002.

25. This paragraph is based on an interview with a senior official who reflected the hawks' point of view.

26. Transcript of Vice President Cheney's press conference with Israeli Prime

Minister Ariel Sharon, March 19, 2002; Michael R. Gordon, "Cheney's Bid to Arafat Aimed to End Violence," *New York Times,* March 21, 2002, p. A16.

27. Interview with an aide to Cheney.

28. Robin Wright, "Powell Talks to Both Sides," *Los Angeles Times,* April 15, 2002, p. A1; Robin Wright, "Powell's Peace Mission Yields No Ceasefire," *Los Angeles Times,* April 18, 2002, p. A1; Alan Sipress, "Policy Divide Thwarts Powell in Mideast Effort," *Washington Post,* April 26, 2002, p. A1.

29. Interview with Paul Wolfowitz, June 19, 2003; Eric Schmitt, "The Busy Life of Being a Lightning Rod for Bush," *New York Times,* April 22, 2002, p. A3.

30. Nick Anderson, "Pro-Israel Demonstration Draws Tens of Thousands to Washington," *Los Angeles Times,* April 16, 2002, p. A10.

31. Wolfowitz interview.

32. Robin Wright and Tracy Wilkinson, "A Vision for Peace—After 28 Drafts," *Los Angeles Times,* June 27, 2002, p. A1; Glenn Kessler, "Cutting Arafat Loose, but Not by Name," *Washington Post,* June 30, 2002; Patrick E. Tyler, David E. Sanger, Todd S. Purdum and Eric Schmitt, "With Time Running Out, Bush Shifted Mideast Policy," *New York Times,* June 30, 2002, p. I12.

33. White House Transcript, "President Bush Calls for New Palestinian Leadership," June 24, 2002.

34. State of the Union address, January 29, 2002; Nicholas Lehman, "The Bush Administration May Have a Brand-New Doctrine of Power," *New Yorker* (April 1, 2002).

35. Transcript, "Remarks by the President at 2002 Graduation Exercise of the United States Military Academy," June 1, 2002.

36. In May 2003, when the Indonesian government launched a military offensive against separatist rebels in Aceh Province, it explicitly cited the Bush administration's doctrine of preemption as justification for the use of force. See Jane Perlez, "Indonesia Says It Will Press Attacks on Separatists in Sumatra," *New York Times,* May 23, 2002, p. A11.

37. Bush West Point speech.

38. John Lewis Gaddis, "A Grand Strategy of Transformation," *Foreign Policy,* issue no. 103 (November–December, 2002), pp. 50–57 and accompanying sidebar, p. 53.

39. National Security Strategy of the United States of America, September 2002, introduction; pp. 3, 6, 15, 30.

40. Richard Falk, "The New Bush Doctrine," *Nation,* vol. 275, no. 3 (July 15, 2002), p. 9.

41. National Security Strategy, p. 15.

42. Bill Bradley foreign policy address, Fletcher School of Law and Diplomacy, November 29, 1999.

43. For views of the hawks: interview with a senior administration official.

CHAPTER TWENTY-ONE: TOWARD WAR WITH IRAQ

1. Michael R. Gordon and David L. Sanger, "Powell Says U.S. Is Weighing Ways to Topple Hussein," *New York Times,* February 13, 2002, p. A1.

2. This list and account of the options were provided by a participant in the interagency discussions.

3. For a discussion and analysis of the enclave option, see Daniel Byman, Kenneth Pollack and Gideon Rose, "The Rollback Fantasy," *Foreign Affairs,* vol. 78, no. 1 (January–February 1999), pp. 24–41.

4. Thom Shanker and David E. Sanger, "U.S. Envisions Blueprint on Iraq Including Big Invasion Next Year," *New York Times,* April 28, 2002, p. A1; William Arkin, "Planning an Iraqi War but Not an Outcome," *Los Angeles Times,* May 5, 2002, part M, p. 1.

5. Debate between Richard Perle and Leon Fuerth, sponsored by University of Maryland School of Public Affairs and Hudson Institute, April 17, 2002; Todd S. Purdum, "After Saddam, What?," *New York Times,* February 17, 2002, section 4, p. 1.

6. Transcript of interview with Richard Perle, *Wide Angle,* July 11, 2002.

7. Perle resigned as chairman of the Defense Policy Board in March 2003 after it was disclosed that he had agreed, for a fee of up to $725,000, to help the U.S.-based telecommunications firm Global Crossing to overcome Defense Department objections to its sale to a venture controlled by Hong Kong and Singaporean investors. See Stephen Labaton, "Pentagon Adviser Is Also Advising Global Crossing," *New York Times,* March 21, 2003, p. C1. After stepping down as chairman, Perle remained a member of the board. The Pentagon inspector general later found that Perle had not violated ethics laws or rules, because his advisory position at the Defense Department required only eight days of work per year, far below the minimum required by these regulations. Stephen Labaton, "Report Finds No Violations at Pentagon by Adviser," *New York Times,* November 15, 2003, p. B1.

8. Interview with James Woolsey, March 29, 2002.

9. Ibid.

10. Interview with Brent Scowcroft, June 6, 2002.

11. Transcript of interview with Brent Scowcroft, *Face the Nation,* August 4, 2002.

12. Interview with Brent Scowcroft, February 20, 2003.

13. Brent Scowcroft, "Don't Attack Saddam," *Wall Street Journal,* August 15, 2002, p. A12.

14. See Todd Purdum and Patrick E. Tyler, "Top Republicans Break with Bush on Iraq Strategy," *New York Times,* August 16, 2002, p. A1.

15. James A. Baker III, "The Right Way to Change a Regime," *New York Times,* August 25, 2002, section 4, p. 9; transcript of Lawrence Eagleburger, *Crossfire,* August 19, 2002.

16. Scowcroft interview, February 20, 2003.

17. Zelikow interview.

18. Walter Gibbs, "Scowcroft Urges Wide Role for the U.N. in Postwar Iraq," *New York Times,* April 9, 2003, p. B6.

19. Interview with a senior aide to Powell; interview with a senior aide to Cheney.

20. Vice President Cheney, speech to Veterans of Foreign Wars' 103rd national convention, August 26, 2002.

21. Hagel quote in Purdum and Tyler, op. cit. For "chicken hawks," see, for example, a Web site called the New Hampshire Gazette, www.nhgazette.com.

22. President Bush, address to the United Nations General Assembly, September 12, 2002.

23. Doyle McManus, "Poll Still Backs Military Move on Iraq," *Los Angeles Times,* September 2, 2002, p. A1; Andrew Kohut, "Simply Put, the Public's View Can't Be Put Simply," *Washington Post,* September 29, 2002, p. B5.

24. Text of congressional joint resolution, published in *Washington Post,* October 11, 2002, p. A12.

25. Interview with James Kelly, September 17, 2002.

26. Interview with a U.S. government official involved in policy toward North Korea.

27. Doug Struck, "Hints on N. Korea Surfaced in 2000," *Washington Post,* October 19, 2002, p. A19.

28. Don Oberdorfer, "My Private Seat at Pyongyang's Table," *Washington Post,* November 10, 2002, Outlook section, p. B3.

29. See Barbara Slavin, "N. Korea Admits Nuclear Program," *USA Today,* October 17, 2002, p. 1A.

30. Interview with Colin Powell, December 29, 2002, *Meet the Press.*

31. Department of Defense transcript, Donald Rumsfeld Remarks to the Reserve Officers Association, January 20, 2002.

32. For detailed accounts of the diplomacy leading up to the resolution, see Tyler Marshall, "A War of Words Led to Unanimous U.N. Vote," *Los Angeles Times,* November 10, 2002, p. I1, and Karen DeYoung, "For Powell, a Long Path to a Victory," *Washington Post,* November 10, 2002, p. A1.

33. Michael O'Hanlon, "How the Hard-Liners Lost," *Washington Post,* November 10, 2002, p. B7.

34. White House transcript, remarks by the president on Iraq, Cincinnati Museum Center, October 7, 2002.

35. Interview with Zalmay Khalilzad, June 3, 2003.

36. Eric Schmitt, "Buildup Leaves U.S. Nearly Set to Start Attack," *New York Times,* December 8, 2002, p. I1.

37. Interview with a senior French official.

38. Ibid.

39. Glenn Kessler, "Moderate Powell Turns Hawkish on War with Iraq," *Washington Post,* January 24, 2003, p. A1; Steven R. Weisman, "Patience Gone, Powell Adopts Hawkish Tone," *New York Times,* January 28, 2003, p. A1; Department of State transcript, press conference of Secretary Colin Powell in Beijing, February 24, 2003; interview with a senior French official.

40. George W. Bush, speech to American Enterprise Institute, February 26, 2003.

41. This account of Powell, Tenet and the UN presentation was offered separately

by two different administration officials who were generally on opposite sides of the administration's internal debates about Iraq.

42. Transcript of Dominique de Villepin's remarks, "France's Response," *New York Times,* February 15, 2003, p. A13.

43. Defense Department transcript, Secretary Rumsfeld briefs at the Foreign Press Center, January 22, 2003.

44. Department of Defense, transcript of news briefing with Secretary Rumsfeld and General Myers, March 11, 2003; Karen DeYoung and Colum Lynch, "Bush Lobbies for Deal on Iraq," *Washington Post,* March 12, 2003, p. A1.

45. Peter Stothard, *Thirty Days: Tony Blair and the Test of History* (New York: HarperCollins, 2003), p. 21.

46. Interview with a senior French official.

47. See Gerard Baker, James Blitz, Judy Dempsey, Robert Graham, Quentin Peel and Mark Turner, "Blair's Mission Impossible," *Financial Times,* May 29, 2003, p. 17.

48. Interview with an American official.

49. NBC News transcript, *Meet the Press* interview with Colin Powell, March 9, 2003.

50. Interview with a senior French official.

51. Governor George W. Bush, "A Distinctly American Internationalism," speech at Ronald Reagan Presidential Library, November 19, 1999.

52. President Bush, address to the nation, March 19, 2003.

CONCLUSION

1. Interview with a senior French diplomat.

2. Press briefing of Deputy Secretary of Defense Paul Wolfowitz, July 23, 2003.

3. White House transcript, "Remarks by the President from the USS *Abraham Lincoln* at Sea Off the Coast of San Diego," May 1, 2003.

4. Vernon Loeb, "'Guerrilla' War Acknowledged; New Commander Cites Problems," *Washington Post,* July 17, 2003, p. A1.

5. Dana Priest and Walter Pincus, "Search in Iraq Finds No Banned Weapons," *Washington Post,* October 3, 2003, p. A1. While finding no stocks of weapons of mass destruction, Kay reported that Iraq had been carrying out research and other activities that were in violation of UN resolutions.

6. Interview with Paul Wolfowitz, June 19, 2003.

7. Robert G. Kaiser, "The Briefing: Rumsfeld's E-Ring Circus," *Washington Post,* March 22, 2003, p. C1.

8. Thom Shanker and John Tierney, "Top General Denounces Internal Dissent," *New York Times,* April 2, 2003, p. A1.

9. Secretary of Defense Donald Rumsfeld and General Richard Myers, Defense Department regular news briefing, April 11, 2003.

10. Newt Gingrich, "Transforming the State Department," speech at American Enterprise Institute, April 22, 2003; Newt Gingrich, "Rogue State Department," *Foreign Policy,* issue 137 (July–August 2003), pp. 42–48; for Armitage quote, Barbara

Slavin, "Gingrich Takes Swipe at State Department," *USA Today,* April 23, 2003, p. 8A.

11. Condoleezza Rice, remarks at 28th Annual Convention of the National Association of Black Journalists, August 7, 2003.

12. Dana Milbank and Mike Allen, "Iraq Flap Shakes Rice's Image," *Washington Post,* July 27, 2003, p. A1.

13. Jane Perlez, "Iraqi Shadow Government Cools Its Heels in Kuwait," *New York Times,* April 3, 2003, p. B9.

14. Wolfowitz interview.

15. Interview with Richard Armitage, June 23, 2003.

16. Walter Pincus and Dana Priest, "Some Iraqi Analysts Felt Pressure from Cheney Visits," *Washington Post,* June 5, 2003, p. A1.

17. Wolfowitz's press secretary Kevin Kellems would not permit the use of the picture in this book.

18. The two exceptions were former Senator Edmund Muskie, who was President Carter's secretary of state, and former Representative Les Aspin, who served as President Clinton's first defense secretary. But each of these men served in their foreign policy jobs for less than a full year.

19. The only time between 1968 and 2004 that the Republicans were out of power for more than a single presidential term was during the Clinton administration. But in that instance, the Republicans took control of Congress after Clinton's first two years, and as chapter fifteen explains, several of the Vulcans worked closely with the Republican leadership on Capitol Hill.

Index